Utilizing
System 360/370
OS and VS
Job Control Language
and Utility Programs

Utilizing
System 360/370
OS and VS
Job Control Language
and Utility Programs

DANIEL H. RINDFLEISCH
USDA Graduate School
Washington, D.C.

PRENTICE-HALL, INC.
Englewood Cliffs, New Jersey 07632

Library of Congress Cataloging in Publication Data

RINDFLEISCH, DANIEL H., (date)
Utilizing system 360/370 OS and VS job control
language and utility programs.

Includes index.
1. IBM 360 (Computer)--Programming.
2. IBM 370 (Computer)--Programming. 3. Utilities
(Computer programs) I. Title.
QA76.8.I12R53   001.6'42   78-12100
ISBN 0-13-939793-0

Editorial/Production supervision by Cathy Van Yperen
Cover design by: Edsal Enterprises
Manufacturing Buyer: Gordon Osbourne

Printed in the United States of America
10 9 8 7 6 5 4 3 2 1

PRENTICE-HALL INTERNATIONAL, INC., London
PRENTICE-HALL OF AUSTRALIA PTY. LIMITED, Sydney
PRENTICE-HALL OF CANADA, LTD., Toronto
PRENTICE-HALL OF INDIA PRIVATE LIMITED, New Delhi
PRENTICE-HALL OF JAPAN, INC., Tokyo
PRENTICE-HALL OF SOUTHEAST ASIA PTE. LTD., Singapore
WHITEHALL BOOKS LIMITED, Wellington, New Zealand

Contents

Preface

Most beginning programmers are shocked to discover that program coding and testing are only half of a programmer's overall duties and responsibilities! After all, appropriate schooling and on-the-job background may have enabled us to master ASSEMBLER's machine-oriented approach, COBOL's business-like report syntax, FORTRAN's mathematical prowess, and/or perhaps PL/1's advantageous combinations of the above features. We need now only bring out the coding sheets and begin to solve our most worldly problems!

It is at this pinnacle of expectation that many beginning programmers are confronted with their first major processing obstacle--Job Control Language (JCL). JCL is a most perplexing problem facing all application and system programmers and analysts. It is the language of the Operating System (OS)--the interface between user and machine. It must be learned and mastered to effectively compile, link, execute, debug, sort, and perform all other processing functions. New programmers especially are adversely affected; and experienced analysts never seem to successfully shake that subtle fear of unexpected JCL failure.

So what's the other half of a programmer's overall duties and responsibilities? To be sure, JCL and Utility Program system flow, coding, execution, error analysis, and debugging (including storage dumps) encompass the bulk of a programmer's remaining time. Utilities are small programs which perform functions common to most users of a dp installation. The infrequent offerings of courses on these subjects in the progressive ADP field is surprising, though improving.

The purpose of this book is to provide a thorough and practical working knowledge of OS and VS JCL and Utility Programs. The book is organized in textbook fashion, such that it can be readily adapted to classroom use if desired. A workshop is provided at the end of all chapters except the first.

Chapter 1 introduces the reader to Operating System concepts, a necessary topic to the understanding of JCL and Utilities. Chapters 2 through 4 describe the three basic JCL statements--the Job statement, the Execute statement, and the Data Definition statement. In addition to a complete detailed presentation of each statement's parameters, an abbreviated and basic format reflective of common parameter use is presented. Chapter 5 discusses catalogued procedures, the most misunderstood aspect of JCL use. The utilization of high level languages (COBOL, FORTRAN, and PL/1), ASSEMBLER language, and Sort procedures are emphasized. Chapters 6 and 7 describe the uses of Utility Programs (Data Set, System, and Independent), a most underrated topic of programmer concern. Chapter 8 presents advanced JCL applications and considerations. Finally, the appendices provide a handy parameter syntax summary, complete catalogued procedure listings, all parameter options of compiler, assembler, linkage editor, loader, and sort/merge programs, a 42-term JCL and Utility Program glossary, and workshop answers for previous exercises.

By the way, I was one of those perplexed programmers who had learned only half of my job and didn't realize it. After picking up pieces here and there, gaining experience day by day, and training myself like so many others, I decided to organize the subject matter and begin teaching it myself. Since that first class in the summer of 1972, I have reorganized and refined the course numerous times while presenting it to over 500 students through the U. S. Department of Agriculture's Graduate School in Washington, D.C. This textbook is a resultant by-product of that experience.

My appreciation is extended to Chuck Tobin and Al Impellitteri for their technical advice and assistance; Charlotte Tsoucalas for her thorough editing and critique; and my wife, Ruth, for her exacting typing reviews. I would also like to thank International Business Machines Corporation for permission to reproduce the JCL Syntax Reference Summary Card as well as follow their specific parameter code notations. Charles Gold of IBM was also most helpful. The IBM JCL Reference Manual, Utilities Manual, and appropriate Programming Language Guide Manuals were handy references on specific occasions.

DANIEL H. RINDFLEISCH

Utilizing
System 360/370
OS and VS
Job Control Language
and Utility Programs

1
Operating System Concepts

A. OS INTRODUCTION

Job Control Language (JCL) is the language of the Operating System (OS) with or without the Virtual Storage (VS) feature. JCL is the interface between the application, data base, or system user and the Operating System. It is the Operating System (software) which activates and supervises the Central Processing Unit (CPU), Control units, Input/Output (I/O) units, etc. (hardware). This concept is depicted in Figure 1.1.

Figure 1.1 The Job Control Language (JCL) Interface

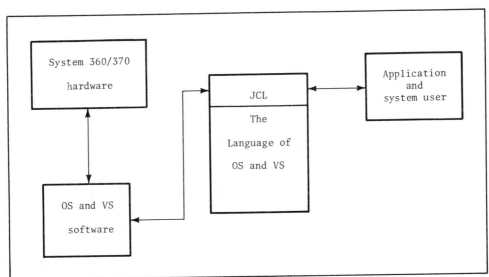

As one can see, JCL is a most powerful language. It commands the Operating System to activate and control millions of dollars worth of data-processing equipment. As such, it is a most strenuous tool. In a like manner, gross errors may result. An anticipated small-volume test run could result in a very expensive JCL timing error. A computer operator may continually receive erroneous JCL-generated messages to mount, then dismount, then mount again, then dismount a tape over and over again on a particular drive. In addition, many JCL logic errors result in abend storage dumps, one of the most perplexing problems facing application and system programmers and analysts. The need to understand and utilize the basics of Job Control Language and Utility Programs is ever-present in all OS and VS data-processing.

The System 360/370 OS and VS approach to JCL is one of processing flexibility and capability. For example, a tape of unique or nonstandard specifications may need to be processed. To be sure, there is a way of describing that file to OS via the JCL language. System 360/370 OS and VS is nonrestrictive by nature. Though processing standards are present, desirable, and useful, one need not necessarily be limited by a nonstandard data-processing situation. There is a way of describing or bypassing various specifications to the Operating System via Job Control Language. This in turn increases the capability of a data-processing system to the user.

The above broad-based approach also increases the complexity of JCL syntax. At first glance, the format of some JCL parameters appears to "boggle the mind". There is little need for concern, however. In my opinion, the 90/10 rule prevails insofar as the basics of OS and VS Job Control Language are concerned. That is, 90% of the syntax is used an average of only 10% of the time. Conversely, and fortunately, 10% of the syntax is used an average of 90% of the time. Chapters 2 though 5 of this text and accompanying workshops emphasize that 10% syntax (90% use), i.e., the basics of Job Control Language, though all parameters are eventually covered. Chapters 6 and 7 concentrate on how to use Utility Programs. Utilities are programs which perform data-processing functions common to most system users, i.e., print, punch, catalogue, update, copy, reformat, etc. In the final chapter advanced JCL considerations for special situations are presented.

B. OS AND VS DEFINITIONS

Operating System (OS) A group of programs (system software) which control, process, translate, and service a computer configuration (hardware), by automatically supervising a computer's operation to the fullest extent possible, thus maximizing thruput of user programs (application software) and file processing.

Key phrases in the above definition of the Operating System have been underlined. First, the Operating System consists of a group of programs, sometimes referred to as "system software" or "the system". Second, these programs perform four basic functions: (1) control of the system itself, (2) processing while under its own control, (3) translation of higher-level programming languages, and (4) servicing user needs. The Operating System directs the Central Processing Unit (CPU), Control units, Input/Output (I/O) units, etc. These various equipment configurations are commonly referred to as "hardware" and do include user terminals connected remotely to the installation or processing site. Third, the Operating System automatically supervises its own operation. There are conditions in all installations, however, when the Operating System cannot completely and automatically supervise its own operation. These conditions commonly result in "bottlenecks" to operations management, e.g., the manual mounting of tapes on drives. However, the Operating System attempts to automatically supervise its own operation to the fullest extent possible. Fourth, thruput is maximized as a result of the Operating System's performance. That is, many user programs, commonly referred to as "application software" or "user software", can be executed concurrently though not simultaneously. While one user's program is waiting for input/output work to be completed, another user's program can be utilizing the Central Processing Unit, etc. This form of resource sharing, as compared to operating systems where each job must process to completion prior to initialization of the next job, results in higher job thruput.

The Virtual Storage (VS) feature of the Operating System is also an attempt to maximize thruput.

Virtual Storage (VS) A feature of the Operating System where main storage requirements are allocated by segments (or pages) as needed by the processing program, thus creating an appearance to the user of unlimited or "virtual" storage.

Key phrases in the above definition of Virtual Storage have been underlined. First, Virtual Storage is a significant feature, but not a completely new operating system. That is, following the above definition, VS is an extension of OS, and a logical one at that. Second, main storage needs are allocated in portions, commonly referred to as "segments", which consist of "pages", but only as needed by the program being executed. The size of each segment may vary depending upon installation and user needs, but in general ranges from over 4,000 bytes to 60,000 bytes. A byte is a unit of main storage measurement, equivalent to eight contiguous bits, and is represented in print form by two hexadecimal characters. Third, this paging technique gives an appearance to the user of unlimited or "virtual" storage. For example, a fictitious 16,384-byte program operating in a small 4,096-byte segment will require four pages of storage. However, only one segment (the one needed at the moment) resides in main storage, the other three being stored on disk until needed. Eventually they replace or overlay the current segment in main storage. This concept is shown in Figure 1.2.

Thus, it can be seen that with the Virtual Storage feature of the Operating System a large program requires a relatively small amount of main storage at a given moment in time.

C. OS COMPONENTS

1. Control Program

The System 360/370 Operating System (OS) with or without Virtual Storage (VS) contains a control program which performs the functions of supervisor, master scheduler, and job scheduler. It is the control program which accepts and initiates jobs, schedules them, and in general supervises the overall work to be performed by the Operating System.

Figure 1.2 VS Main Storage Paging

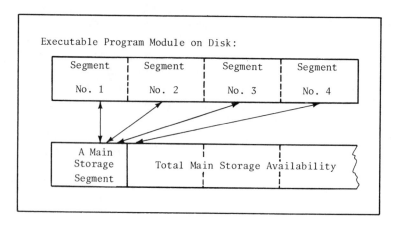

The three main areas of responsibility include: Job Management, Task Management, and Data Management.

a. Job Management

A job can be thought of as a collective unit of work to be performed by the Operating System. It consists of one or more steps. A programmer or systems analyst actually determines the size of a job, large or small, through the Job Control Language (JCL). Within reason, a given job may call many programs and may process many files. Each program to be called should be thought of as one step of a given job. Each step may consist of one or more files to be processed. This concept is shown in Figure 1.3.

Figure 1.3 The Job Step Concept

```
JOB  I  -  Consists of 3 Steps to Be Processed

    STEP  A:  Consists of the Program and 2 Files

            File 1 - Tape Input
            File 2 - Disk Output

    STEP  B:  Consists of the Program and 6 Files

            File 1 - Card Input
            File 2 - Disk Output
            File 3 - Work Disk 1
            File 4 - Work Disk 2
            File 5 - Tape Output
            File 6 - Print Output

    STEP  C:  Consists of the Program and 4 Files

            File 1 - Tape Input
            File 2 - Print Output
            File 3 - Punch Output
            File 4 - Disk Output
```

It is a function of the OS control program to manage the reading, interpreting, scheduling, allocation, initiation, output, recovery, and termination of all jobs that are being submitted, processed, or have completed processing under the supervision of the Operating System. Master scheduler and job scheduler routines control the processing of these jobs. They may be processed concurrently, though not simultaneously. Job priorities are determined in part by a job classification system. Jobs which require a scarce resource (e.g., card punch) or a large amount of a critical resource (e.g., main storage) would be scheduled behind a smaller job requiring less or similar resources. Job execution is also determined by the submission sequence (date and time) of the job relative to others. Job priorities can also be set by the application or system user via JCL as well as set and/or changed by the computer operator.

It is the responsibility of the Operating System to perform and control these Job Management functions.

b. Task Management

A task can be thought of as a unit of work to be performed by the Operating System. Some use the terms "task" and "step" interchangeably, though this is not always technically correct. A step may consist of more than one task or subtask. First, however, main storage requirements must be allocated via Job Control Language specifications or default procedures, and an executable program module loaded into this space. Next, Input/Output (I/O) units such as tape drives, disk drives, etc. must be allocated for each file defined in the program. Processing can then proceed until task completion. This concept is shown in Figure 1.4.

Figure 1.4 The Task Concept

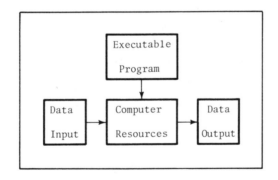

It is the function of the control program to manage the concurrent processing of tasks that will be loaded, have been loaded and are being processed, or have completed processing under the supervision of the Operating System. A supervisor routine controls the concurrent processing of tasks. Resource, program, and data sharing with other tasks are the three primary activities performed. Resource sharing is the most typical, however. For example, one task may need to access the same disk pack as another task running concurrently. Task priorities and execution are determined by similar factors as for a given job, that is, submission sequence, application and system user JCL, resource avail-

5

ability, and the computer operator.

It is the responsibility of the Operating System to perform and control these Task Management functions.

c. Data Management

A data file can be thought of as a collection of logical and physical records. Logical records are usually grouped to form physical blocks, the subunit of a given file. The Operating System performs Input/Output (I/O) operations in terms of these physical blocks. A programmer or systems analyst specifies block size through the Job Control Language (JCL). An example of the physical blocking of logical records is shown in Figure 1.5.

Figure 1.5 The Physical Blocking of Logical Records

Eight 80-Character Logical Records							
80	80	80	80	80	80	80	80

Equals

One 640-Character Physical Record

It is the function of the control program to manage the creation, organization, storage, retrieval, and growth of all data files that are being processed under the supervision of the Operating System. This includes not only data organization, but the management and control of reference libraries and the proper utilization of various access method techniques. In addition to processing in terms of blocks, the data and/or programs may be contained within a private library, may be accessed directly rather than sequentially, may be only partially created in the middle of a system failure, may be shared by other tasks or jobs, and may have originated from one or more remote on-line terminals.

It is the responsibility of the Operating System to perform and control these Data Management functions.

2. Processing Programs

In addition to the Control Program, the System 360/370 Operating System (OS) with or without Virtual Storage (VS) provides processing programs which perform the functions of assembling, compiling, link-editing, loading, sorting, and other utility functions. These programs translate higher-level language programs to machine-readable form as well as provide a service to the system user in other ways.

a. Assemblers and Compilers

To be sure, it is extremely difficult to develop a computer program directly in machine-readable form. With the concept of assembling and compiling came the development of higher-level English-like programming

languages. An assembler is a program which translates an assembly language program (ASSEMBLER) into a nearly 100% machine-readable module,
i.e., an object module. A compiler is a program which translates a
higher-level language program (COBOL, FORTRAN, PL/1, etc.) into such an
object module. Both assemblers and compilers edit for program syntax
errors. The object module they create can always be relocated; that is,
when converted to machine-readable form, it may be loaded into any
appropriate user address locations in main storage. Assemblers generate
machine language statements on a 1-for-1 basis. Macro statements call
more than one assembly statement. However, one assembly language statement still represents only one machine language statement. Compilers
generate machine language statements on a greater-than-1-for-1 basis.
One higher-level program language statement may generate more than one
assembly/machine language statement. These concepts are shown in
Figure 1.6.

Figure 1.6 Assembler and Compiler Concepts

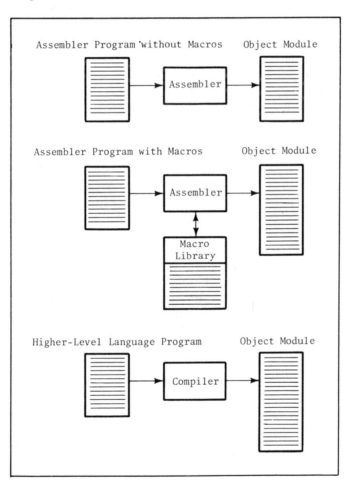

It is the responsibility of the Operating System to provide and
control the assembler and compiler process. The use of assemblers and
compilers will be discussed in detail in Chapter 5.

b. Service Programs

Service programs are provided to perform frequently utilized functions common to all system users. These services include the linkage editor program, the loader, the sort/merge program, as well as utility programs. It is the linkage editor program which converts the object module discussed previously into a 100% machine-executable relocatable module, i.e., a load module. The linkage editor attaches (links) input/output routines and other functions to the object module. It also provides for the program overlay feature if called upon. A loader program combine the linkage and execution of a load module in one step when special features of the linkage editor are not required. The sort/merge program will sort or merge data files into a sequence as specified by the system user. Utility programs (data set, system, independent) perform functions that are simple but common to all system users, e.g., print, punch, reformat, copy, move, catalogue, etc.

It is the responsibility of the Operating System to provide and control numerous service programs. Linking, loading, and the sort/merge process will be discussed in Chapter 5 in addition to assembling and compiling. Data Set Utility programs will be detailed in Chapter 6. System and Independent Utility programs will be covered in Chapter 7.

c. Other Processing Programs

Other service programs provided to the system user include various modules, emulators, and other special program products. Detailed information about these kinds of service can be obtained from the data-processing installation, vendor, and/or related documented sources.

D. OS INTERRUPTS

An interrupt occurs whenever a particular processing activity is halted so that another activity of higher priority can begin. The activity being interrupted may only be (and usually is) temporarily halted. The Operating System keeps track of the status of the halted activity via a program status word and passes control to the supervisor program. The new activity is then directed to begin. Upon completion of this activity, the supervisor regains control, and the original interrupted activity continues again from the point of interruption. The five classes of OS Interruptions in priority order are (1) Machine Check, (2) Supervisor Call, (3) Program, (4) External, and (5) Input/Output.

1. Machine Check Interruption

An OS Machine Check Interruption occurs whenever an activity is interrupted by a machine check signal which is caused by machine malfunctions, and on occasion, by main storage addressing errors. Machine check interruptions assist the system and equipment recovery process by locating the source of the error condition via diagnostic messages.

2. Supervisor Call Interruption

An OS Supervisor Call Interruption occurs whenever the system is interrupted and a switch to a supervisor state occurs. This switch occurs for any one of a broad number of reasons under both normal and abnormal operating conditions. Read and Write user program statements cause supervisor call interrupts, for example. Appropriate action is then provided by the supervisor control program, i.e., a switch to a new task.

3. Program Interruption

An OS Program Interruption occurs whenever the system is interrupted by improper address specifications, invalid use of data, or erroneous program specifications. Errors which cause a program interruption are operator exceptions; execute exceptions; protection, address, and specification exceptions; data errors; fixed-point, decimal, and exponent overflow; fixed-point, decimal, and floating-point divide exceptions; exponent underflows; and significance exceptions. Though occasional corrections are made, these exceptions usually result in abnormal termination of the user task.

4. External Interruption

An OS External Interruption occurs whenever an activity is interrupted by the system timer, interrupt key, or an external signal. The timer occupies a small amount of main storage. The contents of the timer continually change as instructions are executed. Any abnormalities in timing status may cause an external interruption. The Central Processing Unit (CPU) can also be interrupted at any time for any reason from an interrupt key on the computer operator's console panel; for example an operator may wish to send a message to OS. Some operating systems also contain a feature whereby external signals can be received for interruption from other systems, i.e., another CPU. Any of the above conditions may cause an external interruption to occur. Control is then passed to the supervisor state and appropriate attention is directed to a new activity.

5. Input/Output (I/O) Interrupt

An OS Input/Output (I/O) Interrupt occurs whenever the system is interrupted by a request for an I/O operation. Conditions which result in I/O interrupts include unit, program, and protection error checks as well as ending signals from a particular device, channel, or control unit. Any of these conditions as well as attention and busy signals may cause an I/O interruption to occur. Attention is then directed to the I/O operation to be performed.

E. OS CONFIGURATIONS

A dp installation has the option of choosing among certain basic forms of the Operating System when the system is generated within a given facility -- Primary Control Program (PCP), Multiprogramming with a Fixed number of Tasks (MFT), and Multiprogramming with a Variable Number of Tasks (MVT). In addition, the Virtual Storage (VS) feature can be generated for MFT (VS1) and MVT (VS2). An understanding of OS control program configurations will be most helpful to the JCL learning process.

1. Primary Control Program (PCP)

PCP is the simplest form of the Operating System. Under PCP, jobs are processed one at a time in sequential order. Job scheduling is simply a function of when the job was submitted to the system. Only one job step is executed at a time. An example of a PCP configuration is shown in Figure 1.7.

Figure 1.7 PCP Configuration

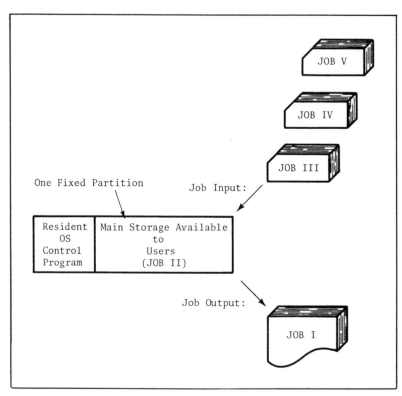

As shown, the PCP option of the Operating System has only one fixed main storage partition for installation users. The nucleus of the Operating System is permanently resident in the low address area of storage. Main storage capacity may total 256,000 (256K) bytes, though an installation can optionally choose less. Common hardware configurations for PCP include System 360, Models 30 and 40.

Due to idle resource time between tasks as well as during task performance, PCP makes the least efficient use of an installation's total resources. Thruput is relatively low, though costs of operation may be low also.

2. Multiprogramming with a Fixed Number of Tasks (MFT)

MFT is a very effective form of the Operating System. Unlike PCP, MFT processes more than one job at the same time. Job scheduling is a function of job characteristics as well as job submission sequence. Though only one job step may be executing at a given moment in time, steps from more than one job may be executing concurrently. That is, while one step is utilizing the Central Processing Unit (CPU), another

10

may be performing necessary Input/Output (I/O) tasks. An example of
a MFT configuration is shown in Figure 1.8.

Figure 1.8 MFT Configuration

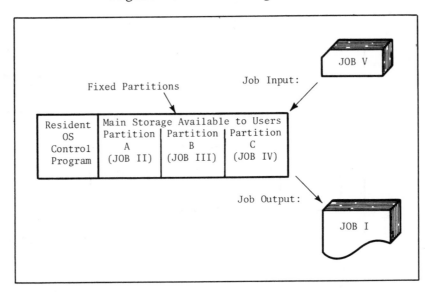

As can be seen, the MFT option of the Operating System may have
more than one fixed main storage partition for installation users. In
fact, up to 15 partitions may be fixed as determined during system
generation by the installation. The nucleus of the Operating System
is permanently resident in the low address area of storage. Main
storage requirements must be at least 128,000 (128K) bytes, though 256K
and 512K capacities are more typical. Common hardware configurations
for MFT include System 360, Models 40 and 50.

Because more than one job step may be executing concurrently (though
not simultaneously), there is a much more efficient use of idle resources
as compared with PCP. This is because many of the tasks to be performed,
though separate and independent of each other, may be accomplished in the
same time frame. A particular job step may need to transfer data from
a buffer area to a physical device; another may need to utilize the Central
Processing Unit; another may be awaiting the mounting of a tape by the
computer operator; and yet another may purposefully run in a background
batch environment waiting for a break in the use of interactive resources.
In other words, system control is purposely planned to be passed back
and forth among jobs at a frequent pace depending upon status, need,
and availability of system resources. Due to this type of resource
sharing, total thruput is much higher than in the PCP version.

3. Multiprogramming with a Variable Number of Tasks (MVT)

MVT is a most effective form of the Operating System. Like MFT,
more than one job may be executing concurrently. Job scheduling is a
function of priority as well as job submission sequence. Priority is
determined by the characterictics of the job as well as a priority
specification or default. Though only one step may be executing at a
given moment in time, steps from more than one job may be executing

11

concurrently. The primary difference between MFT and MVT is under MVT
the number and size of main storage partitions may vary. Partition size
is controlled by the user via a JCL Region parameter. An example of a
MVT configuration is shown in Figure 1.9.

Figure 1.9 MVT Configuration

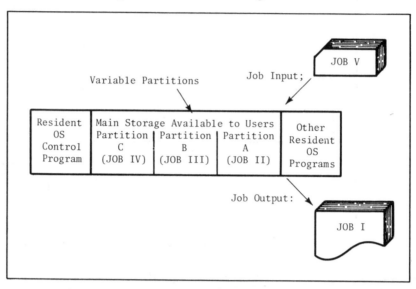

As shown, the MVT option of the Operating System may have a variable
number of main storage partitions (regions) for installation users. In
fact, up to 15 regions are allowed, but are not fixed during system generation as partitions are in MFT. Rather, the user determines when a
partition is needed and what the region size shall be. The nucleus of
the Operating System is permanently resident in the low address area of
storage. OS scheduler and link programs are permanently resident in
the high address area. Main storage requirements should be at least
256,000 (256K) bytes, though 1024K, 2048K, and higher capacities are
more typical. Common hardware configurations for MVT include System 360,
Model 65 as well as the System 370 series.

Because up to 15 variable job steps may be executing concurrently
(though not simultaneously), a more efficient use of idle resources
is accomplished as compared to the fixed-partition nature of MFT. Like
MFT, many of the tasks to be performed, though separate and independent
of each other, may be accomplished in the same time frame. Like MFT,
MVT system control is purposely planned to be passed back and forth among
jobs at a frequent pace depending upon status, need, and availability
of system resources. Due to the nature of this type of variable resource
sharing, total thruput is higher than in the MFT version.

4. Virtual Storage (VS) Operating Systems

a. Virtual Storage 1 (VS1)

VS1 is equivalent to an OS MFT configuration with the virtual storage
feature described earlier in his chapter. As with MFT, partition (segment
and page) characteristics are predefined; that is, they are defined when

12

the system is generated in the dp installation. To the user, main storage requirements are allocated by segments (or pages) as needed by the processing program, thus creating an appearance of unlimited or "virtual" storage.

b. Virtual Storage 2 (VS2)

VS2 is equivalent to an OS MVT configuration with the virtual storage feature described earlier in this chapter. As with MVT, the number of partitions and their size are not predefined; that is, they are defined when needed by the processing program. This concept is commonly referred to as Single Virtual Storage (SVS). Multiple Virtual Storage (MVS) is a multiprocessing extension of SVS which allows for an even larger virtual storage capability.

F. SAMPLE COMPUTER LISTINGS

A listing of pertinent computer run outputs and formats are provided for those readers unfamiliar with JCL, compiler, assembler, and linkage outputs. Figures 1.10 to 1.16 can also be used as a later reference throughout the text.

Figure 1.10 Portion of JCL Listing

```
   2    //STEP1   EXEC COBUCLG,PARM.COB='DMAP,PMAP,XREF',
        //          REGION.GO=30K,TIME.GO=(,20)
   3    XXCOBUCLG PROC PREFIX=SYS1                                      00000010
   4    XXCOB EXEC PGM=IKFCBL00,REGION=130K                             00000020
        *** REVISED 04/27/73 TO GIVE SYMBOLIC DUMP OPTIONS IF           00000030
        *** THE CORRECT CARDS ARE SUPPLIED TO THE GO STEP               00000040
        ***    REVISED 02/22/73 - 166                                   00000050
        *** PROGRAM NAME RUN CHANGED TO GO                              00000060
   5    XXSTEPLIB DD DSN=&PREFIX..COBLIB,DISP=SHR                       00000070
   6    XXSYSPRINT DD SYSOUT=A,SPACE=(3509,(175,50),,,ROUND),           00000080
        XX          DCB=(BLKSIZE=3509,LRECL=121,RECFM=FBA)              00000090
   7    XXSYSUT1  DD  UNIT=SYSDA,SPACE=(460,(700,100),,,ROUND)          00000100
   8    XXSYSUT2  DD  UNIT=SYSDA,SPACE=(460,(700,100),,,ROUND)          00000110
   9    XXSYSUT3  DD  UNIT=SYSDA,SPACE=(460,(700,100),,,ROUND)          00000120
  10    XXSYSUT4  DD  UNIT=SYSDA,SPACE=(460,(700,100),,,ROUND)          00000130
  11    XXSYSUT5  DD UNIT=SYSDA,SPACE=(460,(700,100),,,ROUND),          00000140
        XX          DSN=&&UT5,DISP=(,PASS)                              00000150
  12    XXSYSLIN DD DSN=&LOADSET,DISP=(MOD,PASS),UNIT=SYSDA,            00000160
        XX     SPACE=(80,(2000,1000),RLSE)                             00000170
  13    XXSYSUDUMP DD SYSOUT=A                                          00000180
  14    //COB.SYSIN    DD  *
  15    XXLKED EXEC PGM=IEWL,PARM='LIST,XREF',COND=(5,LT,COB),REGION=100K 00000190
  16    XXSYSLIN  DD DSNAME=&LOADSET,DISP=(OLD,DELETE)                  00000200
  17    XX    DD  DDNAME=SYSIN                                          00000210
  18    XXSYSLMOD DD DSNAME=&GODATA(GO),DISP=(NEW,PASS),UNIT=SYSDA,     00000220
        XX     SPACE=(1024,(200,10,1),,,ROUND)                         00000230
  19    XXSYSLIB  DD  DSNAME=&PREFIX..COBLIB,DISP=SHR                   00000240
  20    XX    DD  DSN=SYS3.PROG,DISP=SHR                                00000250
  21    XXSYSUT1 DD UNIT=SYSDA,                                         00000260
        XX     SPACE=(1024,(50,20),,,ROUND)                            00000270
  22    XXSYSPRINT DD SYSOUT=A                                          00000280
  23    XXSYSUDUMP  DD SYSOUT=A                                         00000290
  24    XXGO  EXEC PGM=*.LKED.SYSLMOD,COND=((5,LT,COB),(5,LT,LKED))     00000300
        *** TO GET A SYMBOLIC DUMP SUPPLY THE FOLLOWING:                00000310
        *** //GO.SYSDBG DD *,DCB=BLKSIZE=80                             00000320
        *** CONTROL CARDS                                              00000330
        ***                                                            00000340
        *** CONSULT IBM OS ANSI COBOL LANGUAGE MANUAL V4                00000350
        ***    #GC28-6396-3 PP. 397-412 OR                             00000360
        ***    IBM OS ANSI PROGRAMMER'S GUIDE V4                        00000370
        ***    #SC28-6456-0 PP. 158-172                                00000380
        *** ON HOW TO FORMAT THE CONTROL CARDS.                         00000390
        *** TO GET A FULL DUMP SUPPLY THE FOLLOWING CARD:               00000400
        *** //GO.SYSUDUMP DD SYSOUT=A                                   00000410
  25    XXSYSPRINT DD SYSOUT=A                                          00000420
  26    XXSYSOUT   DD SYSOUT=A                                          00000430
  27    XXSYSDBOUT DD SYSOUT=A                                          00000440
  28    XXSYSDTERM DD SYSOUT=A                                          00000450
  29    XXDBGDS    DD DSN=&&UT5,DISP=(OLD,DELETE)                       00000460
  30    XXDUMDD DD DSN=&GODATA,DISP=(OLD,DELETE)                        00000470
  31    //GO.INPUT1 DD  *,DCB=BLKSIZE=160
  32    //GO.CDINPUT1  DD  *
  33    //GO.OUTPUT1  DD UNIT=SYSDA,DISP=(NEW,DELETE),
        //     DSN=&&GRDSEL1,SPACE=(4000,4,RLSE),
        //     DCB=(RECFM=FB,LRECL=080,BLKSIZE=4000)
  34    //GO.OUTPUT2  DD UNIT=SYSDA,DISP=(NEW,DELETE),
        //     DSN=&&GRDSEL2,SPACE=(4000,4,RLSE),
        //     DCB=(RECFM=FB,LRECL=080,BLKSIZE=4000)
  35    //GO.MSGOUT    DD  SYSOUT=A,DCB=(RECFM=FBA,LRECL=160,BLKSIZE=3200)
  36    //GO.SYSUDUMP  DD  SYSOUT=A
        //
```

13

Figure 1.11 Portions of Source Program Listings

ANS COBOL:

```
00045     3 1   WORKING-STORAGE SECTION.
00046     3 2   77  STATE4 PICTURE  9(7).
00047           01  INREC.
00048               02  IDENT1     PICTURE 9(7)  OCCURS  5 TIMES.
00049               02  STATE-DATA PICTURE 9(7).
00050               02  IDENT2     PICTURE 9(7)  OCCURS  5 TIMES.
00051               02  FILLER PIC X(3).
00052           01  CARDIN.
00053               02  STATE2     PICTURE X(7).
00054               02  FILLER     PICTURE X(73).
00055     3 3   01  COUNTS.
00056     3 4       02  FILLER PICTURE X(21) VALUE ' RECORDS ON TAPE 1 = '.
00057     3 5       02  CNT1 PICTURE  9(7) VALUE ZEROS.
00058     3 6       02  FILLER PICTURE X(21) VALUE ' RECORDS ON TAPE 2 = '.
00059     3 7       02  CNT2 PICTURE  9(7) VALUE ZEROS.
00060     3 8       02  FILLER PICTURE X(24) VALUE ' NORMAL END OF JOB       '.
00061     4 1   PROCEDURE DIVISION.
00062     4 2       OPEN INPUT CDINPUT1 INPUT1 OUTPUT OUTPUT1 OUTPUT2 TERM-FILE.
00063     4 3       READ CDINPUT1 INTO CARDIN AT END GO TO NORMAL-EOJ.
00064     4 4       MOVE STATE2 TO STATE4.
00065     4 5   PRO-2.
00066     4 6       READ INPUT1 INTO INREC AT END GO TO NORMAL-EOJ.
00067     4 7       IF STATE-DATA = STATE4 GO TO PRO-3.
00068     4 8       WRITE OUTRCD1 FROM INREC.
00069     4 9       ADD 1 TO CNT1.
00070     410       GO TO PRO-2.
00071     411   PRO-3.
00072     412       WRITE OUTRCD2 FROM INREC.
00073     413       ADD 1 TO CNT2.
00074     415       GO TO PRO-2.
00075     416   NORMAL-EOJ.
00076             WRITE TERM-RECORD FROM COUNTS.
00077     418       CLOSE INPUT1 OUTPUT1 OUTPUT2 TERM-FILE CDINPUT1.
00078     419       STOP RUN.
```

FORTRAN IV (G1):

```
          C     PROGRAM TO CREATE CORE DUMPS
0001            COMMON ID(8), M, N, ITEST
0002            READ (5,100) ID, M, N
0003      100 FORMAT (10I2)
0004            CALL COMP
0005            WRITE (6,200) ID, M, N, ITEST
0006      200 FORMAT ('-', T6, '   ID = ', 8I2//,
          1              T6, '    M = ', I2//,
          2              T6, '    N = ', I2//,
          3              T6, 'ITEST = ', I2////,
          4              T6, 'END OF JOB')
0007            STOP
0008            END
```

```
0001            SUBROUTINE COMP
0002            COMMON ID(8), M, N, ITEST
0003      100 ITEST = ID(M) * ID(N)
0004      150 IF( ITEST.GE.2.AND.ITEST.LE.224) GO TO 100
0005            WRITE (6,200)
0006      200 FORMAT ('1', 'ITEST OUT OF LIMITS')
0007      300 RETURN
0008            END
```

PL/1 (F):

```
26             DCL 1 RECIN2,
27               2  REGION2  CHAR  (2),
28               2  STATE2   CHAR  (17),
29               2  FILL3    CHAR  (3),
30               2  BPFYR2   CHAR  (2),
31               2  BPP2     CHAR  (5),
32               2  BPA2     CHAR  (4),
33               2  WQP2     CHAR  (4),
34               2  WQA2     CHAR  (4),
35               2  BAP2     CHAR  (4),
36               2  BAA2     CHAR  (4),
37               2  FILLER   CHAR  (71);
38         DCL (C,D,E,F,G,H,I,J,K,Z,CONV)  FIXED DEC (5);
39         C,D,E,F,G,H,I,J,K,CONV=0;
40             DCL YYMMDD CHAR (6);
41             DCL 1 MMDDYY,
42               2 (MO,DA,YR)  CHAR (2);
43             YYMMDD = DATE;
44         GET STRING (YYMMDD) EDIT (YR,MO,DA) (A(2),A(2),A(2));
45             DCL  PAGENUM FIXED DEC (4);  PAGENUM=1;
46             DCL REG  CHAR (2);  REG=' ';
47             DCL (Y1,Y2,Y3,Y4)  CHAR (2);  Y1,Y2,Y3,Y4=' ';
```

14

```
48          DCL A CHAR (7);  A=(7)'-';  DCL B CHAR (8); B=(8)'-';
49          DCL READIT FILE RECORD INPUT;
50          ON ENDFILE(READIT) GO TO FIN;
51          OPEN FILE (SYSPRINT) LINESIZE (132);
52          REGION2=' ';
53    RD:   READ FILE (READIT) INTO (RECIN);
54          IF BPFYR = ' ' THEN GO TO RD;
55          IF Y4 = ' ' THEN GO TO FORM1;
56    RD1:    IF REG=REGION THEN GO TO FORM2;
57    PUT SKIP EDIT (A,B,A,B,B,A,A,B,B,A,A,B,B,A) (A,A,X(2),A(9),A(10),A(10),
58    A(10),A(3),A(10),A(10),A(11),A(9),A(10),A(10),A);
59    PUT SKIP EDIT ('TOTALS',C,D,E,F,G,H,I,J,K) (X(4),A,X(7),F(5),X(4),F(5),
60    X(15),F(5),X(5),F(5),X(15),F(5),X(4),F(5),X(15),F(5),X(6),F(5),X(4),F(5),X(15),F(5
61    ));
62    C,D,E,F,G,H,I,J,K,CONV=0;
63          PUT PAGE;  PAGENUM=PAGENUM+1;
64    FORM1:   Y4=REGION;
```

ASSEMBLER (F):

```
  LOC   OBJECT CODE      ADDR1 ADDR2   STMT     SOURCE STATEMENT

000000                                  1         START  0
                                        2         PRINT  NOGEN
000000 05C0                             3 BEGIN   BALR   12,0
                           00002        4         USING  *,12
000002 50F0 CCE6           00CE8        5         ST     14,SAVE
000006 D74F CBE9 CBE9 00BEB 00BEB       6         XC     PRINT,PRINT
                                        7         OPEN   (CARDRD,(INPUT))
                                       13         OPEN   (CARDWR,(OUTPUT))
                                       19         OPEN   (PARAM,(INPUT))
                                       25         OPEN   (PARAM1,(OUTPUT))
                                       31         OPEN   (ERFILE,(OUTPUT))
000046 D7CF CCF6 CCF6 00CF8 00CF8      37         XC     EREC,EREC
                                       38 READ5   GET    PARAM,PARMREC
00005A D204 CCF0 CAA2 00CF2 00AA4      43         MVC    SELECT(5),PARMREC
000060 D24F CBE9 CAA2 00BEB 00AA4      44         MVC    PRINT(80),PARMREC
                                       45         PUT    CARDWR,PRINT
000074 FA20 CAF2 CAF5 00AF4 00AF7      50         AP     PARMCNT,ONE
00007A D20C CCD9 C956 00CDB 00958      51         MVC    WID+0(13),CARD
000080 47F0 C0B0           000B2       52         B      COMP
                                       53 READ    GET    CARDRD,CARD
000092 D200 CAF8 CAF7 00AFA 00AF9      58         MVC    I,ZERO
00009B D200 C0C8 CF44 00DCA 00E46      59         MVC    SWT,=C'0'
0000BE FA20 C9A6 CAF5 009A8 00AF7      60         AP     COUNT,ONE
0000A4 D504 C971 CAA2 00973 00AA4      61         CLC    CARD+27(5),PARMREC
0000AA 4770 C0C6           000C8       62         BNE    READ2
0000AE 4780 C0F0           000F2       63         BE     READ4
0000B2 D50C CCD9 C956 00CDB 00958      64 COMP    CLC    WID+0(13),CARD
0000B8 4770 C6A4           006A6       65         BNE    RESET
0000BC D24F CAF9 C956 00AFB 00958      66         MVC    WORK(80),CARD
0000C2 D24F CBE9 C956 00BEB 00958      67         MVC    PRINT(80),CARD
```

Figure 1.12 Portions of Generated Assembly Language Listings

ANS COBOL:

```
 66    READ    000BA2   58 10 C 01C          L     1,01C(0,12)
               0008A6   18 21                LR    2,1
               0008A8   D2 02 2 021 C 019    MVC   021(3,2),019(12)
               0008AE   58 F0 1 030          L     15,030(0,1)
               0008B2   05 EF                BALR  14,15
               0008B4   50 10 D 1F4          ST    1,1F4(0,13)
               0008B8   58 70 D 1F4          L     7,1F4(0,13)
               0008BC   D2 4F 6 008 7 000    MVC   008(80,6),000(7)
               0008C2   47 F0 B 13E          BC    15,13E(0,11)
               0008C6              GN=03     EQU   *
 66    GO      0008C6   47 F0 B 214          BC    15,214(0,11)
               0008CA              GN=04     EQU   *
 67    IF      0008CA   F2 76 D 210 6 028    PACK  210(8,13),028(7,6)
               0008D0   F2 76 D 218 6 000    PACK  218(8,13),000(7,6)
               0008D6   F9 33 D 214 D 21C    CP    214(4,13),21C(4,13)
               0008DC   47 70 B 158          BC    7,158(0,11)
 67    GO      0008E0   47 F0 B 1B6          BC    15,1B6(0,11)
               0008E4              GN=05     EQU   *
 68    WRITE   0008E4   D2 4F 8 000 6 008    MVC   000(80,8),008(6)
               0008EA   58 10 C 020          L     1,020(0,12)
               0008EE   18 21                LR    2,1
               0008F0   92 00 2 07A          MVI   07A(2),X'00'
               0008F4   58 40 2 024          L     4,024(0,2)
               0008F8   92 00 4 014          MVI   014(4),X'00'
               0008FC   96 01 4 01B          OI    01B(4),X'01'
               000900   58 10 C 020          L     1,020(0,12)
               000904   58 00 1 04C          L     0,04C(0,1)
               000908   58 F0 1 030          L     15,030(0,1)
               00090C   44 00 1 060          EX    0,060(0,1)
               000910   58 20 C 020          L     2,020(0,12)
               000914   91 40 2 07A          TM    07A(2),X'40'
```

15

FORTRAN IV (G1):

```
000138            A36    L      13,4(0,13)
00013C                   L      14,12(0,13)
000140                   LM     2,12,28(13)
000144                   MVI    12(13),255
000148                   BCR    15,14
00014A            A20    L      15,100(0,13)        IBCOM#
00014E                   LR     12,13
000150                   LR     13,4
000152                   BAL    14,64(0,15)
000156                   LR     13,12
000158            2      L      15,100(0,13)        IBCOM#
00015C                   BAL    14,0(0,15)
000160                   DC     00000005
000164                   DC     0000009C
000168                   BAL    14,12(0,15)
00016C                   DC     00000000
000170                   DC     04500008
000174                   L      10,72(0,13)
000178                   BAL    14,8(0,15)
00017C                   CC     0450A020
000180                   BAL    14,8(0,15)
000184                   DC     0450A024
000188                   BAL    14,16(0,15)
00018C            4      LA     1,0(0,0)
000190                   L      15,104(0,13)        CCMP
000194                   BALR   14,15
000198            5      L      15,100(0,13)        IBCOM#
00019A                   BCR    0,0
00019C                   BAL    14,4(0,15)
0001A0                   DC     00000006
0001A4                   DC     000000A2
0001A8                   BAL    14,12(0,15)
0001AC                   DC     00000000
0001B0                   CC     04500008
```

PL/1 (F):
```
                 PRS1:    PROC OPTIONS (MAIN);

00104C   47 90 A E9C              BC     9,CK1
001050                    CL.5    EQU    *

* STATEMENT NUMBER   57
001050   92 39 D 063              MVI    99(13),X'39'
001054   41 10 D 130              LA     1,DV..RECIN1.BPP1
001058   41 20 B 5A1              LA     2,DED..RECIN1.BPP1
00105C   41 33 D 1DB              LA     3,Z
001060   41 40 B 5A2              LA     4,DED..Z
001064   58 F0 B 05C              L      15,A..IHEDCN\
001068   05 EF                    BALR   14,15

* STATEMENT NUMBER   58
00106A   92 3A D 063              MVI    99(13),X'3A'
00106E   FA 22 D 1C3 D 1DB        AP     C(3),Z(3)

* STATEMENT NUMBER   59

* STATEMENT LABEL                 CK1
001074   92 3B D 063              MVI    99(13),X'3B'
001078   D5 00 D 299 B 361        CLC    RECIN1.BPA1(1),C..
                                         OF58
00107E   47 70 A EB0              BC     7,CL.23
001082   D5 02 D 29A B 118        CLC    RECIN1.BPA1+1(3),C
                                         ..1554

001088                    CL.23   EQU    *

* STATEMENT NUMBER   60
001088   92 3C D 063              MVI    99(13),X'3C'
00108C   47 90 A EDC              BC     9,CK2
001090                    CL.6    EQU    *

* STATEMENT NUMBER   61
001090   92 3D D 063              MVI    99(13),X'3D'
001094   41 10 D 138              LA     1,DV..RECIN1.BPA1
001098   41 20 B 5A1              LA     2,DED..RECIN1.BPA1
00109C   41 30 D 1DB              LA     3,Z
0010A0   41 40 B 5A2              LA     4,DED..Z
0010A4   58 F0 B 050              L      15,A..IHEDCN\
0010A8   05 EF                    BALR   14,15

* STATEMENT NUMBER   62
0010AA   92 3E D 063              MVI    99(13),X'3E'
0010AE   FA 22 D 1C3 D 1DB        AP     D(3),Z(3)

* STATEMENT NUMBER   63

* STATEMENT LABEL                 CK2
0010B4   92 3F D 063              MVI    99(13),X'3F'
0010B8   D5 00 D 21B B 361        CLC    RECIN.BPP(1),C..OF
                                         58
0010BE   47 70 A EFC              BC     7,CL.24
```

Figure 1.13 Portions of Abbreviated Assembly Listings

ANS COBOL:

CONDENSED LISTING

62	OPEN	00076C	63	READ	000870	63	GO	000894
64	MOVE	000898	66	READ	0008A2	66	GO	0008C6
67	IF	0008CA	67	GO	0008E0	68	WRITE	0008E4
69	ADD	000928	70	GO	00093E	72	WRITE	000942
73	ADD	000986	74	GO	00099C	76	WRITE	0009A0
77	CLOSE	0009E4	78	STOP	0009C			

PL/1 (F):

TABLE OF OFFSETS AND STATEMENT NUMBERS WITHIN ON UNIT

OFFSET (HEX)   0000 0048 0052
STATEMENT NO   23   23

TABLE OF OFFSETS AND STATEMENT NUMBERS WITHIN PROCEDURE   PRS1

OFFSET (HEX) 0000 01D0 020C 0224 0292 0298 029E 02B6 02BC 02C2 02D0 02DA 02E0 02F8 0308 030C 031C 0320 0326 032A 0480
STATEMENT NO   1   6   9   10   12   14   16   18   20   22   24   25   26   27   28   29   30   31   32   33   34

OFFSET (HEX) 0628 0664 0674 067A 0680 074E 078E 07CE 080E 0872 08E2 0938 0978 097E 0984 099C 09A2 0BDA 0C98 0DEE 0F4E
STATEMENT NO   35   36   37   38   39   40   41   42   43   44   45   46   47   48   49   50   51   52   53   54   55

OFFSET (HEX) 0F5E 0F62 0F78 0F7E 0F8E 0F92 0FA8 0FAE 0FBE 0FC2 0FD8 0FDE 0FEE 0FF2 1008 100E 101E 1022 1038 103E 104E
STATEMENT NO   56   57   58   59   60   61   62   63   64   65   66   67   68   69   70   71   72   73   74   75   76

OFFSET (HEX) 1052 1068 106E 107E 1082 1098 10AA 10BA 10BE 10D4 10E6 10F6 10FA 1110 1116 111C 112C 1130 1136 113C 1140
STATEMENT NO   77   78   79   80   81   82   83   84   85   86   87   88   89   90   91   92   93   94   95   96   97

OFFSET (HEX) 1146 115E 116E 1172 1178 117C 118C 1190 11A8 11AC 130A 14BA
STATEMENT NO   98   99 100 101 102 103 104 105 106 107 108 109

Figure 1.14 COBOL and FORTRAN Maps

ANS COBOL Date Map (DMAP):

LVL	SOURCE NAME	BASE	DISPL	INTRNL NAME	DEFINITION	USAGE
FD	INPUT1	DCB=01		DNM=1-073		QSAM
01	INRCD	BL=1	000	DNM=1-092	DS 80C	DISP
FD	OUTPUT1	DCB=02		DNM=1-107		QSAM
01	OUTRCD1	BL=2	000	DNM=1-127	DS 80C	DISP
FD	OUTPUT2	DCB=03		DNM=1-144		QSAM
01	OUTRCD2	BL=3	000	DNM=1-164	DS 80C	DISP
FD	CDINPUT1	DCB=04		DNM=1-181		QSAM
01	CD-IN	BL=4	000	DNM=1-202	DS 80C	DISP
FD	TERM-FILE	DCB=05		DNM=1-220		QSAM
01	TERM-RECORD	BL=5	000	DNM=1-242	DS 80C	DISP
77	STATE4	BL=6	000	DNM=1-263	DS 7C	DISP-NM
01	INREC	BL=6	008	DNM=1-279	DS OCL80	GROUP
02	IDENT1	BL=6	008	DNM=1-297	DS 7C	DISP-NM
02	STATE-DATA	BL=6	02B	DNM=1-313	DS 7C	DISP-NM
02	IDENT2	BL=6	032	DNM=1-333	DS 7C	DISP
02	FILLER	BL=6	055	DNM=1-349	DS 3C	GROUP
01	CARDIN	BL=6	058	DNM=1-360	DS OCL80	DISP
02	STATE2	BL=6	058	DNM=1-379	DS 7C	DISP
02	FILLER	BL=6	05F	DNM=1-395	DS 73C	GROUP
01	COUNTS	BL=6	0A8	DNM=1-409	DS OCL80	DISP
02	FILLER	BL=6	0A8	DNM=1-428	DS 21C	DISP-NM
02	CNT1	BL=6	0BD	DNM=1-442	DS 7C	DISP
02	FILLER	BL=6	0C4	DNM=1-456	DS 21C	DISP-NM
02	CNT2	BL=6	0D9	DNM=1-470	DS 7C	DISP
02	FILLER	BL=6	0E0	DNM=1-484	DS 24C	DISP

FORTRAN IV (G1) Map:

COMMON BLOCK /   / MAP SIZE   2C

SYMBOL	LOCATION	SYMBOL	LOCATION	SYMBOL	LOCATION	SYMBOL	LOCATION
ID	C	M	20	N	24	ITEST	28

SUBPROGRAMS CALLED

SYMBOL	LOCATION	SYMBOL	LOCATION	SYMBOL	LOCATION	SYMBOL	LOCATION
IBCOM#	94	COMP	58				

FORMAT STATEMENT MAP

SYMBOL	LOCATION	SYMBOL	LOCATION	SYMBOL	LOCATION	SYMBOL	LOCATION
100	9C	200	A2				

G. OS CONCEPTS SUMMARY

Job Control Language (JCL) is the language of the Operating System (OS). It is the interface between the user and OS. JCL is designed for processing flexibility and capability. This approach increases the com-

Figure 1.15 Program Cross-Reference Tables

```
ANS COBOL:

                                    CROSS-REFERENCE DICTIONARY

       DATA NAMES                DEFN     REFERENCE

       INPUT1                    000011   000062   000066   000077
       INRCD                     000022   000066
       OUTPUT1                   000012   000062   000068   000077
       OUTRCD1                   000028   000068
       OUTPUT2                   000013   000062   000072   000077
       OUTRCD2                   000033   000072
       CDINPUT1                  000014   000062   000063   000077
       CD-IN                     000039   000063
       TERM-FILE                 000015   000062   000076   000077
       TERM-RECORD               000044   000076
       STATE4                    000046   000064   000067
       INREC                     000047   000066   000068   000072
       IDENT1                    000048
       STATE-DATA                000049   000067
       IDENT2                    000050
       CARDIN                    000052   000063
       STATE2                    000053   000064
       COUNTS                    000055   000076
       CNT1                      000057   000069
       CNT2                      000059   000073



       PROCEDURE NAMES           DEFN     REFERENCE

       PRO-2                     000065   000070   000074
       PRO-3                     000071   000067
       NORMAL-EOJ                000075   000063   000066
```

```
PL/1 (F):

                                    ATTRIBUTE AND CROSS-REFERENCE TABLE

DCL NO.      IDENTIFIER           ATTRIBUTES AND REFERENCES

17           A                    AUTOMATIC,UNALIGNED,STRING(7),CHARACTER
                                  18,33,33,33,33,33,33,53,53,53,53,53,53,53,107,107,107,107,107,107
                                  107

19           B                    AUTOMATIC,UNALIGNED,STRING(8),CHARACTER
                                  20,33,33,33,33,33,33,33,53,53,53,53,53,53,53,107,107,107,107,107,107
                                  107

2            BAA                  IN RECIN,AUTOMATIC,UNALIGNED,STRING(4),CHARACTER

3            BAA1                 IN RECIN1,AUTOMATIC,UNALIGNED,STRING(4),CHARACTER
                                  54,83,85

4            BAA2                 IN RECIN2,AUTOMATIC,UNALIGNED,STRING(4),CHARACTER

2            BAP                  IN RECIN,AUTOMATIC,UNALIGNED,STRING(4),CHARACTER
                                  54,87,89,105

3            BAP1                 IN RECIN1,AUTOMATIC,UNALIGNED,STRING(4),CHARACTER
                                  54,79,81

4            BAP2                 IN RECIN2,AUTOMATIC,UNALIGNED,STRING(4),CHARACTER

2            BPA                  IN RECIN,AUTOMATIC,UNALIGNED,STRING(4),CHARACTER

3            BPA1                 IN RECIN1,AUTOMATIC,UNALIGNED,STRING(4),CHARACTER
                                  54,59,61

4            BPA2                 IN RECIN2,AUTOMATIC,UNALIGNED,STRING(4),CHARACTER

2            BPFYR                IN RECIN,AUTOMATIC,UNALIGNED,STRING(2),CHARACTER
                                  27,47,50
```

18

```
ASSEMBLER (F):

SYMBOL    LEN    VALUE    DEFN    REFERENCES                                                      ASM 0201 16.43 08/03/77

BEGIN     00002  00000000 00003  00746
CARD      00080  00000958 00719  00051 00055 00061 00064 00066 00067 00068 00071 00074 00077 00080 00082 00083 00091 00094
                                  00096 00097 00105 00108 00110 00111 00119 00122 00125 00127 00128 00136 00139 00141 00142
                                  00150 00153 00155 00156 00164 00167 00169 00170 00178 00181 00183 00184 00192 00194 00196
                                  00198 00200 00202 00204 00206 00208 00210 00212 00214 00216 00218 00220 00222 00224 00226
                                  00228 00230 00232 00234 00236 00238 00240 00242 00244 00246 00249 00252 00255 00258 00261
                                  00264 00267 00270 00274 00280 00281 00283 00285 00287 00289 00291 00293 00295 00297 00299
                                  00301 00303 00305 00307 00309 00311 00313 00315 00317 00319 00321 00324 00326 00328 00330
                                  00332 00334 00336 00338 00340 00342 00344 00345 00359 00361 00362 00372 00374 00375 00385
CARDRD    00004  00000778 00453  00011 00054 00419
CARDWR    00004  00000838 00561  00017 00046 00347 00392 00401 00410 00431
CMP       00006  000004A2 00274  00277
CO        00003  000009B1 00723  00356 00399
COMP      00006  000009B2 00064  00052 00386
COUNT     00003  000009A8 00720  00060 00390
FREC      00208  00000CF8 00743  00037 00037 00079 00079 00080 00082 00083 00084 00087 00093 00093 00094 00096 00097 00098
                                  00101 00107 00107 00108 00110 00111 00112 00115 00124 00124 00125 00127 00128 00129 00132
                                  00138 00139 00141 00142 00143 00146 00152 00152 00153 00155 00156 00157 00160 00166
                                  00166 00167 00169 00170 00171 00174 00180 00180 00181 00183 00184 00185 00188 00358 00358
                                  00359 00361 00362 00363 00366 00371 00371 00372 00374 00375 00376 00379
FREILE    00004  000008F8 00669  00035 00086 00100 00114 00131 00145 00159 00173 00187 00365 00378 00443
ERROR     00006  0000062E 00358  00197 00203 00209 00215 00221 00227 00233 00239
ERROR2    00006  0000066A 00371  00243 00245 00269
I         00001  00000AFA 00731  00058
INSERT    00C04  000004B4 00278  00275
LL        00002  00000DC8 00744  00081 00084 00095 00098 00109 00112 00126 00129 00140 00143 00154 00157 00168 00171 00182
                                  00185 00360 00363 00373 00376
MASK      00006  00000CEC 00740  00389 00398 00407
NEXTI1    00006  0000042C 00249  00248
NEXTI3    00006  00000448 00255  00254
NEXTI4    00006  00000456 00258  00257
NEXTI5    0C006  00000464 00261  00260
NEXTI6    00006  00000472 00264  00263
NEXTI7    00006  00000480 00267  00266
```

Figure 1.16 Linkage Cross-Reference Table

```
LINKAGE EDITOR:

F64-LEVEL LINKAGE EDITOR OPTIONS SPECIFIED LIST,XREF
        DEFAULT OPTION(S) USED - SIZE=(196608,65536)

                                        CROSS REFERENCE TABLE

    CONTROL SECTION                 ENTRY
      NAME    ORIGIN   LENGTH          NAME   LOCATION    NAME   LOCATION    NAME   LOCATION    NAME   LOCATION
    A5558      00       C64
    ILBOCOMO*  C68      FA          ILBOCOM    C68

    ILBOEXT *  D68      6A          ILBOEXTO   D6A

    ILBOSRV *  DD8      37C         ILBOSRVO   E12     ILBOSR     E12     ILBOSR3    E12     ILBOSRV1   E16
                                    ILBOSTP1   E16     ILBOST     E1A     ILBOSTPO   E1A

    ILBOBEG *  1158     C2          ILBOBEGO   118A

    ILBOCMM *  1220     3C1         ILBOCMMO   1252    ILBOCMM1   1256

    ILBOMSG *  15E8     DO          ILBOMSGO   161A


    LOCATION   REFERS TO SYMBOL  IN CONTROL SECTION        LOCATION   REFERS TO SYMBOL  IN CONTROL SECTION
       754          ILBOSRVO        ILBOSRV                   758          ILBOSR          ILBOSRV
       75C          ILBOEXTO        ILBOEXT                   760          ILBOSRV1        ILBOSRV
       6CO          ILBOCOMO        ILBOCOMO                  10CO         ILBOCOM         ILBOCOMO
       10C4         ILBOCMMO        ILBOCMM                   10C8         ILBOBEGO        ILBOBEG
       10CC         ILBOMSGO        ILBOMSG
    ENTRY ADDRESS     00

    TOTAL LENGTH     16B8
    ****GO         DOES NOT EXIST BUT HAS BEEN ADDED TO DATA SET
    AUTHORIZATION CODE IS        0.
```

plexity of JCL syntax. In learning JCL basics, however, only a portion of that syntax is necessary, though all aspects will eventually be covered.

The Operating System (OS) is a group of programs which control, process, translate, and service a computer configuration, by automatically supervising its own operations to the fullest extend possible, thus maximizing thruput of user programs and file processing. Likewise, Virtual Storage (VS) is a feature of the basic Operating System where main storage requirements are allocated by segments as needed by the processing program, thus creating an appearance to the user of unlimited or "virtual" storage.

OS components of the System 360/370 Operating System consist of the Control Program, Processing Programs, and other Service Programs. The Control Program performs the functions of supervisor, master scheduler, and job scheduler.   The three main areas of control program responsibility are: Job Management, Task Management, and Data Management. It is the Control Program which accepts and initiates jobs, schedules them, and in general, supervises the overall work to be performed by the Operating System. Processing Programs consist of assemblers, compilers, and service programs such as the linkage editor, loader, sort/merge, utility, graphics, emulators, and other programs. Utility Programs perform relatively simple functions common to most users.

OS operates on an interrupt basis; an interrupt occurs whenever a particular processing activity is halted such that another activity of higher priority can begin. The Operating System keeps track of the status of the halted activity; control passes to the new activity which is eventually completed; control then usually returns to the halted activity. The five classes of OS Interruptions in priority order are Machine Check, Supervisor Call, Program, External, and Input/Output.

Basic OS Configurations consist of Primary Control Program (PCP), Multiprogramming with a Fixed Number of Tasks (MFT), Multiprogramming with a Variable Number of Tasks (MVT), and the Virtual Storage (VS) extension of the Operating System. PCP consists of one partition where jobs are scheduled one at a time in sequential order. MFT consists of multiple fixed partitions where jobs are scheduled based upon selected characteristics. MVT is similar to MFT except that the partitions are variable, that is, their characteristics are determined by the user. The Virtual Storage (VS) feature when implemented under OS MFT is called Virtual Storage 1 (VS1). When implemented under OS MVT it is referred to as Virtual Storage 2 (VS2). VS2 consists of a Single Virtual Storage (SVS) option and an extended Multiple Virtual Storage (MVS) option.

Though this chapter is not intended to make an OS expert of the reader, a basic understanding of OS concepts will greatly assist the the JCL learning process. The computer run listings as depicted in this chapter will also be a valuable reference throughout the text.

2

Job Identification

A. JCL INTRODUCTION

Job Control Language (JCL) is the fundamental interface between the prospective user and the System 360/370 Operating System (OS) with or without Virtual Storage (VS). JCL is the communication tool which application and system programmers and analysts use to activate as well as coordinate the many hardware and software facilities available to accomplish data-processing tasks and objectives. Given this most powerful tool it follows that gross (and costly) errors can also result. Learning to use JCL effectively is as important to the application and system programmer's and analyst's duties as the effective use of one or more of the many available programming languages.

JCL is not as confusing as many presume. Nor is the use of Utilities: those small programs called to perform many functions common to all system users, i.e., print, punch, reformat, copy, move, catalogue, etc. Given a basic set of methodical step-by-step procedures, anyone with a conceptual data-processing background can learn to effectively use System 360/370 OS and VS Job Control Language and Utility Programs.

B. JCL CODE NOTATION

As with all languages, a set of symbols are defined to meet the objectives and purpose of the specific language to be utilized. In order to describe that language's syntax to prospective users, various notations are provided to depict specific formats. Some notations are part of parameter syntax, while others are not.

1. Braces and Brackets

Neither braces {   } nor brackets [   ] are ever coded as part of a

21

parameter's syntax. Both have special explanatory meanings in understanding that syntax, however.

Braces are used to delineate one or a group of items in which one
(and only one) of the items is necessary and therefore required to be
coded if the parameter is to be utilized. For example,

$\begin{Bmatrix} \text{VOLUME} \\ \text{VOL} \end{Bmatrix}$ means that either the letters 'VOLUME' or 'VOL' must be coded
when the volume parameter is utilized.

Brackets are used to delineate one or a group of items in which one
or none of the items is necessary and therefore can be coded at the
option of the user if the parameter is utilized. If not coded, a default
value becomes effective. For example,

$\begin{bmatrix} \text{NEW} \\ \text{OLD} \\ \text{SHR} \\ \text{MOD} \end{bmatrix}$ means that either the letters 'NEW', 'OLD', 'SHR', or 'MOD' can
be coded to indicate the status of a data set. If no speci-
fication is given, a default to the first descriptor, 'NEW',
is to be generally assumed.

Braces and brackets occur quite frequently in the syntax description of JCL parameters. Their interpretation soon becomes second
nature to the system user.

2. Upper- and Lower-Case Characters

Capitalized words are used to describe special key reserved words in
JCL syntax. Keywords must be spelled exactly as described in the
format of the parameter. For example,

PGM=Program Name is a JCL parameter which fetches, loads, and initiates
the execution of a program module in main storage. The exact letters 'PGM' followed by an equal (=) sign indicate that a program
name follows.

Likewise, lower-case words with the first letter capitalized are
used to symbolize parameter variable values. When coded, a character
string must be substituted for the name(s) indicated. For example,

CLASS=Job Class is a JCL parameter which classifies jobs according to
their characteristics. The job class specified is determined by
substituting one or more characters for the words 'Job Class', e.g.,
CLASS=D.

In addition to upper- and lower-case alphabetic and numeric characters, the following special characters are coded directly as is:

    & - Ampersand
    ' - Apostrophe or Single Quote Mark
    * - Asterisk
    @ - At Sign
      - Blank
    , - Comma
    $ - Dollar Sign

```
=  -  Equal Sign
-  -  Hyphen or Minus Sign
(  -  Left Parenthesis
)  -  Right Parenthesis
.  -  Period
+  -  Plus Sign
#  -  Pound Sign
/  -  Slash Character
```

Parentheses are coded to enclose more than one occurrence of subparameter information. In some cases the Apostrophe (or Single Quote Mark) can be used for this purpose. The Apostrophe must be used to enclose literal characters. Commas are used to separate parameter and/or subparameter information. Blanks are used to separate fields in JCL format and to indicate the end of a particular JCL statement. Slashes are used at the beginning of each JCL line. The Equal Sign is used throughout JCL coding to separate keywords from value specifications. The three national characters (At Sign, Dollar Sign, and Pound Sign) can be used in lieu of some alpha character requirements. Hyphens (or Minus Signs) and Plus Signs are used to clarify the readability of some items as well as to specify file generations. Ampersands and Periods have special meaning in some JCL names. The Asterisk is used to read card data. The occurrence of six dots (......) in a JCL parameter's format indicates that the specification preceding the dots can be repeated one or more times. Specific uses for special characters will be described in more detail as they are encountered.

C. GENERAL JCL FORMAT

1. Control Fields

JCL statements can be divided into the following five fields of varying size as depicted in Figure 2.1.

Figure 2.1 JCL Statement Fields

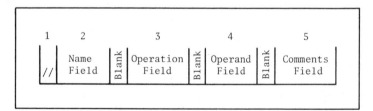

a. Name Field

Following the first field, a // (slash slash) in columns 1 and 2, the Name Field begins in column 3 and is one to eight characters in length. It assigns a name to this particular JCL statement's job, step, or file, thus identifying it for current use and/or later reference.

b. Operation Field

Following the Name Field and at least one blank, the Operation

Field identifies the type of JCL statement to be described, e.g., Job, Exec, or Dd, to be discussed later.

c. Operand Field

Following the Operation Field and at least one blank, the Operand Field contains basic parameter descriptions for the job, step, or file being identified. This is the main descriptor field of a JCL statement. Each parameter specification is separated by a comma.

d. Comments Field

Following the Operand Field and at least one blank, the Comment Field contains any additional information deemed useful by the JCL analyst.

2. Parameter Types

The Operand Field discussed above may contain two basic types of parameter specifications -- Positional Parameters and Keyword Parameters.

a. Positional Parameters

A positional parameter is one whose value is specified by coding the parameter in a certain relative position on the JCL statement. For example,

//GRD1 JOB 8974538 is a portion of a Job statement with a positional account number parameter of '8974538'. It is known to OS that this is an account number only because account information is always positional as the first parameter following the 'JOB' specification.

The absence of a positional parameter value must always be indicated by coding a comma, unless this is the last piece of positional information to be supplied or all available positional parameters are to be omitted.

b. Keyword Parameters

A keyword parameter is one whose value is specified by coding a special system-recognizable name, usually followed by an equal sign. For example,

TIME=(1,30) is a portion of a JCL statement with the keyword TIME followed by an equal sign.

Because keywords are recognized as such, they may be coded in any order following the positional parameter specifications. It should also be pointed out that positional subparameters may follow the equal sign of a keyword. In the above example, one minute and thirty seconds are being specified. These subparameters are positional in the sense that minutes must be specified before seconds.

3. Continuation Rules

JCL statements are continued onto succeeding lines by following a specific set of coding rules:

    a. Operand field parameters must end with a comma prior to column 72; the optional comment field need only end before column 72. (See Figure 2.2.) If a comment is being continued, however, a nonblank character must be coded in column 72.

    b. The second line must contain a // (slash slash) in column 1-2 while column 3 remains blank.

    c. Continuing parameter information or comments must begin in columns 4-16.

Figure 2.2 JCL Statement Continuation Example

```
//GRD1   JOB   8974538,'DHR',MSGLEVEL=1,
//        CLASS=A,TIME=(1,30)
```

The MSGLEVEL specification of '1' in the Job statement in Figure 2.2 is followed by a comma prior to column 72 (actually column 38). The second line begins with // followed by at least one blank. Continued information begins in columns 4-16 (actually 9). The end of the JCL statement is then denoted by the absence of a continuation, i.e., a blank.

D. THE JOB STREAM

A job stream consists of a series of one or more jobs to be read by the Operating System's reader/interpreter for editing and placement into the job queue. It is in this reader/interpreter process that individual jobs, steps, and files as described in the JCL are delineated and made distinct from one another. This task is accomplished by flagging the occurrence of any one of three basic types of JCL statements:

    The JOB (Job) Statement   - one per job;
    The EXEC (Execute) Statement   - one per step;
    The DD (Data Definition) Statement - one per file.

The first statement to be coded in all jobs is the Job statement. Specific jobs are in fact identified and delineated from one another by the occurrence of a Job statement. For example, the beginning of the description of the first job is signified by the occurrence of a Job statement. (See the top half of Figure 2.3.) Similarly, the end of the description of the first job and beginning of the second is signified by the occurrence of a second Job statement, etc. The beginning of the description of the first job step in the first job is denoted by the occurrence of an Exec statement. (See the bottom half of Figure 2.3.) Likewise, the end of the description of the first step and beginning of the second is signified by the occurrence of a second Exec statement, etc., for each job. Finally the beginning of the descrip-

tion of the first file in the first step of the first job is identified
by the occurrence of a Dd statement. (Also see the bottom half of
Figure 2.3.) In like manner, the end of the description of the first
file and beginning of the second is identified by the occurrence of a
second Dd statement, etc., for each step of each job.

Figure 2.3 A Typical Job Stream

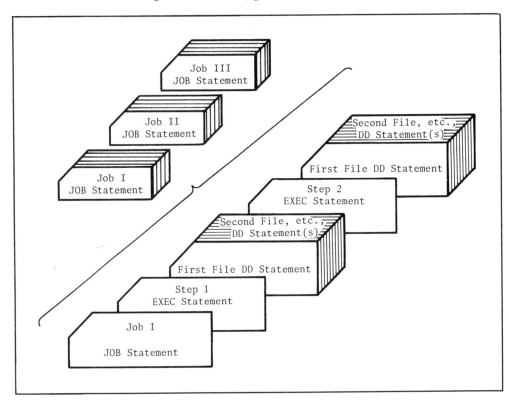

In summary, a job stream is divided into its component parts by
occurrences of the three types of JCL statements, i.e., JOB, EXEC, and
DD.

E. THE JOB STATEMENT

The presence of a Job statement signifies to the OS reader/interpreter
the end of previous JCL job coding and the beginning of the current job.

1. Job Statement Format

Throughout this text two formats will be provided where applicable for
each JCL parameter to be discussed -- a Basic Format and a Complete
Format. The Basic Format is that which the author believes to be common and typical of most System 360/370 OS and VS user applications.
It is, in essence, a practical on-the-job abbreviated version of the
Complete Format. First, however, an overview of Job statement format
should be presented. (See Figure 2.4.)

Figure 2.4 Job Statement Overview

```
 o                                                                          o
 o      //Jobname  JOB  Operand Field  Comment Field                        o
 o                                                                          o
```

    With one exception (the /* delimiter) all JCL statements begin with
a // (slash slash) in columns 1 and 2. This is to distinquish JCL
from non-JCL statements, i.e., programs and/or data. It is possible,
however, to process data with a // in columns 1 and 2 using a /* delimiter. This will be discussed later in the text.
    The // is followed by a mandatory jobname. All JCL identifier
names are 1 to 8 alphanumeric characters in length. The first character must be an alpha character (A - Z) or one of three national (@,$,#)
characters. Remaining characters may be numeric. This rule holds true
for all JCL names, that is, jobnames, ddnames, dsnames, etc. An installation may also define additional JCL naming conventions and rules.
This is more frequently the case with the jobname than any other JCL
specification.
    The symbol 'JOB' follows the jobname after at least one blank. This
symbol does nothing more than indicate that this particular JCL statement is a JOB (Job) statement rather than an EXEC (Execute) statement
or DD (Data Definition) statement.
    The Operand Field follows the symbol 'JOB' after at least one blank.
This field contains one or more positional and/or keyword parameters
describing the characteristics of the job to be executed. Information
such as an account number for billing purposes, programmer name, job
class, priority, time estimate, and messages desired are described
herein. The Operand Field is the body of the Job statement and many
times encompasses more than one line of JCL. Parameter specifications
should end before column 72 but may be continued following the Continuation Rules discussed previously.
    The optional Comment Field follows the Operand Field after at least
one blank. Though nonexecutable, it may be used as desired to exemplify
various JCL specifications. It should also end before column 72 but
may be continued following the Continuation Rules discussed previously.

2. The Jobname

The jobname is used to identify a given job, though system-generated
job numbers may also accomplish this task. As with all JCL identifier
names, the jobname must be 1 to 8 alphanumeric characters in length.
The first character must be an alpha character (A - Z) or one of the
three national characters (@, $, #). Remaining characters may be nu-
meric. Though chosen by the user, jobnames must also conform to any
additional or unique installation standards. Jobs with invalid jobnames are not allowed to enter the job queue for processing. Figure
2.5 depicts both valid and invalid jobname specifications.

Figure 2.5 Jobname Examples

```
┌────────────────────────────────────────────────────────────────────────┐
│  O                                                                    O  │
│  O      Valid:        Invalid:                                        O  │
│  O                                                                    O  │
│  O      //ABC         //1ABC        -  first character numeric        O  │
│  O                                                                    O  │
│  O      //A1B2C3      //A1B2C3D4E   -  name too long                  O  │
│  O                                                                    O  │
│  O      //$XYZ        //*XYZ        -  first character invalid        O  │
│  O                                                                    O  │
│  O      //X           //X=+&        -  characters 2-4 invalid         O  │
│  O                                                                    O  │
│  O      //#XYZ1234    //#XYZ12345   -  name too long                  O  │
│  O                                                                    O  │
└────────────────────────────────────────────────────────────────────────┘
```

Also note that the following jobnames should not be used as they are special computer operator console commands:

A, CONSOLES, N, P, PFK, Q, R, RT, SQA, T, TP, U, and USER

Aside from the above specifications, an installation may define additional job naming conventions and rules. For example,

xxxxyyyz may be a jobname where
    xxxx = customer identification,
     yyy = output bin number, and
       z = @ if job is not to be resubmitted, or
           $ if job needs special paper, or
           # if job requires card punch, or
   blank   if no specification.

The above example of a jobname standard may be a unique generation to a particular installation. Additional system routines are then added to edit and check for user compliance. In summary, it must be noted that the jobname is one of the most frequently installation-modified JCL specifications. Detail jobname format standards should be obtained from your specific dp facility.

3. Positional Parameters

Positional parameters are distinguished by the requirement that they be placed in a specific relative location (or position) on a JCL state-ment. Positional parameters are coded before keyword parameters and their absence accounted for by a comma. The Job statement contains two positional parameters which follow the symbol 'JOB'. They are:

Accounting Information; and

Programmer's Name

a. Accounting Information

Basic Format   : Account Number

Complete Format : (Account Number, Additional Account Information,
                   ......)

The Accounting Information positional parameter contains the Account Number to be used for job billing purposes. Accounting Information may be alphanumeric but must not exceed 142 characters in length.

Additional Accounting Information can also be provided if more detailed billing or user identification is desired. Each item of information (or subparameter) is separated by a comma. If more than one piece of positional information is provided, the total specification must be enclosed in parentheses. Continuation of Accounting Information onto another line also requires parentheses.

Figure 2.6 provides various examples of Accounting Information specifications using both basic and complete formats.

Figure 2.6 Accounting Information Examples

```
Basic Format:

//JCLTEXT   JOB   XYZABC123

//JCLTEXT   JOB   123

//JCLTEXT   JOB   A1B2C3XYZ

Complete Format:

//JCLTEXT   JOB   (XYZ,PROJECT1)

//JCLTEXT   JOB   (123,AGENCY53,DIVISION17,SYSTEMS)

//JCLTEXT   JOB   (A1B2C3,RAR,5,2,1,1484,02,Y,45)
```

In the basic format of the Accounting Information parameter only the Account Number is provided. Utilizing the complete format, Additional Account Information to be supplied must be separated by commas and from the Account Number itself while the whole Accounting Information specification is enclosed in parentheses. A check with the dp installation should be made to determine additional and unique Accounting Information standards.

Common Accounting Information errors should also be pointed out. For example, in //JCLTEXT JOB X ZABC123 the blank between the X and Z would most likely generate a JCL error message. The blank is interpreted as the end of the Job statement; and the ZABC123 is therefore regarded as a portion of the Comment Field. If X ZABC123 is truly a valid Account Number, coding conventions require it to be enclosed within apostrophes, i.e., 'X ZABC123'. In //JCLTEXT JOB XYZPROJECT1 another error message would most likely be generated, this time for an invalid account number. A comma must separate account numbers from additional account information. Similarly, even with //JCLTEXT JOB XYZ,PROJECT1 coded, the PROJECT1 specification would not be picked up as additional account information. With multiple specifications the complete Accounting Information parameter must be enclosed in parentheses. Otherwise PROJECT1 would be interpreted as Programmer's Name, the next positional parameter on the Job statement. In this example, only the //JCLTEXT JOB (XYZ,PROJECT1) coding is correct. Additional Account Information must be separated within itself and from the Account Number itself by the use of commas. When multiple account specifications are utilized, the complete Accounting Information positional parameter must be enclosed within parentheses. The parentheses contain and separate Accounting Information from subsequent parameters such as Programmer's Name.

b. Programmer's Name

Basic and Complete Format: Programmer's Name

The Programmer's Name positional parameter is in essence a comment field for user and installation use. If coded, it must be 1 to 20 characters in length and must follow the previously discussed Accounting Information parameter. If Accounting Information is absent, a comma must be coded prior to the Programmer's Name specification. This is due to the positional nature of Accounting Information relative to Programmer's Name -- a comma must be coded to account for its absence. When the Programmer's Name contains special characters such as blanks it must also be enclosed in apostrophes. To minimize potential errors it is a good habit to code the information in apostrophes whether needed or not.
Figure 2.7 provides various examples of Programmer's Name specifications using the combined basic and complete format.

Figure 2.7 Programmer's Name Examples

```
Basic and Complete Format:

//JCLTEXT   JOB   XYZABC123,TOBIN

//JCLTEXT   JOB   (123,PROJ1),IMPELLITTERI

//JCLTEXT   JOB   A1B2C3XYZ,'DHR - PHONE X71463'

//JCLTEXT   JOB   ,'NO ACCOUNT INFO'
```

A check with the dp installation should be made to determine any additional and unique Programmer's Name standards.
Common Programmer's Name errors should also be pointed out. For example, in //JCLTEXT JOB XYZABC123,TO IN the blank between the TO and IN would be interpreted by the OS reader/interpreter as the end of the Job statement; the IN is therefore regarded as a portion of the Comment Field. If the imbedded blank is a desired specification, however, code //JCLTEXT JOB XYZ,'TO IN' with apostrophes around the Programmer's Name. In //JCLTEXT JOB (123,PROJ1)IMPELLITTERI another error message would be generated for an invalid account number.

30

IMPELLITTERI is ignored as a Programmer's Name; a comma is missing to separate the two positional parameters. Also, if //JCLTEXT JOB A1B2C3XYZ,'DHR - TELEPHONE X71463' were coded, an error message would be generated; the Programmer's Name is greater than 20 characters. Likewise, //JCLTEXT JOB 'NO ACCOUNT INFO' would cause the Programmer's Name literal to be interpreted as Accounting Information; a comma must precede the Programmer's Name to account for the absence of positional Accounting Information specifications.

Finally, no coding action need be taken if it is decided not to code Programmer's Name. Like the Accounting Information preceding it, Programmer's Name is optional unless an installation has taken specific action to make them mandatory. Because Programmer's Name is the last positional specification, a comma need not be coded to indicate its absence. For example, //JCLTEXT JOB XYZ,CLASS=A is a valid Job statement. Though XYZ is Accounting Information, CLASS which follows is a keyword (to be discussed next) and is therefore recognized as a valid keyword parameter specification. Programmer's Name, the last positional parameter, has simply not been coded.

Having completed a discussion of the Job statement's two positional parameters, pertinent keyword parameters can now be presented.

Basic Keyword Parameters

Keyword parameters are distinguished by the occurrence of a special system-recognizable word or character set with no positional restrictions. They follow positional parameters; and because they are recognizable key words, they may be coded in any order. Though separated from other parameters by a comma, their absence as such need not be indicated or accounted for by the coding of a comma such as with positional parameters.

Some keyword parameters which relate to the Job statement can be considered common or typical. Though optional, they are frequently utilized. These will be discussed first. They are:

    CLASS (Job Class);
    COND (Condition);
    MSGLEVEL (Message Level);
    PRTY (Priority);
    TIME (Maximum CPU Time); and
    TYPRUN (Type of Run).

a. CLASS (Job Class)

    Basic and Complete Format: CLASS=Job Class

The purpose of the CLASS keyword parameter is to specify the classification or grouping into which a particular job will be placed. Under the Multiprogramming with a Fixed Number of Tasks (MFT) option of the Operating System (OS), it is the job class which determines the fixed partition to be utilized. Under the Multiprogramming with a Variable Number of Tasks (MVT) option of OS as well as in Virtual Storage (VS) environments, jobs with similar characteristics are grouped into the same job class. An attempt is made by the Operating System to concurrently process jobs with dissimilar characteristics. Jobs with dis-

31

similar characteristics, i.e., in different job classes, provide a good processing mix. They tend to complement rather than compete with each other in terms of their demand upon the need for installation resources. This in turn increases the total thruput of an installation's operation.

All dp installations define their own job classification system. Job class definitions vary from installation to installation, especially under the MVT option of OS with or without VS. Specific job classes are initially defined by an installation after analyzing user needs in conjunction with hardware and software equipment and configurations currently available in the installation itself. Scarce and limited resources are noted, i.e., tape drives, main storage availability, etc. Actual job classes are then defined using these critical resource restraints as a major determinant. For example, if an installation has only one 7-track tape drive available, it would be advisable to define a job class for those jobs requiring that drive. The Operating System can then insure that two or more jobs which happen to require the 7-track tape drive will not be scheduled to be executed concurrently. Rather, jobs of dissimilar characteristics, i.e., different job classes, will be scheduled for concurrent execution, thus reducing competition for an installation's critical resources during a given time period. Requirements for the use of the Central Processing Unit (CPU) and an estimate of the number of print lines to be produced are two additional yet common factors used in defining an installation's job classification system.

Following is an example of a job classification system which the author believes encompasses the broad spectrum of defining job classes. Although it may be called typical by many, one must hesitate to describe any such job classification system as typical. As previously discussed, there are many factors which determine the definition of specific job classes at a particular installation. A job classification example which utilizes many factors common to most dp installations is depicted in Figure 2.8.

In the example in Figure 2.8, the most critical resource in each job class has been encircled with a dotted line for visibility. It is because of the existence of this limiting factor that a job class has been defined. For example, if total Central Processing Unit (CPU) job time is estimated to be less than or equal to 3 minutes, CLASS=C could be coded in the Job statement -- provided that the other less limiting factors for that class are not exceeded. If greater than 3 minutes but less than or equal to 15 minutes of total CPU job time is required, CLASS=G would be necessary, etc. If the largest step of a given job in terms of main storage availability requires more than 128K bytes but less than or equal to 256K bytes, CLASS=H would be coded provided other less limiting factors for that class are not exceeded. If a given job requires no mountable devices (tape or disk) other than an on-line disk, for example, CLASS=A could be coded. Similarly, if the old 7-track drive (usually collecting dust in a far corner of most 9-track-oriented installations) is needed, CLASS=B is necessary. Likewise, if the largest step of a given job in terms of the number of mountable devices to be utilized requires more than 2 mountable devices but less than or equal to 6 mountable devices, CLASS=I would be a most probable alternative. If the total estimated number of print lines for a job is greater than 10K but less than or equal to 30K, CLASS=J is a most likely choice given other limitaions. High-usage classes such as K, L, M, and N are

Figure 2.8 A Job Classification System

Job Class	Job Description	Maximum CPU Use (Minutes)	Maximum Main Storage Use (K) Bytes	Maximum No. Mountable Devices	No. of Print Lines (K)
A	No Mountable Devices	3	128	0	10
B	7-Track Use	3	128	1	10
C	Low Time	3	256	6	30
D	Low Storage	15	128	6	30
E	Low Devices	15	256	2	30
F	Low Print	15	256	6	10
G	Medium Time	15	384	4	20
H	Medium Storage	30	256	4	20
I	Medium Devices	30	384	6	20
J	Medium Print	30	384	4	30
K	High Time	60	256	6	30
L	High Storage	15	512	6	30
M	High Devices	15	256	8	30
N	High Print	15	256	6	100
O	Multiple Use	60	512	8	100

usually available at most installations. Finally, if a given job cannot be classified into any of the previous job classes, CLASS=O must be coded. If a given job exceeds the limitations defined as Class O, it cannot be run in this particular installation as such, but must be broken into two or more separate and smaller jobs.

It should also be pointed out that the smaller the job in terms of resource requirements, the faster job turnaround should be. Likewise, large job classes may be held until the "midnight shift" when more of each resource is readily available, i.e., most jobs have been run and few are being submitted. In a typical batch environment small jobs may be turned around in a few hours, average-size jobs in one day, while large job classes could require a couple of days.

In addition, it should also be pointed out that some installations do not require a Class parameter on their Job statement. Rather, reader/interpreter job input software analyzes the job stream for critical resources and generates a job class. In this instance, the user need not classify and code a Class parameter prior to job submission.

Figure 2.9 depicts various Class parameter specifications utilizing the combined basic and complete format.

Figure 2.9 Class Parameter Examples

```
         Basic and Complete Format:


         //JCLTEXT  JOB  XYZABC123,TOBIN,CLASS=A

         //JCLTEXT  JOB  (123,PROJ1),IMP,CLASS=B

         //JCLTEXT  JOB  A1B2C3XYZ,DANHR,CLASS=H

         //JCLTEXT  JOB  1234,'A LARGE JOB',CLASS=O

         //JCLTEXT  JOB  (ABC,789),'CLASS GENERATED'
```

The first four examples in Figure 2.9 require the user to specify job class, while in the last example the specific job class is generated by the Operating System.

In summary, job class definitions vary from installation to installation as determined by available hardware and software coupled with the general characteristics of user jobs. The objective of all job classifications systems is to obtain a good processing mix, that is, the concurrent processing of jobs with dissimilar characteristics. This in turn increases the total thruput of an installation's operation.

b. COND (Condition)

Basic Format   : COND=(Code,Operator)

Complete Format: COND=((Code,Operator),......)

The purpose of the COND keyword parameter is to specify conditions under which processing is to be discontinued. Condition Codes, sometimes referred to as Return Codes, are generated throughout the processing of a given job and indicate the severity of error occurrences. Standard condition codes referred to by the Operating System are:

    0 - No errors encountered;
    4 - Warning error, execution continues, e.g., field truncation;
    8 - Conditional error, assumption made, e.g., period at end of program sentence;
   12 - Significant error, step terminates, e.g., Input/Output (I/O) error; and
   16 - Severe error, job terminates, e.g., storage dump condition.

Note that processing terminates at either the step or job level when the condition code is greater than 8, that is, 12 or 16. Conversely, processing continues to normal completion provided the condition codes generated remain less than 12, that is, 8, 4, or 0. If one wishes to accept the above default conditions as most applicable to the job being processed, a COND parameter need not be coded. The optional COND parameter should be coded when it is desired to change the above-described step and/or job termination conditions. Perhaps a user wishes to completely terminate a particularly sensitive job if a significant error (code 12) occurs rather than accept step termination and allow the system to attempt to execute other remaining steps in the same job. A user may also wish to terminate a job if a warning (code-4) or conditional (code-8) error occurs. It is within the COND parameter that changes of this nature can be made.

   To code the COND parameter on the Job statement, the following codes are generally used in conjunction with one of six operations:

Codes	Operators
0	GT - Greater Than
4	GE - Greater Than or Equal to
8	EQ - Equal to
12	LE - Less Than or Equal to
16	LT - Less Than
	NE - Not Equal to

   It should be noted that any code from 0 to 4095 can be utilized. This is because programmers can define and generate condition codes within the program itself. This technique is particularly amenable to Assembler and Machine language coding applications. If additional error conditions, whether mild or severe, are desired to be indicated or flagged, additional condition codes may be generated by the executing program. Tests for the occurrence of these conditions may be accomplished via the COND parameter on the Job statement. Processing can then be altered by terminating execution at the job level or continuing as is.

   For example, COND=(12,EQ) indicates that the job is to be terminated if a condition code of 12 is generated at some time during job processing. This specification modifies the code-12 default from step termination to job termination. It should be noted in this example that code-16 job termination also remains in effect. Similarly, COND=(4,LT) indicates that if 4 is less than the highest generated condition (return) code, the job is to be terminated. In other words, 8, 12, or 16 return codes will result in job termination. Code-0 or code-4 generation will not affect job status, i.e., processing will continue. Multiple Or conditions can be specified using the complete format. Figure 2.10 depicts typical COND parameter specifications utilizing both basic and complete Job statement formats.

   The first two basic format examples in Figure 2.10 specify essentially the same condition. If code-12 is generated in the first example, the job will be terminated in addition to the occurrence of any code-16 (default) conditions. In the second case, if 8 is less than the condition (return) code, i.e., 12 or 16, the job will terminate as in the first example. Likewise, the third and fourth basic format examples specify identical conditions. In the third example, if 4 is less than the condition (return) code, i.e., 8, 12, or 16, the job will terminate. Similarly, if 8 is less than or equal to the condition (return) code, i.e., 8, 12, or 16, the job in the fourth example will also terminate. The fifth example depicts an additional test for a

Figure 2.10 Condition Parameter Examples (JOB Statement)

```
Basic Format:

//JCLTEXT  JOB  XYZABC123,TOBIN,CLASS=A,COND=(12,EQ)

//JCLTEXT  JOB  XYZABC123,TOBIN,CLASS=A,COND=(8,LT)

//JCLTEXT  JOB  (123,PROJ1),IMP,CLASS=B,COND=(4,LT)

//JCLTEXT  JOB  (123,PROJ1),IMP,CLASS=B,COND=(8,LE)

//JCLTEXT  JOB  A1B2C3XYZ,DANHR,CLASS=H,COND=(2048,EQ)

//JCLTEXT  JOB  A1B2C3XYZ,DANHR,CLASS=H


Complete Format:

//JCLTEXT  JOB  XYZABC123,TOBIN,CLASS=A,COND=((8,EQ),(12,EQ))

//JCLTEXT  JOB  (123,PROJ1),IMP,CLASS=B,COND=((12,EQ),(2048,EQ))

//JCLTEXT  JOB  A1B2C3XYZ,DANHR,CLASS=H,COND=((4,GT),(2048,LE))
```

program-generated condition (return) code of 2048. Default termination conditions also remain in effect. The last example of the basic format depicts no COND parameter coding. Again, the general default conditions described previously remain in effect -- 0 for no errors, 4 for warning errors, 8 for conditional errors, 12 for significant errors (step termination), and 16 for severe errors (job termination).

The first example of the complete format specifies a multiple Or condition. If 8 or 12 is equal to the condition (return) code, the job will terminate in addition to the occurrence of any code-16 (default) condition. This specification is also equivalent to the COND=(4,LT) and COND=(8,LE) discussed previously. The second example of the complete format specifies another multiple Or condition. If code-12 or program-generated 2048 is equal to the condition (return) code, the job will terminate in addition to the occurrence of any code-16 (default) condition. This is similar in principle to the COND=(8,LT) specification described previously. Finally, the last example of the complete format specifies that if 4 is greater than the condition (return) code, or 2048 is less than or equal to the condition (return) code, the job will be terminated. In other words, only codes 4 through 2047 allow processing to be continued. This last example is one in which a programmer has most likely defined a completely new series of executing conditions via program specifications.

In summary, the Condition parameter specifies selected test conditions under which processing is to be altered (continued or discontinued) from general system default conditions. Additional condition (return) codes can also be program-defined, generated, and tested as desired.

c. MSGLEVEL (Message Level)

Basic and Complete Format: MSGLEVEL=(Statement Code,Message Code)

The purpose of the MSGLEVEL keyword parameter is to specify at what level JCL statements and system messages are to be provided. Valid JCL statement codes are:

0 - Job statement only;
1 - All JCL statements including the input stream, catalogued procedures, and symbolic representations and substitutions; and
2 - Input stream JCL statements only.

Unfortunately, a most frequent default at many dp installations is a 0 specification. Unless modified by a MSGLEVEL parameter, only the Job statement will be written to the user's output job stream file. No other JCL statements will be provided. Concurrently, valid system message codes are:

0 - No allocation and termination messages; and
1 - All allocation and termination messages.

Fortunately, a most frequent default at many dp installations is a 1 specification. Unless modified by a MSGLEVEL parameter, all allocation and termination messages will be written to the user's output job stream file. With a 0 specification, none would be written. Those messages provided with abnormal termination procedures will always be written, however.

In the opinion of the author, all system and application programmers and analysts should ensure that all possible JCL statements and system messages are provided. These are especially significant in debugging situations. Assuming a most frequent default of MSGLEVEL= (0,1), coding MSGLEVEL=(1,1) or MSGLEVEL=1 on a Job statement will modify the Statement Code to a 1 while maintaining the Message Code of

Figure 2.11 Message Level Parameter Examples

```
Basic and Complete Format:

//JCLTEXT   JOB   XYZABC123,TOBIN,CLASS=A,MSGLEVEL=0

//JCLTEXT   JOB   (123,PROJ1),IMP,CLASS=B,MSGLEVEL=2

//JCLTEXT   JOB   A1B2C3XYZ,DANHR,CLASS=H,MSGLEVEL=1

//JCLTEXT   JOB   XYZABC123,TOBIN,CLASS=A,MSGLEVEL=(,0)

//JCLTEXT   JOB   (123,PROJ1),IMP,CLASS=B,MSGLEVEL=(,1)

//JCLTEXT   JOB   (123,PROJ1),IMP,CLASS=B

//JCLTEXT   JOB   A1B2C3XYZ,DANHR,CLASS=H,MSGLEVEL=(1,1)
```

1. This is because these subparameter specifications are positional with respect to one another. With MSGLEVEL=1, the first positional subparameter (Statement Code) is assumed. With MSGLEVEL=(,0) the first positional subparameter specification is bypassed but its absence is accounted for by the comma. The second positional subparameter specification is therefore indicated as a 0, resulting in a MSGLEVEL=(0,0) indication with the first zero an assumed default. Figure 2.11 depicts various MSGLEVEL parameter specifications utilizing the combined basic and complete format.

The first three basic and complete format examples in Figure 2.11 modify the positional subparameter, Statement Code, by 0, 2, and 1. They specify the printing of the Job statement only, input stream JCL, and all JCL statements, respectively. The next two examples bypass the Statement Code specification and modify the second positional subparameter (Message Code) to 0 and 1. They specify no allocation and termination messages and all allocation and termination messages to be printed, respectively. The sixth example depicts no MSGLEVEL parameter specification. It assumes a most frequent installation default of MSGLEVEL=(0,1). The last example modifies both positional pieces of subparameter information. This is recommended to ensure generation of all JCL and system messages at all times for the user.

In summary, the Message Level parameter specifies the level of statements and messages to be issued by the Operating System to the user. All JCL statements and system messages should be provided and/or called for.

d. PRTY (Priority)

Basic and Complete Format: PRTY=Priority Code

The purpose of the PRTY keyword parameter is to specify a processing priority for a job within a given job class. Valid priority codes are:

       0 - Priority 0, the lowest priority specification;
       1 - Priority 1;
       2 -- Priority 2;
       3 - Priority 3, a common default priority;
       4 - Priority 4;
       5 - Priority 5;
       6 - Priority 6, also a common default priority;
       7 - Priority 7;
       8 - Priority 8;
       9 - Priority 9;
      10 - Priority 10;
      11 - Priority 11;
      12 - Priority 12, generally the highest allowable user priority
              specification; and
      13 - Priority 13, the highest system priority.

A zero is the lowest job priority code; 3 or 6 are common defaults when no PRTY parameter is coded; a 12 is generally the highest priority specification allowed; and a 13 is usually reserved for special system use.

Installations attempt to guarantee job turnaround time based upon a combination of job class and priority. The higher the priority, the faster the turnaround. Remember, however, that many dp installation billing algorithms adjust job cost accordingly. For example, a priority-6 may be double the cost of an identical priority-3 job; a priority-9 may triple the cost of an identical priority-3 job; etc. Also keep in mind that no absolute job turnaround times can be given with complete assurance. This is because job priorities are relative -- that is, relative to all other job priorities and classes in a job initiation queue at a given moment in time. If an installation has suffered severe downtime and users become anxious, the job queue may actually consist of many high-priority 9 through 12 specifications. Under these conditions a priority-6 job may await execution for an extended period of time. Job turnaround will still be slow, yet all prioritized jobs may be factored at double or triple the normal user cost! At other times when a dp installation is not behind schedule, a priority-6 job may go into immediate execution upon submission. Data-processing experience coupled with an analysis of the number, class, and priority of jobs awaiting execution in the job queue provide insight into coding the most effective priority specification. As a matter of fact, most jobs should be coded to accept an installation's priority default unless special action can be justified. Figure 2.12 depicts common PRTY parameter specifications utilizing the combined basic and complete format.

Figure 2.12 Priority Parameter Examples

```
   Basic and Complete Format:

   //JCLTEXT   JOB   XYZABC123,TOBIN,CLASS=A

   //JCLTEXT   JOB   XYZABC123,TOBIN,CLASS=A,PRTY=3

   //JCLTEXT   JOB   (123,PROJ1),IMP,CLASS=H,PRTY=6

   //JCLTEXT   JOB   (123,PROJ1),IMP,CLASS=B,PRTY=0

   //JCLTEXT   JOB   A1B2C3XYZ,DANHR,CLASS=H,PRTY=9

   //JCLTEXT   JOB   A1B2C3XYZ,DANHR,CLASS=H,PRTY=12
```

The first three examples in Figure 2.12 are similar. The absence of a priority specification generally defaults to 3 or 6 in most installations. In the fourth example, a slow turnaround (at most likely a less expensive rate) is requested with the priority specification of 0. In the last two examples, high job turnaround priorities of 9 and 12, respectively, have been requested.

It should also be noted that some dp installations may not require or allow the PRTY parameter specification. Also, some installations have defined priority job classes. For example, three jobs normally classified as A, B, and C but desiring priority execution may instead be coded in priority job classes X, Y, and Z, respectively. These classes denote automatic priority (perhaps priority code 8 or 10).

Like priority keyword parameter specifications, the jobs are executed appropriately and users billed accordingly.

In summary, the PRTY parameter specifies relative processing priority within a given job class. Priority specifications affect job turnaround time and costs.

e.   TIME (CPU Time)

Basic Format   :   TIME=CPU Minutes

Complete Format: $\text{TIME=} \begin{Bmatrix} \text{CPU Minutes} \\ \text{(CPU Minutes,CPU Seconds)} \\ 1440 \end{Bmatrix}$

The purpose of the TIME keyword parameter is to specify the maximum amount of Central Processing Unit (CPU) time allowed beyond which processing is to terminate. The Time parameter is thus used as a safety limit to prevent endless program loops and other burdensome program errors from using a needless and unnecessary amount of system resources. It is a method of placing a "lid" on a given job to prevent runaway cost and resource situation from occurring.

CPU time can be specified in terms of maximum CPU minutes, maximum CPU seconds, both minutes and seconds, or the value 1440. There happen to be 1440 minutes in one day (24 X 60). For the purposes of JCL, this value signifies that CPU resources are not to be timed, a very insecure if not dangerous specification. Like most other parameters, the Time parameter need not be coded. In this case only the individual job steps will be timed for termination purposes. Time parameter specifications are in terms of actual CPU use, not wall-clock or elasped execution time, which could be from 2 to 20 or more times longer.

As can be seen, a small budget could be easily wasted by an unforeseen program loop. It is for this reason that the author recommends a Time parameter be coded on the Job statement in addition to regular step specifications. This concept will be expanded upon in the next chapter. Figure 2.13 depicts various TIME parameter specifications utilizing the basic and complete job statement formats.

The first three basic format examples in Figure 2.13 indicate that if a job total of more than 1, 10, and 30 CPU minutes respectively, are utilized, processing for the job should be discontinued. The job time specification should fall within the range of allowable times for the chosen job class. The last example utilized under the basic format contains no Time parameter. In this case only individual step time specifications or defaults will be utilized. The first three examples utilizing the complete format in Figure 2.13 indicate that if a CPU job total of more than 1 minute and 30 seconds, 20 seconds, and 10 minutes and 59 seconds are utilized, respectively, processing of the job should be disontinued. Only seconds specifications of less than 60 seconds are considered valid. Also, as can be seen by the (,20) specification, minutes and seconds are positional -- minutes are to be coded first. A comma must be coded to indicate the absence of a minutes specification, i.e., the presence of a seconds specification.

40

Figure 2.13   Time Parameter Examples (JOB Statement)

```
 o                                                                    o
 o      Basic Format:                                                 o
 o                                                                    o
        //JCLTEXT   JOB   XYZABC123,TOBIN,CLASS=A,TIME=1
 o                                                                    o
        //JCLTEXT   JOB   XYZABC123,TOBIN,CLASS=A,TIME=10
 o                                                                    o
        //JCLTEXT   JOB   XYZABC123,TOBIN,CLASS=A,TIME=30
 o                                                                    o
        //JCLTEXT   JOB   (123,PROJ1),IMP,CLASS=B
 o                                                                    o
 o      Complete Format:                                              o
 o                                                                    o
 o      //JCLTEXT   JOB   A1B2C3XYZ,DANHR,CLASS=H,TIME=(1,30)          o
 o                                                                    o
 o      //JCLTEXT   JOB   A1B2C3XYZ,DANHR,CLASS=H,TIME=(,20)           o
 o                                                                    o
 o      //JCLTEXT   JOB   A1B2C3XYZ,DANHR,CLASS=H,TIME=(10,59)         o
 o                                                                    o
 o      //JCLTEXT   JOB   A1B2C3XYZ,DANHR,CLASS=H,TIME=1440            o
 o                                                                    o
```

Parentheses must be used to encompass more than one piece of positional
subparameter information. If TIME=1,30 without the parentheses were
coded, a JCL error would result. The OS reader/interpreter would
infer that the '30' following the comma was the beginning of the next
keyword, i.e., an invalid keyword. The fourth job statement utilizing
the complete format in Figure 2.13 provides a 1440-minute specification. This is rarely used, as no time limit would now exist for total
CPU job time processing.

In summary, the TIME parameter provides a CPU time limit beyond
which processing will be discontinued.

b. TYPRUN (Type of Run)

Basic and Complete Format: TYPRUN= $\left\{ \begin{array}{c} \text{HOLD} \\ \text{SCAN} \end{array} \right\}$

The purpose of the TYPRUN keyword parameter is to specify that
under certain conditions the initial execution of a job is to be inhibited. If coded, either HOLD or SCAN must be specified. If HOLD
is specified, the job will be placed into a hold condition, that is,
it will not be available for execution until a computer operator releases it. Some installations require TYPRUN=HOLD to be coded for
large-resource-demanding job classes. For example, a given job may
be held during prime work shifts and released during the night shift
after job backlog and resource demands have significantly decreased.
If SCAN is specified, the JCL for the job will be scanned for syntax
errors only and will not enter the job queue for execution. This feature
is particularly important when a job stream has been created for the
first time and and the premature execution of the job prior to complete
testing could result in a costly mistake. Figure 2.14 depicts all

41

coding variations of the TYPRUN parameter utilizing the combined basic and complete format.

Figure 2.14   Type of Run Parameter Examples

```
  o                                                                    o
  o        Basic and Complete Format:                                  o
  o                                                                    o
  o        //JCLTEXT   JOB   XYZABC123,TOBIN,CLASS=A,TYPRUN=HOLD        o
  o                                                                    o
  o        //JCLTEXT   JOB   (123,PROJ1),IMP,CLASS=B,TYPRUN=SCAN        o
  o                                                                    o
  o        //JCLTEXT   JOB   A1B2C3XYZ,DANHR,CLASS=H                    o
  o                                                                    o
```

The first two combined basic and complete format examples specify HOLD and SCAN, respectively. The first job will be held until released by the computer operator. The second job will be scanned for JCL syntax errors only. The third job statement in Figure 2.14 contains no TYPRUN parameter. The job will be available for execution as job class, priority, and resource availability dictate.

In summary, the TYPRUN parameter determines if the initial execution of a job is to be inhibited.

5. Basic Job Statement Examples

The previous discussion has covered JCL introduction, code notation, general JCL format, the job stream, and the Job statement. Eight parameters have been identified as basic or common to most System 360/370 OS and VS users. They are:

Positional	-	Accounting Information; and Programmer's Name.
Keyword	-	Job Class; Condition; Message Level; Priority; CPU Time; and Type of Run.

Other not-so-common keyword parameters will be discussed in this chapter. Figure 2.15 displays a series of typical Job statements utilizing common positional and keyword parameters discussed previously.

The first set of seven examples in Figure 2.15 to be billed to Account XYZABC123 for TOBIN utilize both positional parameters plus from one to all six basic keyword parameters. Only basic formats are utilized. Note that some jobs will terminate if a condition code of 12 (and 16 also) is encountered. All statements and messages will be provided for some jobs via message level specifications. A priority of 9 and a CPU job time limit have also been placed on a few of the

42

Figure 2.15 Typical Job Statement Examples (cont.)

```
//JCLTEXT   JOB   XYZABC123,TOBIN,CLASS=A

//JCLTEXT   JOB   XYZABC123,TOBIN,CLASS=B,COND=(12,EQ)

//JCLTEXT   JOB   XYZABC123,TOBIN,CLASS=C,COND=(12,EQ),MSGLEVEL=(1,1)

//JCLTEXT   JOB   XYZABC123,TOBIN,CLASS=D,COND=(12,EQ),MSGLEVEL=(1,1),

//        PRTY=9

//JCLTEXT   JOB   XYZABC123,TOBIN,CLASS=E,COND=(12,EQ),MSGLEVEL=(1,1),

//        PRTY=9,TIME=5

//JCLTEXT   JOB   XYZABC123,TOBIN,CLASS=F,COND=(12,EQ),MSGLEVEL=(1,1),

//         PRTY=9,TIME=10,TYPRUN=SCAN

//JCLTEXT   JOB   XYZABC123,TOBIN,CLASS=0,COND=(12,EQ),MSGLEVEL=(1,1),

//         PRTY=9,TIME=45,TYPRUN=HOLD


//EXAMPLES   JOB   (123,PROJ1),IMP,CLASS=B

//EXAMPLES   JOB   (123,PROJ1),IMP,CLASS=D,COND=(12,LE)

//EXAMPLES   JOB   (123,PROJ1),IMP,CLASS=F,MSGLEVEL=1

//EXAMPLES   JOB   (123,PROJ1),IMP,PRTY=0

//EXAMPLES   JOB   (123,PROJ1),IMP,CLASS=N,TIME=15

//EXAMPLES   JOB   (123,PROJ1),IMP,TYPRUN=HOLD

//EXAMPLES   JOB   (123,PROJ1),IMP,


//AMIX@     JOB   A1B2C3XYZ,DANHR,MSGLEVEL=1

//AMIX$     JOB   A1B2C3XYZ,'D R',CLASS=E,MSGLEVEL=(1,1),TIME=10

//AMIX#     JOB   A1B2C3XYZ,'D+R',CLASS=G,COND=((8,EQ),(12,EQ)),

//         MSGLEVEL=(0,0)

//@AMIX     JOB   (A1B2C3,XYZ),CLASS=I,PRTY=9,TIME=20

//$AMIX     JOB   (A1B2C3,XYZ),CLASS=0,TIME=20,TYPRUN=HOLD

//#AMIX     JOB   ,DANHR,MSGLEVEL=(1,1),TYPRUN=SCAN

//AMIX@$#   JOB   A1-B2-C3,'DANR',CLASS=K,COND=(8,LE),MSGLEVEL=(1,1),

//          PRTY=4,TIME=45
```

jobs. A scan for JCL errors only and the holding of the job from immediate execution is depicted on the last two job statements, respectively.

The second set of seven examples in Figure 2.15 to be billed to Account 123 and Project PROJ1 for IMP utilize both positional parameters and only a couple of the basic keyword parameters per job statement. Complete formats are also utilized. The following defaults take effect if a keyword is not coded:

Class   - Installation- and/or system-generated;
Condition   - Standard code severity;
Message Level - Generally no statements but with messages;
Priority   - Usually level 3 or 6;
Time   - No job time limit, though step times or step defaults will be in effect; and
Type of Run   - Competes for initiation and execution as soon as possible.

The third set of seven examples in Figure 2.15 to be billed initially to Account A1B2C3XYZ for DANHR utilize both positional parameters and a mixture of basic keyword parameters and formats. As job statements standards vary by installation, these are the broadest of the three sets of examples. Specific defaults in effect are determined by the Operating System as supplied by the vendor as well as installation needs and desires reflected at system generation time, i.e., when the operating system is installed in a particular facility.

It should be noted that one or more Exec statements will be placed behind each Job statement. An Exec statement must be coded for each program or procedure to be called for processing. Exec statements are the topic of the next chapter.

6. Other Positional and Keyword Parameters

   a. Additional Accounting Information

   Many System 360/370 OS and VS facilities define additional account information as follows:

(Account Number, Project/User,aaaa,bbbb,cccc,dddd,ee,f,gg)
     where aaaa = Maximum CPU and/or I/0 Time (Minutes);
           bbbb = Maximum Number of Printed Output Lines (thousands);
           cccc = Maximum Number of Cards to be punched (thousands);
           dddd = Paper Type Specification;
             ee = Number of Times Job Output is to be printed;
              f = Print or No-Print of Spooling Log; and
             gg = Number of Lines to be printed per page.

   A check with your installation should be made to obtain detail coding and format specifications for additional account information.

   b. ADDRSPC (Address Space)

   Basic and Complete Format: ADDRSPC= $\begin{Bmatrix} VIRT \\ REAL \end{Bmatrix}$

The purpose of the ADDRSPC keyword parameter is to specify that real storage is to be used for this job rather than virtual storage. Specific to installations with the Virtual Storage (VS) feature of OS, this parameter when allowed provides the user with a means of bypassing the virtual storage of program load modules and routines.

If not coded, ADDRSPC=VIRT is assumed at VS installations. If ADDRSPC=REAL is coded, a programmer wishes to allocate a complete region of real (or actual) storage for the total load module as under operating systems without the Virtual Storage feature. Both specifications may be coupled with Region parameters as appropriate to be discussed later.

c. MPROFILE (Message Profile)

Basic and Complete Format: MPROFILE='Character String'

The purpose of the MPROFILE keyword parameter is to assign a message class. The 'Character String' must conform to installation standards for providing information to the Message Profile parameter. Message class specifications identify where and how system output is to be written. For example, MPROFILE='STANDARD SIZE SINGLE PAGE' is a syntactically correct specification of message profile provided the particular installation's operating system recognizes the character string as valid. Likewise, MPROFILE=('1468 TYPE PAPER','4 COPIES', '1000 PAGES') is a correct specification given installation standards for multiple recognition. The Message Profile parameter provides a more descriptive method of coding message class to be discussed next.

d. MSGCLASS (Message Class)

Basic and Complete Format: MSGCLASS=Output Class

The purpose of the MSGCLASS keyword parameter is to define the output class to which system messages are to be written. Output classes range from A to Z and 0 to 9. If not coded, MSGCLASS=A is assumed. Output Class A is defined as a standard 11 X 14 7/8 one-part lined paper default at most installations. Other unique paper types, sizes, and number of copies can be specified if desired, however, i.e., MSGLEVEL= X. The Message Profile parameter discussed previously overrides Message Class specifications if both are coded.

e. NOTIFY (Notify)

Basic and Complete Format: NOTIFY=Identification

The purpose of the NOTIFY keyword parameter is to indicate who should be notified under the Time Sharing Option (TSO) that a particular Multiprogramming with a Variable Number of Tasks (MVT) background job has completed execution. An appropriate message is sent to the user as identified during the TSO logon process. NOTIFY=IMPELLITTERI means that the TSO user named 'IMPELLITTERI' will receive a message informing that person of the completion of the job on which the NOTIFY parameter was coded.

f. PROFILE (Profile)

Basic and Complete Format: PROFILE='Character String'

The purpose of the PROFILE keyword parameter is to assign a job class and priority. The 'Character String' must conform to installation standards for providing information to the Profile parameter. Job class and priority specifications identify job requirements. For example, PROFILE='5 CPU AND NO TAPE' is a syntactically correct specification provided that the particular installation's operating system recognizes the character string as valid. Likewise, PROFILE=('10 CPU MINUTES','100K','2 TAPE DRIVES','5000 LINES','PRIORITY 6') is a correct specification given installation standards for multiple-character-string recognition. The PROFILE parameter overrides Job Class and Priority specifications and provides a more descriptive method of coding these items.

g. RD (Restart Definition)

$$\text{Basic and Complete Format:}\quad RD= \cdot \left\{ \begin{array}{l} R \\ RNC \\ NR \\ NC \end{array} \right\}$$

The purpose of the RD keyword parameter is to define or limit job restart capabilities as coded in the JCL and/or operating programs. It is possible for a step which has abnormally terminated to be automatically restarted at the beginning of the step (Automatic Step Restart) or at a specific point within that step (Automatic Checkpoint Restart). When these capabilities are to be utilized but are not desired to a certain degree for this run of the job, the RD parameter should be coded. If not coded, RD=R is assumed, that is, both automatic step restart and automatic checkpoint restart are allowed. If automatic step restart is to be permitted but automatic checkpoint restart is not to be permitted, code RD=RNC. If neither automatic step restart nor automatic checkpoint restart are to be allowed for this run but it is desired to establish checkpoints for a deferred restart, i.e., job pickup and resubmission, code RD=NR. If RD=NC is coded, not only is automatic step restart and automatic checkpoint restart not permitted, but checkpoints are also not established for deferred restarts. RD parameters coded on a Job statement override those which may be coded on Exec statements.

h. REGION (Region)

Basic and Complete Format: REGION=SizeK

The purpose of the REGION keyword parameter is to specify how many 1,000-byte increments of main storage are to be allocated. Actually, a value specification of 1K is equal to 1,024 bytes. (A byte is a unit of main storage measurement, equivalent to eight contiguous bits and represented in print form by two hexadecimal characters.) When coded on the Job statement, a Region parameter applies to each step of the job, e.g., REGION=60K. It is on Exec statements, where program modules and routines are fetched, loaded, and executed in storage, that Region parameters are commonly coded, however. There they are considered one of the basic keyword parameters, whereas on the Job statement they are not. This is becuase main storage requirements for executable modules vary from step to step and should therefore be accounted for and allocated on a step-by-step basic.

i. RESTART (Restart)

Basic Format   :   RESTART=(Stepname,Checkpoint)

Complete Format: RESTART=
$$\left\{ \begin{array}{l} * \\ \text{Stepname} \\ \text{Stepname.ProcStepname} \\ (*,\text{Checkpoint}) \\ (\text{Stepname},\text{Checkpoint}) \\ (\text{Stepname},\text{ProcStepname},\text{Checkpoint}) \end{array} \right\}$$

The purpose of the RESTART keyword parameter is to indicate where in the overall job stream restart is to begin if abnormal termination occurs. Restart can occur at the beginning of a job step (step restart) or at one of many points within a job step (checkpoint restart) as defined in the operating program. An asterisk (*) signifies that restart is to occur in the first job step. Stepnames in combination with Procedure Stepnames also indicate specific job step starting points. Checkpoints are names defined in the operating program at which restart may occur. RESTART=STEP4 indicates that step restart may occur at the beginning of the fourth step. Similarly, RESTART=(STEP2,POINT3) indicates that checkpoint restart may occur at an area in the second step called POINT3. When restart facilities are to be utilized, a SYSCHK DD Statement must also be coded. It should be pointed out that a great deal of programmer and system analyst care is necessary when coding a program to be executed for restart possibilities. The exact status of the program and every file being processed must be taken into account. Though confusing at times, checkpoint and restart capabilities are much more of a system software and programming challenge than they are a JCL coding problem. If not coded, restart capabilities are assumed not to be desired.

j. ROLL (Roll)

Basic and Complete Format: ROLL=(Status,Cause)

The purpose of the ROLL keyword parameter is (1) to signify whether steps of this job may be temporarily rolled out of main storage in favor of another job (Status) and (2) to signify whether steps of this job may cause temporary rollout of another job from main storage in favor of this job (Cause). This parameter is only valid for Multiprogramming with a Variable Number of Tasks (MVT) OS configurations. If not coded, ROLL=(YES,NO) is a common default, that is, this job may be rolled out but may not cause rollout of other jobs. Conversely, ROLL=(NO,YES) signifies that this job may not be rolled out but may cause

47

rollout of other jobs if more main storage than originally requested is desired.

F. JOB STATEMENT WORKSHOP

All allowable positional and keyword parameters which can be coded on a Job statement have been discussed. A workshop is now provided to solidify a working knowledge of basic Job statement JCL coding. Workshop answers can be found in Appendix E.

1. Syntax Check

Review, analyze, and correct the following ten Job statements for syntactical and/or logic coding errors. A given Job statement may contain none, one, or more than one error.

    1. //RUN?   JOB   A5438,CFT,TIME=1,30,MSGLEVEL=(1,1)

    2. //RUN1   JOB   A5438,PROJ1,CFT,CLASS=D   NEED 1484 PAPER

    3. //#RUN   JOB   (A5438,PROJ1),CFT,COND=((8,LE),(8,GT))

    4. //#@$15678   JOB   456,'ARS',CLASS=G,MSGLEVEL=(1,1)

    5. //123456   JOB   456,ARS,CLASE=A,COND=(8,AND)

    6. //A12345678   JOB   456,ARS,MSGLEVEL=(1,2),TIME=2

    7. //XAMPLE   JOB   XYZ,DHR,CLASS=J,PRTY=13,TYPRUN=SCAN

    8. //SAMPLE   JOB   XYZ,'D R',PRTY=6,TYPRUN=HELD

    9. //EXAMPLE   JOB   XYZ,DHR,CLASS=B,COND=(4,LT)

    10. //$123   JOB   (XYZ,123),D*R,CLASS=X,COND=(0,GT),

        //MSGLEVEL=(1,1),TIME=(,45),PRIORITY=9,TYPRUN=HOLD

2. Job Statement Coding

Code ten Job statements based upon the following specifications:

    - Choose your own Jobname but vary it for each job.

48

- Choose your own Account Numbers but supply UPDATE1 as Additional Account Information on the last five statements.
- For the Programmer Name field use your own three initials on the first five statements and two initials with an imbedded blank on the last five statements.
- Insure via the Message Level parameter that all statements and messages are produced.
- Classify the jobs utilizing the following job classification system:

Job Class	Job Description	Maximum CPU USE (Minutes)	Maximum Main Storage Use (K) Bytes	Maximum Number of Mountable Devices
A	No Mountables	3	128	0
B	7-Track Use	3	128	1
C	Low Time	3	128	3
D	Low Storage	10	64	3
E	Low Devices	10	128	1
F	High Time	15	128	3
G	High Storage	10	256	3
H	High Devices	10	128	6
I	Multiple Use	30	512	12

1. A job is estimated to take no longer than 3 minutes of CPU time. Input includes two mountable devices (9-track tape). The program module to be fetched, loaded, and executed requires 100,000 bytes of main storage. Code the Job statement utilizing the MSGLEVEL, CLASS, and TIME keyword parameters.

2. A job will be submitted which requires no mountable devices. Execution time is estimated at 45 seconds maximum. Main storage requirements demand 60,000 bytes. Only Return Codes of less than or equal to 8 are satisfactory for continuing execution. Code the Job statement utilizing the MSGLEVEL, CLASS, TIME, and COND keyword parameters.

3. The next job will take at least 10 minutes of CPU time, no more than 10,000 bytes of main storage, and one 9-track tape drive. Only a JCL scan is desired. Code the Job statement utilizing the MSGLEVEL, CLASS, and TYPRUN keyword parameters.

49

4. This job executes a small program module requiring 20,000 bytes of main storage. The job requires 1½ minutes of CPU time. Input consists of the use of one 7-track tape drive. Code the Job statement utilizing the MSGLEVEL and CLASS keyword parameters.

5. A job requires no mountable devices, but demands 200,000 bytes of main storage and 5 minutes of CPU time. To insure reasonable turnaround, the job should be executed at a priority-8 level. Code the Job statement utilizing the MSGLEVEL, CLASS, and PRTY keyword parameters.

6. This job reads a large amount of data. It needs 5 CPU minutes to execute and six 9-track tape drives. The largest step of the job requires 120,000 bytes of main storage. A Return Code equal to 12 along with the 16 default should terminate job execution. Code the Job statement utilizing the MSGLEVEL, CLASS, and COND keyword parameters.

7. This job requires only 40,000 bytes of main storage, 7 minutes of CPU time, and 2 mountable devices (one 9-track tape and one disk pack). Turnaround must be as quick as possible, so a priority level of 12 should be specified. Code the Job statement utilizing the MSGLEVEL, CLASS, and PRTY keyword parameters.

8. The next job is large and demands at least 15 minutes of CPU time, 200,000 bytes of main storage, and 8 mountable devices. Once submitted it needs to be held for the evening work shift. Code the MSGLEVEL, CLASS, and TYPRUN keyword parameters.

9. Another job requires up to 15 minutes of CPU time, 80,000 bytes of main storage, and one mountable device (9-track tape). Code the Job statement utilizing the MSGLEVEL, CLASS, and TIME keyword parameters.

10. This final job is to be run at an installation where job class is generated and not coded by the user. A CPU time specification of 12 minutes and 30 seconds and priority level of 8 should be coded. Only Return Codes of less than 4 are satisfactory for continuing execution. Code the Job statement utilizing the MSGLEVEL, TIME, PRTY, and COND keyword parameters.

3

Step Identification

A. TASK AND STEP CONCEPTS

It has been noted that a job consists of one or more steps. But what exactly is a step . . . and how can it be defined?

Easily enough in terms of JCL, a step can be delineated from other steps in a given job by the successful completion of the tasks of fetching and loading a program module into main storage for execution purposes. That is, every time the JCL calls for a program to be loaded into main storage, a distinct step of that job can be defined. This is accomplished by coding of an EXEC (Execute) statement. In fact, steps are delineated by the occurrence of Exec statements which call programs. The execution of each step (or program) in a given job is wholly independent of the execution of other steps (or programs) in that same job or other jobs. The overall sequence of events is as follows:

First, the Operating System determines that a given step of a given job should be executed and allocates main storage space.

Second, an executable program module is called by the JCL.

Third, the program is located and fetched from a job stream file or a program library.

Fourth, the program is loaded into main storage for execution purposes.

Fifth, appropriate units and files described in the JCL are assigned and allocated for processing.

Sixth, processing proceeds, given system interrupts, until step (or program) completion.

Seventh, files are deallocated, main storage is freed. The next step (and program) must now compete all over again for system resources with other steps in other jobs to be executed, i.e., the execution of each step (or program) in a given job is wholly independent of the execution of other step (or programs) in that same job or other jobs.

One may think of a three-step example where an IBM utility program is called in the first step to reformat a data file. This new file is then passed as input to a sort program in the second step which sorts the reformatted file into a new sequence. Perhaps the third step of this job calls a user-written program which edits the new sorted file and creates an error listing. Though logically interrelated to one another, each step is independent of the others as far as the Operating System (OS) is concerned. In fact, it is the responsibility of the JCL coder (programmer/analyst) to logically inter-connect the steps of a given job such that new files may be created and passed to succeeding job step for further processing.

B. THE EXEC STATEMENT

The presence of an Exec statement signifies the end of any previous JCL step coding and the beginning of a current step.

1. Exec Statement Format

Prior to Exec statement coding an overview of Exec statement format should be presented. (See Figure 3.1.)

Figure 3.1 EXEC Statement Overview

```
O                                                                     O
O      //Stepname    EXEC    Operand Field    Comment Field           O
O                                                                     O
```

The // (slash slash) is followed by a stepname. As with the job-name, a stepname is 1 to 8 alphanumeric characters in length; the first character must be an alpha character (A - Z) or one of the three national characters (@, $, #); remaining characters may be numeric. Few installations define additional JCL naming conventions and rules for the stepname. As a result, stepnames are almost completely chosen by the user.

The symbol 'EXEC' follows the stepname after at least one blank. This symbol does nothing more than indicate that this particular JCL statement is an EXEC (Execute) statement rather than a JOB (Job) statement or a DD (Data Definition) statement.

The Operand Field follows the symbol 'EXEC' after at least one blank. This field contains one or more positional and/or keyword parameters describing the characteristics of the step to be executed. Information such as the program or catalogued procedure to be called, its size in terms of main storage, and any CPU time limits or other conditions are described herein. The Operand Field is the body of the Exec statement and many times encompasses more than one line of JCL. Parameter specifications should end before column 72 but may be continued following the Continuation Rules discussed in the previous chapter.

The optional Comment Field follows the Operand Field after at least one blank. Though nonexecutable, it may be used as desired to exemplify various JCL specifications. It should also end before column 72 but may͜ continued following the Continuation Rules discussed previously.

2. The Stepname

The stepname is used to identify a given step of a job. It follows the same naming conventions and rules as all other JCL identifier names. Jobs with invalid stepnames and other syntactical errors are not allowed to enter the job queue for processing. In addition to being chosen by the user, stepnames are optional though necessary if referback and other references are desired. At least one blank must be coded to signify a stepname's absence. Figure 3.2 depicts both valid and invalid stepname specifications.

Figure 3.2 Stepname Examples

```
Valid:           Invalid:

//STEP1          //1STEP          - first character numeric

//ASTEP          //ASTEPNAME      - name too long

//$GO            //*GO            - first character invalid

//X              //X=+&           - characters 2 to 4 invalid

//#STEP          //#STEPFOUR      - name too long
```

Other than for the above specifications, few installations define additional stepnaming conventions and rules.

3. Positional Parameters

Positional parameters are distinguished by the requirement that they be placed in a specific relative location (or position) on a JCL statement. The Exec statement contains two positional parameters that are also keywords. These keywords are positional in the sense that one or the other (or its default if not coded) must be accounted for prior to the coding of any additional and optional keyword parameters. They are:

        PGM for Program
                and
        PROC for Procedure

a. PGM (Program)

Basic Format   : PGM=Program Name

Complete Format: PGM= $\left\{ \begin{array}{l} \text{Program Name} \\ \text{*.Stepname.Ddname} \\ \text{*.Stepname.ProcStepname.Ddname} \end{array} \right\}$

The purpose of the PGM positional parameter is to specify the name or reference of the executable program module to be fetched, loaded, and executed. The module must be a member of a Partitioned Data Set (PDS). (PDS's will be covered in detail in Chapter 5.) The parameter is positional in the sense that if PGM is to be coded, it must occur on the Exec statement prior to any keyword parameters. The Program Name specification must conform to the standard naming convention and rules for JCL identifier names. A Program Name is assigned to the program itself during the linkage editor process. (Compiling and linkage editing will also be covered in detail in Chapter 5.) Nevertheless, it must be noted that the program to be fetched, loaded, and executed must at the time of PGM reference be in 100% machine-executable form, i.e., a load module. In other words, the original source language program must have proceeded through an assembler/compiler/linkage process prior to the current reference for execution purposes.

Many times the program name of the program module to be executed is not known. It is in this case that stepname referbacks are necessary. A referback is indicated by coding an asterisk followed by a period, the stepname to be referenced, another period, the procedure stepname to be referenced if an instream or catalogued procedure was called and another period, and finally the ddname of the program file of interest. (see the complete format above.) Procedures (instream and catalogued) are simply a set of JCL given a name for identification and calling purposes. Ddnames are program-defined or compiler-generated names given to program files for JCL reference purposes. (The Dd statement will be covered in detail in the next chapter.) Figure 3.3 depicts various PGM parameter specifications utilizing both the basic and complete formats.

Figure 3.3 Program Parameter Examples

```
Basic Format:

//STEP1   EXEC   PGM=ASUM

//STEP2   EXEC   PGM=X789

// EXEC   PGM=#EDIT321


Complete Format:

//STEP6   EXEC   PGM=*.STEP3.INPUT1

//STEP7   EXEC   PGM=*.STEP4.LKED.SYSLMOD
```

The three basic format examples in Figure 3.3 all call executable program load modules by name following standard naming conventions and rules. The third example does not contain a stepname. It therefore cannot be referenced by another step such as is depicted in the two examples utilizing the complete format. The sixth step (STEP6) references the program to be executed as contained within the third step's (STEP3) ddname file called INPUT1. Similarly, the seventh step (STEP7) references the program to be executed as contained within the fourth step's (STEP4) procedure which contained a linkage editor (LKED) step with a ddname file called SYSLMOD. (Again, the details of compiling and link editing to create 100% machine-executable load modules will be covered in Chapter 5.)

In summary, the PGM parameter calls programs to be fetched, loaded, and executed.

b. PROC (Procedure)

Basic and Complete Format: $\left\{ \begin{array}{l} \text{PROC=Procedure Name} \\ \text{Procedure Name} \end{array} \right\}$

The purpose of the PROC positional parameter is to specify the name of an instream or catalogued procedure to be called and executed. A procedure is simply a set of JCL coded to perform specific functions. If you desire to utilize these functions you need only call the procedure by name, thus eliminating the need to code all other JCL. Instream procedures are part of the job stream and normally deleted at the end of the job. Catalogued procedure characteristics are saved as members of a Partitioned Data Set (PDS) and therefore are not automatically deleted but reserved for future reference. Procedures may and frequently do contain more than one JCL step.

Procedure Name specifications must conform to standard naming convention and rules for JCL identifier names. A Procedure Name is assigned by a utility program control card in the case of catalogued procedures and by JCL specifications in the case of instream procedures. (Both instream and catalogued procedures will be covered in detail in later chapters.) Note in the complete format above that if neither the PGM nor PROC positional parameter is coded, the Procedure Name is assumed. Figure 3.4 depicts various PROC parameter specifications utilizing the combined basic and complete format.

Figure 3.4 Procedure Parameter Examples

```
      Basic and Complete Format:

      //STEP1    EXEC    PROC=COBUCL

      //STEP2    EXEC    PROC=A987

      //STEP3    EXEC    FTG1CLG

      //STEP4    EXEC    @SUM321

      // EXEC    SORT
```

56

The first two examples in Figure 3.4 (STEP1 and STEP2) utilize the PROC keyword to call the procedures COBUCL and A987, respectively. The next two steps (STEP3 and STEP4) do not utilize the PROC keyword. Therefore, it is assumed that FTG1CLG in STEP3 and @SUM321 in STEP4 are procedure names and not program names. In the absence of PGM or PROC, PROC is assumed. The last example also utilizes this default in addition to no stepname. This step cannot be referenced by later steps in this job if desired.

In summary, the PROC parameter references procedures (both instream and catalogued, single-step or multistep) to be called, loaded, and executed.

4. Basic Keyword Parameters

Keyword parameters are distinguished by the occurrence of a special system-recognizable word or character set with no positional restrictions. They follow positional parameters, and because they are recognizable keywords they may be coded in any order.

Some keyword parameters which relate to the Exec statement can be considered common or typical, that is, though optional they are frequently utilized. These will be discussed first. They are:

```
COND   (Condition);
PARM   (Parameter);
REGION (Region); and
TIME   (Maximum CPU Time).
```

a. COND (Condition)

Basic Format   : COND=(Code,Operator,Stepname)

Complete Format:

$$\text{COND=}\begin{bmatrix}(\text{Code,Operator}) \\ (\text{Code,Operator,Stepname}) \\ (\text{Code,Operator,Stepname.ProcStepname})\end{bmatrix}[,......]\begin{bmatrix},\text{Even}) \\ ,\text{ONLY}\end{bmatrix}$$

The purpose of the COND keyword parameter is to specify conditions under which processing is to be discontinued. As discussed with the Job statement in the previous chapter, standard Condition (Return) codes provided by the Operating System are:

0 - No errors encountered;
4 - Warning error, execution continues, e.g., truncation;
8 - Conditional error, assumption made, e.g., period at end of sentence;
12 - Significant error, step terminates, e.g., Input/Output (I/O) error; and
16 - Severe error, job terminates, e.g., storage dump condition.

To code the COND parameter on the Exec statement, similar to the Job statement, the following codes are used in addition to program-generated codes in conjunction with one of six operators:

57

Code	Operators
0	GT - Greater than
4	GE - Greater than or Equal to
8	EQ - Equal to
12	LE - Less than or Equal to
16	LT - Less than
	NE - Not Equal to

For example, COND=(12,EQ,STEP1) coded on STEP2's Exec statement indicates that Step 2 is not to be executed, but control bypassed to the next step if a condition code of 12 is generated at some time during the execution of Step 1. That is, the initiation and execution of the second step is conditional upon the "successful" execution of the first step. In addition, the code-16 job termination default is still in effect. Similarly, COND=(4,LT,STEP2) coded on STEP3's Exec statement indicates that Step 3 is to be bypassed if 4 is less than the highest generated condition (return) code from Step 2. In other words, an 8, 12, or 16 return code from Step 2 will result in Step 3 bypassed. Code 0 or 4 generation in Step 2 will not affect Step 3's status, i.e., Step 3 will be initiated and executed.

Moving away from the basic to the complete format, coding COND=(12,EQ) or COND=(4,LT) without a stepname signifies that the condition to be tested applies to all previous steps. If reference is to be made to a step which called an instream or catalogued procedure, procedure stepnames must also be coded, e.g., COND=(12,EQ,STEP1.GO), COND=(4,LT,STEP2.SORT), etc. If COND=EVEN is coded, the step will be executed, even if a preceding step has abnormally terminated. Likewise, if COND=ONLY is coded, the step will be executed only if a preceding step has abnormally terminated.

Multiple-condition tests can also be made. For example, COND=((8, EQ,STEP1),(4,LT,STEP2)) coded on STEP3's Exec statement indicates that Step 3 is to be bypassed if either of the conditions is satisfied. Multiple tests reflect OR rather than AND conditions. Likewise, COND=((8,EQ,STEP1),(4,LT,STEP2),ONLY) signifies that the step is to be bypassed if one of the first two condition tests is satisfied. However, if one of the first two condition tests is not satisfied, the step should be executed only if a preceding step has abnormally terminated. Figure 3.5 depicts typical COND parameter specifications utilizing both the basic and complete Exec statement formats.

The first two basic format examples in Figure 3.5 specify essentially the same condition as regards Step 1. If code-12 is generated in the first example, Step 2 will be bypassed in addition to the occurrence of any code-16 (job default) conditions. In the second case, if 8 is less than the condition (return) code, i.e., 12 or 16, Step 3 will not be executed, similar to Step 2's condition. Likewise, the third and fourth basic format examples specify identical conditions. In the third example, if 4 is less than the condition (return) code issued by Step 3, i.e., 8, 12, or 16, all of Step 5's procedure steps will be bypassed. Similarly, if 8 is less than or equal to the condition (return) code from Step 3, i.e., 8, 12, or 16, all of Step 8's procedure steps will also not be executed. The fifth example with no stepname depicts an additional test for a program-generated condition (return) code of 2048 in Step 3. Default termination conditions also remain in effect. The last example of the basic format depicts no COND pa-

Figure 3.5 Condition Parameter Examples (Exec Statement)

```
Basic Format:

//STEP2    EXEC    PGM=ASUM,COND=(12,EQ,STEP1)

//STEP3'   EXEC    PGM=X789,COND=(8,LT,STEP1)

//STEP5    EXEC    PROC=COBUCL,COND=(4,LT,STEP3)

//STEP8    EXEC    PROC=FTG1CLG,COND=(8,LE,STEP3)

// EXEC            SORT,COND=(2048,EQ,STEP3)

//STEP9    EXEC    PGM=#EDIT321


Complete Format:

//STEP3    EXEC    PGM=ASUM,COND=((8,EQ),(12,EQ))

//STEP6    EXEC    PGM=*.STEP4.LKED.SYSLMOD,COND=((12,EQ,STEP5),(2048,EQ,STEP5))

//STEP9    EXEC    PROC=COBUCLG,COND=EVEN

//STEPX    EXEC    FTG1CL,COND=(4,LT,STEP9.GO)

//STEP#    EXEC    PGM=IEBGENER,COND=((8,LT,STEPX.FORT),(12,EQ,STEPX.GO),EVEN)

//         EXEC    PROC=SORT,COND=((4,GT,STEP3),(2048,LE,STEP6),ONLY)
```

ameter coding. Again, the general default conditions described previously remain in effect -- 0 for no errors, 4 for warning errors, 8 for conditional errors, 12 for significant error (step termination), and 16 for severe errors (job termination).

The first two examples of the complete format specify a multiple-OR condition. If 8 or 12 is equal to the condition (return) code for any of the previous steps, Step 3 will be bypassed in addition to the occurrence of any code-16 (job default) condition. The second example of the complete format specifies that if code-12 or program-generated 2048 is equal to the condition (return) code issued by Step 5, Step 6 will not be executed in addition to the occurrence of any code-16 (job default) condition. The third example specifies that all of Step 9's procedure steps should be executed even if a previous step has abnormally terminated. The fourth example states that if 4 is less than the condition (return code issued by procedure stepname GO in Step 9 of the JCL, i.e., 8, 12, or 16, all of STEPX's procedure steps should be bypassed. The fifth and sixth examples are multiple-OR conditions. If 8 is less than the code issued by procedure stepname FORT in STEPX of the JCL, i.e., 12, or 16, or if 12 is equal to the code returned by procedure stepname GO in STEPX of the JCL, the step will be bypassed. However, if these conditions are not satisfied, STEP# is to be executed even if a preceding step has abnormally termination. In a like manner, if 4 is greater than the code issued by Step 3 or 2048 is less than or equal to the code returned by Step 6, all of the procedure steps in the last JCL step with no stepname

59

(last step) are to be bypassed. If the above conditions are not met, this last step will be executed only if a preceding JCL step has abnormally terminated. This last example is one in which a programmer has most likely defined a completely new series of executing conditions via program specifications in Step 3 and 6. One must consider any Condition parameters coded on the Job statement to be in effect also.

In summary, the Condition parameter specifies selected test conditions under which processing is to be altered (continued or discontinued) from the general system default condition. Additional condition (return) codes can also be program-defined, generated, and tested as desired.

b. PARM (Parameter)

Basic and Complete Format: PARM=Parameter Information

The purpose of the PARM keyword parameter is to pass specific information to a processing program. The executable program must also be coded to recognize and accept such information utilizing proper programming techniques and parameter tests. This method of passing parameter information from JCL to program is similar in principle to the processing of a control or parameter file by the executing program as described in the JCL. Various program switches, options, and features can be activated utilizing either technique. The advantage of the PARM parameter is that a data file need not be defined and coded in the program to be processed. Although programmers themselves do not frequently utilize this programming technique of accepting PARM information, vendor-supplied assemblers, compilers, linkage editors, sort routines, and related catalogued procedures contain frequent occurrences of PARM information. Therefore, if a programmer is to utilize these programs and functions which one cannot do without, the use of the PARM parameter must be understood.

To code the PARM parameter on the Exec statement, the Parameter Information specification need only be substituted with the information to be passed to the program. In order to be recognized as valid, this information must conform exactly with the character strings defined in the program itself. PARM=ABC789 is a valid specification provided that the processing program recognizes ABC789 as valid parameter information and can act accordingly. Two or more pieces of information must be separated by commas and enclosed with apostrophes or parentheses, e.g., PARM='123,XYZ' or PARM=(123,XYZ). The maximum parameter specification allowed is 100 characters. Parentheses must be used for continuation purposes and special character information must be enclosed in apostrophes. A mixture of parentheses and apostrophes is therefore possible, e.g., PARM=(123,'X*Z'). Figure 3.6 depicts typical PARM parameter specifications utilizing the combined basic and complete format. (Detailed meanings of these specifications will be covered in Chapter 5.)

The first example in Figure 3.6 utilizes the PARM parameter to specify the character string LIST to a program named IEKAAOO (the FORTRAN H-level compiler) to be executed in Step 1. The second example passes LET, LIST, and XREF information to the IEWL-named program called by Step 2. Multiple information must be separated by commas and enclosed within apostrophes or parentheses. Similarily, the third example

Figure 3.6 Parm Parameter Examples

```
Basic and Combined Format:


//STEP1   EXEC   PGM=IEKAAOO,PARM=LIST

//STEP2   EXEC   PGM=IEWL,PARM=(LET,LIST,XREF)

//STEP3   EXEC   PROC=COBUCLG,PARM=(CLIST,DMAP,XREF)

//        EXEC   SORT,PARM=('CORE-40000','MSG=AP')

//STEP5   EXEC   PGM=ASUM,COND=(12,EQ,STEP1),PARM=(ABCDEFGH,

//               IJKLMNOP,ORSTUVWX,YZ)
```

passes CLIST, DMAP, and XREF to a program in the first step of a procedure named COBUCLG called by Step 3. The fourth example with no
stepname provides some special character information (the equal sign)
along with other information to the program called by the SORT procedure. Apostrophes and parentheses have been used appropriately. The
last example depicts a continuation example. Continuation must occur
after a comma; all parameter information must be enclosed in parentheses.

In summary, the Parm Parameter specification is a method of passing information to the processing program. The program must also be
coded to recognize and accept such information so that various program
switches, options, and features can then be utilized.

c. REGION (Region)

    Basic and Complete Format: REGION=SizeK

The purpose of the REGION keyword parameter is to specify how many
1,000 byte increments of main storage are to be allocated in this step
for the program to be executed. Actually, a size specification of
1K is equal to 1,024 bytes, i.e., REGION=60K really allocates 61,440
bytes of main storage. A byte is a unit of main storage measurement
equivalent to eight contiguous bits and represented in print form by
two hexadecimal characters. The amount of main storage to allocate is
determined by adding the executable program load module size to the
total buffer area plus a slight safety factor rounded up to an even
number. The safety factor is utilized for the calling and loading of
unplanned routines, e.g., the storage dump routine such that a dump
may be printed. A load module of 40,000 bytes and a total buffer area
of 14,000 bytes equals approximately 54K. Adding a 10% safety factor
and rounding up to the next even integer results in a value specification of 60K.

Though the Region parameter may be coded on the Job statement, the
author recommends it be coded on Exec statements only. It is on the
Exec statement, where program modules and routines are called and
loaded into main storage for execution. Resource demands are account-

ed for on an individual step-by-step basic. Main storage requirements and allocations usually vary substantially from step to step. Billing and cost algorithms also may include main storage use as a significant factor. When a Region parameter is not coded, a frequent default at many OS installations is 20K.

Installations under Multiprogramming with a Fixed Number of Tasks (MFT) ignore the Region parameter but check for syntax. Some OS Multiprogramming with a Variable Number of Tasks (MVT) installations also provide a main storage hierarchy support feature whereby two-part regions can be allocated. In this case a Region parameter may be coded REGION=(40K,20K) for hierarchy 0 and 1, respectively. The Region parameter also takes on less significance for installations with the Virtual Storage (VS) feature of the Operating System (OS), though it may be used to assist in determining virtual storage disk space requirements. Figure 3.7 depicts typical REGION parameter specifications utilizing the combined basic and complete format.

Figure 3.7 Region Parameter Examples (EXEC Statement)

```
Basic and Combined Format:


//STEP1    EXEC    PGM=ASUM,REGION=60K

//STEP2    EXEC    PGM=*.STEP1.INPUT1,REGION=IOOK

//STEP3    EXEC    PROC=A987,REGION=39K

//STEP4    EXEC    @SUM321,REGION=(30K,20K)

//         EXEC    PGM=#EDIT321
```

The first and second examples of the basic and combined format in Figure 3.7 utilize the REGION parameter to allocate approximately 60,000 and 100,000 bytes of main storage, respectively. In Step 3 a specification of 39K rounds to 40K for all steps of the procedure named A987. In the fourth step values of 30K and 20K are allocated for main storage hierarchy 0 and 1, respectively, in all steps of the procedure named @SUM321. The last example with no stepname also provides no Region specification. In this case the installation main storage allocation default (frequently 20K) is in effect.

d. TIME (Maximum CPU Time)

Basic Format   :   TIME=CPU Minutes

Complete   Format: TIME=$\left\{\begin{array}{l}\text{CPU Minutes} \\ \text{(CPU Minutes,CPU Seconds)} \\ 1440\end{array}\right\}$

The purpose of the TIME keyword parameter is to specify the maximum amount of Central Processing Unit (CPU) time allowed beyond which processing is to terminate. The Time parameter is thus used as a safety limit to prevent endless program loops and other burdensome program errors from using a needless and unnecessary amount of system resources. It is a method of placing a "lid" on a given step to prevent a runaway cost and resource situation from occurring.

CPU time can be specified in terms of maximum CPU minutes, maximum CPU seconds, both minutes and seconds, or the value 1440. There happen to be 1440 minutes in one day (24 x 60). For the purposes of JCL, this value signifies that CPU resources are not to be timed, a very insecure if not dangerous specification. Like most other parameters, the Time parameter need not be coded. In this case, the installation step time default takes effect for termination purposes. A most frequent default at many System 360 installations is 10 minutes; and 1 minute at many System 370 facilities. Time parameter specifications at OS installations are in terms of actual CPU use, not wall-clock or elapsed execution time, which could be from 2 to 20 or more times longer. Ten minutes of actual CPU use on System 370 models in particular is a large amount of processing time, especially when compared to early System 360 counterparts.

As can be seen, a small budget could be easily wasted by an unforeseen program loop. It is for this reason that the author recommends that a Time parameter be coded on all Exec statements other than those which call utility programs or which have Time parameters already contained within instream and catalogued procedure steps. It can be assured that current vendor-supplied utility programs will not go into an accidental program loop. However, it can never be assured that a user program written in any language will not fall into an unforeseen and unplanned loop. User programs should never be without a time limit. The installation default is seldom coincidentally appropriate.

The author also recommends that a Time parameter be coded on the Job statements. Estimates of maximum CPU use at the job level may be less than the sum of the estimates of maximum CPU use for each step. For example, a series of Time parameters could be coded as follows:

    Job: 12 minutes maximum

 Step 1:   5 minutes maximum

 Step 2:   5 minutes maximum

 Step 3:   5 minutes maximum

     +_____

        15 minutes total step maximum compared to only

        12 minutes total job time maximum

Though the above time specifications may appear to be conflicting at first glance, in reality they are most appropriate. It is estimated that Steps 1 through 3 will each take exactly 3 minutes of CPU time. The user has specified 5 minutes for each step to provide a safety margin or error, i.e., if a given step requires 5 minutes of CPU use, we know something is wrong, as our best estimate is 3 minutes. Likewise, specifying 12 minutes (not 15) on the Job statement adds another time limit to the job; i.e., if the job uses 12 minutes of CPU time we know something is wrong, as our best estimate is 9 minutes (3 + 3 + 3). Job and step time coding need not add to nor necessarily agree with each other. Each parameter merely provides an additional time restriction to a given job. Figure 3.8 depicts typical TIME parameter specifications utilizing both the basic and complete format.

Figure 3.8 Time Parameter Examples (EXEC Statement)

```
Basic Format:

//STEP1   EXEC   PGM=ASUM,TIME=1

//STEP2   EXEC   PGM=*.STEP1.INPUT1,TIME=10

//STEP3   EXEC   PROC=A987,TIME=30

//        EXEC   PGM=IEBGENER

//        EXEC   PROC=COBUCL

//        EXEC   PGM=X789


Complete Format:

//STEPX   EXEC   PGM=#EDIT321,TIME=(1,30)

//STEP@   EXEC   PGM=*.STEP4.LKED.SYSLMOD,TIME=(,20)

//XYZ     EXEC   PROC=A987,TIME=(10,59)

//        EXEC   @SUM321,TIME=1440
```

The first three basic format examples in Figure 3.8 indicate that if a JCL step total of more than 1, 10, and 30 CPU minutes are utilized, respectively, processing for the complete job (not just the step) should be discontinued. The first two examples call programs, while the third example calls a procedure. The STEP3 time specification therefore relates to the total of all steps within the procedure. The last three basic format examples in Figure 3.8 with no stepnames contain no Time parameters. The installation default is in effect, as utility program IEBGENER and catalogued procedure COBUCL need no time specifications coded by the user, though it is not an error to do so. One need not worry that vendor-supplied utility programs will slip into an endless program loop. Similarily so with procedure COBUCL. Compilers, linkage editor, and other vendor-supplied programs are also secure from this risk, That last example of the basic format raises some question, however. Program X789 is not vendor-supplied. Presumably, it is installation- or user-written. Though most programs written by an installation to meet common user needs may be wholly debugged, most user programs are not. A time specification is strongly recommended. Many small user budgets have been quickly exhausted due to this oversight.

The first three complete format examples indicate that if a JCL CPU step total of more than 1 minute and 30 seconds, 20 seconds, and 10 minutes and 59 seconds are utilized, respectively, processing for the complete job should be discontinued. The seconds specification must be less than 60. The first two examples call programs, while the third and fourth examples call procedures. The A987 step time specification therefore relates to the total of all steps within the procedure. Similarly, the fourth example with no step relates to procedure @SUM321 and contains a time specification of 1440. This is rarely used, as no time limit would now exist for total procedure CPU step time processing.

In summary, the Time parameter provides a CPU time limit beyond which processing will be discontinued.

5. Basic Exec Statement Examples

The previous discussion has covered task and step concepts and the Exec statement. Six parameters have been identified as basic or common to most System 360/370 OS and VS users. They are:

Positional	-	Program; and
		Procedure.
Keyword	-	Condition;
		Parameter;
		Region; and
		CPU Time.

Other not-so-common Keyword parameters will be covered later in this chapter. Figure 3.9 displays a series of typical Exec statements with Job statements utilizing common positional and keyword parameters discussed previously.

The first set of seven Exec statement examples in Figure 3.9 for TOBIN's JOB1 utilize from one to all four basic keyword parameters when calling programs and procedures. Only basic formats are utilized. The first four steps call user programs with appropriate main storage allocation Region parameters. Time parameters should be coded to place a limit on maximum CPU use. Occasional Condition and Parameter specifications can be found in the job. The last three steps of this set call procedures (presumably catalogued). Time, Region, and Condition parameters as coded refer to all steps of a procedure. The Parm parameter as coded in Step 7 defaults to the first step of the procedure. (Chapter 5's presentation on catalogued procedures will discuss in detail how other steps of a procedure can be individually referenced.)

The second set of the examples in Figure 3.9 for IMP's JOB2 primarily utilize one or two basic keyword parameters per Exec statement. Complete formats are also utilized. The following defaults take effect if a keyword is not coded:

Condition	-	standard code severity;
Parameter	-	no specification;
Region	-	frequently 20K; and
Time	-	frequently 10 minutes and 1 minute at System 360 and 370 installations, respectively.

Figure 3.9 Typical Exec Statement Examples

```
//JOB1    JOB    XYZABC123,TOBIN,MSGLEVEL=(1,1),CLASS=L

//STEP1   EXEC   PGM=EDIT1,REGION=70K

//STEP2   EXEC   PGM=EDIT2,REGION=30K,TIME=1

//STEP3   EXEC   PGM=EDIT3,REGION=50K,TIME=5,

//               COND=(8,LT,STEP2)

//STEP4   EXEC   PGM=EDIT4,REGION=100K,TIME=8,

//               COND=(12,EQ,STEP3),PARM=MATCH

//STEP5   EXEC   PROC=SUM1,TIME=15

//STEP6   EXEC   PROC=SUM2,TIME=10,REGION=180K

//STEP7   EXEC   SUM3,TIME=3,REGION=80K,PARM=TABLE



//JOB2    JOB    (123,PROJ1),IMP,MSGLEVEL=(1,1)

//STEPA   EXEC   PGM=UPDATE1,TIME=1,PARM=('X&Y','I P')

//STB     EXEC   PGM=UPDATE2,REGION=76K,TIME=(,45)

//STC     EXEC   PGM=IEBGENER,COND=EVEN

//STEPD   EXEC   PROC=COBUCLG,PARM=(DMAP,PMAP)

//SP      EXEC   PL1LFCLG,TIME=(2,30),

//               COND=((12,EQ,STB),(4,LE,STEPD.GO))

//        EXEC   PGM=IEBPTPCH

//        EXEC   PGM=SORTD



//JOB3    JOB    A1B2C3XYZ,DANHR,MSGLEVEL=(1,1),CLASS=H,TIME=20

//STEPX   EXEC   PGM=IEBUPDTE,PARM=NEW

//STEPY   EXEC   PGM=USERPROG,REGION=40K,TIME=(1,30)

//STEPZ   EXEC   PGM=IKFCBLOO,REGION=130K

//@ST     EXEC   PGM=IEWL,COND=(4,LT,STEPZ)

//#STP    EXEC   PROC=FTG1CL,PARM='LIST,MAP'

//$STEP   EXEC   COBUCL,PARM=(CLIST,DMAP,XREF)

//        EXEC   PGM=USER1,REGION=220K,TIME=10,COND=(12,EQ)
```

Remember when calling a procedure that some keywords may already be coded therein.

66

The third set of examples in Figure 3.9 for DANHR's JOB3 utilize a mixture of basic keyword parameters and formats. This set is perhaps the most common of the three sets of examples. Remember that defaults may vary from installation to installation. This is because specific defaults are determined not only by the Operating System as supplied by the vendor, but also by installation needs and **desires** reflected at system generation time, i.e., when the operating system is installed at a particular facility.

It should be noted that one or more Dd statements will be placed behind each Exec statement. A Dd statement must be coded for each file to be processed in each step. Dd statements are the topic of the next chapter.

6. Other Keyword Parameters

a. ACCT (Account)

Basic and Complete Format: ACCT=Account Information

The Account keyword parameter contains Account Information to be used for step billing purposes. That is, if one or more individual steps of a given job need to be billed to separate account numbers or if separate subaccounts within the same account number need to be billed on a step-by-step basis, the Account parameter can be utilized, e.g., ACCT=XYZABC123.

If more than one piece of account information (or more than one subparameter) is to be provided as separated by commas, **the** complete account information specification must be enclosed within parentheses. Account information may be alphanumeric but must not exceed 142 characters in length. Continuation of account information onto another line also requires parentheses. Subparameters with special characters must be enclosed in apostrophes.

As a general rule, information coded on a Job statement takes precedence over similar parameter information coded on Exec statements. In the case of the Account parameter, however, one must check with the specific installation to be sure.

b. ADDRSPC (Address Space)

Basic and Complete Format: $\text{ADDRSPC}=\begin{Bmatrix} \text{VIRT} \\ \text{REAL} \end{Bmatrix}$

The purpose of the ADDRSPC keyword parameter is to specify that real storage is to be used for this step rather than virtual storage. Specific to installations with the Virtual Storage (VS) feature of OS, this parameter when allowed provides the user with a means of bypassing the virtual storage of program load modules and routines.

If not coded, ADDRSPC=VIRT is assumed at VS installations. If ADDRSPC=REAL is coded, a programmer wishes to allocate a complete region of real (or actual) storage for the total load module as under operating systems without the virtual storage feature. Both specifications may be coupled with Region parameters as appropriate, to be discussed later.

c. DPRTY (Dispatching Priority)

Basic and Complete Format: DPRTY=(Priority Code1,Priority Code2)

The purpose of the DPRTY keyword parameter is to specify a processing priority for a step of a given job in installations with Multiprogramming with a Variable Number of Tasks (MVT). Installations attempt to guarantee job turnaround time based upon a combination of job class and priority. The higher the priority, the faster the turnaround. Remember however, that many dp installation billing algorithms adjust job cost accordingly.

Priority Code1 functions the same as the priority code specified in the PRTY parameter of the Job statement. The system accesses the priority value, converts it internally (multiplying by 16), and then adds a constant of 11 to the converted figure. This new value becomes the actual dispatching priority used to determine when a given job and/or step will be executed. A priority Code2 value can be added to the converted figure rather than an 11 if desired, e.g., DPRTY=(6,12). Although a priority is assumed and/or coded at the job level, the dispatching priority parameter allows a user to raise or lower this level for one or more steps in a given job.

d. RD (Restart Definition)

$$\text{Basic and Complete Format:} \quad RD=\begin{Bmatrix} R \\ RNC \\ NR \\ NC \end{Bmatrix}$$

The purpose of the RD keyword parameter is to define or limit step restart capabilities as coded in the JCL and/or operating program. It is possible for a step which has abnormally terminated to be automatically restarted at the beginning of the step (Automatic Step Restart) or at a specific point within that step (Automatic Checkpoint Restart). When these capabilities are to be utilized but are not desired to a certain degree for this run of a given step, the RD parameter should be coded. If not coded, RD=R is assumed, that is, both automatic step restart and automatic checkpoint restart are allowed. If automatic step restart is to be permitted but automatic checkpoint restart is not to be permitted, code RD=RNC. If neither automatic step restart nor automatic checkpoint restart are to be allowed for this run of the step but it is desired to establish checkpoints for a deferred restart, i.e., job step pickup and resubmission, code RD=NR. If RD=NC is coded, not only are automatic step restart and automatic checkpoint restart not permitted, but checkpoints are also not established for deferred restarts. Remember, however, that RD parameters coded on a Job statement override those which may be coded on Exec statements.

e. ROLL (Roll)

Basic and Complete Format: ROLL=(Status,Cause)

The purpose of the ROLL keyword parameter is (1) to signify whether a given step of this job may be temporarily rolled out of main storage in favor of another job (Status) and (2) to signify whether a given step of this job may cause temporary rollout of another job from main storage in favor of this job step (Cause). This parameter is only valid for Multiprogramming with a Variable Number of Tasks (MVT) OS configurations. If not coded, ROLL=(YES,NO) is a common default, that is, this step may be rolled out but may not cause rollout of other jobs. Conversely, ROLL=(NO,YES) signifies that this step may not be rolled out but may cause rollout of other jobs if more main storage than originally requested is desired. If the Roll parameter has been coded on the Job statement, Roll parameters on Exec statements are ignored.

C. EXEC STATEMENT WORKSHOP

All allowable positional keyword parameters which can be coded on an Exec statement have been discussed. A workshop is now provided to solidify a working knowledge of basic Exec statement JCL coding. Workshop answers can be found in Appendix E.

1. Syntax Check

Review, analyze, and correct the following ten Exec statements for syntactical and/or logic coding errors. A given Exec statement may contain none, one, or more than one error.

1. //STEP& EXEC PGM=ALOAD,TIME=2,30,REGION=40K

2. //STEP2 EXAC PGM=AAA999,PARM=ON,YES,COND=(4,LT)

3. //#STEP EXEC PROC=SORTW,COND=((4,LT),(4,GE))

4. //$@#12345 EXEC COBUCL,PARM=(CLIST,DMAP,XREF)

5. //7654321 EXEC PGM=EXAM,TYME=1,COND=(12,OR)

6. //Z12345678 EXEC PROC=ABC,TIME=(2,64),REGION=80K

```
7. //      EXEC   PGM=IEBGENER,COND=(8,LT,STEP10)


8. //EIGHTH  EXEC   REGION=140K,TIME=3


9. //EXAMPLE  EXEC   FTG1C,PARM=(LIST,MAP)


10. //STEP10   EXEC   PGM=AEDIT,PARM=10%,REGION=50K


   //           CONDITION=(4,LT,STEP2),TIME=(,45)
```

2. Exec Statement Coding

Code ten Exec statements based upon the following specifications:

- Choose your own stepname but vary it for each step.
- Do not code a stepname for the last step.

1. Execute a catalogued procedure called TAPE which creates a
   tape file from a card deck. No other parameters are necessary.

_____

_____

2. Execute a user-written program called AEDIT which edits the
   tape produced in the first step. The total program module
   requires 70,000 bytes of main storage. Execution should be
   terminated if more than 3 minutes of CPU time are utilized.

_____

_____

3. Call a utility program named IEBPTPCH to print the edited
   tape created by the previous step. System defaults for Region,
   Condition, and Time are acceptable. No information is to be
   supplied via the Parm parameter.

4. Execute a user-written program named AMATCH which matches previous data with a master file. A Time specification of 1 minute is desired. Bypass this step if 4 is less than the condition (return) code issued by the second step.

_____

_____

5. Call a catalogued procedure named COBUC which compiles ANS COBOL Version 4 source programs. Ask for a DMAP and PMAP via the Parm parameter.

_____

_____

6. Call a catalogued procedure called LKED which link-edits the program object module from the preceding step. Specify LET, LIST, and XREF to the linkage editor program via the Parm parameter. Bypass this step if 8 is less than or equal to the condition (return) code issued by the previous step or if 12 is equal to the condition (return) code issued by any preceding step.

_____

_____

7. Execute a user-written program called AREFORM which reformats the matched data from the fourth step. Allocate 200,000 bytes of main storage and limit processing to 90 seconds. Specify YES, OFF, and A*B to the program via the Parm parameter.

_____

_____

8. Call a catalogued procedure named FTG1CLG which compiles, links, and executed FORTRAN G1-Level source programs. Specify LIST and MAP to the compiler program called in the first step of the procedure. Terminate processing if and when a total of 5 CPU minutes have been utilized by the procedure.

----

9. Execute a utility program called IEBGENER which creates a backup copy of a file produced in the eighth step. Bypass this step if 8 is less than the condition code issued by the eighth step.

----

10. Execute a user-written program called FINEE. Allocate 120,000 bytes of main storage. Specify a 4-minute maximum. Bypass this step if 4 is less than or equal to the condition (return) code issued by any preceding step. Supply 4+8 to the program via the Parm parameter.

4

File Identification

A. FILE MANAGEMENT CONCEPTS

Now that the characteristics of a given job and the specifications for each step of that job have been defined, each file to be processed must be described to the Operating System on a step-by-step basis.

First, an Input/Output (I/O) device is assigned to each file, that is, a 9-track tape drive, high-density disk pack, etc. Generally, tape and disk drives are readily available. However, if a card punch is desired and only one is available for all users, the Operating System must be assured of obtaining this unit prior to program execution. Scheduling of this step will be deferred until all files to be processed have been assigned the appropriate I/O device. It is the user who specifies these unit characteristics in the JCL via the Dd statement.

Second, once the proper unit has been assigned, a specific tape reel or disk pack must be mounted on the device, with the exception of those units with volumes already on-line. Many direct-access devices, including disk, drums, and data cells, may be on-line at all times. In addition, some may need to be shared by many users. Those volumes which are off-line must be located and mounted prior to program execution. It is the user who requests specific volumes via the Dd statement.

Third, some direct-access devices require space allocations for output files. That is, the Operating System must be assured that enough space is available on the unit for the creation of a new file. If available space cannot be found, processing will not begin. It is the user who specifies space requirements via the Dd statement.

Fourth, various logical and physical characteristics of each file must be described to the Operating System. Record format, record lengths, blocksizes, etc. need to be provided. In addition, these specifications may not conflict with actual file properties. The user may specify these file characteristics via the Dd statement.

It is not until all units have been assigned, necessary volumes specified and mounted, required space allocated, and appropriate file characteristics described to the Operating System that the initial file management process is complete and program execution can begin. The Dd statement defines these characteristics and requirements for each file in each step of a given job to be processed. Once processing has begun, the Operating System monitors and controls file status. As interruptions occur and control is switched back and forth from Input/Output (I/O) functions to the Central Processing Unit (CPU) and vice versa, file management continues. The system must keep track of the unit being utilized, the volume specified, and the data being processed. The file management process is not complete until all programs have been executed, files processed, and units reallocated, or until abnormal termination has occurred.

B. THE DD STATEMENT

1. Dd Statement Format

Prior to Dd statement coding, an overview of Dd statement format should be presented. See Figure 4.1.

Figure 4.1 Dd Statement Overview

The // (slash slash) is followed by a ddname. As with the jobname and stepname, all JCL identifier names are 1 to 8 alphanumeric characters in length; the first must be an alpha character (A-Z) or one of three national characters (@, $, #); remaining characters may be numeric. Jobs with invalid ddnames and other syntactical errors are not allowed to enter the job queue for processing. Unlike jobnames and stepnames, ddnames are defined in the program to be executed for each file to be processed.

The symbol 'DD' follows the ddname after at least one blank. This symbol does nothing more that indicate that this particular JCL statement is a DD (Data Definition) statement rather than a JOB (JOB) statement or an EXEC (Execute) statement.

The Operand Field follows the symbol 'DD' after at least one blank. This field contains one or more positional and/or keyword parameters describing the nature and characteristics of each file to be processed. Information such as unit, status, disposition, name, volume, and control characteristics are described herein. The Operand Field is the body of the Dd statement and many times encompasses more than one line of JCL. Parameter specifications should end before column 72 but may be continued following the Continuation Rules discussed in Chapter 2.

The optional Comment Field follows the Operand Field after at least one blank. Though nonexecutable, it may be used as desired to exemplify various JCL specifications. It should also end before column 72 but may be continued following the Continuation Rules discussed previously.

2. The Ddname

The ddname is used to identify a given file within the steps of a job. It follows the same naming conventions and rules as all other JCL identifier names. Unlike jobnames and stepnames, ddnames are defined in the program to be executed for each file to be processed. One must code JCL ddnames as chosen by the programmer. The ddname is the only link between the physical file described in the JCL and the corresponding logical file defined in the program. Therefore, the ddname as coded in the program must be coded as such in the JCL. Figure 4.2 shows various program statements which are used at the source language level to assign ddnames to program files. These ddnames are then utilized when coding Dd statements for each file to be processed.

Figure 4.2 Ddname Assignment and Examples

Program Assignment:	JCL Example:
COBOL:	
ASSIGN TO CARDIN	//CARDIN
ASSIGN TO UT-2400-S-WRTOUT	//WRTOUT
ASSIGN TO 'PRTOUT' UTILITY	//PRTOUT
FORTRAN:	
READ (1)	//FT01F001
READ (5,100)	//FT05F001
WRITE (6,200)	//FT06F001
PL/1:	
DECLARE DATAIN	//DATAIN
READ FILE(MASTERIN)	//MASTERIN
OPEN FILE(PRINTOUT)	//PRINTOUT
ASSEMBLY:	
DDNAME=INPUT1	//INPUT1
DDNAME=OUTPUT1	//OUTPUT1
DDNAME=PRINT#	//PRINT#

As one can see, the ddnames as defined in the program must be coded in the JCL. In the FORTRAN example in Figure 4.2 it should be noted that a ddname is generated by the compiler utilizing unit numbers coded in the program. For example, the 5 in READ (5,100) is converted to 05; the characters FT and F001 are generated and placed on each side of the unit designation; i.e., FT05F001. This compiler-generated name is now the ddname for the file to be processed by the READ (5,100) program statement. Also note that the following seven ddnames should not be used, since they are special ddnames with specific purposes which will be discussed later in this chapter: JOBCAT, JOBLIB, STEPCAT, STEPLIB, SYSABEND, SYSUDUMP, and SYSCHK.

3. Positional Parameters

Positional parameters are distinguished by the requirement that they be placed in a specific relative location (or position) on a JCL statement. The Dd statement contains three positional parameters that are reserved words or symbols. They are positional in the sense that if their function is to be utilized, one of the three must be coded on the Dd statement prior to the coding of any keyword parameters. They are:

    * (Asterisk);
    DATA; and
    DUMMY.

a. * (Asterisk)

    Basic and Complete Format: //Ddname DD *

The purpose of the * (Asterisk) positional parameter is to assign a card reader to a given file. The card file to be processed follows this statement in the input stream. In other words, the actual card file is placed directly behind the DD * statement. End of file is indicated by a /* (slash asterisk) in columns 1 and 2, // (slash slash) in columns 1 and 2, or an EOF (End of File) condition at the card reader. Therefore, to ensure that all card data is read it is imperative that the file to be processed not contain /*'s or //'s in columns 1 and 2 or that a pause or command at the card reader does not inadvertently generate an EOF condition in the middle of the card file. It should also be pointed out that only BLKSIZE (Blocksize), BUFNO (Buffer Number), and DLM (Delimeter) subparameters of the DCB (Data Control Block) keyword parameter are valid on a DD * statement. They will be discussed later in this chapter. Also, under the Primary Control Program (PCP) version of OS, only one DD * or DATA statement is allowed per step. No such restrictions exist in MFT, MVT, and VS dp environments. Figure 4.3 depicts two DD * examples utilizing the combined basic and complete format.

The two combined basic and complete format examples in Figure 4.3 both read card input. The first example with ddname CARDIN reads card data from the the input stream. The occurrence of a /* in columns 1 and 2 signifies an EOF (End of File) condition. The second example with ddname SYSIN reads program cards from the input stream. The occurrence of only a // in columns 1 and 2 signifies an EOJ (End of Job) condition. The // could be the beginning of another Job, Exec, or Dd statement,

Figure 4.3 * (Asterisk) Parameter Examples

```
Basic and Complete Format:


//CARDIN  DD  *

      1153210  XYZ CORP.    2110  ⎫
                                  ⎪
      3218736  ABC  INC.    7385  ⎪
                                  ⎬  Data
      8853218  LMN COMPANY 2187   ⎪
                                  ⎪
      8976531  PDQ CO.      1532  ⎭
   /*
//SYSIN  DD  *

      IDENTIFICATION DIVISION     ⎫
                                  ⎪
      PROGRAM ID. UPDATE.         ⎪
                                  ⎬  Data
      CLOSE OUTPUT1.              ⎪
                                  ⎪
      STOP RUN.                   ⎭
```

however. In each case, ddnames CARDIN and SYSIN must have been defined in
the program to be called and executed.

    In summary, the * (Asterisk) parameter assigns the card reader to a
card file in the input stream following the DD * statement. EOF conditions
can be indicated by a /*, //, or an EOF condition at the card reader.

b. DATA (Data)

    Basic and Complete Format: //Ddname DD DATA

    The purpose of the DATA positional parameter is to assign a card
reader to a given file and to designate that the card file to be processed
follows this statement in the input stream. In other words, the card file
is placed directly behind the DD DATA statement. EOF (End of File) is
indicated by a /* or an EOF condition at the card reader. In other words,
cards with a // in columns 1 and 2 are allowed, i.e., JCL, and should be
considered as part of the input data. A job to catalogue a JCL deck as
a procedure is one such example. To ensure that all card data is read
it is imperative either that the file to be processed not contain /*'s or
that a pause or command at the card reader not inadvertantly generate an
EOF condition in the middle of the card file. A // in columns 1 and 2
does not symbolize an EOF condition. It should also be pointed out that,
like the DD * statement, only the BLKSIZE (Blocksize), BUFNO (Buffer
Number), and DLM (Delimiter) subparameters of the DCB (Data Control Block)
keyword parameter are valid on a DD DATA statement. As previously noted,
these subparameters will be discussed later in this chapter. Figure 4.4
depicts two DD DATA examples utilizing the combined basic and complete
format.

77

Figure 4.4 Data Parameter Examples

```
      Basic and Complete Format:


          //SYSUT1   DD   DATA

          //STEP1    EXEC  PGM=IEBGENER        ⎫
                                               ⎬   Data
          //INPUT1   DD   DUMMY                ⎪

          //PRINT1   DD   SYSOUT=A             ⎭

          /*


          //SYSIN  DD   DATA

          1153210  XYZ  CORP.   2110           ⎫
                                               ⎪
          //32187  ABC  INC.    7385           ⎪
                                               ⎬   Data
          88532    LMN  COMPANY 2187           ⎪

          //89765 PDQ CO.       1532           ⎪

          //*  COMMENT                         ⎭

          /*
```

The two combined basic and complete format examples in Figure 4.4
read card input. The first example with ddname SYSUT1 read card data
(JCL) with a // in columns 1 and 2 from the input stream. Presumably
this JCL deck is to be catalogued. The occurrence of a /* in columns
1 and 2 signifies an EOF (End of File) condition. The second example
with ddname SYSIN reads card data (non-JCL) with and without //'s in
columns 1 and 2 from the input stream. Presumably, the // in columns
1 and 2 on some of the data is part of the record's format. The occurrence of a /* (not the //) is columns 1 and 2 signifies and EOF condition.
In each case, ddnames SYSUT1 and SYSIN must have been defined in the
program to be called and executed.

In summary, the DATA parameter assigns the card reader to the card
file in the input stream following the DD DATA statement. EOF conditions
can be indicated by a /* or an EOF condition at the card reader, but not
a //.

c. DUMMY (Dummy)

    Combined Basic and Complete Format: //Ddname   DD   DUMMY

    The purpose of the DUMMY positional parameter is to specify that no
devices are to be assigned to the file and that no Input/Output (I/O)
operations are to be performed. The executing program is not to process
dummied files, though they may be opened. When program input/read statements are encountered, an End of File (EOF) condition is to be assumed.
The program is to follow EOF programmer logic. When program output/write
statements are encountered the respective statement is to be skipped, i.e.,
no operation is to be performed. These situations occur and may be desirable in a testing environment as well as during the initial creation of

master files when input update files are not yet present. Figure 4.5
depicts various DD DUMMY examples utilizing the combined basic and complete format.

Figure 4.5 Dummy Parameter Examples

```
//CARDIN  DD   DUMMY

//SYSIN   DD   DUMMY,DCB=(RECFM=FB,LRECL=080,BLKSIZE=1600)

//SYSUT1  DD   DUMMY,UNIT=2400,DISP=(OLD,KEEP),
//             DSNAME=AMASTER,VOL=SER=007239
```

Basic and Complete Format:

The three combined basic and complete format examples in Figure 4.5
all utilize the dummy file feature. The first example with ddname CARDIN
utilizes only the Dummy parameter. The second example with ddname SYSIN
also specifies the DCB (Data Control Block) information to be covered
later in this chapter. The third example with ddname SYSUT1 specifies
various keyword parameters also to be covered later in this chapter. These
parameters are checked for syntax and ignored on a DD DUMMY statement.

In summary, the DUMMY parameter specifies that no devices or I/O
operations are to be assigned and performed by the executing program for
the specified file.

4. Basic Keyword Parameters

Keyword parameters are distinguished by the occurrence of a special system-
recognizable word or character set with no positional restrictions. They
follow positional parameters and because they are recognizable keywords
they may be coded in any order.

Various keyword parameters which relate to the Dd statement can be
considered common or typical, that is, though optional they are frequently utilized. These will be discussed first. They are:

     DCB   (Data Control Block);
     DISP   (Disposition);
     DSNAME   (Data Set Name);
     LABEL   (Label);
     SPACE   (Space);
     SYSOUT   (System Output);
     UNIT   (Unit); and
     VOLUME   (Volume).

a. DCB (Data Control Block)

     Basic Format   :   DCB=(RECFM=Type,LRECL=Length1,BLKSIZE=Length2)

                          where Type=F (Fixed);

                                     FB (Fixed Block);

FBA (Fixed Block with Carriage Control);

V (Variable);

VB (Variable Block); or

U (Undefined) Record Format.

Length1 = 2-to-5-character Maximum Record Length.

Length2 = 2-to-5-character Maximum Blocksize.

Complete Format :   DCB=(List of Characteristics to be discussed
later in this chapter)

The purpose of the DCB keyword parameter is to describe to the Operating System necessary characteristics of the file to be processed. These characteristics consist of record format, logical record length, maximum blocksize, tape density, tape-recording technique, buffer number, data set organization, key length, error option, and others to be discussed later in this chapter. For now it is best to concern ourselves with the basic format and those few subparameters used so very often. Prior to detail coding of the DCB parameter, however, a discussion of record format, logical record length, and maximum blocksize concepts is in order.

The Operating System performs Input/Output (I/O) operations in terms of physical blocks. An Inter-Record Gap (IRG), sometimes called an Inter-Block Gap (IBG), of 1/2 to 3/4 inch exists between each physical block on tape. An IRG allows space for a tape unit to slow down, stop, start, and speed up again between blocks. The executing program, however, performs read/write operations in term of logical records, i.e., a subunit of a physical block. Logical records may be of fixed, variable, or undefined length.

Presume that a block of data 640 characters in length has just been transferred from a physical device (tape, disk, etc.) through a channel and placed in a single buffer area in main storage. Presume also that the program is coded to process and expects to find 80-character fixed-length logical records from this file. This concept is depicted in Figure 4.6.

Figure 4.6 Blocking 80-Character Fixed-Length Records

Eight Fixed-Length 80-Character Logical Records

| 80 | 80 | 80 | 80 | 80 | 80 | 80 | 80 |

Equals
One 640-Character Physical Record

The program begins processing the first 80 characters as one logical record. The second read brings forward a second set of 80 characters, etc. The eighth read brings forward the eighth set of 80 characters. The ninth read cannot be accomplished in this example, as only eight logical records exist in this block, and they have all been processed. Control now passes from the program back to the Operating System and a second I/O operation is performed to place the second physical block of data into the single buffer area overlaying the first block in main storage. Control now returns to the program, which again processes the 640-character physical block on a fixed 80-character logical record basis. Control switching and processing continues until an EOF (End of File) condition is finally reached.

Frequent I/O interruptions are a primary cause of processing inefficiency and are a significant factor in the billing algorithms of most installations. In the above example, only one I/O interruption occurred for every eight logical records to be processed. If the physical record were the same size as a logical record, e.g., 80-characters each, overall processing time and costs would be greatly increased. If a file contained 64,000 logical and physical fixed-length records of 80 characters each, then 64,000 I/O interruptions would have to occur to process the complete file. Given a physical blocksize of 640 characters (Blocking Factor = 8, or 8 Logical Records per Physical Record), then one-eighth of the above or 8,000 I/O interruptions would occur. If the records were blocked at a 6,400 size (Blocking Factor = 80), then one-eightieth of the above or only 800 I/O interruptions would occur. As physical blocksize increases, the number of required I/O operations decreases.

Why, then, is not the largest allowable blocksize used for all files at all times? The reason is that buffer areas require main storage. A blocksize of 16,000 may well be efficient in terms of I/O operations but wasteful and/or costly in terms of main storage requirements. A blocksize of 16,000 with a single buffering system would require 16K of main storage for just this file above. Likewise, with a double buffering system (now most typical), 32K of main storage would be required for this file. Given four or five files to be processed, main storage requirements for the buffer areas only may be from 128K to 160K in this example. There is a cost for main storage use, i.e., it is not wholly unlimited. This cost must be balanced against I/O cost and overhead. A most frequent compromise by users ranges in the area of 4,000-to-8,000-character physical record lengths.

Logical records need not always be fixed in length, though blocksize must be a multiple of fixed record lengths. Utilizing appropriate program file definition and logic, however, record lengths may be variable within the same file. This concept is depicted in Figure 4.7.

Figure 4.7 Blocking Variable-Length Records

Eight Variable-Length Logical Records

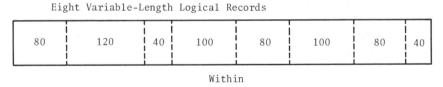

Within

One 640-Character Physical Record

Logical record lengths may be variable from record to record provided the proper programming techniques have been utilized to identify and process appropriate field items. It is recommended that variable-length records also be blocked as in the above example. In this case, maximum-length value are coded. Logical record lengths may also be undefined. In this case it is the responsibility of the executing program to read a physical block as a logical record and internally examine the data block for identifying characteristics to delineate separate records if necessary.

Detail coding of the DCB parameter for the basic format may now begin. The RECFM (Record Format) subparameter is equal to:

F - if the records are fixed;

FB - if the records are fixed and blocked, that is, have a Blocking Factor greater than 1;

FBA - if a standard carriage control character exists in the first byte of each record, and the records are fixed and blocked;

V - if the records are variable;

VB - if the records are variable and blocked, that is, have a Blocking Factor greater than 1; and

U - if the records are undefined.

If the Record Format parameter is not coded, U is assumed. Other less common record format specifications will be covered later in this chapter. The LRECL (Logical Record Length) subparameter is equal to the maximum logical record length occurrence (2 to 5 characters) in the file. The BLKSIZE (Blocksize) subparameter is equal to the maximum physical record length occurrence (2 to 5 characters, highest allowable 32,760) in the file.

It should be pointed out that values for these three basic DCB subparameters may be specified in the program in lieu of the JCL. ASSEMBLY, COBOL, and PL/1 programmers sometimes utilize this technique. FORTRAN programmers cannot. Actually, a DCB is built in main storage prior to execution for each file to be processed. To build a DCB the system checks:

The program first;
The JCL second; and
The header label third (for input files).

To build a Data Control Block in main storage, DCB characteristics must be specified in one or more of these three sources. This concept is depicted in Figure 4.8.

DCB characteristics may be specified in more than one source. If so, they should not conflict with previous specifications. Note in the above example that the record format specification in the JCL, as well as the record format and logical record length specifications in the label, were not referenced for building the DCB since these items had already been previously obtained.

Though the requirements for coding a DCB parameter in the JCL vary depending upon program specifications and the existence of labeled input files, the author recommends coding the three basic DCB subparameters in the JCL for each data file (tape or disk) to be processed. This not only prevents errors in terms of missing DCB information, but documents DCB characteristics as well. In a debugging situation one need not necessarily locate and reference the source program listing just to obtain DCB information. Rather, it is also printed in the JCL listing. The author also recommends that the three basic DCB subparameters not be coded in the JCL for card and print files unless necessary. This is because programmers should follow widely known installation default standards for defining card and print file characteristics in the program. Generally speaking, information which does not change from run

Figure 4.8 DCB Initialization Process

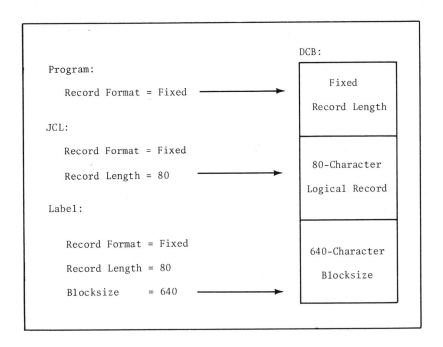

to run should be initially coded in the program, while information which
may change from run to run should be coded in the JCL for ease of reference. The label can then be used for file characteristic verification
purposes as it is originally intended. Figure 4.9 depicts various DCB
parameter specifications utilizing the basic format only.

Figure 4.9 Data Control Block Parameter Examples

```
Basic Format:

//INPUT1    DD  DCB=(RECFM=FB,LRECL=80,BLKSIZE=640)

//SYSIN     DD  DCB=(RECFM=F, LRECL=120,BLKSIZE=120)

//SYSUT1    DD  DCB=(RECFM=V,LRECL=120,BLKSIZE=124)

//SYSIN     DD  DCB=(RECFM=FB,LRECL=120,BLKSIZE=4800)

//SYSUT1    DD  DCB=(RECFM=VB,LRECL=120,BLKSIZE=4804)

//DATAIN    DD  DCB=(RECFM=U,BLKSIZE=3200)

//PRINT1    DD  DCB=(RECFM=FBA,LRECL=133, BLKSIZE=02660)

//DISKFILE  DD  DCB=BLKSIZE=2400

//DISKFILE  DD  DCB=(RECFM=FB,LRECL=60,BLKSIZE=2400)
```

83

The first Dd statement utilizing the basic format in Figure 4.9 with ddname INPUT1 corresponds to previous DCB discussion examples. The second and third Dd statements with ddnames SYSIN and SYSUT1 describe unblocked files. The fourth and fifth Dd statements with the same ddnames as the unblocked files depict how these files can be blocked for more efficient processing. The sixth Dd statement with ddname DATAIN depicts an undefined record format. The seventh Dd statement with ddname PRINT1 indicates that a carriage control character is present in column 1. It also shows that leading zeroes are allowed and in fact recommended to minimize rekeying a complete JCL statement for simple changes in record length or blocksize specifications. The last two Dd statements with ddname DISKFILE presumably depict the same file except that in the first all basic DCB information is not provided. One can assume that the missing information has been coded in the program and/or exists in the label for input files. In either case the latter example is recommended for ease of reference. It should be noted that other Dd statement parameters will need to be coded in the example above.

In summary, the DCB parameter specifies the characteristics of a file to be processed. Utilizing the basic format these items include: Record Format, Logical Record Length, and Blocksize. They may be specified in the program, JCL, and/or input label and are accessed in that order to build a DCB in main storage for each file. Other DCB characteristics will be discussed in detail later in this chapter.

b. DISP (Disposition)

Basic Format   : DISP= ($\begin{bmatrix} \text{NEW} \\ \text{OLD} \end{bmatrix}$ $\begin{bmatrix} \text{,DELETE} \\ \text{,KEEP} \\ \text{,PASS} \end{bmatrix}$)

Complete Format: DISP= ($\begin{bmatrix} \text{NEW} \\ \text{OLD} \\ \text{SHR} \\ \text{MOD} \end{bmatrix}$ $\begin{bmatrix} \text{,DELETE} \\ \text{,KEEP} \\ \text{,PASS} \\ \text{,CATLG} \\ \text{,UNCATLG} \end{bmatrix}$ $\begin{bmatrix} \text{,DELETE} \\ \text{,KEEP} \\ \text{,CATLG} \\ \text{,UNCATLG} \end{bmatrix}$)

The purpose of the DISP keyword parameter is to specify to the Operating System the status and disposition of a data set or file. The first subparameter of the basic format indicates its current status. A data set is NEW if it is to be created in this step; a data set is OLD if it was created prior to this step. The second subparameter of the basic format indicates what is to be done with the data set upon completion of the step. DELETE is coded if the file is to be scratched, i.e., its storage space is to be released for other file use at the end of the step. KEEP is coded if the data set is to be saved and/or not used in subsequent steps of this job. PASS is coded if the data set is to be used in subsequent steps of this job.

If DELETE or KEEP is specified for tape files, the reel will be rewound and dismounted at the end of the step. Mountable disk packs would also be dismounted. KEEP by itself will usually not ensure the saving of tape files for longer than a couple of days. A physical label to be affixed to the outside of the reel may be required by the installation to "save" a tape data set. A retention specification via a Label parameter is required by many tape management systems for save purposes.

Likewise, DELETE may not actually free a tape for other file use. A physical tape label may need to be removed first before an operator will allow the data set to be written over (destroyed or scratched). Similarly, many tape management systems prevent the accidental scratching of saved data sets. It should also be noted that a data set in a PASS condition upon completion of a job will revert to the DELETE status and be handled accordingly.

Utilizing additional specifications with the complete format, SHR (Share) should be coded for the first subparameter if the data set may be shared by other jobs during execution of this step. There is no need to prevent other jobs from accessing a program library file (just because your job has accessed it in this step) until step completion. SHR presumes the data set existed before this step and it will be read only. MOD (Modify) is a handy specification when records need to be added to the end of a large file. MOD activates the read/write head to a position at the end of the last data record. New records can now be written without the reading of all prior existing records by the program. One can understand the significance of this specification if, for example, only a couple of records need to be added to the end of a file containing up to 100,000 current records. If MOD is coded and the file does not exist, a New condition is assumed.

CATLG (Catalogue) should be coded if the data set is to be kept at the end of this step and the characteristics of the data set placed into the System Catalogue. This catalogue merely stores the characteristics of a file (volume, unit, and sequence number) by its data set name and prevents needless duplicative and repetitive coding of JCL characteristics upon access of a given file. This is similar in principle to data sets in a passed state. The System Catalogue also lends itself to the creation and maintenance of generation data sets to be discussed later in this text. Conversely, UNCATLG (Uncatalogue) should be coded if the data set is to be kept at the end of this step and the characteristics of the data set are to be removed from the System Catalogue. Deleted data sets will also be uncatalogued. The third subparameter indicates what is to be done with the data set if this step abnormally terminates. DELETE, KEEP, CATLG, and UNCATLG can be coded appropriately. If the third subparameter is not coded, it automatically assumes the value of the second subparameter, though a new passed data set may be deleted. If all or a protion of the DISP parameter is not coded, NEW is assumed for its status (the first subparameter). DELETE is assumed for its disposition (the second and third subparameters) if the file did not exist prior to this job; KEEP is assumed if it did exist prior to this job. Figure 4.10 depicts typical DISP parameter specifications utilizing the basic and complete formats.

The first two Dd statements utilizing the basic format in Figure 4.10 with ddnames INPUT1 and SYSIN depict input files (Old) created prior to this particular step. The first is not to be used by a subsequent step (Keep), while the second is to be used by a subsequent step (Pass). The next three examples for SYSUT2, DATAOUT, and OUTPUT1 depict output files to be created in this step (New). The first is not to be used by a subsequent step (Keep); the second is to be used by a subsequent step (Pass); while the third is most likely a test file to be scratched or released upon completion of this step. The last example of the basic format with ddname DATAIN depicts an input file (Old) to be scratched or released upon completion of this step. In the case of tapes and other mountable

Figure 4.10 Disposition Parameter Examples

```
Basic Format:

//INPUT1    DD  DISP=(OLD,KEEP)

//SYSIN     DD  DISP=(OLD,PASS)

//SYSUT2    DD  DISP=(NEW,KEEP)

//DATAOUT   DD  DISP=(NEW,PASS)

//OUTPUT1   DD  DISP=(NEW,DELETE)

//DATAIN    DD  DISP=(OLD,DELETE)


Complete Format:

//INPUT1    DD  DISP=(OLD,KEEP,DELETE)

//SYSIN     DD  DISP=(OLD,PASS,KEEP)

//SYSUT2    DD  DISP=(NEW,KEEP,DELETE)

//DATAOUT   DD  DISP=(NEW,PASS,KEEP)

//OUTPUT1   DD  DISP=(NEW,DELETE,KEEP)

//DATAIN    DD  DISP=(OLD,DELETE,KEEP)

//INPUT1    DD  DISP=OLD

//SYSIN     DD  DISP=(,KEEP)

//SYSUT2    DD  DISP=NEW

//OUTPUT1   DD  DISP=(NEW,CATLG,DELETE)

//INPUT1    DD  DISP=(OLD,UNCATLG)

//SYSUT1    DD  DISP=SHR

//DATAOUT   DD  DISP=(MOD,KEEP)

//OUTPUT1   DD  DISP=(MOD,PASS)
```

files, the Delete specification may not actually delete the data set.
Though dangerous to code, a physical label may need to be removed before
an operator will allow the data set to be used for another job and written over. Similarly, a tape management system may perform delete functions.

The first six examples utilizing the complete format are identical
to the six format examples just discussed except that the third subparameter has been coded for abnormal termination conditions. If not coded,
the third subparameter takes on the value of the second subparameter.
This may or may not be desirable depending upon a given situation. The
next three examples for ddnames INPUT1, SYSIN, and SYSUT2 utilize only
one specification. When the second subparameter is not coded, KEEP is

assumed if the file existed prior to this step while DELETE is assumed if the file did not exist prior to this step. If the first subparameter is not coded, NEW is assumed. The next two examples for ddname OUTPUT1 and INPUT1 utilize the System Catalogue. The first catalogues the data set to be created while the second uncatalogues an existing data set. The next example for ddname SYSUT1 utilizes only the Share specification. Other subparameters are not coded because the file to be shared was created prior to this step and therefore will continue to be saved in the absence of other disposition values. Finally, the last two examples for ddnames DATAOUT and OUTPUT1 utilize the MOD specification. The read/write head is positioned at end of file; new records can then be written to expand the file thus bypassing unnecessary reading and writing of existing sequential records. It should be noted that other Dd statement parameters will need to be coded in the examples above.

In summary, the DISP parameter specifies the status and disposition or files to be processed on a step-by-step basis.

c. DSNAME or DSN (Data Set Name)

$$\text{Basic Format: } \begin{Bmatrix} \text{DSNAME} \\ \text{DSN} \end{Bmatrix} = \begin{Bmatrix} \text{Data Set Name} \\ \text{\&\&Data Set Name} \end{Bmatrix}$$

$$\text{Complete Format:} \begin{Bmatrix} \text{DSNAME} \\ \text{DSN} \end{Bmatrix} = \begin{Bmatrix} \text{Data Set Name} \\ \text{\&\&Data Set Name} \\ \text{Data Set Name(Member Name)} \\ \text{Data Set Name(Generation Number)} \\ \text{Data Set Name(Area Name)} \\ \text{\&\&Data Set Name(Member Name)} \\ \text{\&\&Data Set Name(Area Name)} \\ \text{*.Ddname} \\ \text{*.Stepname.Ddname} \\ \text{*.Stepname.ProcStepname.Ddname} \end{Bmatrix}$$

The purpose of the DSNAME or abbreviated DSN keyword parameter is to identify by name the input or output file to be processed as well as to indicate its permanent or temporary nature. It is the data set name which is referenced to locate an input file of interest. Likewise, it is the data set name which identifies an output file. At output time the data set name is stored in the tape header label or the disk volume table of contents. At input time, the data set name coded in the JCL is located on the disk volume of interest or compared with the data set name stored in the tape volume header label. Conflicts will cause abnormal termination of the job to be processed. There are two types of data set names:

    Simple; and
    Qualified.

Simple data set names utilizing the basic format follow the same naming conventions and rules as all other JCL identifier names, e.g., DATA6789. That is, it is 1 to 8 alphanumeric characters in length, the first an alpha character (A-Z) or one of three national characters (@,

$, #). Remaining characters may be numeric. The hyphen (-) and plus zero (12-0 punch) are also valid data set name characters. Qualified data set names are composed of simple data set names separated by a period. They may be up to 44 characters in length, e.g., DSNAME=THE.FIRST. OF.SEVEN.NON.EDITED.INPUT.FILES, for further clarification and identification of a given data set. Though qualified data set names are more cumbersome and prone to keying errors, they are more user-descriptive of the file to be processed and self-documenting.

Temporary data sets may also be defined with the DSNAME or DSN parameter by coding two ampersands (&&) in front of the name of interest, e.g., DSNAME=&&DATA8899. The ampersands are not part of the data set name itself. A temporary data set is defined as a file which is to be created and deleted all within the same job. This can also be accomplished via the Disposition parameter, i.e., DISP=(NEW,PASS) when created and DISP=(OLD,DELETE) in the last step to utilize this file. However, the use of two ampersands in front of the data set name is a technically correct method of coding temporary data set names. If KEEP is coded in the DISP parameter for a file with a temporary data set name, a JCL error message may be generated, depending upon installation standards. Permanent data set names without the two ampersands (&&), e.g., DSNAME=DATA 8899, are not automatically deleted at the end of the job but rather rely on Disposition specifications. The use of one ampersand in front of the data set name also indicates a temporary file, but in addition defines a symbolic specification. The use of symbolic parameters will be described later in the text.

Utilizing the complete format, member names of partitioned data sets (PDS's), generation numbers of generation data sets, and area names of index sequential files can also be specified via the Dsname parameter. PDS program and JCL data set libraries will be covered in the next chapter. The techniques for utilizing generation data sets and index sequential data files will be covered later in the text. Similarly, the JCL technique of backward reference by coding an asterisk and a period (*.) in front of the file to be referenced will be expanded upon in the next chapter and later in the text. It should also be pointed out that data set names containing special characters must be enclosed in apostrophes are not part of the data set name.

If a Dsname parameter is not coded, a temporary qualified data set name is automatically generated by the system. An installation will insure via OS that the name to be generated is unique, that is, it will not be confused with another file of the same name in the job stream. To accomplish this task, such items as date, time of day, and sequence numbers are utilized. To avoid confusion and JCL errors, data set names for separate files within a job stream should be unique whether generated by the system or coded by the user. Figure 4.11 depicts somewhat common DSNAME or DSN parameter specifications utilizing the basic and complete formats.

The first set of three examples utilizing the basic format in Figure 4.11 spell out the keyword DSNAME and describe permanent simple data set names. The second set of three examples above abbreviate the keyword DSN. The file with the ddname DATAOUT depicts a temporary simple data set to be deleted at the end of the job. OUTPUT1's data set name is also temporay but qualified as well. The last example of the basic format for ddname DATAIN describes a permanent qualified data set name.

Figure 4.11 Dsname Parameter Examples

```
       Basic Format:

       //INPUT1    DD  DSNAME=DATAFILE

       //SYSIN     DD  DSNAME=CARDS78

       //SYSUT2    DD  DSNAME=#OUT1

       //DATAOUT   DD  DSN=&&ATEMP

       //OUTPUT1   DD  DSN=&&ATEMP.QUAL.IFIED.DATASET.NAME

       //DATAIN    DD  DSN=APERM.QUAL.IFIED.DATASET.NAME

       Complete Format:

       //INPUT1    DD  DSNAME=DATAFILE(PROG1)

       //SYSIN     DD  DSNAME=CARDS76(+1)

       //SYSUT2    DD  DSNAME=#OUT1(INDEX)

       //DATAOUT   DD  DSN=&&ATEMP(PROC1)

       //OUTPUT1   DD  DSN=&&IND.SEQ.DATA.FILE(PRIME)

       //DATAIN    DD  DSN=*.SYSUT2

       //DATAIN    DD  DSN=*.STEP1.INPUT1

       //DATAIN    DD  DSN=*.STEP2.GO.DATAOUT

       //OUTPUT2   DD  DSN='A$B*C-D'
```

The complete format will be discussed further at various points
throughout the text. The first three examples specify member name PROG1,
generation number +1, and area name INDEX for permanent simple data set
names DATAFILE, CARDS76, and #OUT1, respectively. Similarly, the next
two examples specify member name PROC1 and area name PRIME for temporary
simple and qualified data set names ATEMP and IND.SEQ.DATA.FILE, respectively. The next three examples of the complete format with ddname
DATAIN utilize the technique of backward reference to indicate a data
set name of interest. The SYSUT2 ddname file in the current step, the
INPUT1 ddname file in the step named STEP1, and the DATAOUT ddname file
,in a procedure step named GO in stepname STEP2 are referenced for processing, respectively. The last example for ddname OUTPUT2 utilizes
special characters and must therefore be enclosed in apostrophes. It
should be noted that other Dd statement parameters may need to be coded
in these examples.

In summary, the DSNAME or DSN parameter identifies a data set by name
for processing as well as indicates whether the file is to be considered
permanent or temporary.

d. LABEL (Label)

Basic Format : $\text{LABEL=}\begin{Bmatrix} (1,\text{SL}) \\ (,\text{SL}) \end{Bmatrix}$

Complete Format: $\text{LABEL=(}\begin{bmatrix} \text{Data Set Sequence Number} \end{bmatrix}\begin{bmatrix} \text{,SL} \\ \text{,SUL} \\ \text{,AL} \\ \text{,AUL} \\ \text{,NSL} \\ \text{,NL} \\ \text{,BLP} \\ \text{,LTM} \\ \text{,} \end{bmatrix}$

$\begin{bmatrix} \text{,PASSWORD} \\ \text{,NOPWREAD} \\ \text{,} \end{bmatrix}\begin{bmatrix} \text{,IN} \\ \text{,OUT} \end{bmatrix}\begin{bmatrix} \text{,EXPDT=yyddd} \\ \text{,RETPD=xxxx} \end{bmatrix}\text{)}$

The primary purpose of the LABEL keyword parameter is to describe the type of label associated with a data set. Other functions include spec- ifying the relative position of the data set on the volume, password status, input/output conditions, and the time period to keep a saved data set. It is in the header and trailer labels of a given data set where such items as Data Control Block (DCB) information, data set name, volume serial number, and other characteristics which describe the data set are stored. In other words, the first few records in a file are not necessar- ily your data but rather a series of label records created when the file itself was created. Labels store data set characteristics and are used for verification purposes. Prior to input processing of data, label records are read, edited, and checked against JCL specifications. Any conflicts in file descriptions result in abnormal terminations of the given job. An overview of label record format should be discussed prior to actual Label parameter coding. Figure 4.12 displays a schematic over- view of standard tape label layout.

All of the header and trailer tape label records in Figure 4.12 are 80 characters in length. For the most part they are created when the data itself is created. Prior to processing actual input data, the Initial Volume Record, Header Record #1, and Header Record #2 are read and checked for validity against JCL specifications. As discussed previously, header label DCB characteristics may be used to build a data control block in main storage for each file to be processed. User header and trailer re- cords are usually not utilized but may contain additional information for verification purposes. A magnetic tape mark signifies the end of header label information and the beginning of the actual data to be processed. This data may consist of only one block or many blocks to be read or writ- ten. Another magnetic tape mark signifies the end of actual data and the beginning of trailer label records, i.e., End of Volume (EOV) Records #1 and #2. For large files an end of volume condition may be reached prior to end of file. Multivolume data sets are a subject of discussion later in this chapter. With the usual absence of user trailer records, a magnetic tape mark signifies the end of trailer label information. The

Figure 4.12 Standard Tape Label Overview

Initial Volume Record	- Contains volume serial number and other volume identifiers.
Header Record #1	- Contains data set name, creation date, and other data set identifiers.
Header Record #2	- Contains basic DCB characteristics and other DCB attributes.
User Header Records	- Contains 1 to 8 optional user-specified information records.
Tape Mark	- Signifies end of Header Label.
Actual Data Set	- Data to be processed. One or more physical blocks as described in the DCB.
Tape Mark	- Signifies end of Data.
EOV #1 or EOF #1	- This End Of Volume (EOV) or End Of File (EOF) Record similar to Header Record #1.
EOV #2 or EOF #2	- This End Of Volume (EOV) or End Of File (EOF) Record similar to Header Record #2.
Tape Mark	- Signifies end of Trailer Label.
Tape Mark	- Signifies end of Data Set.

presence of a second magnetic tape mark actually signifies that this is the end of all processing for this particular file. Detail standard tape label record and field layouts will be displayed and discussed later in the text.

Standard tape label principles are used in describing label information on disk packs. Figure 4.13 displays a schematic overview of disk label information layout using disk address pointers.

For the most part disk label information is created when the data itself is created. Prior to processing actual input data, the Initial Volume Record and Volume Table of Contents (VTOC) are located via address pointers, read, and checked for validity against JCL specifications. As discussed previously, Label DCB characteristics may be used to build a data control block in main storage for each file to be processed. Another pointer signifies the beginning of the actual data to be processed.

Figure 4.13 Disk Label Record Overview

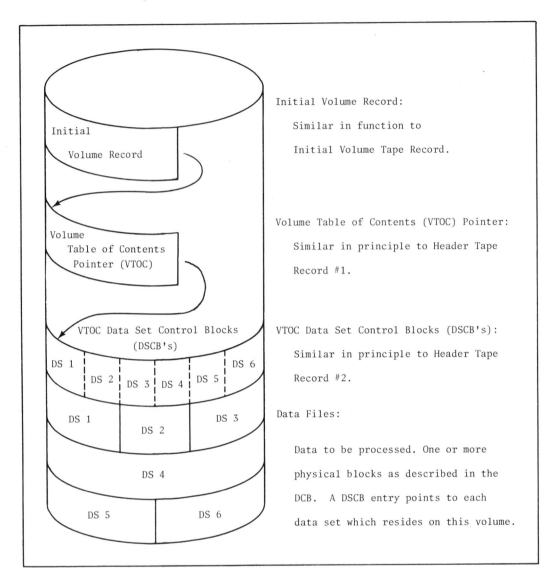

Initial Volume Record:

Similar in function to

Initial Volume Tape Record.

Volume Table of Contents (VTOC) Pointer:

Similar in principle to Header Tape

Record #1.

VTOC Data Set Control Blocks (DSCB's):

Similar in principle to Header Tape

Record #2.

Data Files:

Data to be processed. One or more

physical blocks as described in the

DCB.   A DSCB entry points to each

data set which resides on this volume.

Of course, this data may consist of one or many blocks to be read or written.   In summary, disk label contents are similar in principle to that of standard tape labels.

One specification in the basic format of the Label parameter is LABEL= (1,SL).   The '1' signifies that this data set is the first file on this particular tape volume.   The 'SL' signifies that IBM Standard Labels are to be assumed and utilized.   Standard Labels as previously discussed consist of a field format to be detailed later in the text.   A (,SL) specification is the same as (1,SL), since a '1' is assumed in the absence of a data set sequence number specification.   As a matter of fact, Standard Labels are assumed in the absence of the coding of a Label parameter in most installations.   This is why many Dd statements contain no label parameters.

A brief description of other label specifications contained within the complete format follows.

SUL	-	IBM Standard Label contains IBM User Label records.
AL	-	American National Standard (ANS) Label.
AUL	-	ANS Label contains ANS User Label records.
NSL	-	Nonstandard Label.
NL	-	No Label (typically 7-track tapes).
BLP	-	Bypass Label Processing (not a valid specification at installation).
LTM	-	Leading Tape Mark may be present.
,	-	Standard Label assumed; other subparameters follow.
PASSWORD	-	Operator must supply Password in all cases to utilize data set.
NOPWREAD	-	Operator must supply Password to utilize data set with the exeception of reading the file.
,	-	No Password Protection; other subparameters follow.
IN	-	File to be processed as input only.
OUT	-	File to be processed as output only.
EXPDT	-	Specifices 2-digit year and 3-digit Julian day Expiration Date for file to be saved. Utilized in installations with automated tape library and management system.
RETPD	-	Specifies number of days from creation date as Retention Period for file to be saved. Utilized in installations with automated tape library and management systems.

Some of the above specifications utilized on an occasional basis will be further discussed later in the text. Figure 4.14 depicts various LABEL parameter specifications utilizing the basic and complete formats.

Figure 4.14 Label Parameter Examples

```
Basic Format:

    //INPUT1   DD   LABEL=(1,SL)

    //INPUT1   DD   LABEL=(,SL)


Complete Format:

    //SYSIN    DD   LABEL=(2,SL)

    //SYSUT2   DD   LABEL=(1,NL)

    //DATAOUT  DD   LABEL=(1,SL,PASSWORD)

    //DATAOUT  DD   LABEL=(1,SL,NOPWREAD)

    //INPUT1   DD   LABEL=(1,SL,IN)

    //OUTPUT1  DD   LABEL=(1,SL,,OUT)

    //TAPEOUT  DD   LABEL=(1,SL,PASSWORD,IN,EXPDT=80305)

    //DISKOUT  DD   LABEL=(1,SL,RETPD=475)

    //DISKOUT  DD   LABEL=RETPD=475

    //DATAIN   DD   LABEL=(1,BLP)
```

The two examples utilizing the basic format in Figure 4.14 are essentially the same specification -- the first data set on this particular volume, and the data set contains standard labels. This is the same as the system default when not coding a Label parameter at most installations. As no expiration date or retention period is specified in the basic format, it is assumed that one must follow an installation's manual or semiautomated procedures for saving files. That is, purchase or lease one's own reels and packs and/or permanently affix a physical label to the exterior of the reel or pack indicating the expiration or retention period to be used.

The first example utilizing the complete format in Figure 4.14 indicates that the data set is the second one on this particular volume. The second example indicates that no labels are to be created on output nor exist for processing on input. The next two examples for ddname DATAOUT dictate password restrictions. (JCL security is a topic of the last chapter.) The fifth and sixth examples for ddnames INPUT1 and OUTPUT1 signify input and output processing only, respectively, an occasional installation standard for FORTRAN program executions. The next three examples for ddnames TAPEOUT and DISKOUT specify time periods after which the file will be deleted, or scratched and released for other use. They are the 305th day of 1980 and 475 days after creation date. The two DISKOUT ddname examples are identical specifications at most installations. The last example of the complete format bypasses label processing. This specification may not be valid at your installation as it undermines the primary purpose for using labels -- to verify that the characteristics of the file as described in the Label and the JCL do not conflict, i.e., the proper file has been readied for processing. It should be noted that other Dd statement parameters will need to be coded in the examples above.

In summary, the LABEL parameter describes the nature of the label records, the file's data set sequence, password status, input/output conditions, and the time period to keep a saved data set.

e. SPACE (Space)

Basic Format : SPACE= ({TRK CYL Blocksize} ,Primary Quantity)

Complete Format: SPACE= ({TRK CYL Blocksize} , (Primary Quantity [,Secondary Quantity ,]

[,Directory ,Index] [,RLSE ,] [,CONTIG ,MXIG ,ALX] [,ROUND])

SPACE=(ABSTR,(Primary Quantity,Address [,Directory ,Index]))

94

The purpose of the SPACE keyword parameter is to allocate space and describe the nature of a new data set's space on a direct-access device (usually disk). Space can be allocated (or expressed) in three different ways:

1. By Tracks;
2. By Cylinders; or
3. By Block Size.

An overview of disk pack characteristics should be discussed prior to actual Space parameter coding. Figure 4.15 displays a schematic overview of disk pack layout.

Figure 4.15 Disk Pack Conceptual Overview

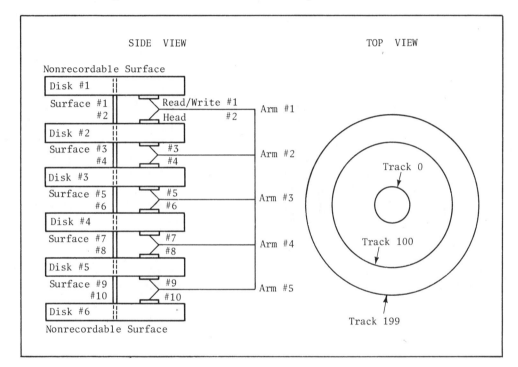

In order to facilitate the discussion of disk pack concepts, a schematic of a Model 2311 has been depicted in Figure 4.15 as it contains only 10 recordable surfaces and 200 primary tracks. An update to more current equipment will be made later.

Note on the side view in Figure 4.15 that this particular pack contains 6 disks. For now think of a single disk as a record album. There are 10 recordable inside surfaces and 2 nonrecordable outside surfaces on this particular disk pack. The disks spin at a high rate of speed. Note that there are 5 Read/Write Arms consisting of a total of 10 Read/Write Heads. Of particular significance, though, is the fact that the 5 arms and 10 heads move as a single unit. They are not independent of one another. Consequently, with one movement (seek) of the read/write unit to a particular area in the pack, 10 surfaces can be accessed. In terms of input/output time this 10-to-1 ratio is certainly an advantage over a 1-to-1 ratio if it were so independently designed.

Next, translate this concept of a disk pack to the top view. Note that in this example there are 200 concentric circles on each recordable surface. This differs from a record album in that a record's circles are in reality not circles but one big spiral running to the center of the record. Each concentric circle can be thought of as one track. With 10 surfaces and 200 tracks it can be calculated that this particular disk pack contains 2000 (10 x 200) tracks. Note again that one movement (seek) of the read/write unit accesses 10 tracks simultaneously. This concept is called a cylinder. That is, at any given point (or track) an imaginary cylinder can be depicted by viewing the location of the read/write heads as underneath one another. There are therefore 200 cylinders on this particular pack; each cylinder contains 10 tracks, that is, one track from each recording surface. Data can therefore be stored and accessed from 10 tracks with only one movement of the read/write unit. This cylinder concept is a significant improvement over storing and accessing 10 tracks of data from 10 different movements of the read/write unit to 10 different cylinder areas.

Space can be allocated in terms of tracks or cylinders via the Space parameter. SPACE=(TRK,10) allocates 10 available tracks to this new data set. Though the system will attempt to allocate these tracks such that read/write head movement is minimized, the cylinder concept cannot be guaranteed. SPACE=(CYL,1) will guarantee a cylinder allocation of 10 tracks in this example. The system will search for one completely available cylinder, and when found will allocate it appropriately. In order to determine how many tracks or cylinders to allocate, one must first find out how many characters, records, or blocks can be stored on one track and then how many characters, records, or blocks of data are expected to be contained within the new file. In the above example, assume one track will hold 3,600 characters. With 10 tracks per cylinder, one cylinder will hold 36,000 characters. Assuming 200 cylinders per pack, one pack will store 7,200,000 characters (or bytes) of data. When allocating disk storage in terms of tracks or cylinders, one must be familar with the physical characteristics and capacities of the units involved. In addition, it is recommended that file blocksize be less than or equal to track capacity. It should also be noted that the Space parameter need only be coded once for a given file, when it is initially created. Figure 4.16 provides a table of safe and approximate direct-access storage device capacities per volume (or pack) for programmer/analyst estimating use.

Specifications for updated equipment, expanded capacities, dual densities, etc., can be obtained from the appropriate vendor or dp installation. One problem now becomes apparent. That is, what happens to user JCL track and cylinder specifications every time storage equipment is updated? Note that a 3330 track will hold about twice as much data as a 2314 track. The answer, unfortunately, is that user JCL must be changed -- unless the blocksize space coding option has been utilized! Allocating space by blocksize allows the system to calculate how many tracks are needed for whatever equipment, model, and volume feature to which the file happens to be allocated. The user need not be particularly concerned with the physical capacities of a disk pack, for example. If SPACE=(6400,100) were coded, the user is simply indicating that enough space should be allocated for 100 blocks of data with a blocksize of 6,400 characters regardless of what the characteristics of the volume are. Let the system determine how many tracks are needed! With 640,000 (100

Figure 4.16 Storage Unit Volume Capacities

Device Type	Tracks Per Cylinder	Cylinders Per Volume	Number of Bytes (Approximate)		
			Per Track	Per Cylinder	Per Volume
Disk:					
Unit 2302, Model 3	46	492	4,900	225,400	110,400,000
Unit 2302, Model 4	46	984	4,900	225,400	220,800,000
Unit 2305, Model 1	8	48	14,000	112,000	5,300,000
Unit 2305, Model 2	8	96	14,000	112,000	10,600,000
Unit 2311	10	200	3,600	36,000	7,200,000
Unit 2314	20	200	7,200	144,000	28,800,000
Unit 3330, Model 1	19	404	13,000	247,000	99,750,000
Unit 3330, Model 11	19	808	13,000	247,000	199,500,000
Unit 3340, 35-Megabyte	12	348	8,300	99,600	34,500,000
Unit 3340, 70-Megabyte	12	696	8,300	99,600	69,000,000
Unit 3350	30	555	19,000	570,000	316,300,000
Drum:					
Unit 2301	8	25	20,400	163,000	4,075,000
Unit 2303	10	80	4,800	48,000	3,800,000
Data Cell:					
Unit 2321	20	980	2,000	40,000	39,000,000

x 6400) characters to be stored, nearly 50 tracks are required on a 3330, while almost twice as many would be needed if 2314's were used. Also, blocksize should be less than track capacity. Changes in equipment configurations, however, do not generally affect user JCL space specifications by blocksize. It is for this reason that the author recommends that the blocksize coding option of the Space parameter be utilized whenever possible to allocate space on direct-access storage devices.

Utilizing the complete format for the Space parameter, it is noted that a Secondary Quantity can be specified in addition to the Primary Quantity, e.g., SPACE=(TRK,(10,2)). A secondary quantity specifies how many additional tracks, cylinders, or equivalent blocks are to be allocated if additional space beyond the primary allocation is required. An attempt is made to allocate secondary space on a contiguous basis, that is, adjacent tracks in the same area of a particular volume. If this is not possible, up to five noncontiguous areas (extents) may be allocated. Every time the data set requires additional space, another allocation is attempted. A total of up to 16 of these extents are allowed. Once this maximum is reached, the job may abnormally terminate unless additional space has been specified. Secondary allocations should only be utilized if significant file growth is expected or its size is largely unknown.

Beyond the secondary quantity a Directory or Index specification can be made. The Directory value specifies the size of the directory for a partitioned data set in terms of the number of 256-byte records required. The Index value specifies the size of the index of an indexed sequential data set in terms of the number of cylinders required. If a directory or index is to be coded but no secondary allocation is desired, its absence must be indicated by a comma, e.g., SPACE=(TRK,(10,,1)).

The importance of the RLSE (Release) keyword of the Space parameter is most often overlooked. This specification releases all unused space upon closing of the new file. If 10 tracks were asked for but only 6 were needed, the remaining 4 would be released if RLSE were coded, e.g., SPACE=(TRK,10,RLSE). One need only ask, how many tracks of an installation's total number available are currently being wasted? This question is one reason why many installations continuously query their users to free unused data space for which future file growth is not expected. Disk space can be a relatively expensive form of data storage, especially if much of it is unused.

The CONTIG (Contiguous) keyword specifies that space is to be allocated on a contiguous basis, that is, adjacent tracks in the same area of a particular volume. This form of space allocation is most effective in terms of time and cost for large files which are accessed frequently. The MXIG (Maximum Contiguous) specification asks for the largest contiguous area available on the volume for the primary allocation. ALX (All Contiguous) specifies that up to five contiguous areas on the volume are to be allocated. The keyword ROUND, used when block size has been specified, indicates that the total amount of calculated space should be rounded up to the next full cylinder.

A second form of coding the Space parameter utilizing the complete format is also possible. The keyword ABSTR (Absolute Track) is coded to indicate that a specific starting location for the data set is to be specified. The Primary Quantity, Directory, and Index all have the same meaning as in the first form just discussed. The Address portion of the specification indicates the relative track number at which data storage is to begin. Figure 4.17 depicts various Space parameter specifications utilizing the basic and complete formats.

The three examples utilizing the basic format in Figure 4.17 each specify a method of allocation (Track, Cylinder, Blocksize) and a primary quantity (40 tracks, 4 cylinders, and 10 data blocks of size 6,400, respectively). Remember that once file size has been estimated by the user, programmer, or analyst it is best to add a safety factor (perhaps 10%) to avoid needless abnormal terminations due to a close estimating error.

The first example utilizing the complete format in Figure 4.17 for ddname OUTPUT1 specifies a secondary allocation of 3 tracks. The second example depicts a value of 6 for the directory (records) or index (cylinders) depending upon whether or not the output file for which space is to be allocated is a partitioned data set or an indexed sequential file. The third example for ddname OUTPUT3 releases any unused calculated space upon completion of file processing for this step. The fourth example for ddname DATAOUT asks for contiguous space. The fifth example with ddname DISKOUT asks that the primary allocation

Figure 4.17 Space Parameter Examples

```
   o                                                                          o
   o       Basic Format:                                                      o
   o                                                                          o
   o       //OUTPUT1   DD   SPACE=(TRK,40)                                     o
   o                                                                          o
   o       //OUTPUT2   DD   SPACE=(CYL,4)                                      o
   o                                                                          o
   o       //OUTPUT3   DD   SPACE=(6400,10)                                    o
   o                                                                          o
   o       Complete Format:                                                   o
   o                                                                          o
   o       //OUTPUT1   DD   SPACE=(TRK,(30,3))                                 o
   o                                                                          o
   o       //OUTPUT2   DD   SPACE=(CYL,(10,,6))                                o
   o                                                                          o
   o       //OUTPUT3   DD   SPACE=(4000,20,RLSE)                               o
   o                                                                          o
   o       //DATAOUT   DD   SPACE=(3200,50,,CONTIG)                            o
   o                                                                          o
   o       //DISKOUT   DD   SPACE=(6400,40,,,ROUND)                            o
   o                                                                          o
   o       //SYSUT2    DD   SPACE=(6400,(40,10),,CONTIG,ROUND)                 o
   o                                                                          o
   o       //OUTPUT4   DD   SPACE=(ABSTR,(10,16))                              o
   o                                                                          o
   o       //FILEOUT   DD   SPACE=(3200,(100,10,10),,CONTIG,ROUND)             o
   o                                                                          o
```

be rounded up to the next fullest cylinder. The sixth example with
ddname SYSUT2 also uses the blocksize option for coding the Space
parameter. In addition, a secondary allocation is coded, all data
space must be contiguous, and all allocations are to be rounded.
The second-to-last example with ddname OUTPUT4 utilizes a second form
of the Space parameter. Relative track number 16 is to be the starting location (or first track) of the data set. The last example
utilizes most options of the Space parameter. It should be noted
that other Dd statement parameters may need to be coded in the examples
above.

    In summary, the SPACE parameter specifies the amount and nature
of the space to be allocated for data sets on direct-access storage
devices.

f. SYSOUT (System Output)

$$
\text{Basic Format} \quad : \quad \text{SYSOUT=} \begin{cases} \text{Output Class} \\ \text{(Output Class,,Paper Type)} \end{cases}
$$

$$
\text{Complete Format:} \quad \text{SYSOUT=} \begin{cases} \text{(Output Class} \begin{bmatrix} \text{,Program Name} \\ \text{,} \end{bmatrix} \begin{bmatrix} \text{,Paper Type} \end{bmatrix}) \\ \text{PROFILE='Character String'} \\ (\begin{bmatrix} \text{,Program Name} \\ \text{,} \end{bmatrix} \begin{bmatrix} \text{,Paper Type} \\ \text{,} \end{bmatrix} \text{,PROFILE='Character String')} \end{cases}
$$

The purpose of the SYSOUT keyword parameter is to describe which system output class a data set is to be written to. The System Output parameter is primarily used for print and punch output files.

In a multiprogramming environment one need not and should not allocate specific print or punch units directly as a standard operating procedure. This is because there are usually many other jobs being executed and competing for the same unit at about the same time. Rather, print and punch output is directed to be temporarily stored on disk. For print files, a carriage control character must be present in column 1. As the printer and/or punch unit becomes free, output written to any one of many contiguous areas of disk (or output classes) by many different jobs are connected with the desired unit and all printing or punching accomplished in one time frame. The items of physical output are then identified and separated from one another by job name or job number. Appropriate print or punch system output disk storage is then automatically deleted.

Though any letter from A to Z as well as numerics 0 to 9 are valid output classes, System Output area A is a typical specification for one-part print on standard 14 7/8 x 11-inch paper, lined or unlined as the installation desires, e.g., SYSOUT=A. System Output B is somewhat of a standard for punch output, e.g., SYSOUT=B. System Output areas C and higher can then be used for special paper types and labels. If special print output is desired, specifications in the Sysout parameter must usually be made to indicate the paper type. Paper type specifications are unique and installation-defined. Examples of paper type definitions are given below.

Specification		Paper Type Definition
1431	-	Paper, standard 14 7/8 x 11 inches, 1-part.
1432	-	Paper, standard 14 7/8 x 11 inches, 2-part.
1434	-	Paper, standard 14 7/8 x 11 inches, 4-part.
1061	-	Paper, regular 10 5/8 x 8 1/2 inches, 1-part.
1062	-	Paper, regular 10 5/8 x 8 1/2 inches, 2-part.
1064	-	Paper, regular 10 5/8 x 8 1/2 inches, 4-part.
1031	-	Paper, regular 10 5/8 x 17 inches, 1-part.
1032	-	Paper, regular 10 5/8 x 17 inches, 2-part.
1034	-	Paper, regular 10 5/8 x 17 inches, 4-part.
1481	-	Paper, regular 14 7/8 x 8 1/2 inches, 1-part.
1482	-	Paper, regular 14 7/8 x 8 1/2 inches, 2-part.
1484	-	Paper, regular 14 7/8 x 8 1/2 inches, 4-part.
1471	-	Paper, regular 14 7/8 x 17 inches, 1-part.
1472	-	Paper, regular 14 7/8 x 17 inches, 2-part.
1474	-	Paper, regular 14 7/8 x 17 inches, 4-part.
1571	-	Paper, photo 14 7/8 x 17 inches, 1-part.
1572	-	Paper, photo 14 7/8 x 17 inches, 2-part.
1521	-	Paper, photo 14 7/8 x 22 inches, 1-part.
1522	-	Paper, photo 14 7/8 x 22 inches, 2-part.
9101	-	Labels, small 3 1/2 x 1 5/16 inches, 1 across.

```
9103      -  Labels, small 3 1/2 x 1 5/16 inches, 3 across.
9151      -  Labels, large 4 x 1 7/16 inches, 1 across.
9153      -  Labels, large 4 x 1 7/16 inches, 3 across.
```

Coding SYSOUT=(C,,1482) will cause program output for this file to be assigned and written to System Output Class C. The second comma bypasses a program name specification. The 1482 designation (installation-defined) is transmitted to the printer prior to actual printing. This informs the print operator to mount regular 2-part 14 7/8 x 8 ½-inch paper for this file, then to start the printer. As you can see, printing system output defined for special paper are a potential bottleneck to installation management. But then this is the primary reason why system output classes for special paper types have been separated from standard classes to begin with. It seems as though more time is expended changing paper at the printer which handles special paper then the actual printing itself. Other less common and unique paper types and classes are also available at most installations, e.g., preprinted forms.

Utilizing the complete format for the Sysout parameter, it is possible to specify the name of a special program to write the output file if one does not desire to use the standard system output writer program. Though used infrequently, perhaps a special program has been written to test for the existence of certain logical conditions prior to the complete or partial printing of a given preprinted form, for example. In lieu of specifying output classes, some installations define a series of recognizable character strings via the PROFILE keyword. They are handled exactly the same way as a specific output class and paper type specification. In fact, the coding of a Profile string overrides output class and paper type specifications on the same Sysout parameter. Figure 4.18 depicts various Sysout parameter specifications using the basic and complete formats.

Figure 4.18 Sysout Parameter Examples

```
Basic Format:


//OUTPUT1    DD   SYSOUT=A

//OUTPUT2    DD   SYSOUT=B

//OUTPUT3    DD   SYSOUT=(C,,1432)

//OUTPUT4    DD   SYSOUT=(Z,,9103)


Complete Format:


//DATAOUT    DD   SYSOUT=(C,FORMA,1571)

//SYSUT2     DD   SYSOUT=PROFILE='PUNCH OUTPUT'

//PRINTOUT   DD   SYSOUT=PROFILE='1-PART 10 5/8 x 8 1/2 INCH PAPER'

//OUTFILE    DD   SYSOUT=(9,,1064,

//                PROFILE='2-PART 10 5/8 x 17 INCH PAPER')
```

The first two examples in Figure 4.18 utilizing the basic format specify output class A (standard 1 part 14 7/8 x 11-inch paper) and B (presumably punch). The next two examples call special paper and label output classes. Remember that specific output class and paper type specifications are installation-defined and thus may deviate in content from previous examples.

The first example of the complete format calls for a program named FORMA to write the file to Output Class C and to use special paper. The next two examples for ddnames SYSUT2 and PRINTOUT use the PROFILE keyword in lieu of output class and/or paper type specifications. The last example presumably depicts a conflict in paper type specifications. In this case the Profile string overrides. It should be noted that other Dd statement parameters will not have to be coded in the examples other than for occasional DCB information.

In summary, the Sysout parameter describes the output class to which an output file (presumably print or punch) is to be written.

g. UNIT (Unit)

Basic Format   :   UNIT={Device Type / Group Name}

Complete Format :   UNIT=([Device Type / Group Name / Unit Address] [,Unit Count / ,P / ,] [,DEFER] [,SEP=Ddname, ...)])
                       UNIT=AFF=Ddname
                       UNIT=Symbolic Address

The purpose of the UNIT keyword parameter is to specify the type and nature of the unit(s) to be allocated to the data sets(s) to be processed. Device Type and Group Name are the two primary specifications utilized. Device types relate in general to equipment model numbers, e.g., UNIT=2400 for tape, UNIT=3330 for disk. Group names are generally installation-defined, e.g., UNIT=TAPE, though UNIT=SYSDA is common for disk and other direct-access files. Figure 4.19 depicts typical unit designations in use at most installations.

Other device types and group names are available for use though they are not as common as those specified, i.e., card punch, printer, etc. Unit SYSSQ, which asks for any available sequential device, is one such example. Many installations place restrictions on unit designation use. For example, though UNIT=SYSDA indicates that a 2311, 2314, or 3330 disk drive should be allocated depending upon the equipment configuration at a particular installations, it may also mean that the data set is temporary, that is, new files which are to be deleted at the end of the job. In other words, an installation may define UNIT=SYSDA for temporary workspace, on-line packs, etc. while UNIT=3330 could be strictly for off-line mountable packs, etc. An installation's user guide should contain specific and unique unit designation standards and definitions.

Utilizing the complete format, a unit address may be specified in lieu of device type or group name. Each device (tape, disk, etc.) is assigned a unique identifying number (unit address), e.g., UNIT=

Figure 4.19 Typical Unit Device Types and Group Names

Standard Device Type	Common Group Names	Unit Definition
Tape:		
Unit 2400 2400-3 2400-4	TAPE TAPE9	9-track tape drives with various density features and capability levels, e.g., Device 2401-4, Models 1 to 6.
Unit 2400-1 2400-2	TAPE TAPE7	7-track tape drives with various density features and capability levels, e.g., Device 2401-4, Models 1 to 6.
Disk:		
Unit 2302	SYSDA DISK	Device 2302 Disk drives, Models 3 and 4.
Unit 2305	SYSDA DISK	Device 2305 Disk drives, Models 1 and 2.
Unit 2311	SYSDA DISK	Device 2311 Disk drive.
Unit 2314	SYSDA DISK	Device 2314 Disk drive.
Unit 3330	SYSDA DISK	Devices 3330 and 3333 Disk drives, Model I.
Unit 3330-1	SYSDA DISK	Devices 3330 and 3333 Disk drives, Model II.
Unit 3340	SYSDA DISK	Device 3340, 35- and 70-Megabyte Models.
Unit 3350	SYSDA DISK	Device 3350 Disk Drive.

Drum:		
Unit 2301	DRUM	Device 2301 Drum unit.
Unit 2303	DRUM	Device 2303 Drum unit.
Data Cell:		
Unit 2321	DATACELL	Device 2321 Data Cell.

OB4.   If a specific unit is required, it can therefore be specified.
Perhaps a particular tape unit is being operationally tested by the
installation.   Operations personnel will want to be assured of allocating the device to be tested.   Application programmers and analysts
should shy away from allocating specific physical units, however.
One does not care which specific tape unit is allocated, for example,
as long as it is one of the dozen or so 9-track tape units available
for use.

A Unit Count is required to be coded at some installations whenever
more than one unit is required for the data, that is, a data set so
large that more than one volume is utilized, as in some direct-access
data base applications. Rather than coding a specific unit count, the
letter P (Parallel) can be coded to indicate that each volume (tape,
pack, etc.) should be assigned a separate unit device for parallel
mounting.   The keyword DEFER indicates that the mounting of the file
to be processed should be deferred until the data set is opened, perhaps eventually well into the processing cycle.   The keyword SEP=
followed by one or more ddnames indicates that this particular file
should be assigned a specific device which is separate (or different)
from the files for which the ddnames are coded, i.e., a different
disk unit.   For some applications which frequently cross-reference
or access the same group of data sets on a repetitive basis, it may
be more efficient to separate them by allocating different units and/
or packs to each file.

The keyword AFF (unit affinity) is the essential opposite of the
keyword SEP (unit separation).   The AFF= indicates that this particular
file should be assigned the same specific device as the file for which
the ddname is coded, i.e., the same tape unit.   This is particularly
significant when the concatenation of sequential data sets is desired.
Concatenation involves the stringing together of physically separate
files into one larger logical file for processing.   (This technique
will be described in the last chapter.)

A Symbolic Address can be specified if the unit to be assigned
is a remote device.   A symbolic type and number defined by the installation would need to be coded.   Figure 4.20 depicts various Unit parameter specifications using the basic and complete formats.

The first two examples utilizing the basic format in Figure 4.20
each ask that a 9-track tape drive be allocated.   The next two examples
perform the same function but for disk drives.   The next two examples
for ddnames OUTPUT1 and OUTPUT2 indicate that a drum and data cell
should be allocated for the files of interest, respectively.

104

Figure 4.20 Unit Parameter Examples

```
Basic Format:

//INPUT1     DD   UNIT=2400

//INPUT1     DD   UNIT=TAPE9

//INPUT2     DD   UNIT=3330

//INPUT2     DD   UNIT=SYSDA

//OUTPUT1    DD   UNIT=2303

//OUTPUT2    DD   UNIT=2321


Complete Format:

//SYSUT1     DD   UNIT=OD3

//SYSUT2     DD   UNIT=(2311,2)

//OUTPUT1    DD   UNIT=(2314,P)

//SYSIN      DD   UNIT=(2400,,DEFER)

//DISKOUT    DD   UNIT=(3330,SEP=OUTPUT1)

//TAPEIN     DD   UNIT=2400

//           DD   UNIT=AFF=TAPEIN

//PRINTOUT   DD   UNIT=RJE009

//FILEOUT    DD   UNIT=(2400,2,DEFER,SEP=(SYSUT2,OUTPUT1))
```

Utilizing the complete format in Figure 4.20 the first example
specifies a unit address of OD3 and is not a valid device type nor a
logical group name. The next two examples specify disk drives. Two
drives are allocated for the SYSUT2 ddname file. A number to be determined by the number of volumes utilized by the data set will be
allocated prior to processing of the OUTPUT1 ddname file. The
fourth example for ddname SYSIN defers the mounting of the tape file
until the file is opened. The fifth example for ddname DISKOUT insures
that the unit on which this file is to be created will be separate
from the unit on which the OUTPUT1 file is created. The TAPEIN ddname
files are concatenated. Because of the AFF specification the second
file with no ddname coded will use the same unit allocated to the
first file. (The technique of concatenation will be covered in Chapter
8.) The next to the last example utilizes the symbolic address method
of unit specification. The last example utilizes most options of the
Unit parameter. It should also be noted that other Dd statement parameters may need to be coded in the examples above.

In summary, the Unit parameter describes the type and nature of the
unit(s) to be allocated for the file(s) to be processed.

h. VOLUME or VOL (Volume)

Basic Format : $\left\{\begin{array}{l}\text{VOLUME}\\\text{VOL}\end{array}\right\}$=SER=Serial Number

Complete Format: $\left\{\begin{array}{l}\text{VOLUME}\\\text{VOL}\end{array}\right\}$=([PRIVATE] $\left[\begin{array}{c},\text{RETAIN}\\,\end{array}\right]$ $\left[\begin{array}{c},\text{Volume Sequence Number}\\,\end{array}\right]$

[,Volume Count] , $\left[\begin{array}{l}\text{SER=(Serial Number,......)}\\\text{REF=Ddname}\\\text{REF=*.Ddname}\\\text{REF=*.Stepname.Ddname}\\\text{REF=*.Stepname.Procstepname.Ddname}\end{array}\right]$

The purpose of the VOLUME keyword parameter is to specify the
volume or volumes (reel, pack, etc.) on which the data set to be
processed currently resides (input) or will reside (output). Most
dp installations have thousands of tape reels and dozens of disk
packs. Each of these physical volumes has been assigned a unique
number or identifying character set. In addition to being stored
internally in the volume label, the volume serial number is also
affixed to the outside of the volume such that it can be readily
identified. Sometimes it is affixed permanently, e.g., paint, felt
pen, etc. While not in use, those volumes which are mountable (off-
line) are stored in sequential fashion in a tape or disk library room.
If a volume request to mount a particular tape reel or disk pack is
issued by the Operating System, e.g., VOLUME=SER=010567, operations
personnel can then readily locate the file of interest. The keyword
'VOLUME' can be abbreviated to the letters 'VOL', i.e., VOL=SER=010567.
If the volume is already mounted (on-line), the volume request merely
indicates the volume of interest.

If no volume serial number is coded on the Dd statement for uncatalogued files, a nonspecific volume request is made in most installations by the Operating System. This means that the user does not
care which specific volume is utilized, i.e., any scratch (previously
deleted) or spare volume can be used. When the job has been completed
and returned to the user, the volume utilized can be obtained from the
job's JCL listing. Some installations require a specific volume request for all tape and disk data files, however. Catalogued data sets,
where the characteristics of the file are stored in a system catalogue,
do not require the coding of a volume serial number in any case. (The
technique of cataloguing data sets will be covered later in this text.)

Utilizing the complete format the keyword PRIVATE insures that no
output data will be written to this volume unless a specific volume
serial number request is also made. This helps to prevent the accidental scratching (deleting) of good data files. The keyword RETAIN
simply means that the volume is to remain mounted on the drive after
the job step, that is, it is needed in a later job step. This is used
when stacking data sets (creating more than one data set or file on
one volume). (The technique of stacking data sets will be described
in the last chapter.) The Volume Sequence Number specifies which
volume of a multivolume data set (one large file on more than one
volume) is to be processed first. If not coded, the default is '1'.

106

The Volume Count specifies the maximum number of volumes that will be necessary for an output data set. This specification is required by some installations when creating multivolume data sets.

The keyword SER (Serial) followed by an equal sign is used to specify the volume serial number, commonly 6 characters. Alpha and numeric characters are allowed, e.g., VOL=SER=PACK01, VOL=SER=MASTER, etc. As SER is a keyword, the absence of previous specifications do not have to be indicated by the coding of one or more commas. The volume serial number is assigned by the installation when the volume is initially logged in. The keyword REF (Reference) is utilized for the JCL technique of backward reference. This is usually accomplished by coding an asterisk and a period (*.) in front of the file to be referenced and will be expanded upon in the next chapter and later in the text. Figure 4.21 depicts common Volume parameter specifications using the basic and complete formats.

Figure 4.21 Volume Parameter Examples

```
Basic Format:

//INPUT1    DD    VOLUME=SER=024673

//TAPEIN    DD    VOL=SER=UPDATES

//DISKOUT   DD    VOL=SER=DISK66


Complete Format:

//SYSUT2    DD    VOL=(PRIVATE,SER=008960)

//DATAOUT   DD    VOL=(PRIVATE,SER=008960)

//TAPEOUT   DD    VOL=(,RETAIN)

//INPUT1    DD    VOL=(,,3)

//OUTPUT    DD    VOL=(,,,3)

//SYSIN     DD    VOL=REF=(TAPE04,TAPE06,TAPE08)

//TAPEIN    DD    VOL=REF=RAWDATA

//INPUT1    DD    VOL=REF=*.TAPEOUT

//INPUT2    DD    VOL=REF=*.STEP1.TAPEIN

//INPUT3    DD    VOL=REF=*.STEP3.GO.DISKOUT

//OUTFILE   DD    VOL=(PRIVATE,RETAIN,,2,SER=008607)
```

The three examples utilizing the basic format in Figure 4.21 depict numeric, alpha, and alphanumeric volume serial numbers, respectively. VOLUME is generally abbreviated to VOL.

Utilizing the complete format, the first two examples specify PRIVATE and a specific volume request. Though identical in coding, perhaps the first case with ddname SYSUT2 creates the file initially while the second case with ddname DATAOUT allows the file to be written over and deleted. The third example retains the file as mounted for use in a later step. The fourth and fifth example with ddnames INPUT1 and OUTPUT1 ask that the third volume be processed first, and that 3 volumes are required, respectively. The sixth example with ddname SYSIN requests three volumes for a multivolume data set. The seventh example with ddname TAPEIN references a passed or catalogued volume with a data set name of RAWDATA. The next three examples of the complete format utilize the technique of backward reference to indicate the volume serial number of interest. The TAPEOUT ddname file in the current step, the TAPEIN ddname file in stepname STEP1, and the DISKOUT ddname file in a procedure step named GO in stepname STEP3 are referenced for processing, respectively. The last example utilizes most options for the Volume parameter. It should be noted that other Dd statement parameters will need to be coded in the examples above.

In summary, the VOLUME or VOL parameter specifies on which volume(s) the file to be processed currently resides or will reside.

5. Basic Dd Statement Examples

The previous discussion has covered file management concepts and the Dd statement. Eleven parameters have been identified as basic or common to most System 360/370 OS and VS users. They are:

```
Positional    -   * (Asterisk)
              -   Data
              -   Dummy

Keyword       -   Data Control Block
              -   Disposition
              -   Data Set Name
              -   Label
              -   Space
              -   System Output
              -   Unit
              -   Volume
```

Other not-so-common keyword parameters will be covered later in this chapter. Figure 4.22 displays three jobs with typical Dd statements and Job Exec statements utilizing common positional and keyword parameters discussed previously.

Figure 4.22 Typical Dd Statement Examples

```
//JOB1   JOB  XYZABC123,TOBIN, MSGLEVEL=(1,1),CLASS=L

//STEP1  EXEC  PGM=EDIT2,REGION=60K,TIME=2

//CARDIN  DD   *

                 Data Card File Goes Here
```

Figure 4.22 Typical Dd Statement Examples (cont.)

```
        /*
//MASTIN   DD   DUMMY
//DISKOUT  DD   UNIT=SYSDA,DISP=(NEW,KEEP,DELETE).
//         DSN=DATAFILE,VOL=SER=0S0609,
//         SPACE=(TRK,10),
//         DCB=(RECFM=FB,LRECL=080,BLKSIZE=3200)
//PRTOUT   DD   SYSOUT=(C,1484)
//SYSUDUMP DD   SYSOUT=A
//


//JOB2   JOB   (123,PROJ1),IMP,MSGLEVEL=(1,1)
//STEPA  EXEC  PGM=IEBGENER
//SYSUT1   DD   UNIT=2400,DISP=(OLD,KEEP),
//         DSN=RAWDATA,VOL=SER=030560,
//         LABEL=(1,SL),
//         DCB=(RECFM=VB,LRECL=100,BLKSIZE=3204)
//SYSUT2   DD   UNIT=TAPE9,DISP=(NEW,PASS,KEEP),
//         DSN=DATACOPY,
//         DCB=(RECFM=VB,LRECL=100,BLKSIZE=6404)
//SYSPRINT DD   SYSOUT=A
//SYSIN    DD   *
             Control Card File Goes Here
  /*
//SYSUDUMP DD   SYSOUT=A
  /*
//STEPB  EXEC  PGM=UPDATE2,REGION=80K,TIME=5
//INPUT1   DD   UNIT=2400,DISP=(OLD,KEEP),
//         DSN=DATACOPY,
//         DCB=(RECFM=VB,LRECL=100,BLKSIZE=6404)
//INPUT2   DD   UNIT=3330,DISP=(OLD,KEEP),
//         DSN=MASTER.OLDDATA,VOL=SER=PACK08,
//         DCB=(RECFM=FB,LRECL=120,BLKSIZE=4800)
//OUTPUT1  DD   UNIT=2314,DISP=(OLD,DELETE),
//         DSN=&&ATEST,SPACE=(CYL,12,RLSE),
//         DCB=(RECFM=FB,LRECL=040,BLKSIZE=4000)
```

Figure 4.22 Typical Dd Statement Examples (cont.)

```
//PUNCH1   DD   SYSOUT=B           PUNCH CARD OUTPUT
//MSGOUT   DD   SYSOUT=A           PRINT MESSAGES
//LABELS   DD   SYSOUT=(C,,9153)   3-ACROSS LABELS
//SYSUDUMP DD   SYSOUT=A           DUMP FILE
//


//JOB3   JOB   A1B2C3XYZ,DANHR,MSGLEVEL=(1,1),
//        CLASS=H,TIME=20
//@STEPX  EXEC  PGM=USERPROG,REGION=100K,TIME=10
//CARDIN  DD   DATA
             JCL-like Card File Goes Here
/*


//TAPEIN  DD   UNIT=(2400-2,,DEFER),DISP=(OLD,PASS),
//        LABEL=(1,NL),VOL=(PRIVATE,SER=(002921,002922))
//DISKIN  DD   UNIT=3330,DISP=SHR,
//        DSN=APDS.DATA.LIBRARY(FILE7),VOL=SER=DISK99
//LISTOUT DD   SYSOUT=A
//LABELOUT DD  SYSOUT=X
//REPORT  DD SYSOUT=(7,,PHOTO)
//SYSUDUMP DD  SYSOUT=A
/*
//STEPY   EXEC  PGM=AUTILITY
//SYSUT1  DD   UNIT=2400-2,DISP=(OLD,KEEP),
//        LABEL=(1,NL),VOL=(PRIVATE,SER=(002921,002922))
//SYSUT2  DD   UNIT=SYSDA,DISP=(NEW,CATLG,DELETE),
//        DSN=CONVERTED.COPY,VOL=SER=COPYLIB,
//        SPACE=(4000,(100,10),RLSE),
//        DCB=(LRECL=200,BLKSIZE=4000)
//SYSPRINT DD  SYSOUT=A
//SYSIN   DD   *
             Control Card File Goes Here
/*
//SYSUDUMP DD  SYSOUT=A
//
```

110

The first job in Figure 4.22 named JOB1 for TOBIN's account number XYZABC123, contains one step named STEP1. A user program called EDIT2 is fetched and loaded into main storage for execution. In this example only very basic Dd statement parameters are utilized. The program reads a card file as input through ddname CARDIN. A /* is utilized at the end of the card file. No master file is to be processed this run, as the MASTIN ddname file is dummied. An output disk file for ddname DISKOUT is created and kept for future reference. Note the presence of a Space parameter. A print on special paper is created for ddname PRTOUT along with a print of a storage dump on standard paper for special ddname SYSUDUMP if one should occur. A Null statement (// in columns 1 and 2 only) has been placed last to indicate the end of the job. Null statements, storage dump files, and other parameters and statements will be covered later in this chapter and the text.

The second job in Figure 4.22, named JOB2 for IMP's account number 123 and project number 1, contains two steps named STEPA and STEPB, respectively. Basic Dd statement parameters are utilized here also. A /* is coded at the end of card files and intermediate job steps. A utility program named IEBGENER is called in the first step. It reads a 9-track tape via ddname SYSUT1 and creates a duplicate tape copy on ddname SYSUT2 with a larger blocksize. Note that a nonspecific volume request is made on output and passed to STEPB. Program messages are written to ddname SYSPRINT. A control file which directs the utility is read as input for ddname SYSIN. A storage dump file description is also provided. A user program called UPDATE2 is located in the second step. Inputs include the passed tape from STEPA for ddname INPUT1 and an old master disk file for ddname INPUT2. Output consists of a temporary data set named ATEST for ddname OUT_-PUT1. An appropriate Space parameter has been coded. A nonspecific volume request has also been made. System output classes for B, A, and C are also described in addition to the storage dump file. Note the utilization of comment fields. A Null statement has been coded to indicate end of job.

The third job in Figure 4.22 named JOB3 for DANHR's account number A1B2C3XYZ, contains two steps named @STEPX and STEPY, respectively. A mild deviation from some Dd statement basics is occasionally utilized. A /* is coded at the end of card files and intermediate job steps. A program named USERPROG is called in the first step. It processes via ddname CARDIN a data card file which happens to have a // in columns 1 and 2. Two private 7-track tapes are deferred and utilized as input to ddname TAPEIN. This nonlabeled file is then passed as input to the second step. DCB information is program-defined. The DISKIN ddname file accesses a member of a partitioned data set. Note that the library file can also be shared by other jobs during execution. DCB information is disk-label-defined. System output classes for A, X, and 7 are defined in addition to the storage dump file. The second step calls AUTILITY program. It utilizes the same tapes as input for ddname SYSUT1 passed from the first step. The output file for ddname SYSUT2 is to be catalogued. An appropriate space parameter is provided along with some DCB information. A print file, control card file, and storage dump file are also defined prior to the Null statement.

6. Other Keyword Parameters

a. AFF (Affinity)

Basic and Complete Format: AFF=Ddname

The purpose of the AFF keyword parameter is to request channel separation in addition to that already requested. A channel is merely a path between main storage and one or more similar units (or devices). In selected situations channel separation may increase processing efficiency by reducing processing time, i.e., read/write head competition, when accessing more than one data set. Unlike the AFF option of the Unit parameter, the Ddname referenced by the AFF keyword must contain a SEP (Separation) keyword parameter. This reference in effect also requests channel separation.

If //INPUT3 DD SEP=(INPUT1,INPUT2) and //OUTPUT1 DD AFF=INPUT3 are coded, the Affinity parameter is in reality requesting channel separation from INPUT1 and INPUT2 as INPUT3 is defined to do. There is this restriction in the use of the Affinity parameter, that is, it can only refer to a Ddname statement which contains a Separation parameter. Also it should be noted that INPUT3 and OUTPUT1 will not necessarily be assigned the same channel. However, they will both be separated from INPUT1 and INPUT2 channels. A Separation parameter coded on the OUTPUT1 Dd statement like the one coded on the INPUT3 Dd statement would have the same effect as the previously coded Affinity parameter.

b. AMP (Access Method Parameter)

Basic and Complete Format: AMP= ['AMORG'][,'BUFND=Number']

[,'BUFNI=Number'][,'BUFSP=Size'] ,['CROPS = $\begin{Bmatrix} \text{RCK'} \\ \text{NCK'} \\ \text{NRE'} \\ \text{NRC'} \end{Bmatrix}$]

[,'OPTCD= $\begin{Bmatrix} \text{I'} \\ \text{L'} \\ \text{IL'} \end{Bmatrix}$] [,'RECFM= $\begin{Bmatrix} \text{F'} \\ \text{FB'} \\ \text{V'} \\ \text{VB'} \end{Bmatrix}$] [,'STRNO=Number']

[,'SYNAD=Name'][,'TRACE']

The purpose of the AMP keyword parameter is to specify the processing attributes to be used for a Virtual Storage Access Method (VSAM) file. This type of file organization technique can be utilized only with System 370 Virtual Storage configurations. Some VSAM file characteristics can also be defined in the program itself. An AMP parameter will modify any of these previously described attributes. A brief summary of AMP parameter specifications follow:

    AMORG - identifies data set as VSAM.
    BUFND - specifies number of data buffers.
    BUFNI - specifies number of index buffers.

112

BUFSP - specifies size (bytes) of buffer areas.
CROPS - indicates restart/checkpoint options, where
     RCK = perform data erase, and data set post checkpoint
        modification tests;
     NCK = do not perform data set post checkpoint modifica-
        tion test;
     NRE = do not perform data erase test; and
     NRC = do not perform either data erase or data set post
        checkpoint modification tests.
OPTCD - defines how Indexed Sequential Access Method (ISAM)
    interface is to handle record deletion conditions, where,
    L = delete if replaced;
    I = let interface determine; and
    IL = delete in all cases.
RECFM - defines record format to ISAM interface, where
    F = fixed-length records;
    FB = blocked fixed-length records;
    V = variable-length records; and
    VB = Blocked variable-length records.
STRNO - specifies number of strings.
SYNAD - indicates program module name.
TRACE - utilizes trace facility.

c. COPIES (Copies)

  Basic and Complete Format: COPIES=Number

  The purpose of the COPIES keyword parameter is to indicate how
many copies are desired of a given Dd statement's output class specification. If not coded, one copy is assumed. A maximum of 255 copies
is allowed. A SYSOUT parameter must have been coded on the Dd statement, e.g., //PRTOUT DD SYSOUT=C,COPIES=4. It should be pointed out
that the file will be printed separately for each copy desired. To
save printing time and costs, a special original-plus-carbon(s) paper
output class should be coded to avoid duplicative print efforts if
possible, i.e., SYSOUT=(C,,1484).

d. DCB (Data Control Block)

Basic Format : Described earlier in this chapter.

Complete Format : DCB= {(List of Characteristics) / ({Dsname / *.Ddname / *.Stepname.Ddname / *.Stepname.Procstepname.Ddname} [List of charac- teristics])}

    where List of Characteristics description follows:
      Dsname is name of catalogued data set for
        which DCB characteristics are to be
        utilized; and
      *. relates to backward references to be dis-
        cussed later in the text.

113

The purpose of the DCB keyword parameter is to describe to the Operating System necessary characteristics of the file to be process-ed. The three basic subparameters covered previously in this chapter were Record Format, Logical Record Length, and Maximum Blocksize. Additional DCB information must be provided if deviations from instal-lation defaults are necessary. Such items as nonsequential file pro-cessing, buffer characteristics, and special services need to be de-cribed via JCL if they do not conform to standard operating procedures and/or installation defaults. References to a catalogued data set, previous file, or special keyword may be coded. A brief summary of these not-so-common DCB parameter specifications follow.

BFALN   - defines buffer alignment for each DCB, where

$$BFALN= \begin{Bmatrix} F \\ D \end{Bmatrix}$$

            for fullword boundary (F); and
            doubleword boundary (D).
            If not coded, D is assumed.

BFTEK   -- defines buffer technique for each DCB when spanning
            unblocked variable-length records, where
            BFTEK=R

            Where necessary, spanning places a portion of
            a logical record at the end of a block and the
            beginning of the next to fill otherwise physical
            record space. If not coded, unspanned records
            are assumed.

BLKSIZE   - specifies maximum Blocksize in bytes as described
            previously in this chapter under the basic format, where

            BLKSIZE=Length

BUFIN   - specifies number of receiving buffers in telecommunica-
            tion environments, where

            BUFIN=Number

            If not coded, 1 is assumed.

BUFL   - specifies buffer length in bytes for each DCB, where

            BUFL=Size
            If not coded, blocksize can be assumed.

BUFMAX   - specifies maximum number of all buffers in telecommu-
            nications environments, where

            BUFMAX=Number

            If not coded, 2 is assumed.

BUFNO   - specifies number of buffers for each DCB, where

        BUFNO=Number

           If not coded, 2 can be assumed.

BUFOFF   - specifies a buffer offset for each variable-length
              ASCII tape record DCB, where

$$\text{BUFOFF}=\begin{Bmatrix} X \\ L \end{Bmatrix}$$

        for the length of the prefix in bytes (X), and
        a 4-byte prefix which contains the block length
        (L).
        If not coded, 0 is assumed.

BUFOUT   - specifies number of sending buffers in telecommu-
              nication environments, where

        BUFOUT=Number

           If not coded, 2 is assumed.

BUFSIZE   - specifies buffer length in bytes for buffers in
              telecommunication environments, where

        BUFSIZE=Size

           If not coded, blocksize can be assumed.

CODE   - describes paper tape code characteristics for each
              DCB punch output, where

$$\text{CODE}=\begin{Bmatrix} A \\ B \\ C \\ F \\ I \\ N \\ T \end{Bmatrix}$$

        for 8-track ASCIL (A);

        7-track Burroughs (B);

        8-track National Cash Register (C);

        8-track Friden (F);

        8-track IBM Binary Coded Decimal (I);

        No conversion (N); and

        5-track Teletype (T).

        If not coded, I is assumed.

CYLOFL   - specifies the number of tracks per cylinder to be
              assigned as overflow tracks for each DCB, where

CYLOFL=Number

DEN   - specifies tape density in terms of the number of Bits Per Inch (BPI) on each track for a given DCB, where

$$DEN= \begin{Bmatrix} 0 \\ 1 \\ 2 \\ 3 \\ 4 \end{Bmatrix}$$

for 7-track 200 BPI (0);
7-track 556 BPI (1);
7 and 9-track 800 BPI (2);
9-track 1600 BPI (3); and
9-track 6250 BPI (4).

If not coded, the highest-density capability for the specific tape unit should be assumed. A check with the installation may be necessary.

DIAGNS   - utilizes diagnostic trace facility for each DCB, where

DIAGNS=TRACE.

-    If not coded, 0 is assumed.

DSORG   - specifies the type of file organization utilized for each DCB, where

$$DSORG= \begin{Bmatrix} CQ \\ CX \\ DA \\ DAU \\ GS \\ IS \\ ISU \\ MQ \\ PO \\ POU \\ PS \\ PSU \end{Bmatrix}$$

for Communications Queue (CQ);

Communications Line (CX);

Direct Organization (DA);

Graphic DCB (GS);

Indexed Sequential (IS);

Message Queue (MQ);

Partitioned Organization (PO); and

Physical Sequential (PS).

The U signifies that the data set may be location-dependent and unmovable. If not coded, PS is assumed.

EROPT - identifies Input/Output (I/O) error options for each DCB, where

$$EROPT=\begin{Bmatrix} ABE \\ ACC \\ SKP \\ T \end{Bmatrix}$$

for Abend if error (ABE);

Accept error block (ACC);

Skip error block (SKP); and

On-line terminal test (T).

If not coded, ABE is assumed.

FRID - specifies a DCB format record identifier, where

FRID=Character String

The Character String may be 1 to 4 alphanumeric characters.

FUNC - identifies a data set function for each DCB, where

$$FUNC=\begin{Bmatrix} I \\ R \\ RP \\ RPD \\ RPW \\ RPWD \\ RPWXT \\ RW \\ RWT \\ PW \\ PWXT \\ WT \end{Bmatrix}$$

for Punch and Print on Cards (I);

Read Cards (R);

Card Punch (P);

Data Protection (D);

Print Data Set (W);

Printer (X); and

2-line Printer (T).

If not coded, R on input and P on output are assumed.

GNCP   - specifies the maximum number of Input/Output (I/O) macro instructions to be issued prior to a Wait macro instruction, where

GNCP=Numer

If not coded, 1 is assumed.

KEYLEN   - specifies key length in bytes for each DCB, where

KEY=Length

If not coded, key requests may not be made.

LIMCT   - specifies the number of blocks or tracks to be searched for free space depending upon addressing technique utilized, where

LIMCT=Number

If not coded, the search option may not be utilized.

LRECL   - specifies Logical Record Length in bytes as described previously in this chapter under the basic format, where

LRECL=Length

MODE   - specifies a card reader and/or punch mode of operation for each DCB, where

$$\text{MODE}=\begin{Bmatrix} C \\ E \end{Bmatrix}\begin{bmatrix} O \\ R \end{bmatrix}$$

for Card Image mode (C);

EBCDIC mode (E);

Optical Mark Read mode (O); and

Read-Column-Eliminate mode (R).

If not coded, E is assumed.

NCP   - specifies the maximum number of Read/Write (R/W) macro instructions to be issued for each DCB prior to a Check macro instruction, where

NCP=Number

    If not coded, 1 is assumed.

NTM   - number of tracks in master index of indexed sequential data set, where

    NTM=Number

    If not coded, master index not assumed.

OPTCD   - requests optional services to be performed for each DCB, where

    OPTCD=Code

        The code may be one of, or various combinations of, the following specifications:

        A = Unit Addresses specified

        B = Disregard End of File

        C = Use Chain Scheduling

        E = Perform Extended Search

        F = I/O Feedback requested

        H = Hopper Exit requested

        I = Use Independent Overflow Areas

        L = Delete Records Indicator

        M = Create/Maintain Master Index

        Q = ASCII Translation required

        R = Block Addresses specified

        T = User Totaling Facility requested

        U = Analyze Print Data Checks and Error

        W = Validity Check requested

        Y = Use Cylinder Overflow Areas

        Z = Shorten Error Recovery procedure

PCI   - specifies nature of Program Check Interruptions, where

$$PCI = \begin{cases} Code \\ (Code1,Code2) \end{cases}$$

        The code may be one or a pair of the following specifications for receiving and sending operations, respectively:

        A=If PCI, free first buffer, allocate second buffer

        N=No PCI operations on buffers

        R=If PCI, free first buffer, do not allocate second buffer

        If not coded, A is assumed.

PRTSP   - specifies line spacing, where

$$PRTSP=\begin{Bmatrix} 0 \\ 1 \\ 2 \\ 3 \end{Bmatrix}$$

      for suppressed (0),

      single (1),

      double (2), and

      triple (3) spacing.

      If not coded, 1 is assumed.

RECFM   - defines Record Format as described previously in
         this chapter under the basic format, where

RECFM=Type

      Additional specifications not previously discussed
      include the following:

      D=Variable-length ASCII tape records

      M=Machine code carriage control character in
        first byte

      S=Records may span more than one block to use

        unfilled block space

      T=Write to Overflow Tracks

      If not coded, U (Undefined record format) is
      assumed.

REPOS   - requests tape repositioning if block count error, where

$$REPOS=\begin{Bmatrix} N \\ Y \end{Bmatrix}$$

      for No Repositioning (N), and

      Repositioning (Y).

      If not coded, N is assumed.

RESERVE   - specifies number of bytes for Datetime and Sequence
         buffers, where

RESERVE=(Size1,Size2)

      for first and following buffers, respectively.

RKP   - indicates relative position of record key, where

RKP=Number

    If not coded, 0 is assumed.

STACK   - specifies card stacker bin, where

$$\text{STACK} = \begin{Bmatrix} 1 \\ 2 \end{Bmatrix}$$

- for the first or second stacks, respectively.
If not coded, 1 is assumed.

THRESH   - specifies percentage of disk space at which point
message queue is considered full, where

THRESH=Percentage

If not coded, 95 is assumed.

TRTCH   - defines Tape Recording Technique utilized for 7-track
tape, where

$$\text{TRTCH} = \begin{Bmatrix} C \\ E \\ T \\ ET \end{Bmatrix}$$

for Odd Parity, no BCD Translation, with 7- to
9-track Conversion (C);

Even Parity, no BCD Translation, no 7- to 9 track
Conversion (E);

Odd Parity, BCD Translation, no 7- to 9 track
Conversion (T); and

Even Parity, BCD Translation, no 7- to 9-track
Conversion (ET).

If not coded, Odd Parity, no BCD Translation,
and no 7- to 9-track Conversion are assumed.

e. DDNAME (Data Definition Name)

Basic and Complete Format: DDNAME=Ddname

The purpose of the DDNAME keyword parameter is to defer the definition of a data set. The data set is initially defined by a Dd
statement with a Ddname coded after the DDNAME parameter, e.g., DDNAME=
SYSIN. It is later defined by a Dd statement using that particular
Ddname.

A common example of this keyword is found when using catalogued
procedures. Some Dd statements within a catalogued procedure may
contain the DDNAME=Ddname parameter specification in lieu of actually
describing the data set. It is generally expected that the user will
supply a Dd statement with the indicated Ddname and describe the file
when calling the procedure. This technique and the desirability for
its occasional use will be expanded upon in the next chapter.

f. DEST (Destination)

Basic and Complete Format: DEST=Identification

The purpose of the DEST keyword parameter is to specify in a remote environment where a particular system output data set is to be routed. That is, the Destination parameter can only be coded in conjunction with a SYSOUT (System Output) parameter, e.g., //PRINT1 DD SYSOUT= A,DEST=RJ009. Specific identification of the remote destination is installation-defined but must contain from 1 to 7 alphanumeric characters. If a Destination parameter is not coded, the general default is the remote station from which the job was submitted.

g. DLM (Delimiter)

Basic and Complete Format: DLM=Delimiter

The purpose of the DLM keyword parameter is to change the standard end-of-file delimiter from /* (slash asterisk) to another 2-character delimiter set, e.g., DLM=A1. This will allow the /* to be read as part of the input data when desired to do so. As such, the Delimiter parameter only has meaning on DD * or DD DATA statements. Apostrophes must be utilized if special characters are used as part of the new 2-character delimiter, e.g., DLM='%&'.

h. FCB (Forms Control Buffer)

Basic and Complete Format: FCB=(Identification$\left[\begin{array}{l}\text{,ALIGN}\\\text{,VERIFY}\end{array}\right]$)

The purpose of the FCB keyword parameter is to specify the nature and form of control to be utilized for a given output data set on a Model 3211 printer or 3525 card punch. Identification is installation-defined but must contain 1 to 4 alphanumeric or national characters. This name symbolizes a predefined forms-control character set. The keyword ALIGN asks the operator to align the paper prior to printing. VERIFY does the same but in addition displays the desired forms control, e.g., FCB=TAB1, FCB=(TAB2,VERIFY). If the Model 3211 card punch is not utilized, Forms Control Buffer specifications are ignored.

i. HOLD (Hold)

Basic and Complete Format: HOLD=$\left\{\begin{array}{l}\text{NO}\\\text{YES}\end{array}\right\}$

The purpose of the HOLD keyword parameter is to indicate whether this particular system output data set should be held for future release. To be released, the computer operator or user must issue a Route or Release command. If NO is coded, output operations are to proceed normally. This is also the default if the Hold parameter is not coded. This parameter can only be coded in conjunction with a SYSOUT (System Output) parameter, e.g., //PRINT1 DD SYSOUT=A,HOLD= YES.

j. OUTLIM (Output Limit)

Basic and Complete Format: OUTLIM=Number

The purpose of the OUTLIM keyword parameter is to specify the maximum allowable number of records which can be created in a system output data set. If this number should be exceeded, a job will generally terminate unless interceded by a specially written user routine. The highest number which can be specified is over 16 million, though installation standards generally interrupt prior to this point. Output limits prevent wasted time, cost, and paper from accidental program loops. This parameter must be coded in conjunction with a SYSOUT (System Output) parameter, e.g., //PRINT1 DD SYSOUT=A, OUTLIM=10000.

k. QNAME (Queue Name)

Basic and Complete Format: QNAME=Name

The purpose of the QNAME keyword parameter is to specify the name of a teleprocessing function which indicates where messages produced by the executing program are to be routed. Name is installation-defined but must contain 1 to 4 alphanumeric or national characters. This name symbolizes a predefined message queue area, e.g., //OUTPUT1 DD QNAME=SYS1. As such, the DCB parameter is the only other allowable specification if the Queue Name parameter is utilized.

l. SEP (Separation)

Basic and Complete Format: SEP=(Ddname$\left[,......\right]$)

The purpose of the SEP keyword parameter is to request channel separation. A channel is merely a path between main storage and one or more similar units (or devices). In selected situations channel separation may increase processing efficiency by reducing processing time, i.e., read/write head competition, when accessing more than one data set. If //INPUT3 DD SEP=(INPUT1,INPUT2) were coded, the Separation parameter would be requesting channel separation from INPUT1 and INPUT2. That is, a device on another channel will be allocated for INPUT3.

m. SPLIT (Split)

Basic Format   :   SPLIT= $\begin{cases} \text{Number} \\ \text{(Number,CYL,Primary Quantity)} \end{cases}$

Complete Format: SPLIT= $\begin{cases} \text{Number} \\ \text{(Number,CYL,(Primary Quantity} \left[,\text{Secondary Quantity}\right]\text{))} \\ \text{Percent} \\ \text{(Percent,Blocksize,(Primary Quantity} \left[,\text{Secondary Quantity}\right]\text{))} \end{cases}$

123

The purpose of the SPLIT keyword parameter is to allocate space for a new data set on a direct-access device and share (or split) that space with other data sets on the same cylinders. In selected situations cylinder sharing may increase processing efficiency by minimizing read/write head movement when accessing more than one data set.

Utilizing the basic format, SPLIT=(5,CYL,50) allocates 50 cylinders for all data sets and specifies that only 5 tracks per cylinder may be utilized for this particular data set. Once a SPLIT parameter has been coded along with volume and unit specifications, only the number of tracks per cylinder need be specified if desired for remaining Dd statements in the same step, e.g., SPLIT=2.

Utilizing the complete format, secondary quantities, percent of tracks per cylinder, and the blocksize option can be coded. If SPLIT=(25,6400,(100,10)) were coded, then enough cylinder space for 100 blocks of 6,400-byte size would be allocated for all data sets and only 25% of each cylinder rounded down to the nearest full track may be utilized for this particular data set. Ten more blocks are to be allocated given extent limitations if the data set requires more space. For remaining Dd statements in the same step only the percent of tracks per cylinder need be specified if desired, e.g., SPLIT=40. Whether this number is to be interpreted as the number of tracks or percent of cylinder use is determined by the initial allocation, i.e., in terms of cylinders or blocksize.

n. SUBALLOC (Sub-Allocate)

Basic Format : SUBALLOC=$\begin{cases} \text{(TRK} \\ \text{CYL} \\ \text{Blocksize} \end{cases}$,Primary Quantity)

Complete Format: SUBALLOC=$\begin{cases} \text{(TRK} \\ \text{CYL} \\ \text{Blocksize} \end{cases}$,(Primary Quantity $\begin{bmatrix} \text{,Secondary} \\ \text{,\quad Quantity} \end{bmatrix}$

$\begin{bmatrix} \text{,Directory} \end{bmatrix}$) $\begin{cases} \text{,Ddname} \\ \text{,Stepname.Ddname} \\ \text{,Stepname.Procstepname.Ddname} \end{cases}$)

The purpose of the SUBALLOC keyword parameter is to allocate a contiguous series of new data sets in one area of a direct-access device. In selected situations, contiguous suballocation may increase processing efficiency by minimizing read/write head movement when serially accessing more than one data set. Once an area has been allocated via the Space parameter, a series of smaller data sets may be suballocated in this same space via a referback with the Sub-Allocation parameter.

Utilizing both the basic and complete formats, TRK, CYL, Blocksize, Primary Quantity, Secondary Quantity, and Directory definitions are the same as with the Space parameter. Utilizing the Stepname, Procedure stepname, and Ddname referback option, SUBALLOC=(CYL,50,STEP1.GO. OUTPUT1) would be a valid Sub-Allocation parameter specification. Indexed sequential files may not be created with this parameter, however.

If SPACE=(CYL,100) for Ddname OUTPUT1 and Dsname MASTER on a Dd
statement were followed by SUBALLOC=(CYL,25,OUTPUT1) for Dsname FILE1
on another Dd statement, a new file would be suballocated within the
first. The initial file called MASTER would contain 100 cylinders
of space, though less is presumably filled. The second called FILE1
would contain 25 unused cylinders within the initial 100. It may or
may not be filled to capacity also. With another suballocation two
contiguous files would exist, one next to the other in the same area
of direct-access space.

o. TERM (Terminal)

    Basic and Complete Format: TERM=RT

The purpose of the TERM keyword parameter is to indicate that
output should be routed directly to a remote unit record device.
If coded, normal device-allocation procedures should be bypassed.
A Unit parameter needs be coded to indicate the specific remote
device to be utilized, e.g., printer.

p. UCS (Universal Character Set)

    Basic and Complete Format: UCS=(Set Name $\begin{bmatrix} ,\text{FOLD} \\ , \end{bmatrix}$ $\begin{bmatrix} ,\text{VERIFY} \end{bmatrix}$)

The purpose of the UCS keyword parameter is to specify the name
of a character set to be used on a Model 1403 or 3211 printer. Set
names are predefined but must contain 1 to 4 alphanumeric or national
characters. The name symbolizes a specific character set. The keyword FOLD signifies a fold mode, that is, when data is to be printed
in the upper case. The Fold specification requests that the chain
or print train for this particular character set in the fold mode
should be mounted and strung by the print operator. VERIFY asks the
operator to check that the correct chain or print train has been
mounted and strung appropriately, e.g., UCS=(STND,FOLD,VERIFY). A
character set display is printed prior to the check. Spooled output
data does not utilize UCS parameter information. Similarly, if the
parameter is not coded but valid, a standard default character set is
used for print purposes.

7. Other JCL Statements

    There are three basic types of JCL statements -- JOB (Job), EXEC
(Execute), and DD (Data Definition). They account for the bulk of
JCL coding usage. In reality, however, there are six additional,
less frequently utilized types of JCL statements. They are:

    ' The COMMAND,
        COMMENT,
        DELIMITER,
        NULL,
        PEND, and
        PROC statements.

a. The COMMAND Statement

General Format: // Command Field   Operand Field   Comment Field

The purpose of the Command statement is to describe the operator command to be issued and performed. It may be placed before a Job, Exec, Delimiter statement or another Command statement. In no case should another statement be interrupted, however. A // (slash slash) is coded in columns 1 and 2 followed by at least one blank. One of the following commands is then coded:

BRDCST (Broadcast),
CANCEL,
CENOUT (Central Output),
DISPLAY,
HOLD,
LISTBC (List Broadcast),
LOG,
LOGOFF,
MODIFY,
MONITOR,
MOUNT,
MSG (Message),
RELEASE,
REPLY,
RESET,
ROUTE,
SEND,
SET,
SHOW,
START,
STOP,
STOPMN (Stop Monitor),
UNLOAD,
USERID (User Identification),
VARY,
WRITELOG, or
WRITER.

The command is followed by at least one blank. One of a long series of operands can then be coded in the optional Operand Field. The operands are specific to each command, i.e., CANCEL Job Number, SEND Message, etc. Specific operand formats and their range of possibilities may be obtained from appropriate operator reference manuals. The Operand Field is followed by at least one blank. An optional Comment Field is then provided.

b. The COMMENT Statement

General Format: //*Comment Field

The purpose of the Comment statement is to clarify and/or expand upon any item of interest within a given set of JCL. The Comment statement is nonexecutable, though it does appear in the output JCL listing with asterisks in columns 1-3. It does not appear on an operator's console. It may be placed anywhere in a given job stream, though another statement should not be interrupted. A //* (slash slash asterisk) is coded in columns 1, 2, and 3. Any comment may now be coded in columns 4 to 80. Continuation is accomplished simply by coding another Comment statement. Typical uses include:

1. Inform installation of advance paper or punch needs. Code Comment statement after Job statement:

   //* THIS JOB REQUIRES REGULAR 14 7/8 X 8½ INCH 2-PART PAPER.

2. Inform installation of unique program execution requirements. Code Comment statement before or after identified Exec statement:

   //* IF STEP ABNORMALLY TERMINATES, PHONE MAINTENANCE SECTION.

3. Inform installation of unique file execution requirements. Code Comment statement before or after identified Dd statement:

   //* IF TAPE I/O PROBLEMS, PLEASE CLEAN AND RESUBMIT.

4. Document job setup procedures for future users. Code Comment statements as appropriate:

   //* GO TO LAST MONTH'S EDIT RUN AND OBTAIN VOLUME SERIAL

   //* NUMBER FOR CURRENT MASTER FILE. ENTER NUMBER HERE.

The JCL job stream will need to be scanned by appropriate operation or maintenance personnel prior to job submission to obtain provided comments.

c. The DELIMITER Statement

   General Format: /*Comment Field

The purpose of the Delimiter statement is to signify an end-of-data condition for files submitted through the input job stream, i.e., via a DD * or DD DATA statement. This statement does not appear in the output JCL listing. A /* (slash asterisk) is coded in columns 1 and 2 to indicate end of file. Any comment can now be coded starting in column 3. Continuation is not allowed.

A delimiter is not needed for data being read via a DD * statement. End of file in this case is indicated by the occurrence of a // in columns 1 and 2 (the next JCL statement) or an end-of-job condition. In the above case the presence of a /* will indicate end of file, however. If a /* should accidentally be placed in the middle of a card deck, only one-half of the file will be read and processed. The other half is generally flushed by the Operating System but may be picked up by the presence of a SYSIN ddname file defined in the program.

A delimiter is needed for data being read via a DD DATA statement. Records with a // in columns 1 and 2 are technically accepted as data (not JCL). The only way for other remaining and executable JCL of your job to be recognized as such is to delineate it from the data with the presence of a delimiter or an end-of-job condition. If a /* should accidentally be placed in the middle of a card deck, only one-half of the file will be read and processed. The other half with //'s in columns 1 and 2 may well be interpreted as executable JCL! Though such situations generally end with an error message and/or a storage dump, this author will not attempt to predict what might have taken place beforehand!

Keep in mind that if the data contains /*'s in columns 1 and 2, the delimiter can be temporarily changed by coding a DLM (Delimiter) keyword parameter on the Dd statement reading the file, e.g., //INPUT1   DD   DATA,DLM=EF.

Programmers generally place a /* after each job step, though at this location it has no executable or end-of-file meaning. As discussed previously, the same is sometimes true with the DD * statement. To avoid confusion, assist documentation, and provide standardization, the author recommends that a delimiter be coded at the end of all data files being read by a DD * or DD DATA statement as well as at the end of each job step. The liberal use of comments via the Comment statement is also recommended, as the Delimiter statement does not print in the user's output JCL listing.

d. The NULL Statement

Specific Format: //

The purpose of the Null statement is to signify an end-of-job condition. A // (slash slash) is coded in columns 1 and 2. No comments are allowed.

A pause at the input reader as well as the occurrence of the next Job statement also signifies end of job. A problem occurs, however, if, there is an error in the Job statement behind your job. In this case it will not be recognized as a valid Job statement and will therefore be considered as part of your job. The next morning may prove disheartening when you find the latter portion of your job contains an error message for which the JCL is not even a part. Meanwhile, the user of the job which was immediately behind yours begins to search frantically for their output JCL listing. This situation may prove solace to those of us who daily proclaim, "It's always other people who cause my problems!" Needless to say, the author strongly recommends the use of a Null statement at the end of each job.

e. The PEND Statement

General Format: //Name   PEND   Comment Field

The purpose of the Pend (Procedure End) statement is to signify the end of an instream (not-catalogued) procedure. A // is coded in columns 1 and 2 followed by a optional instream procedure name.

After at least one blank the keyword PEND must be coded. After another blank optional comments may also be coded.

Instream procedures are utilized to test JCL prior to cataloguing. Their use will be discussed in detail in the last chapter.

f. The PROC Statement

General Format: //Name   PROC   Comment Field

The purpose of the Proc (Procedure) statement is to signify the beginning of an instream (not-catalogued) procedure and to assign that procedure a temporary name for subsequent calling purposes within the job to be executed. Proc statements can also to used to assign values to symbolic parameters. When used this way in catalogued procedures the name field is optional. A // is coded in columns 1 and 2 followed by an instream procedure name. After at least one blank, the keyword PROC must be coded. After another blank, optional comments may also be coded.

Instream procedures are utilized to test JCL prior to cataloguing. Their use as well as symbolic parameters will be discussed in detail in the last chapter.

8. Special Ddnames

Ddnames defined in the program and coded in the JCL to identify files to be processed are generally assigned by the programmer. There are seven special ddnames which serve a particular system function and should never be utilized in a program. They are:

JOBCAT,
JOBLIB,
STEPCAT,
STEPLIB,
SYSABEND,
SYSCHK, and
SYSUDUMP.

a. Ddname JOBCAT (Job Catalogue)

A Dd statement utilizing the ddname of JOBCAT makes available special Virtual Storage Access Method (VSAM) user catalogues for the duration of the job. A VSAM catalogue stores the characteristics of catalogued data sets as well as other system information. A Jobcat Dd statement follows the Job statement and/or a Joblib Dd statement. The name of the user data set (or catalogue) is provided by a Dsname parameter. The Disposition of the catalogue itself is generally Old or Share. For example,

//JOBCAT   DD   DSN=A.USER.CATALOG,DISP=SHR

allows access of a catalogue named A.USER.CATALOG for data set or other VSAM system information. If not coded, a standard systemwide catalogue remains available for all users and system personnel. A Jobcat Dd statement is only required if additional catalogues are desired by the user. For management purposes and to avoid duplication, user catalogue names are many times assigned by the dp installation and/or follow their naming conventions. The technique of cataloguing data sets will be described in detail in the last chapter of this text.

b. Ddname JOBLIB (Job Library)

A Dd statement utilizing the ddname of JOBLIB makes available special user private libraries for the duration of the job, i.e., it "opens the door" of a private library for member access. A library consists of a data set (generally disk) which has been partitioned to store separate and independent members. Partitioned Data Sets (PDS's) and library use will be described later in the text.

Private libraries are created by a utility program or a complete description of a new library on a Joblib or Steplib Dd statement. Libraries are generally used to store executable program load modules (program library) or catalogued JCL procedure statements (procedure library). They are most handy in eliminating the need to handle many cards and other program or procedure statements. As such, they tend to streamline JCL coding and operating procedures.

A Joblib Dd statement follows the Job statement and/or a Jobcat Dd statement. The name of the private data set (or library) is provided by a Dsname parameter. The Disposition of the library itself is generally Old or Share. For example,

        //JOBLIB   DD   DSN=A.USER.LIBRARY,DISP=SHR

allows access of a library named A.USER.LIBRARY for program modules. If not coded, the standard systemwide public libraries remain available for all users and system personnel. A Joblib Dd statement is only required if additional libraries are desired by the user. This library may be shared by other users during the duration of this job per Disposition parameter specifications. For management purposes and to avoid duplication, private library names are many times assigned by the dp installation and/or follow their naming conventions. The technique of creating libraries and accessing library members will be described throughout the text.

c. Ddname STEPCAT (Step Catalogue)

A Dd statement utilizing the ddname of STEPCAT makes available special Virtual Storage Access Method (VSAM) user catalogues for the duration of the step. A VSAM catalogue stores the characteristics of catalogued data sets as well as other system information. A Stepcat Dd statement follows the Exec statement and/or a Steplib Dd statement. The name of the user data set (or catalogue) is provided by a Dsname parameter. The Disposition of the catalogue itself is generally Old or Share. For example,

        //STEPCAT   DD   DSN=A.USER.CATALOG,DISP=SHR

allows access of a catalogue named A.USER.CATALOG for data set or other VSAM system information. If not coded, a standard systemwide catalogue remains available for all users and system personnel. A

Stepcat Dd statement is only required if additional catalogues are desired by the user. For management purposes and to avoid duplication, user catalogue names are many times assigned by the dp installation and/or follow their naming conventions. The technique of cataloguing data sets will be described in detail in the last chapter of this text.

d. Ddname STEPLIB (Step Library)

A Dd statement utilizing the ddname of STEPLIB makes available special user private libraries for the duration of the step, i.e., it "opens the door" of a private library for member access. A library consists of a data set (generally disk) which has been partitioned to store separate and independent members. Partitioned Data Sets (PDS's) and library use will be described later in the text.
Private libraries are created by a utility program or a complete description of a new library on a Joblib or Steplib Dd statement. Libraries are generally used to store executable program load modules (program library) or catalogued JCL procedure statements (procedure library). They are most handy in eliminating the need to handle many cards and other program or procedure statements. As such they tend to streamline JCL coding and operating procedures.
A Steplib Dd statement follows the Exec statement and/or a Stepcat Dd statement. The name of the private data set (or library) is provided by a Dsname parameter. The Disposition of the library itself is generally Old or Share. For example,

```
//STEPLIB  DD  DSN=A.USER.LIBRARY,DISP=SHR
```

allows access of a library named A.USER.LIBRARY for program modules. If not coded, the standard systemwide public libraries remain available for all users and system personnel. A Steplib Dd statement is only required if additional libraries are desired by the user. This library may be shared by other users during the duration of this step per Disposition parameter specifications. For management purposes and to avoid duplication, private library names are many times assigned by the dp installation and/or follow their naming conventions. The techniques of creating libraries and accessing library members will be described throughout the text.

e. Ddname SYSABEND (System Abnormal End)

A Dd statement utilizing the ddname of SYSABEND describes the file to which a system-oriented storage dump should be written, i.e., usually print. A storage dump is simply a printed representation of a significant portion of main storage at the time a specific task is interrupted and/or abnormally terminated. It is in essence a debugging tool or "picture" of the contents of main storage.
A Sysabend Dd statement produces a hexadecimal print of main storage contents relating to the load module being executed, the system nucleus, and a system trace table. For example,

```
//SYSABEND  DD  SYSOUT=A
```

is a typical abend dump print file definition. Due to the large and sometimes cumbersome amount of print resulting from a Sysabend dump, a user-oriented Sysudump to be discussed later is generally recommended. A Sysabend dump can be valuable in debugging severe system problems, however. It does contain additional information as compared to a Sysudump. If either statement is not provided in a particular step and a storage dump situation occurs, a message will be issued giving the nature of the problem; however, the storage dump will not be printed.

f. Ddname SYSCHK (System Checkpoint)

A Dd statement utilizing the ddname of SYSCHK describes the file to which checkpoint restart information is to be written, i.e., tape or disk. Deferred checkpoint restart is an option whereby an operating program can be restarted at a particular point in its execution if it had abnormally terminated for any reason. This is a common programming technique for the execution of necessarily large and expensive computer runs and files.

The Syschk Dd statement is used in conjunction with the Restart parameter on the Job statement and/or the Restart Definition parameter on the Job and Exec statement. This Dd statement simply describes the file in which checkpoint information is stored. For example,

```
//SYSCHK   DD   UNIT=2400,DISP=(OLD,KEEP),

//          DSN=CHECK.POINT,VOL=SER=018761
```

defines a tape file for checkpoint information. The Syschk Dd statement must be located after the Job statement and any Joblib statements but before the first Exec statement.

g. Ddname SYSUDUMP (System User Dump)

A Dd statement utilizing the ddname of SYSUDUMP describes the file to which a user-oriented storage dump should be written, i.e., usually print. A storage dump is simply a printed representation of a significant portion of main storage at the time a specific task is interrupted and/or abnormally terminated. It is in essence a debugging tool or "picture" of the contents of main storage.

A Sysudump Dd statement produces a hexadecimal print of main storage contents relating only to the load module being executed, a most helpful area. For example,

```
//SYSUDUMP   DD   SYSOUT=A
```

is a typical user dump print file definition. In most cases, the information provided by a Sysudump Dd statement is sufficient to meet the needs of application and system programmers and analysts. Only when severe system problems persist is there a need for a Sysabend Dd statement. It is for this reason that the author recommends the use of a Sysudump Dd statement, producing a print of main storage as it relates only to the specific load module, rather than the much more lengthy and sometimes cumbersome storage dump created by a

Sysabend Dd statement. This recommendation becomes even more significant in remote batch communication environments where terminal print
time may be a critical performance factor. If either statement is
not provided in a particular step and a storage dump situation occurs,
a message will be issued giving the nature of the problem; however,
the storage dump will not be printed.

C. DD STATEMENT WORKSHOP

All allowable positional and keyword parameters which can be coded
on a Dd statement have been discussed. A workshop is now provided
to solidify a working knowledge of basic Dd statement as well as
complete JCL job coding. Workshop answers can be found in Appendix
E.

1. Syntax Check

Review, analyze, and correct the following ten Dd statements for
syntactical and/or logic coding errors. A given Dd statement may
contain none, one, or more than one error.

```
1. //INPUT%   DD   UNIT=SYSDA,DISP=OLD,KEEP,


   //         DSN=MASTER,VOL=SER=018762


2. //SYSUT2  DB  DSN=INDATA,


   //         LABEL=1,SL,DISP=SHR


3. //SYSIN  DD   *,DCB=BLKSIZE=4800


4. //OUTPUT1  DD   UNIT=2400,DISP=(KEEP,PASS,DELETE),


   //         DSN=AFILE.ONE,VOL=SER=TAPE18


   //         DCB=(RECFM=FB,LRECLE=80,BLKSIZE=3160)


5. //2INPUT  DD UNIT=3330,DISP=(NEW,PASS),
```

```
//          SPICE=(4000,20,RLSE),


//          DSN=&&TEMFILE,VOL=SER=PACK77,


//          DCB=(RECFM=AB,LRECL=100,BLKSIZE=4000)
```

6. //APRINTOUT DD SYSOUT=(C,1484)   NEED SPECIAL PAPER

7. //   DD DISP=(MOD,KEEP),DSN=.STEP1.GO.OUTPUT2

8. //CARDIN DD DATA,UNIT=2400

9. //PROGOUT DD UNIT=DISK=(NEW,CATLG,DELETE),


```
//          LABEL=(1,SL),VOLUME=SER=DISK02,


//          DSN=A.PRGM.LIBRY(MEMBER),


//          DCB=(RECFM=VB,BLKSIZE=3204)
```


10. //SYSPRINT DD SYSTEMOUT=A

2. Dd Statement and Job Coding Project

Code the Job statement, all Exec statements, and all Dd statements for
the three-step job depicted by the system flowchart in Figure 4.23.
Pertinent Job statement information (Account, Message Level, Time,
and Class) is displayed thereon. Choose your own jobname and programmer
name, however.
Pertinent Exec statement information (Program or Procedure Name,
Region, and Time) are displayed as appropriate on the flowchart.
Choose your own stepnames, however. Provide 'CORE=30000' Parm

parameter information to the second step. Code a Condition parameter such that if 8 is less than the return code issued by the first step, processing of the third step will be bypassed.

Pertinent Dd statement information (Ddname, Unit, Disposition, Volume, Space, DCB, and Sysout) are displayed as appropriate. Use 2400 for tape unit allocations, 3330 for permanent disk unit, and SYSDA for temporary disk unit allocations. Code only the first two subparameters of the Disposition parameter, keeping all tapes and permanent disk files and eventually deleting all temporary disk files. Release newly created but unused disk space. Choose your own data set names but make them temporary in nature for output disk files. Use DD * for card files with no other parameters. Also, code no parameters other than SYSOUT for print files. Assume standard labels are utilized and therefore need not be described. Insert a Joblib Dd statement after the Job statement. Choose your own shared library name. Insert a Sysudump Dd statement at the end of the first and third steps.

To assist your coding efforts, follow these step-by-step instructions:

Figure 4.23 Dd Statement And Job Coding System Flowchart

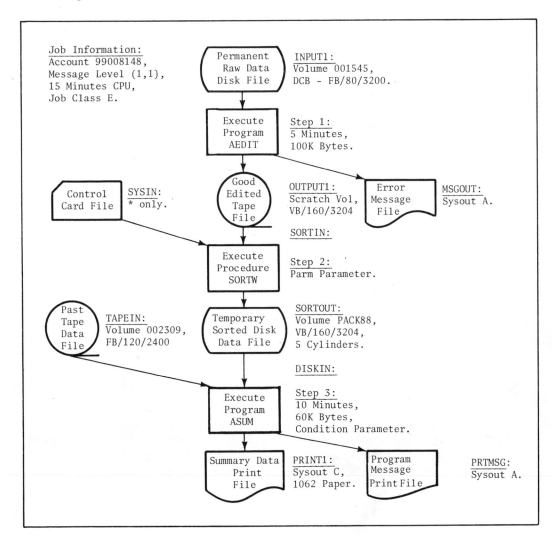

135

1. Code the Job statement. Then comment that this job requires 5,000 lines of 1062 paper. Finally, code a Joblib Dd statement using any shared program library name.

_____

_____

_____

_____

2. Code Step 1's Exec statement with Time and Region parameters. Code four Dd statements -- the first for ddname INPUT1, a second for ddname OUTPUT1, a third for ddname MSGOUT, and the fourth for a user storage dump file. Then code a step Delimiter statement.

_____

_____

_____

_____

_____

_____

_____

_____

_____

_____

_____

3. Code Step 2's Exec statement with a Parm parameter. Code three Dd statements -- the first for ddname SYSIN followed by a Delimiter statement, a second for ddname SORTIN, and the third for ddname SORTOUT. Then code a step Delimiter statement.

_____

_____

_____

_____

_____

_____

_____

_____

_____

_____

_____

4. Code Step 3's Exec statement with Time, Region, and Condition
   parameters. Code five dd statements -- the first for ddname
   TAPEIN, a second for ddname DISKIN, a third for ddname PRINT1,
   a fourth for Ddname PRTMSG, and the fifth for a user storage
   dump file. Then code a Null statement to indicate an end-of-
   job condition.

_____

_____

_____

_____

_____

_____

_____

_____

_____

_____

_____

_____

5

Catalogued Procedures

A. PARTITIONED DATA SET AND LIBRARY CONCEPTS

Now that basic JCL job characteristics, step specifications, and file descriptions have been provided for the Operating System, a detailed discussion on the use of catalogued procedures can begin. Though procedure use has been addressed on occasion in previous chapters, specifics on the topic have been purposefully bypassed until the basics of JCL coding were discussed.

A procedure is simply a set of precoded JCL which has been assigned a unique name. If this particular JCL provides functions which you wish to perform, you need only call upon the procedure via the Exec statement's PROC parameter. In the absence of the PGM (Program) parameter, PROC is assumed. Calling procedures saves considerable JCL coding. They are primarily utilized for functions common to most users, that is, compile, link, execute, sort, etc. There are two types of procedures which may be called. They are:

         Catalogued Procedures
                  and
         Instream Procedures.

Catalogued procedures consist of a set of JCL identified by a unique name which has been stored in a select area of direct-access storage, usually disk. Instream procedures are similar except they have not been so stored. Rather, they exist in the input job stream only. The technique of utilizing instream procedures will be described in the last chapter. The remainder of this text will concentrate on the catalogued version, the most common and frequently utilized technique.

Prior to creating and storing catalogued procedures, a Partitioned Data Set (PDS) must be created utilizing a utility program to be discussed in the next chapter. A Partitioned Data Set (PDS) is nothing more than a file which has the capability of being partitioned (or subdivided) into separate member areas. Members may be individual programs, subfiles, or JCL procedures. These PDS's are commonly referred to as program libraries, data libraries, and procedure libraries, respectively. Though one can intermix the purpose or functions of PDS members, it is best for operational and management purposes to create three separate libraries. All libraries must be PDS's. Figure 5.1 depicts the concept of Libraries and Partitioned Data Sets.

Figure 5.1 Partitioned Data Set Disk Concepts

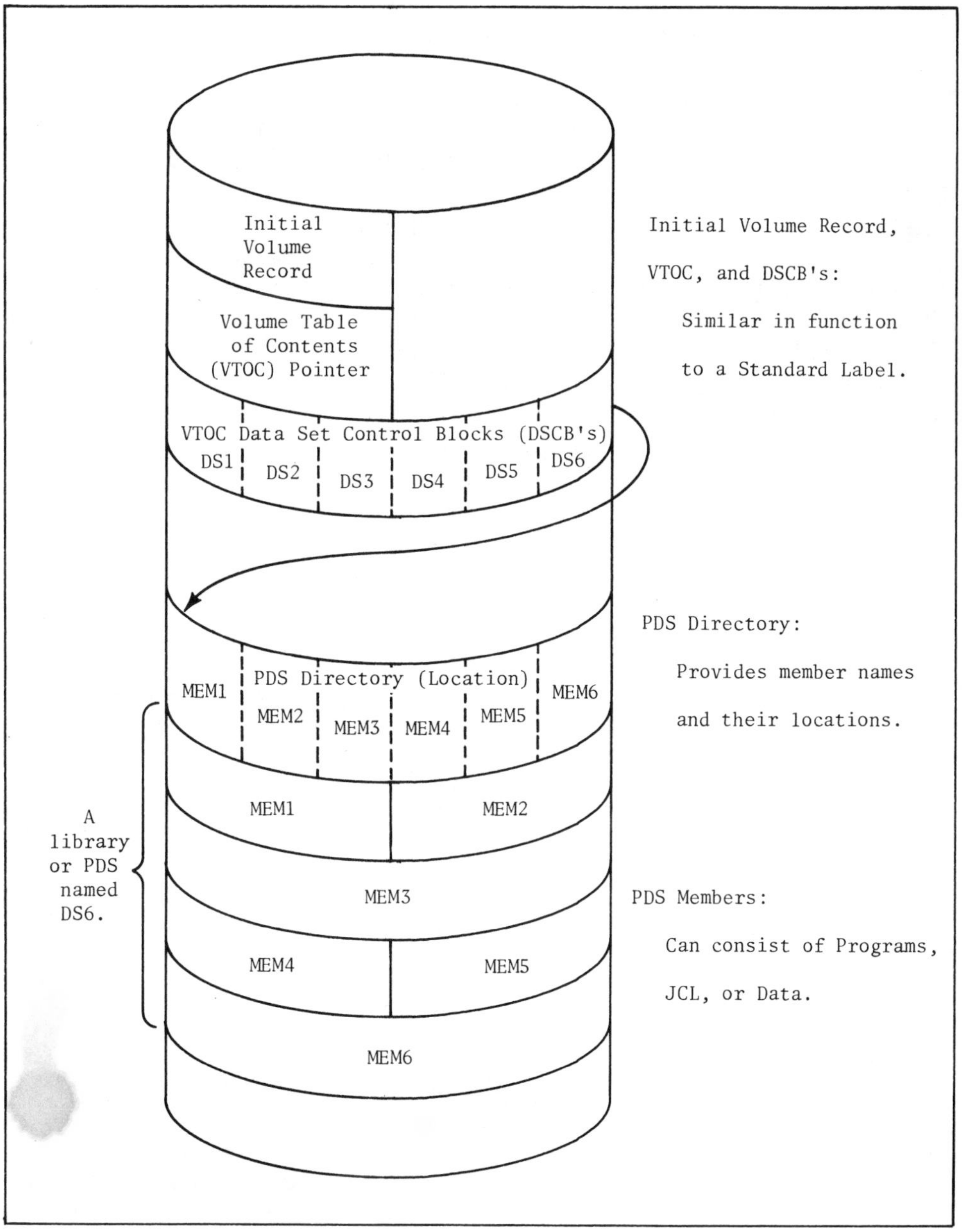

139

Three types of libraries may be accessed. They are:

Temporary Libraries,
System Libraries, and
Private Libraries.

Temporary libraries are created in a given job stream, then
deleted at or before job completion. Many catalogued procedures
which compile, link, and execute user programs create and/or access
libraries for temporary storage of programs. Fetching the program
module (member) to be executed can be accomplished by coding a
referback to a previous step on the PGM parameter. Calling the
program at a later time via a program name requires a JOBLIB or
STEPLIB Dd statement to "open the door" of the library.

A System library contains members which are common to many
users. Compiler programs, the linkage editor program, sort program,
and procedures which compile, link, and sort are examples of common
user functions. In the absence of a JOBLIB or STEPLIB Dd statement,
system libraries are always searched first for the program member
of interest. SYS1.LINKLIB is the name of the systemwide program
library. SYS1.PROCLIB is the name of the systemwide procedure library. A dp installation may create additional system libraries for
customer use. Members in a program library are accessed by either
a name or referback on a PGM (Program) parameter. Members in the
procedure library are accessed by coding a name on the PROC
(Procedure) parameter. In the absence of the PGM keyword, PROC
is assumed.

A Private library contains members which are common only to a
subset of users, i.e., a specific office or organization. Like
temporary libraries, most private libraries are user-created. Unlike temporary libraries, they are permanently maintained. Most
are program libraries, some are procedure libraries, a few are
data libraries. Fetching a program module to be executed can be
accomplished by coding a referback to a previous step on the PGM
parameter. Calling a program at a later time via a program name
requires a JOBLIB or STEPLIB Dd statement to "open the door" of
the library. Members in user procedure libraries are accessed by
coding a name on the PROC parameter. Data libraries are accessed
by coding the data set (or library) name via a DSNAME keyword
parameter. Specific members within the library are accessed by
coding the member name in parentheses behind the library name.

The above techniques will all be utilized in the discussion to
follow.

B. CATALOGUED PROCEDURE CONCEPTS

1. Catalogued Procedure Listing

As previously discussed, JCL procedures are commonly catalogued
and stored in partitioned data set libraries. Frustrations experienced by programmers and analysts in using catalogued procedures
are most frequently caused by the absence of a catalogued procedure
listing. How can one utilize a given catalogued procedure and debug

its problems if specific contents of the procedure are not known? Yet how many system and application programmers and analysts in all dp environments consistently call and utilize catalogued procedures not knowing the statements from which they are made?

A catalogued procedure listing can be easily obtained using a utility program to be discussed in the next chapter. Until then, specific catalogued procedures will be displayed as they are discussed in this chapter. Appendix B also provides a listing of the most common and frequently used procedures. It should be pointed out that many dp installations sometimes modify standard vendor-supplied procedures somewhat to suit user preferences. A '//' in columns 1 and 2 of a given job listing indicates JCL statements, a 'XX' in columns 1 and 2 identifies actual procedure statements, while a 'X/' in columns 1 and 2 depicts overridden procedure statements. Though the author will generally attempt to display procedures as originally supplied by the vendor, procedures displayed in this text may occasionally reflect other slight but common dp installation standards.

2. Procedure Call

Catalogued procedures are called by coding the Proc keyword on an Exec statement. In the absence of a Program keyword, the Procedure keyword is assumed. For example,

```
//STEP1   EXEC   PROC=EXAMPLE
```

and

```
//STEP1   EXEC   EXAMPLE
```

are identical procedure calls. The EXAMPLE procedure discussed below is fictitious. It is merely used to show how one can call upon many JCL statements and steps with only a single procedure call. This concept is depicted in Figure 5.2.

In the example in Figure 5.2, one JCL statement calls nine other statements (13 lines). Using the Procedure keyword in this example has the same effect as coding all 13 lines. Note near the arrows in Figure 5.2 that the procedure consists of two steps, ST1 and ST2. Stepname STEP1 coded in the JCL in reality has called a twostep procedure. These are two independent steps and are treated as such by the Operating System. The first step utilizes ddname files DD1, DD2, and SYSUDUMP. The second step utilizes ddname files SYSUT1, SYSUT2, SYSIN, SYSPRINT, and SYSUDUMP.

3. Procedure Modification

Though procedures can be easily called, seldom can they be created to satisfy all specific user needs for the procedure. That is, a few small but temporary modifications to the procedural input stream are usually required to suit individual user needs and job requirements. For example, how much time should be allowed for program execution? Or what specific volume is required to locate and process a given file? These specifics must usually be supplied by the user at execution time. Therefore,

Figure 5.2 Procedural Call

```
    JCL Code:                           EXAMPLE Procedure Listing:

//STEP1  EXEC  PROC=EXAMPLE         //ST1 EXEC PGM=AEDIT,REGION=60K

                                    //DD1 DD UNIT=2400,DISP=(OLD,PASS),

                                    //    DSN=AFILE,VOL=SER=TAPE99

                                    //DD2 DD SYSOUT=A

                                    //SYSUDUMP DD SYSOUT=A

                                    //ST2 EXEC PGM=IEBGENER

                                    //SYSUT1 DD DSN=AFILE,DISP=(OLD,KEEP)

                                    //SYSUT2 DD UNIT=3330,DISP=(NEW,KEEP),

                                    //    DSN=BACKUP.FILE,VOL=SER=PACK01,

                                    //    SPACE=(3200,(20,2),RLSE),

                                    //    DCB=(RECFM=FB,LRECL=80,BLKSIZE=3200)

                                    //SYSPRINT DD SYSOUT=A

                                    //SYSUDUMP DD SYSOUT=A
```

they may not necessarily be contained within a given catalogued
procedure. When called, the procedure need be slightly and
temporarily modified to suit these individual run requirements.

a. Execute Statements

     Let us assume in Figure 5.2 that three modifications to
Exec statements contained within the procedure must be or
are desired to be made. First, the Region parameter in step ST1
must be changed from 60K to 80K. Second, a Time parameter in
step ST1 must be added to specify 2 minutes rather than the
installation default. Third, a Condition parameter is desired
to indicate that the second step should be bypassed if 8 is less
than or equal to the return code issued by the first step. This
can be accomplished by calling the procedure, then coding appropriate modifications to specific keyword parameters. Keyword
format to modify Exec statement parameters is:

     Parameter.Procedure Stepname=

     Coding REGION.ST1=80K, TIME.ST1=2, and COND.ST2=(8,LE,ST1)
on the calling Exec statement will accomplish the objectives
stated above. The Procedure stepname is coded to indicate
which step the modifications apply to. The complete Exec statement
is as follows:

142

```
//STEP1   EXEC   PROC=EXAMPLE,REGION.ST1=80K,
//          TIME.ST1=2,COND.ST2=(8,LE,ST1)
```

Note the order in which these three procedure modifications occur. First, any or all changes to the initial step occur first followed by additions; any or all changes to the second step occur next followed by additions; etc. Second, any or all changes within a given step occur in the same order as they exist in the procedure followed by additions. This is why the Time parameter addition to the first step follows the Region parameter modification for the first step, and why the Condition parameter addition to the second step follows the other two. Figure 5.3 depicts the effective job stream created by calling procedure EXAMPLE and modifying or adding Exec statement parameters accordingly.

Figure 5.3 Procedure Execute Statement Modifications

Note the three previously discussed changes made to the procedure in the effective job stream near the arrows in Figure 5.3. Remember that these changes are temporary to the job stream and do not affect the actual makeup of the procedure itself. Those parameters which are to remain unchanged need not be specified in the JCL code. It should also be noted that individual steps within a procedure can only call programs, e.g., AEDIT, IEBGENER, etc., and not other procedures. That is, procedures cannot call other procedures. Only programs can be called by their Exec statements.

Finally, if an Exec statement parameter is not qualified by a stepname when making modifications or additions, the following basic defaults are in effect:

COND (Condition)   - applies to and/or overrides the condition of all steps in the procedure.

PARM (Parameter)   - applies to and/or overrides parameter information for only the first step of the procedure.

REGION (Region)   - applies to and/or overrides main storage allocation for each step in the procedure.

TIME (Maximum CPU Time) - applies to and/or overrides total time of all steps in the procedure.

Other Exec Parameters - generally apply to and/or override all steps of the procedure.

To avoid confusion, the author recommends a stepname be coded to indicate as well as document to which step or steps modifications and/or additions apply.

b. Dd Statements

Let us presume in previously discussed Figure 5.2 that three modifications to Dd statements contained within the procedure must be or are desired to be made. First, the Volume parameter on the first step's DD1 ddname file needs to be changed from TAPE99 to REEL07. Second, a DCB parameter specifying fixed-block, 80-character record length and 3,200 blocksize needs to be added to that same Dd statement. Third, a complete Dd statement with ddname SYSIN must be added to the second step to read a control card file. This can be accomplished by calling the procedure, then coding appropriate modifications to specific keyword parameters. Ddname format to modify Dd statement parameters is:

//Procedure Stepname.Ddname   DD   etc.

Coding ST1.DD1 ddname for VOL=SER=REEL07 and DCB=(RECFM=FB, LRECL=80,BLKSIZE=3200) along with ST2.SYSIN ddname with an asterisk (*) will accomplish the objectives stated above. The procedure stepname should be coded to indicate to which step the modifications apply. The complete Dd statements are as follows:

```
//ST1.DD1  DD  VOL=SER=REEL07,
//        DCB=(RECFM=FB,LRECL=80,BLKSIZE=3200)
//ST2.SYSIN  DD  *
   -  -  -  - Control Card File Here  -  -  -  -
/*
```

Note the order in which these three procedure modifications occur. First, any or all changes to the initial step occur first, followed by additions; any or all changes to the second step occur next, followed by additions; etc. Second, any or all changes within a given step occur in the same order as they exist in the procedure, followed by additions. This is why the DCB parameter addition to the first step's DD1 file follows the Volume parameter modification for the same step and file and why the DD * statement addition for ddname SYSIN to the second step follows the other two. Figure 5.4 depicts the effective job stream created by calling procedure EXAMPLE and modifying or adding Dd parameters and statements accordingly.

Figure 5.4 Procedure Dd Statement Modification

```
JCL Code:                              Effective Job Stream:


//STEP1  EXEC  PROC=EXAMPLE            //ST1 EXEC PGM=AEDIT,REGION=60K

//ST1.DD1  DD  VOL=SER=REEL07,         //DD1 DD UNIT=2400,DISP=(OLD,PASS),

//         DCB=(RECFM=FB,LRECL=80,     //     DSN=AFILE,VOL=SER=REEL07,

//               BLKSIZE=3200)         //     DCB=(RECFM=FB,LRECL=80,BLKSIZE=3200)

//ST2.SYSIN  DD  *                     //DD2 DD SYSOUT=A

----Control Card File Here----         //SYSUDUMP DD SYSOUT=A

/*                                     //ST2 EXEC PGM=IEBGENER

                                       //SYSUT1 DD DSN=AFILE,DISP=(OLD,KEEP)

                                       //SYSUT2 DD UNIT=3330,DISP=(NEW,KEEP),

                                       //      DSN=BACKUP.FILE,VOL=SER=PACK01,

                                       //      SPACE=(3200,(20,2),RLSE),

                                       //      DCB=(RECFM=FB,LRECL=80,BLKSIZE=3200)

                                       //SYSPRINT DD SYSOUT=A

                                       //SYSUDUMP DD SYSOUT=A

                                       //SYSIN  DD  *

                                       ----Control Card File Here----

                                       /*
```

Note the three previously discussed changes made to the procedure in the effective job stream near the arrows in Figure 5.4. Remember that these changes are temporary to the job stream and do not affect the actual makeup of the procedure itself. Those parameters which are to remain unchanged need not be specified in the JCL code. It should also be noted that it is technically unfeasible to catalogue procedures which contain a DD * statement. This is because one must call and code a Dd * statement modification anyhow such that the card file itself can be inserted directly behind the DD *. This is why in the previous example the SYSIN ddname file was added to the procedure at execution time to provide a Control Card File. It is also technically unfeasible to catalogue procedures which contain a Job statement, a Joblib Dd statement, a Dd Data statement, or an Execute statement which calls another procedure.

Finally, if a Dd statement ddname is not qualified by a stepname when making modifications or additions, a default to the first step is assumed, with one exception. If a previous modification or addition has been made to a succeeding step, a default to that step is assumed. To avoid confusion, the author strongly recommends that a stepname always be coded to indicate as well as document to which step a particular modification or addition applies.

C. PROGRAM TRANSLATION AND CONVERSION

After a computer program has been written (coded), it must be translated and converted to executable machine language form. This overall operation consists of three primary processes. They are:

Compilation;
Linkage; and
Execution.

Many catalogued procedures can be called to accomplish one or a combination of these processes for each programming language and its levels.

1. Compilation

The Compilation process consists of three primary functions -- Interpretation, Translation, and Assembly. All higher-level English-like source programs must be compiled. Assembler language source programs need only be interpreted and assembled. Figure 5.5 displays a typical flowchart of the compilation process.

Figure 5.5 Compilation Process Flowchart

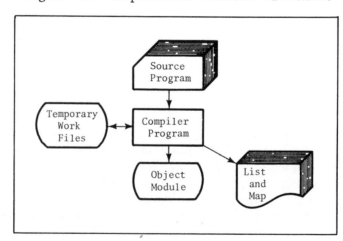

The flowchart in Figure 5.5 depicts a couple of significant points. First, the source program is not really a program at this stage. Rather, it is nothing more than an input file to the compiler program. Each compiler is uniquely written for each programming language and level. Second, the main output from the compiler is an object module. An object module is in nearly 100% machine-executable form. Temporary work files are also required by the compilation process. Various printed outputs, of which program listings and maps are the most critical, are created.

The sequence of compiling activities is as follows. A source program is read as input by the Compiler or Assembly program. For Assembler source programs, individual Assembly statements are generated from macro instructions. The Compiler or Assembler program next checks for syntax errors according to the rules and conventions of the programming language and level utilized (Interpretation). Program logic can also be examined to a small degree. A series of one or more Assembler statements are next generated for each higher-level English-like program statement (Translation). A list of the source program and resulting assembly language representation can be optionally printed for future debugging purposes. Assembler statements and symbolic addresses are next converted to absolute machine statements and relative address on a one-for-one basis (Assembly). The program is now relocatable, i.e., it can be stored in any area of available main storage. Those statements which call or reference external program modules, routines, and functions must await the linkage process to be satisfied. Input/Output (I/O) routines which must be linked to the main program are a common example. Therefore, the output object module is considered close to, but not yet completely in, 100% machine-executable form. Object modules are generally stored as temporary disk files.

2. Linkage

The Linkage process consists of two primary functions -- Module Linkage and Segment Overlay, though other, less frequently utilized linkage functions can be performed. The linkage program is referred to as the Linkage Editor. It is not unique to specific programming languages or levels. Program object modules are linked to satisfy external references and overlay techniques utilized in the source program. Figure 5.6 displays a typical flowchart of the linkage process.

The flowchart in Figure 5.6 depicts a couple of significant points. First, the program object module is still not a completely executable program at this stage. Rather, it is an input file to the Linkage Editor program. Linkage program IEWL is common to all programming languages and levels. Second, the main output from the linkage editor is a load module. A load module is in 100% machine-executable form. All call statements to external references have been satisfied by accessing various system program libraries and obtaining the modules or routines of interest, e.g., I/O routines, mathematical functions, data conversion, etc. Once located, they are attached (or linked) to the object module, thus forming a load module. References to specific segments within an overlay tree structure are also generated. The overlay feature is a technique which calls and loads only those routines which need to reside in main storage at the same time. Main storage requirements are minimized using this module-swapping tech-

Figure 5.6 Linkage Process Flowchart

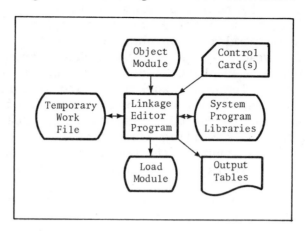

nique. A temporary work file is required by the linkage editor program. One or more control cards may also be required to handle the
assignment of program names, to direct overlay references, and to
perform other linkage functions. Various printed outputs, of which
a cross-reference table is the most critical, are also created.

The sequence of linkage activities is as follows. An object
module is read as input by the linkage editor program along with
perhaps one or more control cards to direct linkage functions. The
program accesses available system libraries for the called program
modules or routines of interest. They are then linked to the main
program module. Appropriate overlay references are also set up.
Optional output tables are then printed. The output load module
is now in 100% machine-executable form and may be stored, fetched,
and/or loaded into main storage as a program module. Load modules
are generally stored on disk, usually permanently or at least until
replaced by an updated version.

It should be pointed out that the Loader process can be utilized
in lieu of linkage functions if specific features of the linkage
editor program are not desired. Loader techniques will be discussed
later in this chapter.

3. Execution

Now that a fully executable load module has been created, it can
be fetched and loaded into main storage for execution. This is
accomplished via the Program (PGM) parameter on an Exec statement.
Of course, other Exec keyword parameters may need to be provided
in addition to a Dd statement for each file to be processed.

D. CATALOGUED PROCEDURE UTILIZATION

Various catalogued procedures are available to accomplish compilation, linkage, and execution. The three most frequently utilized are
Compile Only, Compile and Link, and Compile and Link and Execute. Other
combinations will also be discussed. Many dp installations modify
standard vendor-supplied procedures somewhat to suit user preferences
and standards. Though the author will generally attempt to display
procedures as originally supplied by the vendor, procedures displayed
in this text occasionally reflect slight but common dp installation

148

modifications. A catalogued procedure listing depicting specific procedure content in a dp installation can easily be obtained using a utility program to be discussed in the next chapter.

1. Compile Only

At least one catalogued procedure which compiles only is available at dp installations for each programming language supported. Compile Only procedures are used in the early stages of program syntax testing when there is no particular need to link and execute. They are also used when the output object module is to be stored rather than linked. Figure 5.7 displays four catalogued procedures which compile American National Standard (ANS) COBOL Version 4, FORTRAN IV G1-Level, PL/1 F-Level, and ASSEMBLER F-Level source programs. Standard names for these procedures are COBUC, FTG1C, PL1FC, and ASMFC, respectively. The last letter 'C' stands for Compile. The letter(s) next to the last character are an indication of programming language level, e.g., 'G1' for Level G1, while the first two or three characters are an abbreviation of the programming language utilized.

Figure 5.7 Compile Only Procedures

```
COBUC:

//COB EXEC PGM=IKFCBL00,REGION=130K,
//        PARM='NOLOAD'
//STEPLIB DD DSNAME=SYS1.COBLIB,DISP=SHR
//SYSPRINT DD SYSOUT=A
//SYSPUNCH DD SYSOUT=B
//SYSUT1 DD UNIT=SYSDA,DSNAME=&SYSUT1,SPACE=(460,(700,300),RLSE)
//SYSUT2 DD UNIT=SYSDA,DSNAME=&SYSUT2,SPACE=(460,(700,300),RLSE)
//SYSUT3 DD UNIT=SYSDA,DSNAME=&SYSUT3,SPACE=(460,(700,300),RLSE)
//SYSUT4 DD UNIT=SYSDA,DSNAME=&SYSUT4,SPACE=(460,(700,300),RLSE)
_____
FTG1C:

//FORT EXEC PGM=IGIFORT,REGION=130K
//STEPLIB DD DSNAME=SYS1.FORTLIB,DISP=SHR
//SYSPRINT DD SYSOUT=A
//SYSPUNCH DD SYSOUT=B
//SYSLIN DD UNIT=SYSDA,DISP=(MOD,PASS),
//        DSNAME=&LOADSET,DCB=BLKSIZE=3200,
//        SPACE=(3200,(60,60),RLSE)
```

Figure 5.7 Compile Only Procedures (cont.)

```
PL1LFC:

//PL1L EXEC PGM=IEMAA,REGION=100K,
//       PARM='NOLOAD'
//SYSPRINT DD SYSOUT=A
//SYSPUNCH DD SYSOUT=B
//SYSUT3 DD UNIT=SYSDA,
//       DSNAME=&SYSUT3,DCB=BLKSIZE=3200,

//       SPACE=(3200,(10,10))
//SYSUT1 DD UNIT=SYSDA,
//       DSNAME=&SYSUT1,DCB=BLKSIZE=1024,
//       SPACE=(1024,(60,60)
```

```
ASMFC:

//ASM EXEC PGM=IEUASM,REGION=80K,
//       PARM='LIST'
//SYSPRINT DD SYSOUT=A
//SYSPUNCH DD SYSOUT=B
//SYSUT1 DD UNIT=SYSDA,DSNAME=&SYSUT1,SPACE=(3200,(80,80))
//SYSUT2 DD UNIT=SYSDA,DSNAME=&SYSUT2,SPACE=(3200,(80,80))
//SYSUT3 DD UNIT=SYSDA,DSNAME=&SYSUT3,SPACE=(3200,(80,80))
//SYSLIB DD DSNAME=SYS1.MACLIB,DISP=SHR
```

The first statement in the procedures in Figure 5.7 calls the appropriate language compiler or assembly program, allocates main storage for this program, and usually modifies program default parameter information via the Parm parameter. Specific compiler level libraries may be called to supplement a given compiler's capabilities. The next two statements describe the compiler or assembly program message file and an optional object module punch file for ddnames SYSPRINT and SYSPUNCH, respectively. Next, any statement with ddname SYSUT1 through SYSUT4 defines temporary work files. The coding of one ampersand (&) in front of a data set name defines that specification as a symbolic option and/or temporary data set. (The use of symbolic parameters will be described in the last chapter of this text.) The object module is described via ddname SYSLIN in the FORTRAN procedure, while the macro statement library is described via ddname SYSLIB in the ASSEMBLER procedure. The Dd * statement to read the source file as input to the compiler is not included as part of the procedure. Dd * statements are not allowed in procedures. This is because they must be coded anyhow when the procedure is called such that the source program can be inserted directly behind it. The actual coding of JCL to call these procedures can now begin.

a. COBOL Programs

Assume that one has just coded an American National Standard (ANS) COBOL program and wishes to test-edit for syntax and obvious logic errors. Linkage and execution are not desired at this point. Rather, we wish to compile only. An example of JCL which could be coded to meet this objective is as follows:

```
//JCLTEXT  JOB  XYZABC123,TOBIN,MSGLEVEL=(1,1),CLASS=A
//STEP1  EXEC  PROC=COBUC
//COB.SYSIN  DD  *
    - - - - ANS COBOL Program Here - - - -
//
```

Following the appropriate Job statement is an Exec statement which calls the one-step procedure of interest, COBUC. See the first procedure listed in Figure 5.7. A region size of 130,000 bytes of main storage has been specified for compiler program IKFCBL00. NOLOAD has been specified via the Parm parameter. NOLOAD requests that an output object module not be created and passed to a linkage step. If it were created, a SYSLIN ddname file would need to be described and added to the compile step. There is no particular need at this time to modify or add new Exec statement parameter information. Similarly, there is no need to modify existing Dd statements for ddnames SYSPRINT, SYSPUNCH, and SYSUT1 through SYSUT4, as they are required by the compiler and have been set up accordingly. SYSPRINT is a compiler message file; SYSPUNCH is a punch file if the DECK option has been specified via a Parm parameter; and SYSUT1 through SYSUT4 are temporary disk compiler work files.

What is missing in the procedure, however, is the Dd * statement to read the input source program file. It needs to be added to the COB step. Coding //COB.SYSIN DD * in the JCL job stream effectively adds a temporary Dd * statement named SYSIN to the COB (first) step of the procedure. This is followed by the source program itself, as the compiler contains a description for a file named SYSIN which defines the source program as input. A Null statement follows the program to indicate the end of this particular job stream. Printed output includes a JCL listing with file allocation and termination messages, a compiler listing of the source program, and a program error listing. Other printed outputs such as maps, a deck, cross-references, etc., may be requested via the Parm parameter. They will be covered

151

in the Compile and Link section of this chapter, where they are more frequently utilized.

A comparable Compile Only catalogued procedure exists for other COBOL programming levels as well. The names of the procedures are only slightly changed. Instead of COBUC, for example, the catalogued procedure to compile Level-F COBOL programs is named COBFC. That is, the letter 'U' is replaced by the letter 'F'. Other levels also reflect comparable name changes. The only essential difference among these procedures is that a different compiler program is called. Aside from that, the method of calling the procedure is the same; the technique of modifying or adding to the procedure is identical; and other than procedure and compiler names, the content of the procedure itself is essentially the same as other COBOL programming levels. A check with the dp installation should be made, as unique user standards and preferences may affect the specific makeup of a given procedure.

b. FORTRAN Programs

Assume that one has just coded a FORTRAN IV Level-G1 program and wishes to test-edit for syntax and obvious logic errors. Linkage and execution are not desired at this point. Rather, we wish to compile only. An example of JCL which could be coded to meet this objective is as follows:

```
//JCLTEXT   JOB   XYZABC123,TOBIN,MSGLEVEL=(1,1),CLASS=A
//STEP1   EXEC   PROC=FTG1C,
//          PARM.FORT='NOLOAD'
//FORT.SYSIN   DD   *
   -   -   -   -   FORTRAN IV (G1) Program Here   -   -   -   -
//
```

Following the appropriate Job statement is an Exec statement which calls the one-step procedure of interest, FTG1C. See the second procedure list in Figure 5.7. A region size of 130,000 bytes of main storage has been specified for compiler program IGIFORT. NOLOAD has not been specified via the Parm parameter. LOAD, which is the compiler's default, requests that an output object module be created and passed to a linkage step. Assuming we do not desire an object module, coding PARM.FORT='NOLOAD' in the JCL job stream effectively adds a temporary specification of NOLOAD to the compiler via a Parm parameter on the Exec statement in the FORT step of the procedure. Otherwise, there is no particular need at this time to modify or add new Exec statement parameter information. Similarly, there is no need to modify existing Dd statements for ddnames SYSPRINT, SYSPUNCH, and SYSLIN. An object module would have been created for the SYSLIN ddname file had NOLOAD not been specified when calling the procedure. This technique will be discussed in the Compile and Link section of this chapter.

What is missing in the procedure, however, is the Dd * statement to read the input source program file. It needs to be added to the

FORT step. Coding //FORT.SYSIN DD * in the JCL job stream effectively adds a temporary Dd * statement named SYSIN to the FORT (first) step of the procedure. This is followed by the source program itself, as the compiler contains a description for a file name SYSIN which defines the source program as input. A Null statement follows the program to indicate the end of this particular job stream. Output includes a JCL listing with file allocation and termination messages, a listing of the source program, and a syntactical program error listing. Other printed outputs such as maps, a deck, cross-references, etc. may be requested via the Parm parameter. They will be covered in the Compile and Link section of this chapter where they are more frequently utilized.

A comparable Compile Only catalogued procedure exists for other FORTRAN programming levels as well. The names of the procedures are only slightly changed. Instead of FTG1C, for example, the catalogued procedure to compile Level-H FORTRAN IV programs is named FORTHC. Other levels also reflect comparable name changes. The only essential difference among these procedures is that a different compiler is called for execution purposes. Compiler work files may also be provided on occasion. Other than that, the method of calling the procedure is the same; the technique of modifying or adding to the procedure is identical; and other than procedure and compiler names, the content of the procedure itself is essentially the same as for other FORTRAN programming levels. A check with the dp installation should be made, as unique user standards and preferences may affect the specific makeup of a given procedure.

c. Programming Language/One (PL/1) Differences

Assume that one has just coded a PL/1 Level-F program and wishes to test-edit for syntax and obvious logic errors. An example of JCL which could be coded to meet this objective is as follows:

```
//JCLTEXT  JOB  XYZABC123,TOBIN,MSGLEVEL=(1,1),CLASS=A
//STEP1  EXEC  PROC=PL1LFC
//PL1L.SYSIN  DD  *
   -  -  -  -  PL/1 (F) Program Here  -  -  -  -
//
```

See the third procedure list in Figure 5.7. NOLOAD has been specified to the compiler program via the Parm parameter. As a result, an output module will not be created and passed to a linkage step. If it were created, a SYSLIN ddname file would need to be described and added to the compile step. Other ddnames defined in this procedure also have similar functions as discussed in preceding examples.

A Dd * statement to read the input source program file is also missing and needs to be added to the PL1L step. Coding //PL1L.SYSIN DD * in the JCL job stream effectively adds a temporary Dd * statement named SYSIN to the PL1L (first) step of the procedure. This is followed by the source program itself. Outputs are the same as discussed in preceding examples.

153

A comparable Compile Only catalogued procedure exists for other PL/1 programming levels as well. The names of the procedures are only slightly changed to reflect the programming level utilized, though a check with your dp installation should be made.

d. ASSEMBLER and Other Program Language Considerations

Assume that one has just coded an ASSEMBLER Level-F program and wishes to test-edit for syntax and obvious logic errors. An example of JCL which could be coded to meet this objective is as follows:

```
//JCLTEXT  JOB  XYZABC123,TOBIN,MSGLEVEL=(1,1),CLASS=A
//STEP1  EXEC  PROC=ASMFC
//ASM.SYSIN  DD  *
    -  -  -  -  ASSEMBLER (F) Program Here  -  -  -  -
//
```

See the fourth procedure list in Figure 5.7. LIST has been specified to the assembly program via the Parm parameter, as NOLIST is the assembly program's default. LIST will generate a source program assembler language listing as output. If an object module were to be created, a SYSGO ddname file would need to be described and added to the assembly step. This differs from previous procedures where ddname SYSLIN represented the object module. LOAD would also need to be specified to the assembly program, as NOLOAD is the default. Also note the presence of a SYSLIB Dd statement describing a macro library as input to the assembly program. The program accesses this appropriate macro library to generate individual ASSEMBLER statements from macro instructions representing an overall function to be performed. Other ddnames defined in this procedure have similar functions as discussed in preceding examples.

A Dd * statement to read the input source program file is also missing and needs to be added to the ASM step. Coding //ASM.SYSIN DD * in the JCL job stream effectively adds a temporary Dd * statement named SYSIN to the ASM (first) step of the procedure. This is followed by the source program itself. Outputs are the same as discussed in preceding examples.

A comparable Assemble Only catalogued procedure exists for other ASSEMBLER programming levels as well. The names of the procedures are only slightly changed to reflect the programming level utilized. Other program languages also follow these same concepts and principles. The procedure name follows previously discussed standards. That is, procedure RPGEC would be called to compile only a Report Program Generator (RPG) Level-E program. Various programming levels are also reflected in the procedure name. A unique compiler name would be coded in the procedure itself. Exec statement parameters and ddnames defined in these procedures have similar functions as discussed in preceding examples. A check with the dp installation should be made, as unique user standards and preferences may affect the specific makeup of any given procedure.

2. Compile and Link

At least one catalogued procedure which compiles and links is available at dp installations for each programming language supported. Compile and Link catalogued procedures are generally used after program testing is completed and/or after needed minor changes are made. At this point the load module is ready to be permanently stored in a program library. Figure 5.8 displays four catalogued procedures which compile and link American National Standard (ANS) COBOL Version 4, FORTRAN IV G1-Level, PL/1 F-Level, and ASSEMBLER F-Level source programs. Standard names for these procedures are COBUCL, FTG1CL, PL1LFCL, and ASMFCL, respectively. The last two letters 'CL' stand for Compile and Link; the letter(s) next to the last two characters are an indication of programming language level, e.g., 'G1' for Level G1, while the remaining first two or three characters are an abbreviation of the programming language utilized.

Figure 5.8 Compile and Link Procedures

```
COBUCL:

//COB EXEC PGM=IKFCBLOO,REGION=130K
//STEPLIB DD DSNAME=SYS1.COBLIB,DISP=SHR
//SYSPRINT DD SYSOUT=A
//SYSPUNCH DD SYSOUT=B
//SYSUT1 DD UNIT=SYSDA,DSNAME=&SYSUT1,SPACE=(460,(700,300),RLSE)
//SYSUT2 DD UNIT=SYSDA,DSNAME=&SYSUT2,SPACE=(460,(700,300),RLSE)
//SYSUT3 DD UNIT=SYSDA,DSNAME=&SYSUT3,SPACE=(460,(700,300),RLSE)
//SYSUT4 DD UNIT=SYSDA,DSNAME=&SYSUT4,SPACE=(460,(700,300),RLSE)
//SYSLIN DD UNIT=SYSDA,DISP=(MOD,PASS),
//         DSNAME=&LOADSET,DCB=BLKSIZE=3200,
//         SPACE=(3200,(20,20),RLSE)
//LKED EXEC PGM=IEWL,REGION=100K,
//         PARM='LET,LIST,XREF',
//         COND=(4,LT,COB)
//SYSPRINT DD SYSOUT=A
//SYSUT1 DD UNIT=SYSDA,DSNAME=&SYSUT1,SPACE=(1024,(50,20))
//SYSLIN DD DSNAME=&LOADSET,DISP=(OLD,DELETE)
//         DD DDNAME=SYSIN
//SYSLIB DD DSNAME=SYS1.COBLIB,DISP=SHR
//SYSLMOD DD UNIT=SYSDA,DISP=(NEW,PASS),
//
//         DSNAME=&GOSET(RUN),DCB=BLKSIZE=1024,
//         SPACE=(1024,(50,20,1),RLSE)
```

```
FTG1CL:


//FORT EXEC PGM=IGIFORT,REGION=130K
//STEPLIB DD DSNAME=SYSL.FORTLIB,DISP=SHR
//SYSPRINT DD SYSOUT=A
//SYSPUNCH DD SYSOUT=B
//SYSLIN DD UNIT=SYSDA,DISP=(MOD,PASS),
//       DSNAME=&LOADSET,DCB=BLKSIZE=3200,
//       SPACE=(3200,(60,60),RLSE)
//LKED EXEC PGM=IEWL,REGION=100K,
//       PARM='LET,LIST,XREF',
//       COND=(4,LT,FORT)
//SYSPRINT DD SYSOUT=A
//SYSUT1 DD UNIT=SYSDA,DSNAME=&SYSUT1,SPACE=(1024,(20,20))
//SYSLIN DD DSNAME=&LOADSET,DISP=(OLD,DELETE)
//       DD DDNAME=SYSIN
//SYSLIB DD DSNAME=SYS1.FORTLIB,DISP=SHR
//SYSLMOD DD UNIT=SYSDA,DISP=(NEW,PASS),
//       DSNAME=&GOSET(MAIN),DCB=BLKSIZE=1024,
//       SPACE=(1024,(20,20),1),RLSE)
```

```
PL1LFCL:

//PL1L EXEC PGM=IEMAA,REGION=100K
//SYSPRINT DD SYSOUT=A
//SYSPUNCH DD SYSOUT=B
//SYSUT3 DD UNIT=SYSDA,
//       DSNAME=&SYSUT3,DCB=BLKSIZE=3200,
//       SPACE=(3200,(10,10))
//SYSUT1 DD UNIT=SYSDA,
//       DSNAME=&SYSUT1,DCB=BLKSIZE=1024,
//       SPACE=(1024,(60,60))
//SYSLIN DD UNIT=SYSDA,DISP=(MOD,PASS),
//       DSNAME=&LOADSET,DCB=BLKSIZE=3200,
//       SPACE=(3200,(10,10),RLSE)
```

```
//LKED EXEC PGM=IEWL,REGION=100K,
//         PARM='LET,LIST,XREF',
//         COND=(4,LT,PL1L)
//SYSPRINT DD SYSOUT=A
//SYSUT1 DD UNIT=SYSDA,DSNAME=&SYSUT1,SPACE=(1024,(200,20))
//SYSLIN DD DSNAME=&LOADSET,DISP=(OLD,DELETE)
//       DD DDNAME=SYSIN
//SYSLIB DD DSNAME=SYS1.PL1LIB,DISP=SHR
//SYSLMOD DD UNIT=SYSDA,DISP=(MOD,PASS),
//         DSNAME=&GOSET(GO),DCB=BLKSIZE=1024,
//         SPACE=(1024,(50,20),RLSE)
```

ASMFCL:

```
//ASM EXEC PGM=IEUASM,REGION=80K,
//         PARM='LOAD,LIST,XREF'
//SYSPRINT DD SYSOUT=A
//SYSPUNCH DD SYSOUT=B
//SYSUT1 DD UNIT=SYSDA,DSNAME=&SYSUT1,SPACE=(3200,(80,80))
//SYSUT2 DD UNIT=SYSDA,DSNAME=&SYSUT2,SPACE=(3200,(80,80))
//SYSUT3 DD UNIT=SYSDA,DSNAME=&SYSUT3,SPACE=(3200,(80,80))
//SYSLIB DD DSNAME=SYS1.MACLIB,DISP=SHR
//SYSGO DD UNIT=SYSDA,DISP=(MOD,PASS),
//         DSNAME=&LOADSET,DCB=BLKSIZE=3200,
//         SPACE=(3200,(10,10),RLSE)
//LKED EXEC PGM=IEWL,REGION=100K,
//         PARM='LET,LIST,XREF,NCAL',
//         COND=(4,LT,ASM)
//SYSPRINT DD SYSOUT=A
//SYSUT1 DD UNIT=SYSDA,DSNAME=&SYSUT1,SPACE=(1024,(50,50))
//SYSLIN DD DSNAME=&LOADSET,DISP=(OLD,DELETE)
//       DD DDNAME=SYSIN
//SYSLMOD DD UNIT=SYSDA,DISP =(MOD,PASS),
//         DSNAME=&GOSET(GO),DCB=BLKSIZE=1024,
//         SPACE=(1024,(50,20),RLSE)
```

The first statement in each of the two-step procedures in Figure 5.8 calls the same language compiler or assembly program and allocates the same amount of storage as in the previous Compile Only procedure examples. In addition, a Parm parameter is provided in the ASSEMBLER Compile and Link procedure to specify LOAD, LIST, and XREF in lieu of comparable program defaults. Specific compiler level libraries may be called to supplement a given compiler's capabilities. The next two statements in each procedure describes the compiler or assembly program message file and an optional object module punch file. Next, any statement with ddnames SYSUT1 through SYSUT4 defines temporary work files. The coding of one ampersand (&) in front of a data set name defines that specification as a symbolic option and/or temporary data set. (The use of symbolic parameters will be described in the last chapter of this text.) Next, a macro statement library named SYS1.MACLIB is described via ddname SYSLIB in the ASSEMBLER procedure. Finally, an object module is described via ddname SYSLIN or SYSGO in all procedures. This file is passed to the linkage step. A Dd * statement to read the input source program via ddname SYSIN is not allowed to be catalogued and therefore is not present.

The first statement in the second step of each of the above two-step procedures calls the same linkage editor program, IEWL. The linkage editor is not specific to the original source language utilized. This statement also allocates an identical amount of main storage in each case as well as provides LET, LIST, and XREF parameter information to the linkage program. NCAL is also specified in the Assembler procedure. LET allows the output load module to be marked as executable even though one or more errors occurred during the linkage process. LIST specifies that the control card(s) supplied to the linkage program should be listed as part of print output. XREF requests that a cross-reference table of external references including a map of relative module locations also be printed as output. NCAL indicates that an Assembler library search should not be made; a SYSLIB DD Statement is not provided. A Condition parameter on each of these Exec statements specifies that if 4 is less than the return code issued by the first step, the linkage step should be bypassed. In other words, there is no need to link a program which still contains conditional-level errors.

The next statement in each procedure with ddname SYSPRINT describes the linkage editor message file. This is followed by a SYSUT1 ddname temporary disk work file. The object module passed from the compile or assembly step is described next for ddname SYSLIN as input to the linkage program. It is deleted at the end of the step. A file which defers the definition of a data set to be later identified with the ddname of SYSIN is concatenated to the input object module. A specific use for this file will be discussed shortly. With the exception of the ASSEMBLER procedure, appropriate program libraries are accessed next via the SYSLIB Dd statement. Appropriate ASSEMBLER macro libraries had been accessed in the assembly step. Finally, a SYSLMOD ddname file describes the output load module as a disk data set to be passed to another step. The JCL for this file will need to be modified. Depending upon use, one may also need to provide a SYSIN Dd * statement to read one or more linkage editor input control card(s). The actual coding of JCL to call these procedures can now begin.

a. COBOL Programs

Assume that one has coded and fully tested an American National
Standard (ANS) COBOL program and wishes to store the executable program load module into a private partitioned data set library. Execution is not desired at this point. Rather, we wish to compile and
link only. An example of JCL which could be coded to meet this objective is as follows:

```
//EXAMPLE  JOB   (123,PROJ2),IMP,MSGLEVEL=(1,1),CLASS=A
//STEP1 EXEC   PROC=COBUCL,
//        PARM.COB='CLIST,DMAP,XREF'
//COB.SYSIN  DD  *

   -  -  -  - ANS COBOL Program Here  -  -  -  -

/*
//LKED.SYSLMOD   DD   DSNAME=A.PROGRAM.LIBRARY,DISP=SHR
//LKED.SYSIN  DD   *
   NAME   AEDIT(R)
//
```

Following the appropriate Job statement is an Exec statement which
calls the two-step procedure of interest, COBUCL. See the first procedure listed in Figure 5.8. A region size of 130,000 bytes of main
storage has been specified for compiler program IKFCBLOO.

No Parm parameter specifications have been provided, though at this
stage in program development some parameter information is desired.
CLIST, DMAP, and XREF should be provided to the COB step via a Parm
parameter. This has been accomplished in the above job stream example.
A Condensed Listing (CLIST) is an abbreviated print of the assembly
language listing in that it shows the relative length of each source
statement into the program module. A Data Map (DMAP) provides a listing of program variable names, their relative location, level, field
length, type of data representation utilized, and other characteristics
for each program variable defined in the program. A Cross-Reference
Table (XREF) is a listing of program variable names as well as paragraph names depicting in which source statement they are defined and
referenced within the program. These three outputs are very handy
references in program-debugging situations. Requesting a Procedure
Map (PMAP) in combination with a DMAP in lieu of a CLIST will generate a complete assembly language listing if desired, e.g., PARM.COB=
'DMAP,PMAP,XREF'. A complete description of all compiler options is
presented in Appendix C. Other than the above, there is no need to
modify or add new Exec statement parameter information.

There is also no need to modify existing Dd statements in the COB step for ddnames SYSPRINT, SYSPUNCH, SYSUT1 through SYSUT4, and SYSLIN, as they are required by the compiler and have been accounted for accordingly. The ddname SYSLIN disk file is the compiler output object module which is subsequently passed to the linkage step. What is missing in the compiler step of the procedure, however, is the Dd * statement to read the input source program file. It needs to be added to the COB step. Coding //COB.SYSIN DD * in the JCL job stream effectively adds a temporary Dd * statement named SYSIN to the COB (first) step of the procedure. This is followed by the source program itself as the compiler contains a description for a file named SYSIN which defines the source program as input.

The second step of the COBUCL procedure named LKED calls the linkage editor program. A region size of 100,000 bytes of main storage has been specified for program IEWL. LET, LIST, and XREF have been specified to the LKED step via the Parm parameter. A Condition parameter has also been coded in the procedure to avoid occasional needless linkage processing. There is no particular need to modify or add new Exec statement parameter information for this application. Similarly, there is no need to modify existing Dd statements in the linkage step for ddnames SYSPRINT, SYSUT1, SYSLIN, and SYSLIB, as they are required by the linkage editor and have been accounted for accordingly.

What needs to be modified in the linkage step of the procedure, however, is the Dd statement's description of the SYSLMOD ddname disk file. This file is the linkage editor's program load module output and is now in 100% machine-executable form. Also, a Dd * statement to read an input program card is not included in the procedure. Both of these changes should be made to the linkage step when calling this procedure. Coding

```
//LKED.SYSLMOD  DD  DSNAME=A.PROGRAM.LIBRARY,DISP=SHR
```

in the JCL job stream effectively modifies the Dd statement named SYSLMOD in the LKED (second) step of the procedure. The load module will now be placed into a private library named A.PROGRAM.LIBRARY. The partitioned data set (PDS) is also shared concurrently by other users per Disposition parameter specifications. (The technique of creating PDS libraries will be described in the next chapter.) Next, coding //LKED.SYSIN DD * in the JCL job stream effectively adds a temporary Dd * statement named SYSIN to the linkage step of the procedure. This is followed by a program name card, as the linkage editor contains a description for a file named SYSIN which defines this control card and others as input. Referencing the input ddname SYSLIN file, it can be seen that this SYSIN file is concatenated to the input object module. The Ddname keyword parameter specified that its definition be delayed -- until now, that is! The Program Name Control Card is represented by the following format:

```
NAME    Program Name(R)
```

leaving at least column 1 blank, then coding the actual characters 'NAME', then coding the program name desired using standard naming conventions and rules, and finally coding an 'R' in parentheses. The

R stands for Replace; that is, if a module by an identical name already exists in the library, it is to be replaced by the current one. It is a good standard to always code the R. If a module by the indicated name does not exist, it will automatically be added to the library anyhow. In the preceding JCL job stream example, a program name of AEDIT was chosen. The load module named AEDIT will be placed as a member into the partitioned data set library named A.PROGRAM.LIBRARY. AEDIT will be flagged as the most current, thus replacing any members previously named AEDIT. An alternative method of specifying program name will be discussed later in this chapter.

A Null statement follows the program name card to indicate the end of this particular job stream. Printed output includes a JCL listing with file allocation and termination messages, a compiler listing of the source program, a program error listing, condensed assembly language listing, data map, cross-reference table, a linkage editor message indicating that the new load module has been added to the library or replaced an existing member, and a cross-reference control section listing from the linkage editor. These are standard compiler and linkage editor outputs which should be requested via JCL Parm parameter specifications discussed previously if they are not a default of the compiler, linkage editor, or procedure itself. Compiler and linkage editor options and their functions are depicted in Appendix C.

A comparable Compile and Link catalogued procedure exists for other COBOL programming levels as well. The names of the procedures are only slightly changed. Instead of COBUCL, for example, the catalogued procedure to compile and link Level-F COBOL program is named COBFCL. That is, the letter 'U' is replaced by the letter 'F'. Other levels also reflect comparable name changes. The only essential difference among these procedures is that a different compiler program is called. Aside from that, the method of calling the procedure is the same; the technique of modifying or adding to the procedure is identical; and other than procedure and compiler names, the content of the procedure itself is essentially the same as other COBOL programming levels. A check with the dp installation should be made, as unique user standards and preferences may affect the specific makeup of a given procedure.

b. FORTRAN Programs

Assume that one has coded and fully tested a FORTRAN IV Level-G1 program and wishes to store the executable program load module into a private partitioned data set library. Execution is not desired at this point. Rather, we wish to compile and link only. An example of JCL which could be coded to meet this objective is as follows:

```
//EXAMPLE  JOB  (123,PROJ2),IMP,MSGLEVEL=(1,1),CLASS=A
//STEP1 EXEC  PROC=FTG1CL,
//       PARM.FORT='LIST'
//FORT.SYSIN  DD  *
     -  -  -  - FORTRAN IV (G1) Program Here -  -  -  -
```

```
          /*
          //LKED.SYSLMOD  DD   DSNAME=A.PROGRAM.LIBRARY,DISP=SHR
          //LKED.SYSIN DD   *
             NAME  ASUM(R)
          //
```

Following the appropriate Job statement an Exec statement calls
the two-step procedure of interest, FTG1CL. See the second procedure
listed in Figure 5.8'. A region size of 130,000 bytes of main storage
has been specified for compiler program IGIFORT.

No Parm parameter specifications have been provided in the compile
step, though at this late stage in program development some parameter
information is desired. LIST should be provided to the FORT step via
a Parm parameter. This has been accomplished in the above job stream
example. List (LIST) refers to the generation and printing of a complete assembly language listing. A Map (MAP) should also be specified
and generated if the NOMAP option has been coded in the procedure.
These two outputs are very handy references in program-debugging
situations. Unfortunately, a Condensed Listing (CLIST) of the assembly language representation of the source program is not a valid
FORTRAN option. A complete description of all compiler options is
presented in Appendix C. Other than the above, there is no need to
modify or add new Exec statement parameter information.

There is also no need to modify existing Dd statements in the
FORT step for ddnames SYSPRINT, SYSPUNCH, and SYSLIN, as they are
required by the compiler and have been accounted for accordingly.
The ddname SYSLIN disk file is the compiler output object module
which is subsequently passed to the linkage step. What is missing
in the compile step of the procedure, however, is the Dd * statement
to read the input source program file. It needs to be added to the
FORT step. Coding //FORT.SYSIN DD * in the JCL job stream effectively
adds a temporary Dd * statement named SYSLIN to the FORT (first) step
of the procedure. This is followed by the source program itself,
as the compiler contains a description for a file named SYSIN which
defines the source program as input.

The second step of the FTG1CL procedure named LKED calls the linkage editor program. A region size of 100,000 bytes of main storage
has been specified for program IEWL. LET, LIST, and XREF have been
specified to the LKED step via the Parm parameter. A Condition parameter has also been coded to avoid occasional needless linkage
processing. There is no particular need to modify or add new Exec
statement parameter information for this application. Similarly,
there is no need to modify existing Dd statements in the linkage
step for ddnames SYSPRINT, SYSUT1, SYSLIN, and SYSLIB, as they are
required by the linkage editor and have been accounted for accordingly.

What needs to be modified in the linkage step of the procedure,
however, is the Dd statement's description of the SYSLMOD ddname disk
file. This file is the linkage editor's program load module output
and is now in 100% machine-executable form. Also, a Dd * statement
to read an input program card is not included in the procedure. Both
of these changes should be made to the linkage step when calling this

162

procedure. Coding

```
//LKED.SYSLMOD  DD  DSNAME=A.PROGRAM.LIBRARY,DISP=SHR
```

in the JCL job stream effectively modifies the Dd statement named
SYSLMOD in the LKED (second) step of the procedure. The load module
will now be placed into a private library named A.PROGRAM.LIBRARY.
The partitioned data set (PDS) is also shared concurrently by other
users per Disposition parameter specifications. (The technique of
creating PDS libraries will be discussed in the next chapter.) Next,
coding //LKED.SYSIN DD * in the JCL job stream effectively adds
a temporary Dd * statement named SYSIN to the linkage step of the
procedure. This is followed by a program name card as the linkage
editor contains a description for a file named SYSIN which defines
the control card and others as input. Referencing the input ddname
SYSIN file, it can be seen that this delayed SYSIN file is concatenated to the input object module. This card file is supplied last,
as its definition had been deferred. In the preceding JCL job
stream example, a program name card of NAME ASUM(R) was coded.
The load module named ASUM will be placed as a member into the
partitioned data set library named A.PROGRAM.LIBRARY. ASUM will
be flagged as the most current, thus replacing any members previously named ASUM. An alternative method of specifying program
name will be discussed later in this chapter.

A Null statement follows the program name card to indicate the
end of this particular job stream. Printed output includes a JCL
listing with file allocation and termination messages, and compiler
listing of the source program, a program error listing, assembly
language listing, program map, a linkage editor message indicating
that the new named load module has been added to the library or
replaced an existing member, and a cross-reference control section
listing from the linkage editor. These are standard outputs which
should be requested via JCL Parm parameter specifications discussed
previously if they are not a default of the compiler, linkage
editor, or procedure itself. Compiler and linkage editor options
and their functions are depicted in Appendix C.

A comparable Compile and Link catalogued procedure exists for
other FORTRAN programming levels as well. The names of the procedures are only slightly changed. Instead of FTG1CL, for example,
the catalogued procedure to compile and link Level-H FORTRAN IV
programs is named FORTHCL. Other levels also reflect comparable
name changes. The only essential difference among these procedures
is that a different compiler program is called for execution purposes.
Compiler work files may also be provided on occasion. Other than
that, the method of calling the procedure is the same; the technique
of modifying or adding to the procedure is identical; and other than
procedure and compiler names, the content of the procedure itself
is essentially the same as other FORTRAN programming levels. A
check with the dp installation should be made, as unique user standards and preferences may affect the specific makeup of a given procedure.

c. Programming Language/One (PL/1) Differences

Assume that one has coded and fully tested a PL/1 Level-F program and wishes to store the executable program load module into a private partitioned data set library. An example of JCL which could be coded to meet this objective is as follows:

```
//EXAMPLE  JOB   (123,PROJ2),IMP,MSGLEVEL=(1,1),CLASS=A
//STEP1  EXEC  PROC=PL1LFCL,
//        PARM.PL1L='LIST,XREF'
//PL1L.SYSIN  DD  *
   -  -  -  -  PL/1  (F)  Program Here  -  -  -  -
/*
//LKED.SYSLMOD  DD  DSNAME=A.PROGRAM.LIBRARY,DISP=SHR
//LKED.SYSIN  DD  *
   NAME  AREFORM(R)
//
```

See the third procedure list in Figure 5.8. No Parm parameter specifications have been provided in the compile step, though at this late stage in program development some parameter information is desired. LIST and XREF should be provided to the PL1L step via a Parm parameter. This has been accomplished in the above job stream example. A Cross-Reference Table (XREF) is a listing of program variable names depicting in which source statement they are defined and referenced within the program. In the absence of a List (LIST) specification, the NOLIST compiler default is in effect. LIST generates a complete assembly language listing, though a Table of Offsets can also be obtained. This table is similar in concept to the Condensed Listing (CLIST) option of the COBOL compiler discussed previously in that it shows the relative length into the program module of each source statement. These two outputs are very handy references in program-debugging situations.

A Dd * statement is also missing and needs to be added to the PL1L step. Coding //PL1L.SYSIN DD * in the JCL job stream effectively adds a temporary Dd * statement named SYSIN to the PL1L (first) step of the procedure. This is followed by the source program itself.

What needs to be modified in the linkage step of the procedure is the Dd statement's description of the SYSLMOD ddname disk file. This file is the linkage editor's program load module output and is now in 100% machine-executable form. Also, a SYSIN Dd * statement to read an input program card is not included in the procedure and should be added to the LKED step. Both of these changes should be made to the linkage step when calling this procedure. In the preceding JCL job stream example, a program name card of   NAME   AREFORM(R) was then coded.

A comparable Compile and Link catalogued procedure exists for other PL/1 programming levels as well. The names of the procedures

164

are only slightly changed to reflect the programming level utilized, though a check with your dp installation should be made.

d. ASSEMBLER and Other Program Language
   Considerations

Assume that one has coded and fully tested an ASSEMBLER Level-F program and wishes to store the executable program load module into a private partitioned data set library. An example of JCL which could be coded to meet this objective is as follows:

```
//EXAMPLE  JOB  (123,PROJ2),IMP,MSGLEVEL=(1,1),CLASS=A
//STEP1  EXEC  PROC=ASMFCL
//ASM.SYSIN  DD  *
   -  -  -  -  ASSEMBLER (F) Program Here  -  -  -  -
/*
//LKED.SYSLMOD  DD  DSNAME=A.PROGRAM.LIBRARY,DISP=SHR
//LKED.SYSIN  DD  *
   NAME   ACONVERT(R)
//
```

See the fourth procedure list in Figure 5.8. Three Parm parameter specifications have been provided in the assembly step. LOAD creates the object module output file. Note that the ddname for the object module in the procedure is SYSGO, not SYSLIN as in previous procedures of other languages. LIST generates a complete source program assembly language listing. A Cross-Reference Table (XREF) is also printed. This list of program variable names depicts in which source statement they are defined and referenced within the program. This output is a very handy reference in program-debugging situations.

A Dd * statement to read the input source program file is also missing and needs to be added to the ASM step. Coding //ASM.SYSIN DD * in the JCL job stream effectively adds a temporary Dd * statement named SYSIN to the ASM (first) step of the procedure.

What needs to be modified in the linkage step of the procedure is the Dd statement's description of the SYSLMOD ddname disk file. This file is the linkage editor's program load module output and is now in 100% machine-executable form. Also, a SYSIN Dd * statement to read an input program card is not included in the procedure and should be added to the LKED step. Both of these changes should be made to the linkage step when calling this procedure. In the preceding JCL job stream example, a program name card of   NAME ACONVERT(R)   was then coded.

A comparable Compile and Link catalogued procedure exists for other ASSEMBLER programming levels as well. The names of the procedures are only slightly changed to reflect the programming level utilized. Other programming languages also follow these same concepts and principles. That is, RPGECL would be called to compile and link a Report Program Generator (RPG) Level-E program. Various programming levels are also reflected in the procedure name. A unique compiler name would be coded in the procedure itself. Exec statement parameters and ddnames defined in these procedures have similar functions as discussed in preceding examples. A check with the dp installation should be made, however, as unique user standards and preferences may effect specific makeup of any given procedure.

3. Compile, Link, and Execute

At least one catalogued procedure which compiles, links, and executes is available at dp installations for each programming language supported. Compile, Link, and Execute catalogued procedures are generally used during program test stages after initial syntax errors have been eliminated and logic program changes still need to be made. At this point the load module is not ready to be stored in a program library. Figure 5.9 displays four catalogued procedures which compile, link, and execute American National Standard (ANS) COBOL Version 4, FORTRAN IV G1-Level, PL/1 F-Level, and ASSEMBLER F-Level source programs. Standard names for these procedures are COBUCLG, FTG1CLG, PL1LFCLG, and ASMFCLG, respectively. The last three letters 'CLG' stand for Compile, Link, and Go (execute); the letter(s) next to the last three characters are an indication of programming language level, e.g., 'G1' for Level G1, while the remaining first two or three characters are an abbreviation of the programming language utilized.

Figure 5.9 Compile, Link, and Execute Procedures

```
COBUCLG:


//COB EXEC PGM=IKFCBL00,REGION=130K

//STEPLIB DD DSNAME=SYS1.COBLIB,DISP=SHR

//SYSPRINT DD SYSOUT=A

//SYSPUNCH DD SYSOUT=B

//SYSUT1 DD UNIT=SYSDA,DSNAME=&SYSUT1,SPACE=(460,(700,300),RLSE)

//SYSUT2 DD UNIT=SYSDA,DSNAME=&SYSUT2,SPACE=(460,(700,300),RLSE)

//SYSUT3 DD UNIT=SYSDA,DSNAME=&SYSUT3,SPACE=(460,(700,300),RLSE)

//SYSUT4 DD UNIT=SYSDA,DSNAME=&SYSUT4,SPACE=(460,(700,300),RLSE)

//SYSLIN DD UNIT=SYSDA,DISP=(MOD,PASS),

//         DSNAME=&LOADSET,DCB=BLKSIZE=3200,

//         SPACE=(3200,(20,20),RLSE)

//LKED EXEC PGM=IEWL,REGION=100K,

//         PARM='LET,LIST,XREF',
```

Figure 5.9 Compile, Link, and Execute Procedures (cont.)

```
//          COND=(4,LT,COB)
//SYSPRINT DD SYSOUT=A
//SYSUT1 DD UNIT=SYSDA,DSNAME=&SYSUT1,SPACE=(1024,(50,20))
//SYSLIN DD DSNAME=&LOADSET,DISP=(OLD,DELETE)
//          DD DDNAME=SYSIN
//SYSLIB DD DSNAME=SYS1.COBLIB,DISP=SHR
//SYSLMOD DD UNIT=SYSDA,DISP=(NEW,PASS),
//          DSNAME=&GOSET(RUN),DCB=BLKSIZE=1024,
//          SPACE=(1024,(50,20,1),RLSE)
//GO EXEC PGM=*.LKED.SYSLMOD,
//          COND=((r,LT,COB),(4,LT,LKED))
//SYSUDUMP DD SYSOUT=A
//SYSOUT DD SYSOUT=A
```

```
FTG1CLG:

//FORT EXEC PGM=IGIFORT,REGION=130K
//STEPLIB DD DSNAME-SYS1.FORTLIB,DISP=SHR
//SYSPRINT DD SYSOUT=A
//SYSPUNCH DD SYSOUT=B
//SYSLIN DD UNIT=SYSDA,DISP=(MOD,PASS),
//          DSNAME=&LOADSET,DCB=BLKSIZE=3200,
//          SPACE=(3200,(60,60),RLSE)
//LKED EXEC PGM=IEWL,REGION=100K,
//          PARM='LET,LIST,XREF',
//          COND=(4,LT,FORT)
//SYSPRINT DD SYSOUT=A
//SYSUT1 DD UNIT=SYSDA,DSNAME=&SYSUT1,SPACE=(1024,(20,20))
//SYSLIN DD DSNAME=&LOADSET,DISP=(OLD,DELETE)
//          DD DDNAME=SYSIN
//SYSLIB DD DSNAME=SYS1.FORTLIB,DISP=SHR
//SYSLMOD DD UNIT=SYSDA,DISP=(NEW,PASS),
//          DSNAME=&GOSET(MAIN),DCB=BLKSIZE=1024,
//          SPACE=(1024,(20,20,1),RLSE)
//GO EXEC PGM=*.LKED.SYSLMOD,
```

Figure 5.9 Compile, Link, and Execute Procedures (cont.)

```
//          COND=((4,LT,COB),(4,LT,LKED))
//SYSUDUMP DD SYSOUT=A
//FT05F001 DD DDNAME=SYSIN
//FT06F001 DD SYSOUT=A
//FT07F001 DD SYSOUT=B
```

```
PL1LFCLG:


//PL1L EXEC PGM=IEMAA,REGION=100K
//SYSPRINT DD SYSOUT=A
//SYSPUNCH DD SYSOUT=B
//SYSUT3 DD UNIT=SYSDA,
//          DSNAME=&SYSUT3,DCB=BLKSIZE=3200,
//          SPACE=(3200,(10,10))
//SYSUT1 DD UNIT=SYSDA,
//          DSNAME=&SYSUT1,DCB=BLKSIZE=1024,
//          SPACE=(1024,(60,60))
//SYSLIN DD UNIT=SYSDA,DISP=(MOD,PASS),
//          DSNAME=&LOADSET,DCB=BLKSIZE=3200,
//          SPACE=(3200,(10,10),RLSE)
//LKED EXEC PGM=IEWL,REGION=100K,
//          PARM='LET,LIST,XREF',
//          COND=(4,LT,PL1L)
//SYSPRINT DD SYSOUT=A
//SYSUT1 DD UNIT=SYSDA,DSNAME=&SYSUT1,SPACE=(1024,(200,20))
//SYSLIN DD DSNAME=&LOADSET,DISP=(OLD,DELETE)
//          DD DDNAME=SYSIN
//SYSLIB DD DSNAME=SYS1.PL1LIB,DISP=SHR
//SYSLMOD DD UNIT=SYSDA,DISP=(MOD,PASS),
//          DSNAME=&GOSET(GO),DCB=BLKSIZE=1024,
//          SPACE=(1024,(50,20,1),RLSE)
//GO EXEC PGM=*.LKED.SYSLMOD,
//          COND=((4,LT,PL1L),(4,LT,LKED))
//SYSUDUMP DD SYSOUT=A
//SYSPRINT DD SYSOUT=A
```

Figure 5.9 Compile, Link, and Execute Procedures (cont.)

```
ASMFCLG:


//ASM EXEC PGM=IEUASM,REGION=80K,
//         PARM='LOAD,LIST,XREF'
//SYSPRINT DD SYSOUT=A
//SYSPUNCH DD SYSOUT=B
//SYSUT1 DD UNIT=SYSDA,DSNAME=&SYSUT1,SPACE=(3200,(80,80))
//SYSUT2 DD UNIT=SYSDA,DSNAME=&SYSUT2,SPACE=(3200,(80,80))
//SYSUT3 DD UNIT=SYSDA,DSNAME=&SYSUT3,SPACE=(3200,(80,80))
//SYSLIB DD DSNAME=SYS1.MACLIB,DISP=SHR
//SYSGO DD UNIT=SYSDA,DISP=(MOD,PASS),
//         DSNAME=&LOADSET,DCB=BLKSIZE=3200,
//         SPACE=(3200,(10,10),RLSE)
//LKED EXEC PGM=IEWL,REGION=100K,
//         PARM='LET,LIST,XREF,NCAL",
//         COND=(4,LT,ASM)
//SYSPRINT DD SYSOUT=A
//SYSUT1 DD UNIT=SYSDA,DSNAME=&SYSUT1,SPACE=(1024,(50,20))
//SYSLIN DD DSNAME=&LOADSET,DISP=(OLD,DELETE)
//         DD DDNAME=SYSIN
//SYSLMOD DD UNIT=SYSDA,DISP=(MOD,PASS),
//         DSNAME=&GOSET(GO),DCB=BLKSIZE=1024,
//         SPACE=(1024,(50,20),RLSE)
//GO EXEC PGM=*.LKED.SYSLMOD,
//         COND=((4,LT,ASM),(4,LT.LKED))
//SYSUDUMP DD SYSOUT=A
```

    The first statement in each of the three-step procedures in
Figure 5.9 calls the same language compiler or assembly program
and allocates the same amount of storage as in the previous Compile
and Link procedure examples. In addition, a Parm parameter is
provided in the ASSEMBLER Compile, Link, and Execute procedure to
specify LOAD, LIST, and XREF in lieu of comparable program defaults.

Specific compiler level libraries may be called to supplement a given compiler's capabilities. The next two statements in each procedure describe the compiler or assembly message file and an optional object module punch file. Next, any statements with ddnames SYSUT1 through SYSUT4 define temporary work files. The coding of one ampersand (&) in front of a data set name defines that specification as a symbolic option and/or temporary data set. (The use of symbolic parameters will be described in the last chapter of this text.) Next, a macro statement library named SYS1.MACLIB is described via ddname SYSLIB in the ASSEMBLER procedure. Finally, an object module is described via ddname SYSLIN or SYSGO in all procedures. This file is passed to the Linkage step. A Dd * statement to read the input source program via ddname SYSIN is not allowed to be catalogued and therefore is not present.

The first statement in the second step of each of the above three-step procedures calls the same linkage editor program, IEWL. The linkage editor is not specific to the original source language utilized. This statement also allocates an identical amount of main storage in each case as well as providing LET, LIST, and XREF parameter information to the linkage program. NCAL is also specified in the Assembler procedure. LET allows the output load module to be marked as executable even though one or more errors occurred during the linkage process. LIST specifies that the control card(s) supplied to the linkage process should be listed as part of print output. XREF requests that a cross-reference table of external references including a map of relative module locations also be printed as output. NCAL indicates that an Assembler library search should not be made; a SYSLIB Dd statement is not provided. A Condition parameter on each of these Exec statements specifies that if 4 is less than the return code issued by the first step, the linkage step should be bypassed. In other words, there is no need to link a program which still contains conditional syntactical errors.

The next statement in each procedure with ddname SYSPRINT describes the linkage editor message file. This is followed by a SYSUT1 ddname temporary disk work file. The ddname SYSLIN or SYSGO object module passed from the compile or assembly step is described next for ddname SYSLIN as input to the linkage process. It is deleted at the end of the step. A file which defers the definition of a data set to be later identified with the ddname of SYSIN is concatenated to the input object module. A specific use for the file will be discussed shortly. With the exception of the ASSEMBLER procedure, appropriate program libraries are accessed next via the SYSLIB Dd statement. Appropriate ASSEMBLER macro libraries had been accessed in the assembly step. Finally, a SYSLMOD ddname file describes the output load module as a disk data set to be passed to another step.

The first statement in the third step of each of the above three-step procedures refers back to the LKED step and the SYSLMOD file. An '*.' indicates a referback. It is used when the actual file name may not be known yet the file is desired for access. The Program (PGM) keyword parameter loads this file into main storage as a 100% machine-executable program load module. As long as the Pass condition of the SYSLMOD file in the linkage step is not changed to Keep, the program module file will automatically be deleted at the end of the job. This is generally desired during the testing phase. A Condition parameter in each of the GO (execute) step's Exec statements specifies that if 4 is less than the return code issued by either the first or second step, the execute step should be bypassed. In other words, there is no need to execute a program which still contains conditional level or linkage errors.

The next statement in each procedure is ddname SYSUDUMP which describes the print file to which a storage dump will be written if this condition occurs. Ddname SYSOUT in the COBUCLG procedure describes the print file to which the program DISPLAY command generates output. Ddnames FT05F001, FT06F001, and FT07F001 in the FTG1CLG procedure describe potential SYSIN card input, print output, and punch output, respectively. To be utilized, a Read on Unit 5, a Write on Unit 6, or a Write on Unit 7 may be coded in the source program, respectively. Ddname SYSPRINT in the PL1LFCLG procedure also describes an output print file. Most user program files cannot be described in catalogued procedures, as their characteristics vary widely and are unknown at the time the procedure is catalogued. Therefore, these Dd statements will need to be temporarily added to the GO step when the procedure is called. The actual coding of JCL to call these procedures can now begin.

a. COBOL Programs

Assume that one has coded and is now testing an American National Standard (ANS) COBOL program. Compilation, linkage, and execution are all desired, though the executable program load module need not be saved. An example of JCL which could be coded to meet this objective is as follows:

```
//AMIX    JOB A1B2C3XYZ,DANHR,MSGLEVEL=(1,1),
//          CLASS=C,TIME=3
//STEP1   EXEC  PROC=COBUCLG,
//          PARM.COB='CLIST,DMAP,XREF',
//          REGION.GO=100K,TIME.GO=(1,30)
//COB.SYSIN  DD   *

    -  -  -  - ANS COBOL Program Here  -  -  -  -
/*
//GO.INPUT1   DD   UNIT=2400,DISP=(OLD,KEEP),
//          DSNAME=AMASTER,VOL=SER=TAPE88,
//          DCB=(RECFM=FB,LRECL=120,BLKSIZE=6400)
//GO.CARDIN   DD   *

    -  -  -  - Card File Here  -  -  -  -
/*
//GO.OUTPUT   DD   UNIT=SYSDA,DISP=(NEW,KEEP),
```

```
//          DSNAME=UPDATED,VOL=SER=001873,
//          SPACE=(6400,(20,2),RLSE),
//          DCB=(RECFM=FB,LRECL=120,BLKSIZE=6400)
//GO.PRINT1  DD   SYSOUT=(C,,1484)
//
```

Following the appropriate Job statement is an Exec statement which calls the three-step procedure of interest, COBUCLG. See the first procedure list in Figure 5.9. A region size of 130,000 bytes of main storage has been specified for compiler program IKFCBLOO.

No Parm parameter specifications have been provided in the cata- logued procedure, though at this stage in program testing some para- meter information is desired. CLIST, DMAP, and XREF should be pro- vided to the COB step via a Parm parameter. This has been accomplished in the above job stream example. A Condensed Listing (CLIST) is an abbreviated print of the assembly language listing in that it shows the relative length of each source statement into the program module. A Data Map (DMAP) provides a listing of program variable names, their relative location, level, field length, type of data representation utilized, and other characteristics for each program variable defined in the program. A Cross-Reference Table (XREF) is a listing of program variable names as well as paragraph names depicting in which source statement they are defined and referenced with the program. These three outputs are very handy references in program-testing situations. Requesting a Procedure Map (PMAP) in combination with a DMAP in lieu of a CLIST will generate a complete assembly language listing if desired, i.e., PARM.COB='DMAP,PMAP,XREF'. A complete description of all compiler options and their functions is depicted in Appendix C.

In addition to the above, a need exists to specify region size and time requirements to the GO (or execute) step. None are specified in the procedure as program size and time demands for its many applications are not known when cataloguing a procedure. Output from the linkage editor includes a 'TOTAL LENGTH xxxxxx' message, where xxxxxx equals region requirements in hexadecimal, i.e., TOTAL LENGTH EA60. Hexadecimal EA60 converts to 60,000 bytes of main storage re- quired for the program. Adding buffer requirements (times 2 for double buffering systems) of 30,000 bytes plus a 10% safety factor calculates to approximately 100,000 bytes of total main storage needed, i.e., REGION.GO=100K. With a count of the number and type of records to be tested and processed, in addition to experience with COBOL per- formance, a maximum allowable CPU time estimate was made, i.e., TIME.GO= (1,30). There is no quick and easy way to estimate initial program time demands until the program has been executed at least once. A Time parameter should always be coded, however. At this stage of program development it is quite easy for user programs to fall into endless loops and utilize an unnecessarily high and expensive amount of resources.

There is no need to modify existing Dd statements in the COB step for ddnames SYSPRINT, SYSPUNCH, SYSUT1 through SYSUT4, and SYSLIN, as they are required by the compiler and have been accounted for accord- ingly. What is missing in the compile step of the procedure, however,

is the Dd * statement to read the input source program file. It needs
to be added to the COB step. Coding //COB.SYSIN DD * in the JCL
job stream effectively adds a temporary Dd * statement named SYSIN
to the COB (first) step of the procedure. This is followed by the
source program itself, as the compiler contains a description for
a file named SYSIN which defines the source program as input.

The second step of the COBUCLG procedure named LKED calls the
linkage editor program. A region size of 100,000 bytes of main
storage has been specified for program IEWL. LET, LIST, and XREF
have been specified to the LKED step via the Parm parameter. A Condition parameter has also been coded to avoid occasional needless
linkage processing. There is no particular need to modify or add
new Exec statement parameter information here for this application.
Linkage options and their functions are depicted in Appendix C.
Similarly, there is no need to modify or add Dd statements in the
linkage step for ddnames SYSPRINT, SYSUT1, SYSLIN, SYSLIB, and
SYSIN, as they are required by the linkage editor and have been
accounted for accordingly. In lieu of a SYSIN Dd * statement, a
default program name of RUN has been assigned by the procedure.
However, it need not be accessed via its name for this application
and is deleted at the end of the execute step.

The third step of the COBUCLG procedure named GO refers back
to the SYSLMOD Dd statement in the LKED step and loads the appropriate program load module into main storage. This is accomplished
by coding an '*.' for referback purposes, i.e., PGM=*.LKED.SYSLMOD.
A Condition parameter has also been coded in the procedure to avoid
occasional needless execution processing. Region and Time parameters
were previously provided to the GO step when the procedure was
called.

A SYSUDUMP Dd statement for abnormal conditions and a SYSOUT Dd
statement for the program DISPLAY command have been provided in
the GO step of the procedure. Note that no other Dd statements have
been provided to this execute step. Why not?? There is no way to
determine which program ddnames a programmer/analyst had chosen.
Furthermore, even if a strict ddname standard were devised and
adhered to, there is no way to determine all appropriate file
descriptions. Tape? Disk? Disposition? Data Set Name? Volume?
Space? System Output? Data Control Block? As a result, those
programmer/analyst choices are commonly left out of catalogued
procedures. Therefore, they must be added to the GO (execute)
step when the procedure is called. The preceding JCL job stream
example adds user Dd statements to the GO step for ddnames INPUT1,
CARDIN, OUTPUT1, and PRINT1 for a tape, card, disk, and print file,
respectively. In this example, the user program contains a
description for each of these files and expects respective input
and output data.

A Null statement follows the above Dd statement additions to
indicate the end of this particular job stream. Printed output
includes a JCL listing with file allocation and termination messages, a compiler listing of the source program, a program error
listing, condensed assembly language listing, data map, cross-
reference table, a linkage editor message indicating that a load
module has been created, a cross-reference control section listing
from the linkage editor, and those outputs as defined and created

by the user program during its execution. Standard compiler and linkage editor outputs should be requested via JCL Parm parameters specifications discussed previously if they are not a default of the compiler, linkage editor, or procedure itself. Compiler and linkage editor defaults are defined in detail in Appendix C.

A comparable Compile, Link, and Execute catalogued procedure exists for other COBOL programming levels as well. The names of the procedures are only slightly changed. Instead of COBUCLG, for example, the catalogued procedure to compile, link, and execute Level-F COBOL programs is named COBFCLG. That is, the letter 'U' is replaced by the letter 'F'. Other levels also reflect comparable name changes. The only essential difference among these procedures is that a different compiler program is called. Aside from that, the method of calling the procedure is the same; the technique of modifying or adding to the procedure is identical; and other than procedure and compiler names, the content of the procedure itself is essentially the same as other COBOL programming levels. A check with the dp installation should be made, as unique user standards and preferences may affect the specific makeup of a given procedure.

b. FORTRAN PROGRAMS

Assume that one has coded and is now testing a FORTRAN IV Level-G1 program. Compilation, linkage, and execution are all desired, though the executable program load module need not be saved. An example of JCL which could be coded to meet this objective is as follows:

```
//AMIX   JOB   A1B2C3XYZ,DANHR,MSGLEVEL=(1,1),
//            CLASS=C,TIME=3
//STEP1  EXEC  PROC=FTG1CLG,
//            PARM.FORT='LIST',
//            REGION.GO=120K,TIME.GO=2
//FORT.SYSIN  DD   *
     -  -  -  -  FORTRAN IV (G1) Program Here -  -  -  -
/*
//GO.FT01F001  DD   UNIT=SYSDA,DISP=(OLD,KEEP),
//        DSNAME=OLDDATA,VOL=SER=PACK07,
//        DCB=(RECFM=VB,LRECL=120,BLKSIZE=3204)
//GO.FT08F001  DD   UNIT=2400,DISP=(NEW,KEEP),
//        DSNAME=NEWDATA,
//        DCB=(RECFM=VB,LRECL=120,BLKSIZE=6204)
//GO.SYSIN  DD   *
     -  -  -  -  Card File Here  -  -  -  -
//
```

Following the appropriate Job statement is an Exec statement which calls the three-step procedure of interest, FTG1CLG. See the second procedure list in Figure 5.9. A region size of 130,000 bytes of main storage has been specified for compiler program IGIFORT.

No Parm parameter specifications have been provided in the catalogued procedure, though at this stage in program testing some parameter information is desired. LIST should be provided to the FORT step via a Parm parameter. This has been accomplished in the above JCL job stream example. List (LIST) refers to the generation and printing of a complete assembly language listing. A Map (MAP) should also be specified and generated if the NOMAP option has been coded in the procedure. These two outputs are very handy references in program-testing situations. Unfortunately, a condensed listing of the assembly language representation of the source program is not a valid FORTRAN option. A complete description of all compiler options and their functions is depicted in Appendix C.

In addition to the above, a need exists to specify region size and time requirements to the GO (or execute) step. None are specified in the procedure, as program size and time demands for its many applications are not known when cataloguing a procedure. Output from the linkage editor includes a 'TOTAL LENGTH xxxxxx' message, where xxxxxx equals region requirements in hexadecimal, i.e., TOTAL LENGTH 11170. Hexadecimal 11170 converts to 70,000 bytes of main storage required for the program. Adding buffer requirements (times 2 for double buffering systems) of 40,000 bytes plus a 10% safety factor calculates to approximately 120,000 bytes of total main storage needed, i.e., REGION.GO=120K. With a count of the number and type of records to be tested and processed, in addition to experience with FORTRAN performance, a maximum allowable CPU time estimate was made, i.e., TIME.GO=2. There is no quick and easy way to estimate initial program time demands until the program has been executed at least once. A Time parameter should always be coded, however. At this stage of program development it is quite easy for user programs to fall into endless loops and utilize an unnecessarily high and expensive amount of resources.

There is no need to modify existing Dd statements in the FORT step for ddnames SYSPRINT, SYSPUNCH, and SYSLIN, as they are required by the compiler and have been accounted for accordingly. What is missing in the compile step of the procedure, however, is the Dd * statement to read the input source program file. It needs to be added to the FORT step. Coding //FORT.SYSIN DD * in the JCL job stream effectively adds a temporary Dd * statement named SYSIN to the FORT (first) step of the procedure. This is followed by the source program itself as the compiler contains a description for a file named SYSIN which defines the source program as input.

The second step of the FTG1CLG procedure named LKED calls the linkage editor program. A region size of 100,000 bytes of main storage has been specified for program IEWL. LET, LIST, and XREF have been specified to the LKED step via the Parm parameter. A Condition parameter has also been coded to avoid occasional needless linkage processing. There is no particular need to modify or add new Exec statement parameter information here for this application. Linkage editor options and their functions are depicted in Appendix C. Similarly, there is no need to modify or add Dd statements in the linkage step for ddnames SYSPRINT, SYSUT1, SYSLIN, SYSLIB, and SYSIN, as they are required by the linkage editor and have been accounted for accordingly. In lieu of a SYSIN Dd * statement, a default program name of MAIN has been assigned by the procedure. However, it need not be accessed via its name for this application and is to be deleted at the end of the execute step.

The third step of the FTG1CLG procedure named GO refers back to the SYSLMOD Dd statement in the LKED step and loads the appropriate program load module into main storage. This is accomplished by coding an '*.' for referback purposes, i.e., PGM=*.LKED.SYSLMOD. A Condition parameter has also been coded in the procedure to avoid occasional needless execution processing. Region and Time parameters were previously provided to the GO step when the procedure was called.

A SYSUDUMP Dd statement for abnormal conditions and Dd statements for ddnames FT06F001, FT07F001, and FT05F001 for print, punch, and card files, respectively, have been provided in the GO step of the procedure. The card file is supplied last, as its definition had been deferred. No other Dd statements have been provided to this execute step. Other than the above ddname standards, there is no way to determine which program logical units a programmer/analyst had chosen. Furthermore, even if a broader unit/ddname standard were devised and adhered to, there is no way to determine all appropriate file descriptions. As a result, many programmer/analyst choices are commonly left out of catalogued procedures. Therefore, they must be added to the GO (execute) step when the procedure is called. In this example, the user program contains a description for the FT06F001, FT07F001, and FT05F001 ddname files and expects respective input and output data.

A Null statement follows the above Dd statement additions to indicate the end of this particular job stream. Printed output includes a JCL listing with file allocation and termination messages, a compiler listing of the source program, a program map, a linkage editor message indicating that a load module has been created, a cross-reference control section listing from the linkage editor, and those outputs as defined and created by the user program during its execution. Standard compiler and linkage editor outputs should be requested via JCL Parm parameters specifications discussed previously if they are not a default of the compiler, linkage editor, or procedure itself. Compiler and linkage editor defaults are defined in detail in Appendix C.

A comparable Compile, Link, and Execute catalogued procedure exists for other FORTRAN programming levels as well. The names of the procedures are only slightly changed. Instead of FTG1CLG, for example, the catalogued procedure to compile and link Level-H FORTRAN IV programs is named FORTHCLG. Other levels also reflect comparable name changes. The only essential difference among these procedures is that a different compiler program is called. Compiler work files may also be provided on occasion. Aside from that, the method of calling the procedure is the same; the technique of modifying or adding to the procedure is identical; and other than procedure and compiler names, the content of the procedure itself is essentially the same as other FORTRAN programming levels. A check with the dp installation should be made, as unique user

standards and preferences may affect the specific makeup of a
given procedure.

c. Programming Language/One (PL/1) Differences

Assume that one has coded and is now testing a PL/1 Level-F program. Compilation, linkage, and execution are all desired, though
the executable program load module need not be saved. An example
of JCL which could be coded to meet this objective is as follows:

```
//AMIX    JOB   A1B2C3XYZ,DANHR,MSGLEVEL=(1,1),
//        CLASS=C,TIME=2
//STEP1   EXEC  PROC=PL1LFCLG,
//        PARM.PL1L='LIST,XREF',
//        REGION.GO=80K,TIME.GO=1
//PL1L.SYSIN  DD   *
   -  -  -  -  PL/1 (F) Program Here  -  -  -  -
/*
//GO.READIN   DD   UNIT=2400,DISP=(OLD,KEEP),
//        DSNAME=RAWDATA,VOL=SER=022183,
//        DCB=(RECFM=FB,LRECL=400,BLKSIZE=4000)
//GO.PARMCARD  DD   *
   -  -  -  -  Card File Here  -  -  -  -
/*
//GO.WRTOUT   DD   UNIT=3330,DISP=(NEW,KEEP,DELETE),
//        DSNAME=EDITDATA,
//        SPACE=(4000,(40,4),RLSE),
//        DCB=(RECFM=FB,LRECL=400,BLKSIZE=4000)
//GO.PUNCHOUT  DD   SYSOUT=B
//
```

See the third procedure list in Figure 5.9. No Parm parameter
specifications have been provided in the compile step of the catalogued procedure, though at this stage in program testing some parameter information is desired. LIST and XREF should be provided to
the PL1L step via a Parm parameter. This has been accomplished in
the above job stream example. A Cross-Reference Table (XREF) is a
listing of program variable names depicting in which source statement
they are defined and referenced within the program. In the absence
of a List (LIST) specification, the NOLIST compiler default is in
effect. LIST generates a complete assembly language listing, though
a Table of Offsets can also be obtained. This table is similar in
concept to the Condensed Listing (CLIST) option of the COBOL
compiler discussed previously in that it shows the relative length

into the program module of each source statement. These two outputs are very handy references in program-testing situations.

In addition to the above, a need exists to specify region size and time requirements to the GO (or execute) step. None are specified in the procedure, as program size and time demands for its many applications are not known when cataloguing a procedure. Region size can be determined by adding the length indication output of the linkage editor to total buffer requirements plus a 10% safety factor, i.e., REGION.GO=80K. Time estimates are based upon data volume and type, program performance, and experience, i.e., TIME.GO=1. There is no quick and easy way to estimate initial program time demands until the program has been executed at least once.

A Dd * statement is also missing and needs to be added to the PL1L step. Coding //PL1L.SYSIN DD * in the JCL job stream effectively adds a temporary Dd * statement named SYSIN to the PL1L (first) step of the procedure. This is followed by the source program itself.

The second step of the PL1LFCLG procedure named LKED calls the linkage editor program. There is no particular need to modify or add new Exec statement nor Dd statement information here for this application.

The third step of the PL1LFCLG procedure named GO refers back to the SYSLMOD Dd statement in the LKED step and loads the appropriate program load module into main storage. A SYSUDUMP Dd statement for abnormal conditions and a SYSPRINT Dd statement print file have been provided in the GO step of the procedure. No other Dd statements have been provided to this execute step. Therefore, they must be added to the GO (execute) step when the procedure is called. The preceding JCL stream example adds Dd statements for ddnames READIN, PARMCARD, WRTOUT, and PUNCHOUT for a tape, card, disk, and punch file, respectively.

A comparable Compile, Link, and Execute catalogued procedure exists for other PL/1 programming levels as well. The name of the procedures are only slightly changed to reflect the programming level utilized, though a check with the dp installation should be made.

d. ASSEMBLER and Other Program Language Considerations

Assume that one has coded and is now testing an ASSEMBLER Level-F program. Compilation, linkage, and execution are all desired, though the executable program load module need not be saved. An example of JCL which could be coded to meet this objective is as follows:

```
//AMIX    JOB   A1B2C3XYZ,DANHR,MSGLEVEL=(1,1),
//            CLASS=C,TIME=2
//STEP1   EXEC  PROC=ASMFCLG,
//            REGION.GO=60K,TIME.GO=1
//ASM.SYSIN  DD   *

     - - - - ASSEMBLER (F) Program Here  - -  ·· -
```

```
/*
//GO.DATAIN    DD   UNIT=SYSDA,DISP=(OLD,KEEP),
//            DSNAME=MASTIN,
//            DCB=(RECFM=FB,LRECL=80,BLKSIZE=3200)
//GO.PARAMIN   DD   *

     -  -  -  -  Card File Here  -  -  -  -

/*
//GO.DATAOUT   DD   UNIT=2400,DISP=(NEW,KEEP),
//            DSNAME=MASTOUT,VOL=SER=TAPE07,
//            DCB=(RECFM=FB,LRECL=80,BLKSIZE=3200)
//GO.PRTOUT    DD   SYSOUT=A
//
```

See the fourth procedure list in Figure 5.9. Three Parm parameter specifications have been provided in the assembly step. LOAD creates the object module output file. Note that the ddname for the object module in the procedure is SYSGO, not SYSLIN as in previous procedures of other languages. LIST generates a complete source program assembly language listing. A Cross-Reference Table (XREF) is also printed. This list of program variable names depicts in which source statement they are defined and referenced within the program. This output is a very handy reference in program-debugging situations.

In addition to the above, a need exists to specify region size and time requirements to the GO (or execute) step. None is specified in the procedure, as program size and time demands for its many applications are not known when cataloguing a procedure. Region size can be determined by adding the length indication output of the linkage editor to total buffer requirements plus a 10% safety factor, i.e., REGION.GO=60K. Time estimates are based upon data volume and type, program performance, and experience, i.e., TIME.GO=1. There is no quick and easy way to estimate initial program time demands until the program has been executed at least once.

A Dd * statement to read the input source program file is also missing and needs to be added to the ASM step. Coding //ASM.SYSIN DD * in the JCL job stream effectively adds a temporary Dd * statement named SYSIN to the ASM (first) step of the procedure. This is followed by the source program itself.

The second step of the ASMFCLG procedure named LKED calls the linkage editor program. There is no particular need to modify or add new Exec statement nor Dd statement information here for this application.

The third step of the ASMFCLG procedure named GO refers back to the SYSLMOD Dd statement in the LKED step and loads the appropriate program load module into main storage. A SYSUDUMP Dd statement for abnormal conditions has been provided in the GO step of the procedure. No other Dd statements have been provided to this execute step. Therefore, they must be added to the GO (execute)

179

step when the procedure is called. The preceding JCL job stream example adds Dd statements for ddnames DATAIN, PARAMIN, DATAOUT, and PRTOUT for a disk, card, tape, and print file, respectively.

A comparable Compile, Link, and Execute catalogued procedure exists for other ASSEMBLER programming levels as well. The names of the procedures are only slightly changed to reflect the programming level utilized. Other programming languages also follow these same concepts and principles. That is, RPGECLG would be called to compile, link, and execute a Report Program Generator (RPG) Level-E program. Various programming levels are also reflected in the procedure name. A unique compiler name would be coded in the procedure itself. Exec statement parameters and ddnames defined in these procedures have similar functions as discussed in preceding examples. A check with the dp installation should be made, however, as unique user standards and preferences may affect specific makeup of any given procedure.

4. Link and Execute

At least one catalogued procedure which links and executes is available at most dp installations for each programming language supported. Link and Execute catalogued procedures are used in environments where program object decks or modules are commonly saved. One must assume that an object deck exists or that the object module of interest has been stored in a program library. Figure 5.10 displays four catalogued procedures which link and execute American National Standard (ANS) COBOL Version 4, FORTRAN IV G1-Level, PL/1 F-Level, and ASSEMBLER F-Level source programs. Standard names for these procedures are COBULG, FTG1LG, PL1LFLG, and ASMFLG, respectively. Though the linkage editor is source-program-language-independent, a procedure has nevertheless been set up for each programming language. They contain JCL in the GO (execute) steps which are unique to each language utilized. This is the only essential difference among Link and Execute catalogued procedures.

The first statement in each of the two-step procedures in Figure 5.10 calls the same linkage editor program as in previous examples, IEWL. The linkage editor is not specific to the original source language utilized. This statement also allocates an identical amount of main storage in each case as well as providing LET, LIST, and XREF parameter information to the linkage program. NCAL is also specified in the ASSEMBLER procedure. The next statement in each procedure with ddname SYSPRINT describes the linkage editor message file. This is followed by a SYSUT1 ddname temporary disk work file.

The ddname SYSLIN input object module or deck is described next. The Ddname keyword defers the definition of a data set to be later identified with the ddname of SYSIN. With the exception of the ASSEMBLER procedure, appropriate program libraries are accessed next via the SYSLIB Dd statement. Appropriate ASSEMBLER macro libraries have been accessed in an assembly step. Finally, a SYSLMOD ddname file describes the output load module as a disk data set to be passed to another step.

The first statement in the second step of each of the above two-step procedures refers back to the LKED step and the SYSLMOD file. The Program (PGM) keyword parameter loads this file into main storage as a 100% machine-executable program load module. As long as

180

Figure 5.10 Link and Execute Procedures

```
COBULG:

//LKED   EXEC  PGM=IEWL,REGION=100K,
//        PARM='LET,LIST,XREF'
//SYSPRINT  DD  SYSOUT=A
//SYSUT1   DD  UNIT=SYSDA,DSNAME=&SYSUT1,SPACE=(1024,(50,20))
//SYSLIN   DD  DDNAME=SYSIN
//SYSLIB   DD  DSNAME=SYS1.COBLIB,DISP=SHR
//SYSLMOD  DD  UNIT=SYSDA,DISP=(NEW,PASS),
//        DSNAME=&GOSET(RUN),DCB=BLKSIZE=1024,
//        SPACE=(1024,(50,20,1),RLSE)
//GO   EXEC  PGM=*.LKED.SYSLMOD,
//        COND=(4,LT,LKED)
//SYSUDUMP  DD  SYSOUT=A
//SYSOUT   DD  SYSOUT=A
```

```
FTG1LG:

//LKED   EXEC  PGM=IEWL,REGION=100K,
//        PARM='LET,LIST,XREF'
//SYSPRINT  DD  SYSOUT=A
//SYSUT1   DD  UNIT=SYSDA,DSNAME=&SYSUT1,SPACE=(1024,(50,20))
//SYSLIN   DD  DDNAME=SYSIN
//SYSLMOD  DD  UNIT=SYSDA,DISP=(NEW,PASS),
//        DSNAME=&GOSET(MAIN),DCB=BLKSIZE=1024,
//        SPACE=(1024,(50,20,1),RLSE)
//GO   EXEC  PGM=*.LKED.SYSLMOD,
//        COND=(4,LT,LKED)
//SYSUDUMP  DD  SYSOUT=A
//FT05F001  DD  DDNAME=SYSIN
//FT06F001  DD  SYSOUT=A
//FT07F001  DD  SYSOUT=B
```

Figure 5.10 Link and Execute Procedures (cont.)

```
        PL1LFLG:

        //LKED  EXEC  PGM=IEWL,REGION=100K,
        //        PARM='LET,LIST,XREF'
        //SYSPRINT  DD   SYSOUT=A
        //SYSUT1   DD   UNIT=SYSDA,DSNAME=&SYSUT1,SPACE=(1024,(50,20))
        //SYSLIN   DD   DDNAME=SYSIN
        //SYSLIB   DD   DSNAME=SYS1.PL1LIB,DISP=SHR
        //SYSLMOD  DD   UNIT=SYSDA,DISP=(MOD,PASS),
        //        DSNAME=&GOSET(GO),DCB=BLKSIZE=1024,
        //        SPACE=(1024,(50,20,1),RLSE)
        //GO  EXEC  PGM=*.LKED.SYSLMOD,
        //        COND=(4,LT,LKED)
        //SYSUDUMP  DD   SYSOUT=A
        //SYSPRINT  DD   SYSOUT=A
```

```
        ASMFLG:

        //LKED  EXEC  PGM=IEWL,REGION=100K,
        //        PARM='LET,LIST,XREF,NCAL'
        //SYSPRINT  DD   SYSOUT=A
        //SYSUT1   DD   UNIT=SYSDA,DSNAME=&SYSUT1,SPACE=(1024,(50,20))
        //SYSLIN   DD   DDNAME=SYSIN
        //SYSLMOD  DD   UNIT=SYSDA,DISP=(MOD,PASS),
        //        DSNAME=&GOSET(GO),DCB=BLKSIZE=1024,
        //        SPACE=(1024,(50,20,1),RLSE)
        //GO  EXEC  PGM=*.LKED.SYSLMOD,
        //        COND=(4,LT,LKED)
        //SYSUDUMP  DD   SYSOUT=A
```

182

the Pass condition of the SYSLMOD file in the linkage step is not changed to Keep, the program module file will automatically be deleted at the end of the job. A Condition parameter on each of the GO (execute) step's Exec statements specifies that if 4 is less than the return code issued by the first step, the execute step should be bypassed. In other words, there is no need to execute a program which still contains conditional level linkage errors.

The next statement in each procedure is ddname SYSUDUMP, which describes the print file to which a storage dump will be written if this condition occurs. Ddname SYSOUT in the COBULG procedure describes the print file to which the program DISPLAY command generates output. Ddnames FT05F001, FT06F001, and FT07F001 in the FTG1LG procedure describe potential SYSIN card input, print output, and punch output, respectively. To be utilized, a Read on Unit 5, a Write on Unit 6, or a Write on Unit 7 may be coded in the source program, respectively. Ddname SYSPRINT in the PL1LFLG procedure also describes an output print file. Most user program files can not be described in catalogued procedures, as their characteristics are widely varied and unknown at the time the procedure is catalogued. Therefore, these Dd statements will need to be temporarily added to the GO step when the procedure is called.

a. COBOL Programs

Assume that one has compiled and saved in program object module form an American National Standard (ANS) COBOL program. Linkage and execution are both desired, though the executable program load module need not be saved. An example of pertinent JCL which could be coded to meet this objective is as follows:

```
//AMIX   JOB   A1B2C3XYZ,DANHR,MSGLEVEL=(1,1),
//            CLASS=C,TIME=3
//STEP1  EXEC  PROC=COBULG,
//            REGION.GO=100K,TIME.GO=(2,30)
//LKED.SYSIN   DD   DSNAME=A.PROGRAM.LIBRARY(EDIT),DISP=SHR
//GO.INPUT1   DD   UNIT=2400,DISP=(OLD,KEEP),
//            DSNAME=EDITDATA,VOL=SER=TAPE99
//GO.CARDIN   DD   *
    -  -  -  -  Card File Here  -  -  -  -
//GO.OUTPUT1  DD   UNIT=SYSDA,DISP=(NEW,KEEP,DELETE),
//            DSNAME=GOODDATA,VOL=SER=SCRTCH,
//            SPACE=(6400,(30,3),RLSE)
//GO.PRINT1   DD   SYSOUT=(C,,1473)
//
```

Following the appropriate Job statement is an Exec statement which calls the two-step procedure of interest, COBULG. See the first procedure list in Figure 5.10. A region size of 100,000 bytes of main storage has been specified for linkage editor program IEWL. LET, LIST, and XREF have been specified to the LKED step via the Parm parameter. There is no particular need to modify or add new Exec statement parameter information for this application. However, a need exists to specify region size and time requirements to the GO (or execute) step. None is specified in the procedure as program size and time demands for its many applications are not known when cataloguing a procedure. Upon calling the procedure a Region and Time parameter should be coded as above, e.g., REGION.GO=100K,TIME.GO=(1,30).

There is no need to modify existing Dd statements in the LKED step for ddnames SYSPRINT, SYSUT1, SYSLIB, and SYSLMOD, as they are required by the linkage editor and have been accounted for accordingly. What needs to be modified in the linkage step of the procedure, however, is the SYSLIN Dd statement to read the input program object module. Its definition was deferred in the procedure. Coding a LKED.SYSIN Dd statement satisfies this deferment for ddname SYSLIN, e.g.,

```
//LKED.SYSIN   DD   DSNAME=A.PROGRAM.LIBRARY(EDIT),DISP=SHR
```

Program object module EDIT was presumably stored in a partitioned library and is now being called as input to the linkage step. If an object deck had previously been created, a Dd * statement would need to be coded followed by the deck itself. In either case, ddname SYSLIN in the procedure must be modified to accept the object module as input.

The second step of the COBULG procedure named GO refers back to the SYSLMOD Dd statement in the LKED step and loads the appropriate program load module into main storage. A Condition parameter has also been coded in the procedure to avoid occasional needless execution processing. Region and Time parameters were previously provided to the GO step when the procedure was called.

A SYSUDUMP Dd statement for abnormal conditions and a SYSOUT Dd statement for the program DISPLAY command have been provided in the GO step of the procedure. Note that no other Dd statements have been provided to this execute step. There is no way to determine which program ddnames a programmer/analyst had chosen. Furthermore, even if a strict ddname standard were devised and adhered to, there is no way to determine all appropriate file descriptions. As a result, those programmer/analyst choices are commonly left out of catalogued procedures. Therefore, they must be added to the GO (execute) step when the procedure is called. The preceeding JCL job stream example adds user Dd statements to the GO step for ddnames INPUT1, CARDIN, OUTPUT1, and PRINT1 for a tape, card, disk, and print file, respectively.

A Null statement follows the above Dd statement additions to indicate the end of this particular job stream. Printed output includes a JCL listing with file allocation and termination messages, a linkage editor message indicating that a load module has been created, a cross-reference control section listing from the linkage editor, and those outputs as defined and created by the user program during its execution. Standard linkage editor outputs should be requested via JCL Parm parameters specifications discussed previously if they are not a default of the linkage editor or procedure itself. Linkage editor defaults are defined in detail in Appendix C.

A comparable Link and Execute catalogued procedure exists for other COBOL programming levels as well. The names of the procedures are only slightly changed. Instead of COBULG, for example, the catalogued procedure to link and execute Level-F COBOL programs is named COBFLG. The only essential difference among these procedures is that some blocksizes and main storage requirements may vary. Aside from that, the method of calling the procedure is the same; the technique of modifying or adding to the procedure is identical; and other than procedure names and storage requirements, the content of the procedure itself is essentially the same as for other COBOL programming levels. A check with the dp installation should be made, as unique user standards and preferences may affect the specific makeup of a given procedure.

b. FORTRAN Programs

Assume that one has compiled and saved in program object module form a FORTRAN IV Level-G1 program. Linkage and execution are both desired, though the executable program load module need not be saved. An example of pertinent JCL which could be coded to meet this objective is as follows:

```
//AMIX    JOB   A1B2C3XYZ,DANHR,MSGLEVEL=(1,1),
//           CLASS=C,TIME=3
//STEP1   EXEC  PROC=FTG1LG,
//           REGION.GO=120K,TIME.GO=(2,30)
//LKED.SYSIN  DD   DSNAME=A.PROGRAM.LIBRARY(SUM),DISP=SHR
//GO.FT01F001  DD   UNIT=3330,DISP=(OLD,KEEP),
//           DSNAME=DISKDATA,VOL=SER=PACK44,
//           DCB=(RECFM=FB,LRECL=100,BLKSIZE=4000)
//GO.FT08F001  DD   UNIT=2400,DISP=(NEW,KEEP),
//           DSNAME=TAPEDATA,VOL=SER=017538,
//           DCB=(RECFM=FB,LRECL=100,BLKSIZE=4000)
//GO.SYSIN  DD   *
    -  -  -  - Card File Here  -  -  -  -
//
```

Following the appropriate Job statement is an Exec statement which calls the two-step procedure of interest, FTG1LG. See the second procedure list in Figure 5.10. A region size of 100,000 bytes of main storage has been specified for linkage editor program IEWL. LET, LIST, and XREF have been specified to the LKED step via the Parm parameter. There is no particular need to modify or add new Exec statement parameter information for this application. However, a need exists to specify region size and time requirements to the GO (or execute) step. None is specified in the procedure, as program size and time demands for its many applications are not known when cataloguing a procedure. Upon calling the procedure, a Region and Time parameter should be coded as above, e.g., REGION.GO=120K,TIME.GO=(2,30).

There is no need to modify existing Dd statements in the LKED step for ddnames SYSPRINT, SYSUT1, SYSLIB, and SYSLMOD, as they are required by the linkage editor and have been accounted for accordingly. What needs to be modified in the linkage step of the procedure, however, is the SYSLIN Dd statement to read the input program object module. Its definition was deferred in the procedure. Coding a LKED. SYSIN Dd statement satisfies this deferment for ddname SYSLIN, e.g.,

    //LKED.SYSIN DD DSNAME=A.PROGRAM.LIBRARY(SUM),DISP=SHR

Program object module SUM was presumably stored in a partitioned library and is now being called as input to the linkage step. If an object deck had previously been created, a Dd * statement would need to be coded followed by the deck itself. In either case, ddname SYSLIN in the procedure must be modified to accept the object module as input.

The second step of the FORTGLG procedure named GO refers back to the SYSLMOD Dd statement in the LKED step and loads the appropriate program load module into main storage. A Condition parameter has also been coded in the procedure to avoid occasional needless execution processing. Region and Time parameters were previously provided to the GO step when the procedure was called.

A SYSUDUMP Dd statement and Dd statements for ddnames FT06F001, FT07F001, and FT05F001 have been provided for print, punch, and card files, respectively. The card file is supplied last, as its definition had been deferred in the GO step of the procedure. Note that no other Dd statements have been provided to this execute step. There is no way to determine which program logical units a programmer/ analyst had chosen. Furthermore, even if a broader unit/ddname standard were devised and adhered to, there is no way to determine all appropriate file descriptions. As a result, many programmer/ analyst choices are commonly left out of catalogued procedures. Therefore, they must be added to the GO (execute) step when the procedure is called.

A Null statement follows the above Dd statement additions to indicate the end of this particular job stream. Printed output includes a JCL listing with file allocation and termination messages, a linkage editor message indicating that a load module has been created, a cross-reference control section listing from the linkage editor, and those outputs as defined and created by the user program during its execution. Standard linkage editor outputs should be requested via JCL Parm parameters specifications discussed previously if they are not a default of the linkage editor or procedure itself. Linkage editor defaults are defined in detail in Appendix C.

A comparable Link and Execute catalogued procedure exists for other FORTRAN programming levels as well. The name of the procedures is only slightly changed. Instead of FTG1LG, for example, the catalogued procedure to link and execute Level-H FORTRAN IV programs is named FORTHLG. The only essential difference among these procedures is that some blocksizes and main storage requirements may be different. Aside from that, the method of calling the procedure is the same; the technique of modifying or adding to the procedure is identical; and other than procedure names and storage requirements, the content of the procedure itself is essentially the same as for other FORTRAN programming levels. A check with the dp installation should be made, as unique user standards and preferences may affect the specific makeup of a given procedure.

c. Programming Language/One (PL/1) Differences

Assume that one has compiled and saved in program object module form a PL/1 Level-F program. Linkage and execution are both desired, though the executable program load module need not be saved. An example of pertinent JCL which could be coded to meet this objective is as follows:

```
//AMIX   JOB  A1B2C3XYZ,DANHR,MSGLEVEL=(1,1),
//          CLASS=C,TIME=(2,30)
//STEP1  EXEC  PROC=PL1LFLG,
//          REGION.GO=80K,TIME.GO=2
//LKED.SYSIN  DD  DSNAME=A.PROGRAM.LIBRARY(REFORM),DISP=SHR
//GO.READIN  DD  UNIT=2400,DISP=(OLD,KEEP),
//          DSNAME=UNFORM,VOL=SER=OS1786,
//          DCB=(RECFM=FB,LRECL=120,BLKSIZE=4800)
//GO.PARMCARD  DD  *
  - - - - Card File Here - - - -
/*
//GO.WRTOUT  DD  UNIT=SYSDA,DISP=(NEW,KEEP),
//          DSNAME=REFORM,
//          DCB=(RECFM=FB,LRECL=120,BLKSIZE=6400)
//GO.PNCHOUT  DD  SYSOUT=B
//
```

See the third procedure list in Figure 5.10. A need exists to specify region size and time requirements to the GO (or execute) step, e.g., REGION.GO=80K,TIME.GO=1. None is specified in the procedure as program size and time demands for its many applications are not known when cataloguing a procedure.

There is no need to modify existing Dd statements in the LKED step for ddnames SYSPRINT, SYSUT1, SYSLIB, and SYSLMOD, as they are required by the linkage editor and have been accounted for accordingly. What needs to be modified in the linkage step of the procedure, however, is the SYSLIN Dd statement to read the input program object module. Its definition was deferred in the procedure. Coding a LKED.SYSIN Dd statement satisfies this deferment for ddname SYSLIN, e.g.,

```
//LKED.SYSIN  DD  DSNAME=A.PROGRAM.LIBRARY(REFORM),DISP=SHR
```

187

Program object module REFORM was presumably stored in a partitioned library and is now being called as input to the linkage step. If an object deck had previously been created, a Dd * statement would need to be coded followed by the deck itself. In either case, ddname SYSLIN in the procedure must be modified to accept the object module as input.

The third step of the PL1LFLG procedure named GO refers back to the SYSLMOD Dd statement in the LKED step and loads the appropriate program load module into main storage. A SYSUDUMP Dd statement for abnormal conditions and a SYSPRINT Dd statement print file have been provided in the GO step of the procedure. No other Dd statements have been provided in the GO step of the procedure. No other Dd statements have been provided to this execute step. Therefore, they must be added to the GO (execute) step when the procedure is called. The preceding JCL job stream example adds Dd statements for ddnames READIN, PARMCARD, WRTOUT, and PNCHOUT for a tape, card, disk, and punch file, respectively.

A comparable Link and Execute catalogued procedure exists for other PL/1 programming levels as well. The names of the procedures are only slightly changed to reflect the programming level utilized, though a check with the dp installation should be made.

d. ASSEMBLER and Other Program Language
   Considerations

Assume that one has assembled and saved in program object module form an ASSEMBLER Level-F program. Linkage and execution are both desired, though the executable program load module need not be saved. An example of JCL which could be coded to meet this objective is as follows:

```
//AMIX    JOB   A1B2C3XYZ,DANHR,MSGLEVEL=(1,1),
//             CLASS=C,TIME=(1,30)
//STEP1   EXEC  PROC=ASMFLG,
//             REGION.GO=60K,TIME.GO=1
//LKED.SYSIN  DD  DSNAME=A.PROGRAM.LIBRARY(CONVERT),DISP=SHR
//GO.DATAIN  DD  UNIT=DISK,DISP=(OLD,KEEP),
//             DSNAME=OLDDATA,VOL=SER=005697
//GO.PARAMIN  DD  *
   -  -  -  -  Card File Here  -  -  -  -
/*
//GO.DATAOUT  DD  UNIT=2400,DISP=(NEW,KEEP,DELETE),
//             DSNAME=NEWDATA,VOL=SER=TAPE56
//GO.PRTOUT  DD  SYSOUT=A
//
```

See the fourth procedure list in Figure 5.10. A need exists to specify region size and time requirements to the GO (or execute) step, e.g., REGION.GO=60K,TIME.GO=1. None is specified in the procedure, as program size and time demands for its many applications are not known when cataloguing a procedure.

There is no need to modify existing Dd statements in the LKED step for ddname SYSPRINT, SYSUT1, SYSLIB, and SYSLMOD, as they are required by the linkage editor and have been accounted for accordingly. What needs to be modified in the linkage step of the procedure, however, is the SYSLIN Dd statement to read the input program object module. Its definition was deferred in the procedure. Coding a LKED.SYSIN Dd statement satisfies this deferment for ddname SYSLIN, e.g.,

      //LKED.SYSIN   DSNAME=A.PROGRAM.LIBRARY(CONVERT),DISP=SHR

Program object module CONVERT was presumably stored in a partitioned library and is now being called as input to the linkage step. If an object deck had previously been created, a Dd * statement would need to be coded followed by the deck itself. In either case, ddname SYSLIN in the procedure must be modified to accept the object module as input.

The third step of the ASMFLG procedure named GO refers back to the LKED step and loads the appropriate program load module into main storage. A SYSUDUMP Dd statement for abnormal conditions has been provided in the GO step of the procedure. No other Dd statements have been provided to this execute step. Therefore, they must be added to the GO (execute) step when the procedure is called. The preceding JCL job stream example adds Dd statements for ddnames DATAIN, PARAMIN, DATAOUT, and PRTOUT for a disk, card, tape, and print file, respectively.

A comparable Link and Execute catalogued procedure exists for other ASSEMBLER programming levels as well. The names of the procedures are only slightly changed to reflect the programming level utilized. Other programming languages also follow these same concepts and principles. That is, RPGELG would be called to link and execute a Report Program Generator (RPG) Level-E program. Various programming levels are also reflected in the procedure name. The only essential difference among these procedures is that some blocksizes and main storage requirements may be changed. Exec statement parameters and ddnames defined in these procedures have similar functions as discussed in preceding examples. A check with the dp installation should be made, however, as unique user standards and preferences may affect specific makeup of any given procedure.

5. The Linkage Editor (Link Only)

Up to this point in the text, the linkage editor program has been used to accomplish two objectives: (1) to access system libraries and attach (or link) called modules to the main program, and (2) to assign a name to the program output load module. Other functions which can be performed by the linkage editor include assigning alias member names, changing external program symbols, specifying program entry points, assigning module storage hierarchies, identifying data for program entry, including other program modules, inserting other program modules, calling additional libraries, defining overlay segments, replacing program modules, and providing selected information to the program directory. These functions will be discussed further throughout the text only to the degree that they are commonly used in most dp environments.

a. Link Only

A one-step catalogued procedure which calls the linkage editor program to link only is available at most dp installations. The linkage editor is common to all programming languages and levels. One must assume that an object deck exists or that the object module of interest has been stored in a program library. Figure 5.11 displays a catalogued procedure which links program object modules regardless of the original source language utilized. The standard name for this procedure is LKED.

Figure 5.11 Link Only Procedure

```
LKED:

//LKED EXEC PGM=IEWL,REGION=100K,
//          PARM='XREF,LIST,LET,NCAL'
//SYSPRINT DD SYSOUT=A
//SYSUT1 DD UNIT=SYSDA,DSNAME=&SYSUT1,SPACE=(1024,(200,20))
//SYSLIN DD DDNAME=SYSIN
//SYSLMOD DD UNIT=SYSDA,DISP=(MOD,PASS),
//          DSNAME=&GOSET(GO),DCB=BLKSIZE=1024,
//          SPACE=(1024,(200,20))
```

The first statement in the one-step procedure in Figure 5.11 calls the linkage editor program, IEWL. Program LINKEDIT is also available in some installations. This statement also allocates 100,000 bytes of main storage as well as providing XREF, LIST, LET, and NCAL parameter information to the linkage program. If MAP is specified in lieu of XREF, a Map listing of the relative location and length of each program and subprogram module is provided. When XREF is specified, not only is a Map provided, but a Cross-Reference Table as well which lists external references and their relative locations in each program and subprogram module. LIST requests the linkage editor to print all control cards utilized. LET allows the program load module to be marked as executable even though one or more errors exist. NCAL (No Call) indicates that any libraries described on a SYSLIB Dd statement should not be accessed to satisfy program external references. A description for the ddname SYSLIB library file need not be provided.

190

These libraries may or may not be accessed later, depending upon the specific application involved.

The next statement in this procedure with ddname SYSPRINT describes the linkage editor message file. This is followed by a SYSUT1 ddname temporary disk work file. The ddname SYSLIN input object module or deck is described next. The Ddname keyword defers the definition of a data set to be later identified with the ddname of SYSIN. Finally, a SYSLMOD ddname file describes the output load module as a disk data set to be passed to another step.

Assume that one has assembled and saved in program object module form an ASSEMBLER program. Linkage only is desired. The executable program load module need also be stored in a private partitioned data set library. An example of JCL which could be coded to meet this objective is as follows:

```
//LINKONLY  JOB  L5438,DANHR,MSGLEVEL=(1,1),
//        CLASS=A
//STEP1  EXEC  PROC=LKED
//LKED.SYSLMOD  DD  DSNAME=A.PROGRAM.LIBRARY(APROG),DISP=SHR
//LKED.SYSIN  DD  *
   -  -  -  - Program Object Deck Here  -  -  -  -
//
```

Following the appropriate Job statement is an Exec statement which calls the one-step procedure of interest, LKED. There is no particular need to modify or add new Exec statement parameter information for this application. Similarly, there is no need to modify existing Dd statements for ddnames SYSPRINT and SYSUT1, as they are required by the linkage editor and have been accounted for accordingly. A SYSLIB Dd statement is not required either, as NCAL has been specified in the LKED procedure.

One statement which needs to be modified in the procedure is the SYSLMOD ddname disk file. This file is the linkage editor's program load module output and will be in 100% machine-executable form if all external references are satisfied. Due to the NCAL option discussed previously, these references are most likely not all satisfied. Rather, the load module is to be placed into a library to await further linkage with other program modules nearer execution time. Coding

```
//LKED.SYSLMOD  DD  DSNAME=A.PROGRAM.LIBRARY(APROG),DISP=SHR
```

would satisfy this requirement and provide a name of APROG to the module. A Program Name Control Card is not required. This technique of coding the member name in parentheses behind the data set library name is a frequently utilized alternative to the NAME control statement. It is also not limited to just linkage editor applications, but rather is common throughout all JCL partitioned data set coding.

Another statement which needs to be modified in the procedure is the SYSLIN Dd statement to read the input program object module. This file is described last, as its definition had been deferred. Coding a LKED.SYSIN Dd statement satisfies this deferment for ddname SYSLIN, e.g., //LKED.SYSIN DD *. The program object deck was presumably recently created and physically stored in card form and is now being used as input to the linkage step. In this example, an input program object module stored in library form is not being utilized.

A Null statement follows the SYSIN Dd statement to indicate the end of this particular job stream. Printed output includes a JCL listing with file allocation and termination messages, a linkage editor message indicating that the new load module has been added to the library or replaced an existing member, and a cross-reference control section listing. These are standard linkage editor outputs which should be requested via JCL Parm parameter specifications discussed previously if they are not a default of the linkage editor program or procedure itself. All linkage editor options are defined in detail in Appendix C. A check with the dp installation should be made, as unique user standards and preferences may affect the specific makeup of a given procedure.

b. Linkage Control Statements

The linkage editor can perform many specialized functions. Figure 5.12 displays the function and specific formats of all linkage editor program control statements. Column 1 must remain blank.

Figure 5.12 Linkage Editor Control Statement Function and Format

Alias Statement: Specifies alternate module names and entry points.

ALIAS
$$\left\{ \begin{array}{l} \text{Symbol Name} \\ \text{Symbol Name},\ldots\ldots \\ \text{External Name} \\ \text{External Name},\ldots\ldots \end{array} \right\}$$

where Symbol Name specifies an alias name for the load

module; and

External Name specifies an entry point within the module.

Change Statement: Changes external symbol name.

CHANGE
$$\left\{ \begin{array}{l} \text{Old Name(New Name)} \\ \text{Old Name(New Name)},\ldots\ldots \end{array} \right\}$$

where Old Name is the name of an external symbol to

be changed to the New Name.

192

Figure 5.12 Linkage Editor Control Statement Function and Format (cont.)

Entry Statement: Specifies first program instruction to be executed.

ENTRY   External Name

where External Name is a program entry name or a control
section name.

Hiarchy Statement: Assigns control sections to storage hierarchies.

HIARCHY $\left\{\begin{array}{l} \text{Hierarchy, Control Section Name} \\ \text{Hierarchy, Control Section Name,......} \end{array}\right\}$

where Hierarchy equals 0 or 1 for Storage Hierarchies 0 and 1,
respectively; and
Control Section Name is the section assigned to the hierarchy.

Identify Statement: Provides identifying information to control
section identification records.

IDENTIFY $\left\{\begin{array}{l} \text{Control Section Name('Id Info')} \\ \text{Control Section Name ('Id Info'),......} \end{array}\right\}$

where Control Section Name is the section to which identification
information (Id Info) will be provided to identification records.

Include Statement: Specifies additional sequential data sets and
Partitioned Data Set (PDS) libraries to be made
available for input.

INCLUDE $\left\{\begin{array}{l} \text{Ddname} \\ \text{Ddname(Member Name)} \\ \text{Ddname(Member Name,......)} \end{array}\right\}$ [,......]

where Ddname is name of appropriate Dd statement; and
Member Name is name of PDS member.

Insert Statement: Rearranges control section positions.

193

Figure 5.12 Linkage Editor Control Statement Function and Format (cont.)

INSERT $\begin{Bmatrix} \text{Control Section Name} \\ \text{Control Section Name,......} \end{Bmatrix}$

where Control Section Name is the section to be rearranged
according to the order of Insert statements.

Library Statement: Specifies additional libraries to be made
available for access, and external references
which need not be resolved.

LIBRARY $\begin{Bmatrix} \text{Ddname(Member Name)} \\ \text{Ddname(Member Name,......)} \\ \text{(External Reference)} \\ \text{(External Reference,......)} \\ \text{*(External Reference)} \\ \text{*(External Reference,......)} \end{Bmatrix}$ [,......]

where Ddname is name of appropriate Dd statement;

Member Name is name of PDS member;

External Reference is name which is not to be resolved

this run via an automatic library call; and

* indicates that the external reference is never to be

solved via an automatic library call.

Name Statement: Assigns program name to output load module.

NAME $\begin{Bmatrix} \text{Member Name} \\ \text{Member Name(R)} \end{Bmatrix}$

where Member Name is name of PDS member; and,

R specifies that this member is to replace

existing member of the same name within the PDS

library.

Overlay Statement: Specifies the beginning of an overlay segment
or region.

194

Figure 5.12 Linkage Editor Control Statement Function and Format (cont.)

```
OVERLAY     ⎧ Overlay Name          ⎫
            ⎨                       ⎬
            ⎩ Overlay Name(REGION)  ⎭
```

where Overlay Name is a symbolic name given to an overlay

segment or region; and

REGION identifies the name as an overlay region.

Replace Statement: Replaces control sections; deletes control

                     sections and entry names.

```
            ⎧ Control Section Name1                       ⎫
            ⎪                                             ⎪
REPLACE     ⎨ Control Section Name1(Control Section Name2)⎬  [,......]
            ⎪                                             ⎪
            ⎩ Entry Name                                  ⎭
```

where Control Section Name1 is name of control section

to be deleted or replaced;

Control Section Name2 is name of control section

which replaces Control Section Name1; and,

Entry Name is name of entry to be deleted.

Setssi Statement: Provides information to be set into System

                    Status Index (SSI) of directory entry of

                    load module.

SETSSI   xxxxxxxx

where xxxxxxxx is appropriate hexadecimal information.

   This being a major subject in and by itself, a more detailed
description of the many unique functions of the Linkage Editor can be
obtained from the Linkage Editor and Loader manual.

6. The Loader (Compile And Execute)

   When special features of the linkage editor are not required, the
Loader program may be called instead. Program LOADER combines into
one step the basic functions of linkage with the loading and execution
of a program module. The Loader does not create load modules to be
saved in program libraries. Nor does it have the capability to create

195

overlay program structures. Rather, simple external references are
resolved and a quick execution of the program is accomplished.

a. Loader Use

   At least one catalogued procedure which compiles and loads (or
executes) is available at dp installations for each programming
language supported. Figure 5.13 displays four catalogued procedures
which compile and execute American National Standard (ANS) COBOL
Version 4, FORTRAN IV G1-Level, PL/1 F-Level, and ASSEMBLER F-Level
source programs. Standard names for these procedures are COBUCG,
FTG1CG, PL1LFCG, and ASMFCG, respectively.
   The compile step in each of the two-step procedures in Figure 5.13
is identical to previous examples of each programming language utilized.
The first statement in the second step of each of the procedures calls
the loader program, LOADER. The loader is not specific to the original
source language utilized. This statement also allocates an identical
amount of main storage in each case as well as providing MAP and LET

Figure 5.13 Compile and Load (Execute) Procedures

```
COBUCG:

//COB EXEC PGM=IKFCBL00,REGION=130K

//STEPLIB DD DSNAME=SYS1.COBLIB,DISP=SHR

//SYSPRINT DD SYSOUT=A

//SYSPUNCH DD SYSOUT=B

//SYSUT1 DD UNIT=SYSDA,DSNAME=&SYSUT1,SPACE=(460,(700,300),RLSE)

//SYSUT2 DD UNIT=SYSDA,DSNAME=&SYSUT2,SPACE=(460,(700,300),RLSE)

//SYSUT3 DD UNIT=SYSDA,DSNAME=&SYSUT3,SPACE=(460,(700,300),RLSE)

//SYSUT4 DD UNIT=SYSDA,DSNAME=&SYSUT4,SPACE=(460,(700,300),RLSE)

//SYSLIN DD UNIT=SYSDA,DISP=(MOD,PASS),

//       DSNAME=&LOADSET,DCB=BLKSIZE=3200,

//       SPACE=(3200,(20,20),RLSE)

//GO EXEC PGM=LOADER,REGION=100K,

//       PARM='MAP,LET',

//       COND=(4,LT,COB)

//SYSLOUT DD SYSOUT=A

//SYSLIB DD DSNAME=SYS1.COBLIB,DISP=SHR

//SYSLIN DD DSNAME=&LOADSET,DISP=(OLD,DELETE)

//SYSUDUMP DD SYSOUT=A

//SYSOUT DD SYSOUT=A
```

Figure 5.13 Compile and Load (Execute) Procedures (cont.)

```
FTG1CG:

//FORT EXEC PGM=IGIFORT,REGION=130K
//STEPLIB DD DSNAME=SYS1.FORTLIB,DISP=SHR
//SYSPRINT DD SYSOUT=A
//SYSPUNCH DD SYSOUT=B
//SYSLIN DD UNIT=SYSDA,DISP=(MOD,PASS),
//        DSNAME=&LOADSET,DCB=BLKSIZE=3200,
//        SPACE=(3200,(60,60),RLSE)
//GO EXEC PGM=LOADER,REGION=100K
//        PARM='MAP,LET',
//        COND=(4,LT,FORT)
//SYSLOUT DD SYSOUT=A
//SYSLIB DD DSNAME=SYS1.FORTLIB,DISP=SHR
//SYSLIN DD DSNAME=&LOADSET,DISP=(OLD,DELETE)
//SYSUDUMP DD SYSOUT=A
//FT05F001 DD DDNAME=SYSIN
//FT06F001 DD SYSOUT=A
//FT07F001 DD SYSOUT=B


PL1LFCG:

//PL1L EXEC PGM=IEMAA,REGION=100K
//SYSPRINT DD SYSOUT=A
//SYSPUNCH DD SYSOUT=B
//SYSUT3 DD UNIT=SYSDA,
//       DSNAME=&SYSUT3,DCB=BLKSIZE=3200,
//       SPACE=(3200,(10,10))
//SYSUT1 DD UNIT=SYSDA,
//       DSNAME=&SYSUT1,DCB=BLKSIZE=1024,
//       SPACE=(1024,(60,60))

//SYSLIN DD UNIT=SYSDA,DISP=(MOD,PASS),
//       DSNAME=&LOADSET,DCB=BLKSIZE=3200,
//       SPACE=(3200,(10,10),RLSE)
```

Figure 5.13 Compile and Load (Execute) Procedures (cont.)

```
//GO EXEC PGM=LOADER,REGION=100K,
//        PARM='MAP,LET",
//        COND=(4,LT,PL1L)
//SYSLOUT DD SYSOUT=A
//SYSLIB DD DSNAME=SYS1.PL1LIB,DISP=SHR
//SYSLIN DD DSNAME=&LOADSET,DISP=(OLD,DELETE)
//SYSUDUMP DD SYSOUT=A
//SYSPRINT DD SYSOUT=A


ASMFCG:


//ASM EXEC PGM=IEUASM,REGION=80K,
//        PARM='LOAD,LIST,XREF'
//SYSPRINT DD SYSOUT=A
//SYSPUNCH DD SYSOUT=B
//SYSUT1 DD UNIT=SYSDA,DSNAME=&SYSUT1,SPACE=(3200,(80,80))
//SYSUT2 DD UNIT=SYSDA,DSNAME=&SYSUT2,SPACE=(3200,(80,80))
//SYSUT3 DD UNIT=SYSDA,DSNAME=&SYSUT3,SPACE=(3200,(80,80))
//SYSLIB DD DSNAME=SYS1.MACLIB,DISP=SHR
//SYSGO DD UNIT=SYSDA,DISP=(MOD,PASS),
//        DSNAME=&LOADSET,DCB=BLKSIZE=3200,
//        SPACE=(3200,(10,10),RLSE)
//GO EXEC PGM=LOADER,REGION=100K,
//        PARM='MAP,LET,NOCALL',
//        COND=(4,LT,ASM)
//SYSLOUT DD SYSOUT=A
//SYSLIN DD DSNAME=&LOADSET,DISP=(OLD,DELETE)
//SYSUDUMP DD SYSOUT=A
```

parameter information to the loader program. NOCALL is also specified in the Assembler procedure. The MAP option provides a listing of external names and their storage addresses. LET allows program execution to continue even though one or more errors occurred during the loader process. NOCALL indicates that an Assembler library search should not be made; a SYSLIB Dd statement is not provided. All Loader options and their functions are depicted in Appendix C. A Condition parameter on each of these Exec statements specifies that there is no need to load a program which still contains conditional errors.

The next statement in each procedure with ddname SYSLOUT describes the loader message file. The ddname SYSLIN object module passed from the compile or assembly step is described next for ddname SYSLIN as input to the linkage program. With the exception of the ASSEMBLER procedure, appropriate program libraries are accessed next via the SYSLIB Dd statement. Appropriate ASSEMBLER macro libraries had been accessed in the assembly step. Note the absence of a SYSLMOD ddname file which described the output load module in linkage steps, but do not need to be described for the loader process. Remaining statements in each procedure describe the same files as in other GO (or execute) steps described previously.

b. Loader Examples

<u>COBOL Programs:</u>

Assume that one has coded and is now testing an American National Standard (ANS) COBOL program. Compilation and execution are desired, and the special features of the linkage editor are not required. An example of JCL which could be coded to meet this objective is as follows:

```
//AMIX   JOB   A1B2C3XYZ,DANHR,MSGLEVEL=(1,1),
//          CLASS=C,TIME=3
//STEP1  EXEC  PROC=COBUCG,
//          PARM.COB='CLIST,DMAP,XREF',
//          REGION.GO=100K,TIME.GO=(1,30)
//COB.SYSIN  DD   *
    -   -   -   - ANS COBOL Program Here  -   -   -   -
/*
//GO.INPUT1  DD   UNIT=2400,DISP=(OLD,KEEP),
//          DSNAME=AMASTER,VOL=SER=TAPE88,
//          DCB=(RECFM=FB,LRECL=120,BLKSIZE=6400)
//GO.CARDIN  DD   *
    -   -   -   - Card File Here  -   -   -   -
/*
//GO.OUTPUT1  DD   UNIT=SYSDA,DISP=(NEW,KEEP),
//          DSNAME=UPDATED,VOL=SER=001873,
//          SPACE=(6400,(20,2),RLSE),
//          DCB=(RECFM=FB,LRECL=120,BLKSIZE=6400)
//GO.PRINT1  DD   SYSOUT=(C,,1484)
//
```

Note that the only difference between the above job stream and a previous one which called procedure COBUCLG is the name of the called procedure itself, COBUCG. A comparable Compile and Execute catalogued procedure exists for other COBOL programming levels as well. The names of the procedures are only slightly changed. Instead of COBUCG, for example, the catalogued procedure to compile and execute Level-F COBOL programs is named COBFCG. That is, the letter 'U' is replaced by the letter 'F'. Other levels also reflect comparable name changes. The only essential difference among these procedures is that a different compiler program is called. Aside from that, the method of calling the procedure is the same; the technique of modifying or adding to the procedure is identical; and other than procedure and compiler names, the content of the procedure itself is essentially the same as other COBOL programming levels. A check with the dp installation should be made, as unique user standards and preferences may affect the specific makeup of a given procedure.

FORTRAN Programs:

Assume that one has coded and is now testing a FORTRAN IV Level-G1 program. Compilation and execution are desired, and the special features of the linkage editor are not required. An example of JCL which could be coded to meet this objective is as follows:

```
//AMIX   JOB   A1B2C3XYZ,DANHR,MSGLEVEL=(1,1),
//         CLASS=C,TIME=3
//STEP1  EXEC  PROC=FTG1CG,
//         PARM.FORT='LIST',
//         REGION.GO=120K,TIME.GO=2
//FORT.SYSIN  DD  *
    -  -  -  - FORTRAN IV (G1) Program Here  -  -  -  -
/*
//GO.FT01F001  DD  UNIT=SYSDA,DISP=(OLD,KEEP),
//         DSNAME=OLDDATA,VOL=SER=PACK07,
//         DCB=(RECFM=VB,LRECL=120,BLKSIZE=3204)
//GO.FT08F001  DD  UNIT=2400,DISP=(NEW,KEEP),
//         DSNAME=NEWDATA,
//         DCB=(RECFM=VB,LRECL=120,BLKSIZE=6204)
//GO.SYSIN  DD  *
    -  -  -  - Card File Here  -  -  -  -
//
```

Note that the only difference between the above job stream and a previous one which called procedure FTG1CLG is the name of the called procedure itself, FTG1CG.

A comparable Compile and Execute catalogued procedure exists for other FORTRAN programming levels as well. The names of the procedures are only slightly changed. Instead of FTG1CG, for example, the catalogued procedure to compile and execute Level-H FORTRAN IV programs is named FORTHCG. Other levels also reflect comparable name changes. The only essential difference among these procedures is that a different compiler program is called. Compiler work files may also be provided on occasion. Aside from that, the method of calling the procedure is the same; the technique of modifying or adding to the procedure is identical; and other than procedure and compiler names, the content of the procedure itself is essentially the same as other FORTRAN programming levels. A check with the dp installation should be made, as unique user standards and preferences may affect the specific makeup of a given procedure.

Programming Language/One (PL/1) Differences:

Assume that one has coded and is now testing a PL/1 Level-F program. Compilation and execution are desired, and the special features of the linkage editor are not required. An example of JCL which could be coded to meet this objective is as follows:

```
//AMIX    JOB   A1B2C3XYZ,DANHR,MSGLEVEL=(1,1),
//        CLASS=C,TIME=2
//STEP1   EXEC  PROC=PL1LFCG,
//        PARM.PL1L='LIST,XREF',
//        REGION.GO=80K,TIME.GO=(1,30)
//PL1L.SYSIN  DD   *

   -  -  -  -  PL/1 (F) Program Here  -  -  -  -

/*
//GO.READIN   DD   UNIT=2400,DISP=(OLD,KEEP),
//        DSNAME=RAWDATA,VOL=SER=022183,
//        DCB=(RECFM=FB,LRECL=400,BLKSIZE=4000)
//GO.PARMCARD  DD   *

   -  -  -  -  Card File Here  -  -  -  -

/*
//GO.WRTOUT   DD   UNIT=3330,DISP=(NEW,KEEP,DELETE),
//        DSNAME=EDITDATA,
//        SPACE=(4000,(40,4),RLSE),
//        DCB=(RECFM=FB,LRECL=400,BLKSIZE=4000)
//GO.PNCHOUT  DD   SYSOUT=B
//
```

Note that the only difference between the above job stream and a previous one which called procedure PL1LFCLG is the name of the called procedure itself, PL1LFCG.

A comparable Compile and Execute catalogued procedure exists for other PL/1 programming levels as well. The names of the procedures are only slightly changed to reflect the programming level utilized, though a check with the dp installation should be made.

ASSEMBLER and Other Program Language Considerations:

Assume that one has coded and is now testing an ASSEMBLER Level-F program. Compilation and execution are desired, and the special features of the linkage editor are not required. An example of JCL which could be coded to meet this objective is as follows:

```
//AMIX   JOB  A1B2C3XYZ,DANHR,MSGLEVEL=(1,1),
//          CLASS=C,TIME=2
//STEP1  EXEC  PROC=ASMFCG,
//          REGION.GO=60K,TIME.GO=(1,30)
//ASM,SYSIN  DD   *
   -  -  -  - ASSEMBLER (F) Program Here  -  -  -  -
/*
//GO.DATAIN   DD  UNIT=SYSDA,DISP=(OLD,KEEP),
//          DSNAME=MASTIN,VOL=SER=REEL99,
//          DCB=(RECFM=FB,LRECL=80,BLKSIZE=3200)
//GO.PARAMIN  DD   *
   -  -  -  - Card File Here  -  -  -  -
/*
//GO.DATAOUT  DD  UNIT=2400,DISP=(NEW,KEEP),
//          DSNAME=MASTOUT,VOL=SER=TAPE07,
//          DCB=(RECFM=FB,LRECL=80,BLKSIZE=3200)
//GO.PRTOUT  DD  SYSOUT=A
//
```

Note that the only difference between the above job stream and a previous one which called procedure ASMFCLG is the name of the called procedure itself, ASMFCG.

A comparable Compile and Execute catalogued procedure exists for other ASSEMBLER programming levels as well. The names of the procedure are only slightly changed to reflect the programming level utilized. Other programming languages also follow these same concepts and principles. That is, RPGECG would be called to compile and execute a Report Program Generator (RPG) Level-E program. Various programming levels are also reflected in the procedure name. A unique compiler name would be coded in the procedure itself. Exec statement parameters and ddnames defined in these procedures have similar functions as discussed in preceding examples. A check with the dp installation should be made, however, as unique user standards and preferences may affect specific makeup of any given procedure.

7. Sort and Merge Procedures

Most programs to be executed require the data to be processed in a specific order. Sort procedures are perhaps the most frequently called procedures of all. They are used by application and system programmers and analysts on a day-by-day basis. Merging is also possible, that is, the collating of two or more files already in a desired sequence.

a. Sort/Merge Use

One-step catalogued procedures which call sort/merge programs are available at most dp installations. Figure 5.14 displays two standard catalogued procedures which sort or merge input data files. Their names are SORTD and SORT. A third and typical installation-defined sort procedure is also displayed.

The first three statements in each of the procedures in Figure 5.14 calls the sort/merge program, IERRCO00. A main storage region allocation is also made. No Parm parameter information is provided, though Appendix C depicts some optional specifications. Ddname SYSOUT defines a sort message file. The Sort library is also accessed for sort/merge modules via a SORTLIB Dd statement. This completes the SORTD procedure, whereas the other two procedures are continued.

The SORTD procedure may be used when linkage editor sort services are not utilized. The SORT procedure contains four additional Dd statements for linkage use. The SYSPRINT ddname file defines linkage editor messages, SYSLMOD for linkage output, SYSLIN for linkage input, and SYSUT1 for a linkage editor work file. The installation-defined procedure is identical to SORTD except that six sort work files have been added. These most desired files have been left out of the SORTD and SORT procedures. As a result, most installations define their own sort procedures to include required work files such that a user need not code them.

b. Sort/Merge File Descriptions

Three basic Dd statements have been purposely left out of the previously discussed sort/merge procedures. Their ddnames are SORTIN, SORTOUT, and SYSIN, where:

SORTIN describes the input file(s) to be sorted;
SORTOUT describes the sorted output file; and
SYSIN describes the sort control file.

In lieu of ddname SORTIN, the ddnames for merging are SORTIN01, SORTIN02, etc., where:

SORTIN01 describes the first input file to be merged; and
SORTINxx describes the xxth input file to be merged, etc.

Figure 5.14 Sort/Merge Procedures

```
        SORTD:

        //SORT EXEC PGM=IERRCO00,REGION=26K

        //SYSOUT  DD  SYSOUT=A

        //SORTLIB  DD  DSNAME=SYS1.SORTLIB,DISP=SHR


        SORT:

        //SORT EXEC PGM=IERRCO00,REGION=98K

        //SYSOUT DD SYSOUT=A

        //SORTLIB DD DSNAME=SYS1.SORTLIB,DISP=SHR

        //SYSPRINT DD DUMMY

        //SYSLMOD DD DSNAME=&GOSET,UNIT=SYSDA,SPACE=(3600,(20,20,1))

        //SYSLIN DD DSNAME=&LOADSET,UNIT=SYSDA,SPACE=(80,(10,10))

        //SYSUT1 DD DSNAME=&SYSUT1,SPACE=(1000,(60,20)),

        //       UNIT=(SYSDA,SEP=(SORTLIB,SYSLMOD,SYSLIN))

        Installation-Defined:

        //SORT EXEC PGM=IERRCO00,REGION=98K

        //SYSOUT DD SYSOUT=A

        //SORTLIB DD DSNAME=SYS1.SORTLIB,DISP=SHR

        //SORTWK01 DD UNIT=SYSDA,SPACE=(TRK,(100),,CONTIG)

        //SORTWK02 DD UNIT=SYSDA,SPACE=(TRK,(100),,CONTIG)

        //SORTWK03 DD UNIT=SYSDA,SPACE=(TRK,(100),,CONTIG)

        //SORTWK04 DD UNIT=SYSDA,SPACE=(TRK,(100),,CONTIG)

        //SORTWK05 DD UNIT=SYSDA,SPACE=(TRK,(100),,CONTIG)
```

These files have been left out because their descriptions are not
known until the user calls the procedure of interest. They must therefore be temporarily added back to the procedure when called. A control
file must also be created by the user. Figure 5.15 displays all sort/
merge control statement formats and functions. Column 1 must remain
blank. Though the list appears lengthy, it will be seen that only a
small portion of the full syntax is necessary for most applications
of the sort/merge program.

Figure 5.15 Sort/Merge Control File Statements

Sort Statement:

SORT FIELDS=$\begin{Bmatrix} (a,b,c,d,\ldots\ldots) \\ (a,b,d,\ldots\ldots),FORMAT=c \end{Bmatrix}$ [,SIZE=y][,SKIPREC=z][,CKPT]

to describe desired sort order and characteristics on a
field-by-field basis from major to minor,
where a = starting location of field of interest;

    b = length of field;

    c = form of data representation utilized;

        CH - Character

        BI - Binary

        FI - Fixed Point

        FL - Floating Point

        PD - Packed Decimal

        ZD - Zoned Decimal;

    d = ordering sequence;

        A   - Ascending

        D   - Descending

        E   - User Modification;

    y = actual or estimated number of input records to

           (if estimated, code the letter 'E'

           in front of y-value);

    z = number of initial records to skip in the sort

        process; and

  CKPT activates the checkpoint facility.

Merge Statement:

MERGE $\begin{Bmatrix} (a,b,c,d,\ldots\ldots) \\ (a,b,d,\ldots\ldots),FORMAT=c \end{Bmatrix}$ [,SIZE=y]

  to describe desired merge order and characteristics on a

  field-by-field basis from major to minor,

  where a through d and y are identical in form to the

    Sort statement.

Figure 5.15 Sort/Merge Control File Statements (cont.)

Record Statement:

$$\text{RECORD} \begin{Bmatrix} \text{TYPE=F,LENGTH=(a,b,c)} \\ \text{TYPE=V,LENGTH=(a,b,c,d,e)} \end{Bmatrix}$$

to indicate changing user program record types and lengths,

where F = Fixed-length records;

V = Variable-length records;

a = maximum input record length;

b = maximum sort record length;

c = maximum output record length;

d = minimum input record length; and

e = most frequent input record length.

Mods Statement:

MODS Exit Name=(a,b,c $\begin{bmatrix} ,N \\ ,S \end{bmatrix}$)[,......]

to transfer control as desired from sort/merge program to

user programs(s),

where Exit Name is one of 17 program modification names;

a = user routine name;

b = user routine storage requirements;

c = ddname which describes routine;

N indicates that routine has been link-edited; and

S indicates that routine has not been link-edited.

End Statement:

END

to delimit control statements from user routines placed

before the /* delimiter.

The actual coding of sort and merge JCL can now begin.

c. JCL Examples

Assume that one has just created a series of records on tape which need to be sorted into a specific sequence for input to the next program. An example of JCL which could be coded to meet this objective is as follows:

```
//AMIX   JOB  A1B2C3XYZ,DANHR,MSGLEVEL=(1,1),
//          CLASS=E,TIME=1
//STEP1  EXEC  PROC=SORTW
//SORT.SORTIN  DD  UNIT=2400,DISP=(OLD,KEEP),
//          DSNAME=NEW.MASTER,VOL=SER=SRS007,
//          DCB=(RECFM=FB,LRECL=100,BLKSIZE=3200)
//SORT.SORTOUT  DD  UNIT=2400,DISP=(NEW,KEEP),
//          DSNAME=SORTED.MASTER,VOL=SER=SCRTCH,
//          DCB=(RECFM=FB,LRECL=100,BLKSIZE=3200)
//SORT.SYSIN  DD  *
  SORT  FIELDS=(20,2,D,1,9,A),FORMAT=CH,SIZE=E10000
//
```

Following an appropriate Job statement is an Exec statement which calls the one-step procedure of interest, SORTW. Let's assume that this name has been chosen for the third and installation-defined procedure listed in Figure 5.14. Sort work files have been included in its makeup. There is no need to modify any of the statements already contained within the procedure. What needs to be added to the SORT step are the Dd statements for the SORTIN, SORTOUT, and SYSIN files. Note that the procedure name and stepname within the procedure are the same.

Let's assume that a 2-character state code is present in columns 20 and 21 of the input records to be sorted. Also, a Social Security number is present in columns 1 to 9. The sort control file in the example above specifies the state code field as major (coded first) and the Social Security number as minor (coded last). Intermediate fields could also be used for sort control if desired. The Sort control statement indicates that the major field begins in column 20, has a length of 2 bytes, and should be sorted in descending order. In addition, the minor field begins in column 1, has a length of 9 bytes, and should be sorted within the major field in ascending order. The Character form of data representation has been utilized to define these fields on the input record. An estimated file size of 10,000 records has been specified to assist the sort program in setting intermediate storage space limits. Thus a file of (unsorted) sample records would be sorted as follows:

Unsorted		Sorted	
890123456	30	123456789	60
123459999	60	123459999	60
111111112	40	999999999	50
777777777	10	111111111	40
901234567	30	111111112	40
123456789	60	999999999	40
789012345	30	789012345	30
111111111	40	890123456	30
999999999	50	901234567	30
999999999	40	777777777	10

The author also recommends that a SYSUDUMP Dd statement be added to the SORT step for abnormal terminations. It should also be pointed out that if procedure SORTD or SORT were called, sort work files would need to be added, e.g.,

```
//SORT.SORTWKxx   DD   UNIT=SYSDA,SPACE=(TRK,(100),,CONTIG)
```

where xx = 01, 02, 03, 04, 05, 06, etc., depending upon file size considerations. Specifications of this nature can be obtained from the Sort/Merge manual. A check with the dp installation should also be made as unique user installation standards and preferences may affect the specific makeup of a given procedure.

Assume that one has just created two files in the same sequence which need to be merged into one file of the same sequence for input to the next program. An example of JCL which could be coded to meet this objective is as follows:

```
//AMIX   JOB   A1B2C3XYZ,DANHR,MSGLEVEL=(1,1),
//        CLASS=C,TIME=1
//STEP1  EXEC   PROC=SORTD
//SORT.SORTIN01   DD   UNIT=3330,DISP=(OLD,KEEP),
//        DSNAME=RAWDATA1,VOL=SER=PACK67,
//        DCB=(RECFM=VB,LRECL=100,BLKSIZE=3204)
//SORT.SORTIN02   DD   UNIT=3330,DISP=(NEW,KEEP),
//        DSNAME=RAWDATA2,VOL=SER=PACK89,
//        DCB=(RECFM=VB,LRECL=100,BLKSIZE=3204)
//SORT.SORTOUT   DD   UNIT=2400,DISP=(NEW,KEEP),
```

```
//        DSNAME=MERGED.DATA,VOL=SER=REEL54,
//        DCB=(RECFM=VB,LRECL=100,BLKSIZE=3204)
//SORT.SYSIN  DD  *
 MERGE  FIELD=(5,4,BI,A,9,4,BI,D,17,16,CH,A)
//
```

Following an appropriate Job statement is an Exec statement which calls the procedure SORTD. Sort work files are not required for merging. There is also no need to modify any of the statements already contained within the procedure. What needs to be added to the SORT step are the Dd statements for the SORTIN01, SORTIN02, SORTOUT, and SYSIN files.

Let's assume that a 4-byte county code is present in columns 5 to 8 of the input records to be merged. A land plot number exists in columns 9 to 12. Also, a township name is present in columns 17 to 32. With variable-length records a 4-byte record length field is present at the beginning of each record. It must be accounted for in determining columnar control. Therefore, column 5 is really the beginning of the first field as viewed from a programmer's standpoint. The merge control file in the example above specifies the county code field as major (coded first), the land plat number field as intermediate (coded second or next), and township name as minor (coded last). More than one intermediate field could also be used for merge control if desired. The Merge control statement indicates that the major field begins in column 5, has a length of 4 bytes, uses binary form, and is to be merged in existing ascending order. The intermediate field begins in column 9, has a length of 4 bytes, uses binary form, and is to be merged in existing descending order. Finally, the minor field begins in column 17, has a length of 16 bytes, uses character form, and is to be merged in existing ascending order.

A major subject in and by itself, a detailed description of the many features of the Sort/Merge program can be obtained from the Sort/Merge manual. Those uses common to all dp environments have been covered in this chapter. In addition, Appendix C contains a listing and description of sort/merge options which can be provided via a Parm parameter.

E. CATALOGUED PROCEDURES WORKSHOP

All common and frequently utilized catalogued procedures which can be called have been discussed. A workshop is now provided to solidify a working knowledge of basic catalogue procedure use and JCL job coding. Workshop answers can be found in Appendix E.

1. Program Test Environment

A newly written ANS COBOL edit program needs to be tested with sorted test data. Code the Job statement, all Exec statements, and all Dd statements for the multistep job depicted by the system flowchart in Figure 5.16.

Pertinent Job statement information is displayed thereon. Choose your own jobname and programmer name, however.

Pertinent Exec statement information is displayed as appropriate in the flowchart. Choose your own stepnames, however. Provide CLIST, DMAP, and XREF Parm parameter information to the COB step. Code a condition parameter such that if 8 is less than the return code issued by the SORT step, processing of the GO step will be bypassed.

Pertinent Dd statement information is displayed as appropriate. Use 2400 for tape unit allocations, 3330 for permanent disk units, and SYSDA for temporary disk unit allocations. Code only the first two subparameters of the Disposition parameter, keeping all tapes and permanent disk files and eventually deleting all temporary disk files. Sort the test data such that columns 20 to 27 are major character ascending and columns 3 to 6 are minor character descending. Release newly created unused disk space. Choose your own data set names but make them temporary when appropriate. Use DD * for card files with no other parameters. Also, code no parameters other than SYSOUT for print files. Assume standard tape labels are utilized and therefore need not be described.

To assist your coding efforts, follow the step-by-step instructions below.

Figure 5.16 Catalogued Procedure Program Test System Flowchart

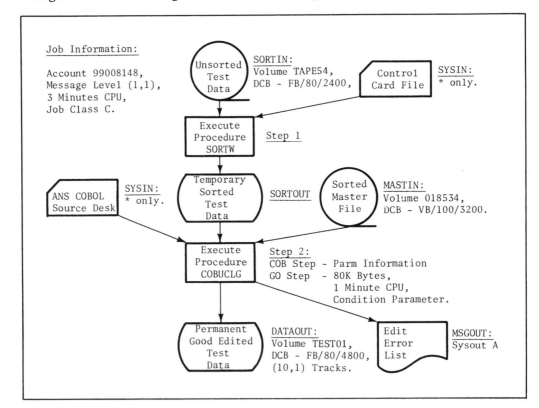

1. Code the Job statement.

2. Code Step 1's Exec statement and Dd statements. Add three Dd statements to the SORT step -- the first for ddname SORTIN, a second for ddname SORTOUT, and the third for ddname SYSIN. Then code the control card file followed by a file/step Delimiter statement.

_____

_____

_____

_____

_____

_____

_____

_____

_____

3. Code Step 2's Execute statement. Provide Parm parameter information to the COB step and Region, Time, and Condition specifications to the GO step.

_____

_____

_____

_____

_____

4. Code Step 2's Dd statements. Add one Dd statement to the COB step for ddname SYSIN. Leave one line for the source program, then code a file Delimiter statement. Add four Dd statements to the GO step -- the first for ddname DATAIN, a second for ddname MASTIN, a third for ddname DATAOUT, and the fourth for ddname MSGOUT. Then code a Null statement to indicate an end-of-job condition.

_____

_____

_____

_____

_____

_____

_____

_____

_____

_____

_____

_____

_____

2. Production Run Environment

An established FORTRAN Level-G1 summary program needs to be changed and replaced in a program library. The program should be executed after a merge of two input files. Code the Job statement, all Exec statements, and all Dd statements for the multistep job depicted by the system flowchart in Figure 5.17.

Pertinent Job statement information is displayed thereon. Choose your own jobname and programmer name, however.

Pertinent Exec statement information is displayed as appropriate in the flowchart. Choose your own stepnames, however. Provide LIST and MAP Parm parameter information to the FORT step. Code a Condition parameter such that if 4 is less than the return code issued by the LKED step, processing of the program's execute step will be bypassed.

Pertinent Dd statement information is displayed as appropriate. Use 2400 for tape unit allocations, 3330 for permanent disk unit, and SYSDA for temporary disk unit allocations. Code only the first two subparameters of the Disposition parameter, keeping all tapes and permanent disk files and eventually deleting any temporary disk files. Merge the edited data such that columns 10 to 13 are major character descending and columns 28 to 37 are minor character ascending. Release newly created unused disk space. Choose your own data set and library names but make them temporary when appropriate. Use DD * for card files with no other parameters. Also, code no parameters other than SYSOUT for print files. Assume standard tape labels are utilized and therefore need not be described.

To assist your coding efforts, follow the step-by-step instructions described below.

Figure 5.17 Catalogued Procedure Production Run System Flowchart

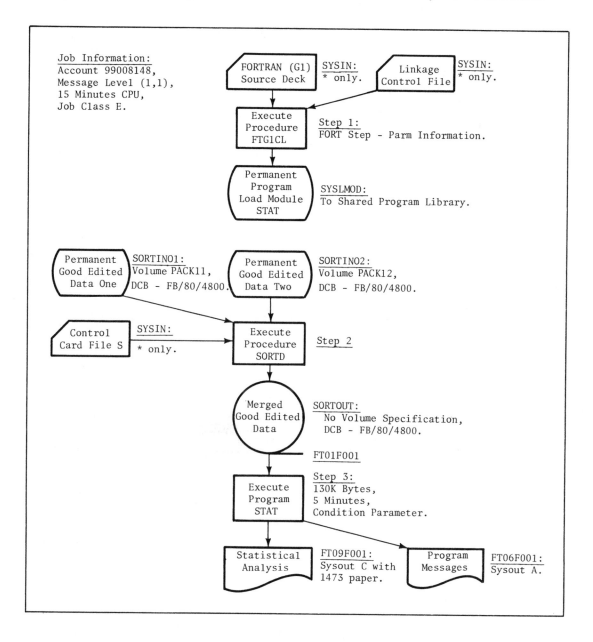

1. Code the Job statement. Then comment that this job requires
   3,000 lines of 1473 paper. Finally, code a Joblib statement
   using any shared program library name.

_____

_____

_____

_____

213

2. Code Step 1's Exec statement. Provide Parm parameter information to the FORT step. Then add one Dd statement in the
FORT step for ddname SYSIN. Leave one line for the source
program, then code a file Delimiter statement. Next modify
the existing SYSLMOD Dd statement such that a shared private
library is described for storage of the program load module.
Then code a Dd statement for ddname SYSIN to the LKED step.
Assign the program name and follow by a file/step Delimiter
statement.

_____

_____

_____

_____

_____

_____

_____

_____

_____

_____

_____

3. Code Step 2's Exec statement and Dd statements. Add four
Dd statements to the SORT step -- the first for ddname
SORTIN01, a second for ddname SORTIN02, a third for ddname
SORTOUT, and the fourth for ddname SYSIN. Then code the
control card file followed by a file/step Delimiter state-
ment.

_____

_____

_____

_____

_____

_____

_____

_____

_____

_____

_____

_____

4. Code Step 3's Exec statement with Region, Time, and Condition
   parameters. Code three Dd statements -- the first for ddname
   FT01F001, a second for ddname FT09F001, and the third for
   ddname FT06F001. Then code a Dd statement for ddname SYSUDUMP,
   though not shown on the flowchart. Finally, code a Null statement to indicate an end-of-job condition.

_____

_____

_____

_____

_____

_____

_____

_____

_____

_____

6

Data Set Utility Programs

A. UTILITY CONCEPTS

Dictionaries define "utilities" as items which are "useful," or possess "usefulness." Though utility programs are also useful, this definition is not exclusive enough for data-processing use. Utilities are relatively small and simple programs which perform common functions on a somewhat frequent basis.

In this light, compilers, linkage editors, sort, and "one-shot" programs are not utilities. Compiler and linkage editor programs are medium to large in size. Both are complex in nature, especially compilers. Sort programs are generally considered medium in size and program complexity. Conversely, though "one-shot" programs may be small and relatively simple in many cases, by definition they are not required on a frequent basis. They possess little commonality of need among users.

Programs which should be considered as utilities are those which perform simple and frequently utilized functions such as print, punch, sequence, copy, allocate, library maintenance, etc. They may be written by installation users, system programmers, or vendor personnel. They should be documented and instructions for their use widely distributed throughout the user community. Though some utilities are written with specific user and installation functions in mind, those covered in this chapter and the next are vendor-supplied and common to all System 360/370 OS and VS environments.

B. DATA SET UTILITY USE

Utility programs are classified as either

Data Set;
System; or
Independent Utilities.

Data set utilities are those which access and print, punch, or otherwise manipulate data sets. Input/Output files may be sequential, index-sequential, or of partitioned data set organization. In general, they are application-oriented and frequently utilized by the user of a dp installation. Data set utility programs and a summary of their most common functions follow:

```
IEBCOMPR - Compare.
IEBCOPY  - Copy, compress, merge, replace.
IEBDG    - Create pattern test data.
IEBEDIT  - Copy JCL.
IEBGENER - Copy, convert, reformat.
IEBISAM  - Convert index-sequential.
IEBPTPCH - Print, punch.
IEBTCRIN - Convert tape cartridge.
IEBUPDAT - Modify symbolic libraries.
IEBUPDTE - Update sequential or partitioned files.
```

C. BASIC DATA SET UTILITY PROGRAMS

Some data set utilities can be considered basic to the performance of a programmer's duties, that is, they are common to the needs of most application and system programmers and analysts. These are IEBCOPY, IEBGENER, IEBPTPCH, and IEBUPDTE.

1. IEBCOPY (Copy)

a. Purpose

The purpose of utility program IEBCOPY is to copy and/or merge one or more partitioned data sets (PDS's). Selected members of a PDS can be either included or excluded from consideration. IEBCOPY thus not only copies, but compresses and merges one or more partitioned data sets. In addition, it can replace and/or rename selected members of a given PDS. As such, this utility is most handy for maintaining program libraries.

b. Files and Use

Standard utility ddnames and their functions are:

```
Ddname1  - Input PDS File.
Ddname2  - Output PDS File.
SYSIN    - Utility Control File.
SYSPRINT - Utility Message File.
SYSUT3   - Input Overflow File.
SYSUT4   - Output Overflow File.
SYSUDUMP - Storage Dump File.
```

Ddname1 and Ddname2 are input and output ddnames which are speci-

fied by the user in the utility control file via INDD and OUTDD parameter specifications. They must both be partitioned data sets, and
as such are generally disk file libraries. The SYSIN ddname file
describes the control file, usually cards. The utility control file
must not be dummied due to the necessity of specifying a ddname. The
ddname SYSPRINT file defines a utility message file for copy, compress,
merge, and replace operations. SYSUT3 and SYSUT4 define input and
output overflow areas in case the PDS directory becomes full. Room
for internal directory sorting may also be needed. A SYSUDUMP Dd
statement describes the storage dump file if this type of abnormal
termination should occur.

The JCL example below compresses a PDS disk file, that is, it
maintains only the most current members, thus freeing up library
space for further use:

```
//UTIL    JOB   99008148,DHR,MSGLEVEL=(1,1),CLASS=A

//STEP1   EXEC   PGM=IEBCOPY

//SYSUT1   DD   UNIT=SYSDA,DISP=(OLD,KEEP),

//          DSNAME=A.PROGRAM.LIBRARY,VOL=SER=DISK88

//SYSIN   DD   *

 COPY   OUTDD=SYSUT1,INDD=SYSUT1

/*

//SYSPRINT   DD   SYSOUT=A

//SYSUT3   DD   UNIT=SYSDA,SPACE=(TRK,1)

//SYSUT4   DD   UNIT=SYSDA,SPACE=(TRK,1)

//SYSUDUMP   DD   SYSOUT=A

//
```

Following an appropriate Job statement, utility program IEBCOPY
is called above. No other Exec statement parameters are necessary, as
all defaults are acceptable. Dd statement SYSUT1 (so named per
utility control record) describes the input and output PDS disk
library. The SYSIN ddname control file contains a COPY statement. Keywords OUTDD and INDD specify ddnames to be utilized for the same output and input file, respectively. Utility messages are provided by
the SYSPRINT ddname print file. Ddnames SYSUT3 and SYSUT4 describe
temporary overflow files for input and output directories, respectively. Default temporary Dsnames, Volumes, and Data Control Block
information are accepted. Finally, a SYSUDUMP Dd statement and Null
statement are coded. This type of program library maintenance must
be done on a regularly scheduled basis.

In order to more fully utilize the capabilities of this utility
program, an expanded utility control file must be described. Figure
6.1 depicts parameter options and syntax for IEBCOPY control file
records.

The Copy statement is mandatory, as file ddnames must be specified. Conversely, the Select and Exclude statements are optional.

Figure 6.1 Utility IEBCOPY Control File Parameters

Copy Statement:

$$[Label] \; COPY \; OUTDD=Ddname2 \; \begin{cases} ,INDD=Ddname1 \\ ,INDD=(Ddname1,R) \\ ,INDD=Ddname1,...... \\ ,INDD=((Ddname1,R),......) \end{cases} \; [,LIST=NO]$$

to copy PDS files,

where Ddname2 is the user-assigned ddname for the Output PDS File;

Ddname1 is the user-assigned ddname for the Input PDS File(s);

R specifies that all input members are to be copied and

replaced by any identically named members already on

the output data set; and

LIST=NO indicates that copied members are not to be written

to the SYSPRINT ddname print file.

Select Statement:

$$[Label] \; SELECT \; MEMBER= \; \begin{cases} Name \\ (Name,R) \\ (Name,New \; Name) \\ (Name,New \; Name,R) \\ Name,...... \\ ((Name,R),......) \\ ((Name,New \; Name),......) \\ ((Name,New \; Name,R),......) \end{cases}$$

to select PDS members,

where Name is the Member Name of interest to be selected;

R specifies that the input member is to be copied and is to

replace any identically named member on the output

data set; and

New Name specifies a member's name change.

219

Figure 6.1 Utility IEBCOPY Control File Parameters (cont.)

Exclude Statement:

[Label] EXCLUDE MEMBER= $\begin{Bmatrix} \text{Name} \\ \text{(Name,......)} \end{Bmatrix}$

to exclude PDS members,

where Name is the Member Name of interest to be excluded.

When used, however, they should be coded in the order described in Figure 6.1 and must begin with a label or blank in column 1. Labels, which follow standard JCL naming conventions, are used as comments to delineate operations.

c. JCL Examples

The two JCL examples below copy, compress, merge, and replace catalogued partitioned disk data set libraries and members:

```
//UTIL   JOB   99008148,DHR,MSGLEVEL=(1,1),CLASS=A
//STEP1  EXEC  PGM=IEBCOPY
//INPUT1   DD  DSNAME=OLDLIB1,DISP=(OLD,KEEP)
//INPUT2   DD  DSNAME=OLDLIB2,DISP=(OLD,KEEP)
//OUTPUT1  DD  DSNAME=NEWLIB1,DISP=(OLD,KEEP)
//SYSIN   DD  *
 COPY  OUTDD=OUTPUT1,INDD=((INPUT1,R),(INPUT2,R))
 EXCLUDE  MEMBER=(AEDIT,SUM)
/*
//SYSPRINT  DD  SYSOUT=A
//SYSUT3   DD  UNIT=SYSDA,SPACE=(TRK,1)
//SYSUT4   DD  UNIT=SYSDA,SPACE=(TRK,1)
//SYSUDUMP  DD  SYSOUT=A
//
```

Following an appropriate Job statement utility program IEBCOPY is called above. Dd statements INPUT1 and INPUT2 describe two old input program libraries. Dd statement OUTPUT1 describes a previously created output program library. A control file for ddname SYSIN specifies user ddnames for the output and input files. The 'R' indicates that any identically named members in the input files are to replace those same members on the output file. Utility control file statements are continued by coding a comma, a continuation character in column 72, and leaving column 1 of the next line blank. Program member names

AEDIT and SUM are to be excluded from the copy process. Presumably, they have been replaced by more updated versions of a different name. Utility program messages including a list of member names are written to the SYSPRINT ddname print file. A SYSUDUMP Dd statement and Null statement should also be provided. Another IEBCOPY example is as follows:

```
//UTIL   JOB   99008148,DHR,MSGLEVEL=(1,1),CLASS=A
//STEP1  EXEC  PGM=IEBCOPY
//LIBIN  DD    DSNAME=OLDLIB3,DISP=(OLD,KEEP)
//LIBOUT DD    DSNAME=NEWLIB1,DISP=(OLD,KEEP)
//SYSIN  DD    *
 COPY   OUTDD=LIBOUT,INDD=LIBIN
 SELECT MEMBER=(REFORM,(CONVERT,R),(TAB1,TAB1A,R))
/*
//SYSPRINT  DD   SYSOUT=A
//SYSUT3    DD   UNIT=SYSDA,SPACE=(TRK,1)
//SYSUT4    DD   UNIT=SYSDA,SPACE=(TRK,1)
//SYSUDUMP  DD   SYSOUT=A
//
```

Following an appropriate Job statement, utility program IEBCOPY is called above. Dd statements LIBIN and LIBOUT describe the input and output files, respectively. A control file for ddname SYSIN specifies user ddnames for the output and input files. Only program member names REFORM, CONVERT, and TAB1 are to be selected for the copy process. The latter two will replace any members currently in the new library by the same name. The latter member's name will also be changed to TAB1A when copied. Utility program messages including a list of member names are to be written to the SYSPRINT ddname print file. A SYSUDUMP Dd statement and Null statement should also be provided.

In summary, utility program IEBCOPY copies, compresses, and/or merges one or more partitioned data sets (PDS's). Selected PDS members may also be copied and replaced or excluded from the copy process. This utility is frequently utilized in program library maintenance environments.

2. IEBGENER (Generate)

a. Purpose

The purpose of utility program IEBGENER is to create backup, converted, and/or reformatted copies of a given sequential or partitioned data set (PDS). The creation of backup file copies is particularly efficient with this utility. How many times have programmers needlessly written, tested, and debugged new programs to perform the simple functions of data conversion and record reformat? Conversion from one form of data representation to another, the rearrangement or reformatting of data fields, and the creation of PDS's are other significant functions of this utility. As such, this utility is probably the most frequently utilized of all available to application and system programmers and analysts.

b. Files and Use

Standard utility ddnames and their functions are:

SYSUT1   - Input Sequential File or PDS Member.
SYSUT2   - Output Sequential File, PDS, or PDS Member.
SYSIN   - Utility Control File.
SYSPRINT - Utility Message File.
SYSUDUMP - Storage Dump File.

Ddnames SYSUT1 and SYSUT2 Dd statements describe the input and output files for utility program IEBGENER. They may be sequentially organized, PDS members, or a complete PDS (output only). The SYSIN ddname file describes the control file, usually cards. If an identical backup copy of the input file is desired, the utility control file should be dummied. When fully described, conversion and reformat operations can be accomplished. The ddname SYSPRINT file defines a utility message file for these backup, conversion, and reformat operations. A SYSUDUMP Dd statement describes the storage dump file if this type of abnormal termination should occur.

The JCL example below creates a tape backup file copy:

```
//UTIL   JOB  99008148,DHR,MSGLEVEL=(1,1),CLASS=C
//STEP1  EXEC  PGM=IEBGENER
//SYSUT1   DD  UNIT=2400,DISP=(OLD,KEEP),
//         DSNAME=MASTER.FILE,VOL=SER=001849,
//         DCB=(RECFM=VB,LRECL=120,BLKSIZE=3204)
//SYSUT2   DD  UNIT=2400,DISP=(NEW,KEEP),
//         DSNAME=BACKUP.COPY,VOL=SER=OS0924,
//         DCB=(RECFM=VB,LRECL=120,BLKSIZE=3204)
//SYSIN   DD  DUMMY
//SYSPRINT  DD  SYSOUT=A
//SYSUDUMP  DD  SYSOUT=A
//
```

Following an appropriate Job statement, utility program IEBGENER is called above. No other Exec statement parameters are necessary, as all defaults are acceptable. Dd statements SYSUT1 and SYSUT2 describe input and output tape files, respectively. The SYSIN ddname control file has been dummied. Program IEBGENER will thus create a backup copy on SYSUT2 identical to the input file described on SYSUT1.

Utility messages are provided by the SYSPRINT ddname print file. Finally, a SYSUDUMP Dd statement and Null statement are coded. Back-up operations of this type are a most frequent application in all system programmer and analyst environments.

In order to more fully utilize the capabilities of this utility program, an expanded utility control file must be described. Figure 6.2 depicts parameter options and syntax for IEBGENER control file records.

Figure 6.2 Utility IEBGENER Control File Parameters

```
Generate Statement:


[Label] GENERATE [MAXFLDS=w]

                 [,MAXLITS=x]

                 [,MAXGPS=y]

                 [,MAXNAME=z]



     to specify control file characteristics,

     where w is greater than or equal to the number of Field

               parameters in Record statements;

          x is greater than or equal to the number of Literal

            characters in Field parameters of Record statements;

          y is greater than or equal to the number of Ident

            parameters in Record statements; and

          z is greater than or equal to the number of Member

            Names specified in Member statements.



Exits Statement:


[Label] EXITS [INHDR=Routine Name]

              [,OUTHDR=Routine Name]

              [,INTLR=Routine Name]

              [,OUTTLR=Routine Name]

              [,KEY=Routine Name]

              [,DATA=Routine Name]

              [,IOERROR=Routine Name]

              [,TOTAL=(Routine Name,Size)]
```

Figure 6.2 Utility IEBGENER Control File Parameters (cont.)

to indicate user exit routines,

where Routine Name is name of user routine to process user input

header labels, user output header labels, user input

trailer labels, user output trailer labels, to create

output record key, to modify physical record, to process

permanent input/output errors, and to handle totaling

routine, respectively. Table size in bytes must also

be specified for the last of the operations.

Labels Statement:

[Label] LABELS DATA= { NO YES ALL ONLY INPUT }

to specify user label processing,

where NO specifies that user labels are not to be processed;

YES means they are;

ALL that they are to be processed regardless of condition

code;

ONLY when user labels are to be processed only; and

INPUT if user labels are being supplied via ddname

SYSLMOD file.

Member Statement:

[Label] MEMBER NAME= { Name (Name,Alias Name) (Name,Alias Name,......) }

to indicate member names and aliases,

where Name specifies a PDS Member Name optionally followed

by one or more Aliases.

224

Figure 6.2 Utility IEBGENER Control File Parameters (cont.)

Record Statement:

[Label] RECORD [IDENT=(Length,'Name',Input Location)]

                [,FIELD=([Length][,Input Location]

                        [,Conversion Code][,Output Location])]

                [,FIELD=([Length][,'Actual Literal']

                        [,Conversion Code][,Output Location])]

                [,LABELS=x]

    to specify groups and reformat specifications,

        where IDENT signifies end of group identification;

            FIELD describes reformat specifications;

            Length equals field length in bytes;

                Name specifies exact character string of a record group;

    Input Location is starting column for input field of interest;

    Conversion Code equals PZ for Packed to Unpacked data,

                    ZP for Unpacked to Packed data,

                    HE for BCD to EBCDIC conversion;

    Output Location is starting column for output field

            of interest;

        Actual Literal is just that; and

                x equals number of input user label records being

                    supplied via ddname SYSIN file.

Generate, Exits, Labels, Member, and Record statements are all optional, but when used should be coded in the order described in Figure 6.2. Each must begin with a label or blank in column 1. Labels, which follow standard JCL naming conventions, are used as comments to delineate utility operations.

c. JCL Examples

The two JCL examples below convert and reformat both sequential and partitioned data sets:

```
//UTIL   JOB   99008148,DHR,MSGLEVEL=(1,1),CLASS=C
//STEP1  EXEC   PGM=IEBGENER
//SYSUT1  DD   UNIT=SYSDA,DISP=(OLD,KEEP),
```

225

```
//         DSNAME=GOODDATA,VOL=SER=ALPHA88,
//         DCB=(RECFM=FB,LRECL=160,BLKSIZE=3200)
//SYSUT2  DD   UNIT=2400,DISP=(NEW,KEEP),
//         DSNAME=CONVDATA,VOL=SER=013796,
//         DCB=(RECFM=FB,LRECL=160,BLKSIZE=3200)
//SYSIN  DD   *
 GENERATE   MAXFLDS=4,MAXLITS=6
 RECORD   FIELD=(160,1,,1),                                         X
          FIELD=(9,11,,22),                                         X
          FIELD=(6,'*   76',,52),                                   X
          FIELD=(4,88,PZ,86)
 /*
//SYSPRINT  DD   SYSOUT=A
//SYSUDUMP  DD   SYSOUT=A
//
```

Following an appropriate Job statement, utility program IEBGENER
is called above. Dd statement SYSUT1 describes a disk input file to
be converted and reformatted. Dd statement SYSUT2 describes the output tape file. The control file for ddname SYSIN consists of Generate
and Record statements. The Generate statement specifies that a maximum of four Field parameters and six literal characters within these
parameters exist in the control file. The first Field parameter in
the Record statement moves the complete contents of each input record
to the output record area. The second Field parameter moves a 9-
character field starting in column 11 to a field beginning in column
22 of the output record area. The third Field parameter creates a
6-character field literal of '*   76' starting in column 52 of the output record. Finally, the last Field parameter converts and moves a
4-character packed field starting in column 88 to an unpacked field
beginning in column 86 of the output area. The utility program then
writes the output record as structured. Utility control card statements are continued by coding a comma, a continuation character in
column 72, and leaving column 1 of the next line blank. Utility program messages are written to the SYSPRINT ddname print file. A SYSU-
DUMP Dd statement and Null statement should also be provided. Another IEBGENER example is as follows:

```
//UTIL  JOB  99008148,DHR,MSGLEVEL=(1,1),CLASS=A
//STEP1  EXEC  PGM=IEBGENER
//SYSUT1  DD   UNIT=SYSDA,DISP=(OLD,KEEP),
//         DSNAME=LOADMOD,VOL=SER=OS1828,
//         DCB=(RECFM=FB,LRECL=080,BLKSIZE=3200)
//SYSUT2  DD   UNIT=3330,DISP=(NEW,CATLG),
```

```
//              DSNAME=ANEW.LIB,VOL=SER=PACK66,
//              DCB=(RECFM=FB,LRECL=080,BLKSIZE=3200,DSORG=PO),
//              SPACE=(TRK,(50,10,5))
//SYSIN   DD   *
 GENERATE   MAXNAME=1
 MEMBER   NAME=(PROG01,SUB1)
/*
//SYSPRINT   DD   SYSOUT=A
//SYSUDUMP   DD   SYSOUT=A
//
```

Following an appropriate Job statement, utility program IEBGENER
is called above. Dd statement SYSUT1 describes a sequential disk
input file to be partitioned. Dd statement SYSUT2 describes a new
catalogued output PDS library file. The control file for ddname SYSIN
consists of Generate and Member statements. The Generate statement
specifies that a maximum of one Name parameter exists within the
control file. The Name parameter on the Member statement assigns a
member name of PROG01 with an alias name of SUB1. Utility program
messages are written to the SYSPRINT ddname print file. A SYSUDUMP
Dd statement and Null statement should also be provided.

In summary, utility program IEBGENER copies, converts, reformats,
and creates sequential or partitioned data set files. This utility
is perhaps the most frequently utilized of all by dp installation
users. As can be seen from Figure 6.2, space does not permit a full
display of all possible combinations of IEBGENER functions. Rather,
the basic functions -- those most common in all dp environments --
have been discussed. The Utilities manual is also a handy detailed
technical reference for more unique applications.

3. IEBPTPCH (Print and Punch)

    a. Purpose

    The purpose of utility program IEBPTPCH is to print or punch a
given sequential or partitioned data set (PDS). These functions are
particularly efficient with this utility. How many times have programmers needlessly written, tested, and debugged new programs to
perform the simple functions of data file printing and punching?
Straight listings of selected records, with or without headings,
realigning print fields, and the punching of selected records are
all significant functions of this utility. As such, IEBPTPCH is probably the second (to IEBGENER) most frequently utilized utility
of all available to application and system programmers and analysts.

    b. Files and Use

    Standard utility ddnames and their functions are:

227

```
SYSUT1    - Input Sequential, PDS File, or PDS Member.
SYSUT2    - Print or Punch Output File.
SYSIN     - Utility Control File.
SYSPRINT  - Utility Message File.
SYSUDUMP  - Storage Dump File.
```

Ddnames SYSUT1 and SYSUT2 Dd statements describe the input and output files for utility program IEBPTPCH. Whereas output is always sequentially organized, input may be sequential or partitioned. The SYSIN ddname file describes the control file, usually cards. If a single-spaced print or direct punch of the complete output file is desired, the characters 'PRINT' or 'PUNCH' need only be supplied as the control file. When fully described, easy-to-read print lines and headings can be created. The ddname SYSPRINT file defines a utility message file for these print and punch operations. A SYSUDUMP Dd statement describes the storage dump file if this type of abnormal termination should occur.

The JCL example below creates a single-spaced print of every record in the input file:

```
//UTIL    JOB   99008148,DHR,MSGLEVEL=(1,1),CLASS=C

//STEP1   EXEC  PGM=IEBPTPCH

//SYSUT1  DD    UNIT=2400,DISP=(OLD,KEEP),

//              DSNAME=MASTER,VOL=SER=TAPE89,

//              DCB=(RECFM=FB,LRECL=100,BLKSIZE=3200)

//SYSUT2  DD    SYSOUT=A

//SYSIN   DD    *

 PRINT

/*

//SYSPRINT  DD   SYSOUT=A

//SYSUDUMP  DD   SYSOUT=A

//
```

Following an appropriate Job statement, utility program IEBPTPCH is called above. No other Exec statement parameters are necessary, as all defaults are acceptable. Dd statements SYSUT1 and SYSUT2 describe input and output files, respectively. PRINT has been specified to the SYSIN ddname control file. Program IEBPTPCH will thus create a single-spaced listing on SYSUT2 of all records in the input file described on SYSUT1. A given print line consists of 8 characters of data, then 2 blanks, 8 characters of data, 2 blanks, etc., as depicted below:

xxxxxxxx xxxxxxxx xxxxxxxx xxxxxxxx xxxxxxxx xxxxxxxx etc.

No headings will be printed. Though this particular print format is not the easiest to read, a quick and simple output of this nature is handy to reference in debugging situations, i.e., when a print of

a problem file is desired. Reportlike formats will be discussed
shortly. Utility messages are provided by the SYSPRINT ddname print
file. Finally, a SYSUDUMP Dd statement and Null statement are coded.
Quick and easy prints of this nature for problem files are a frequent application in all system programmer and analyst environments.

In order to more fully utilize the capabilities of this utility
program, an expanded utility control file must be described. Figure
6.3 depicts parameter options and syntax for IEBPTPCH control file
records.

Figure 6.3 Utility IEBPTPCH Control File Parameters

Print Statement:

[Label] PRINT [MAXFLDS=a]

              [,MAXLITS=b]

              [,MAXGPS=c]

              [,MAXNAME=d]

              [,MAXLINE=e]

              [,INITPG=f]

              [,CNTRL=g]

              [,STRTAFT=h]

              [,STOPAFT=i]

              [,SKIP=j]

              [,PREFORM=k]

              [,TYPORG=1]

              [,TOTCONV=m]

      to specify print and control file characteristics,

      where a is greater than or equal to the number of Field

            parameters in Record statements;

           b is greater than or equal to the number of Literal

              characters in Ident parameters of Record statements;

           c is greater than or equal to the number of Ident

              parameters in Record statements;

           d is greater than or equal to the number of Member Names

              specified in Member statements;

           e is the maximum number of lines to be printed per page;

           f is the initial page number;

Figure 6.3 Utility IEBPTPCH Control File Parameters (cont.)

g equals 1 for single spacing,

2 for double spacing,

3 for triple spacing;

h is the number of records to skip prior to initial printing;

i is the number of records to be printed;

j specifies that every jth record is to be printed;

k equals A if ASA carriage control character is present

in column 1,

M if machine-code carriage control character is

present in column 1;

l equals PS if input file is physically sequential,

PO if input file is partition-organized; and

m equals PZ if data is to be converted from packed to

unpacked form,

XE if data is to be printed in hexadecimal form.

Punch Statement:

[Label] PUNCH [MAXFLDS=a]

[,MAXLITS=b]

[,MAXGPS=c]

[,MAXNAME=d]

[,CDSEQ=e]

[,CDINCR=f]

[,CNTRL=g]

[,STRTAFT=h]

[,STOPAFT=i]

[,SKIP=j]

[,PREFORM=k]

[,TYPORG=l]

[,TOTCONV=m]

to specify punch and control file characteristics,

where a-d are identical to Print statement specifications;

e is initial sequence number in columns 73 to 80;

f is the increment of the sequence numbers to be generated; and

g-m are identical to Print statement specifications.

Figure 6.3 Utility IEBPTPCH Control File Parameters (cont.)

Member Statement:

[Label] MEMBER NAME= $\begin{Bmatrix} \text{Name} \\ \text{Alias} \end{Bmatrix}$

to indicate member name and alias,

where Name and Alias specify a PDS Member Name.

Record Statement:

[Label] RECORD [IDENT=(Length,'Name',Input Location)]

        [,FIELD=([Length][,Input Location]

           [,Conversion Code][,Output Location])]

to specify groups and reformat specifications,

where IDENT signifies end-of-group identification;

    FIELD describes reformat specifications;

    Length equals field length in bytes;

    Name specifies exact character string of a record group;

    Input Location is starting column for input field of interest;

    Conversion Code equals PZ for Packed to Unpacked data,

       XE for hexadecimal print form; and

    Output Location is starting column for output file

       of interest.

Title Statement:

[Label] TITLE ITEM=('Title'[,Output Location])[,ITEM=......]

to specify heading and subheading information,

where ITEM provides title information and location;

    Title is the 40-character maximum heading and subheading

       to be printed at the top of each page; and

    Output Location is starting column for title of interest.

231

Figure 6.3 Utility IEBPTPCH Control File Parameters (cont.)

Exits Statement:

[Label] EXITS [INHDR=Routine Name]

               [,INTLR=Routine Name]

               [,INREC=Routine Name]

               [,OUTREC=Routine Name]

   to indicate user exit routines,

   where Routine Name is name of user routine to process user

        input header labels, process user input trailer

        labels, manipulate input records, and manipulate

        output records.

Labels Statement:

[Label] LABELS DATA= $\begin{Bmatrix} NO \\ YES \\ ALL \\ ONLY \end{Bmatrix}$

   to specify user label processing,

   where NO specifies that user labels are not to be processed;

      YES when they are;

      ALL that they are to be processed regardless of

        condition code; and

      ONLY when user labels are to be processed only.

Either a Print or Punch statement is mandatory. Title, Exits, Member, Record, and Labels statements are optional but when used should be coded in the order described in Figure 6.3. Each must begin with a label or blank in column 1. Labels, which follow standard naming conventions, are used as comments to delineate utility operations.

c. JCL Examples

The two JCL examples below print and punch both a sequential data set and partitioned data set members:

```
//UTIL  JOB  99008148,DHR,MSGLEVEL=(1,1),CLASS=A
//STEP1  EXEC  PGM=IEBPTPCH
```

```
//SYSUT1   DD   UNIT=SYSDA,DISP=(OLD,KEEP),
//         DSNAME=GOODDATA,VOL=SER=ALPHA88,
//         DCB=(RECFM=FB,LRECL=120,BLKSIZE=3200)
//SYSUT2   DD   SYSOUT=(C,,1482)
//SYSIN    DD   *
  PRINT MAXFLDS=1,MAXLINE=30,CNTRL=2,                              X
              STRTAFT=1000,STOPAFT=500,SKIP=10
  TITLE ITEM=('PRINT OF GOOD DATA',12)
  TITLE ITEM=('FOR ADDITIONAL REVIEW',10)
  RECORD FIELD=(120,1,,1)
/*
//SYSPRINT  DD   SYSOUT=A
//SYSUDUMP  DD   SYSOUT=A
//
```

Following an appropriate Job statement, utility program IEBPTPCH
is called above. Dd statement SYSUT1 describes a disk input file to
be printed. Dd statement SYSUT2 describes the new output print file
to system output area C on 1482 type paper. The control file for
ddname SYSIN consists of Print, Title, and Record statements. The
Print statement inserts a carriage control character in output column
1, specifies that a maximum of one Field parameter exists in the
control file, a maximum of 30 lines is to be printed per page, printing is to be double-spaced, the first 1,000 records are to be bypassed,
500 records are to be printed, and every tenth record is to be printed.
That is, the 1,001st, 1,011th, 1,021st, 1,031st, etc. records are
printed until 500 have been reached. Utility control card statements
are continued by coding a comma, a continuation character in column
72, and leaving column 1 of the next line blank. Any standard recognizable character is sufficient. The two Title statements specify
a heading and subheading to begin at the top of each page in columns
12 and 10, respectively. The Record statement moves the complete contents of each input record to the output record area. This is done
to avoid the default of the alternating 8-character, 2-blank format
described previously. A solid line of printed data with no blank
interruptions will result. The utility program writes the output
record as structured. Utility program messages are written to the
SYSPRINT ddname print file. A SYSUDUMP Dd statement and Null statement should also be provided. Another IEBPTPCH example is as follows:

```
//UTIL   JOB   99008148,DHR,MSGLEVEL=(1,1),CLASS=A
//STEP1  EXEC  PGM=IEBPTPCH
//SYSUT1 DD   UNIT=3330,DISP=SHR,
//         DSNAME=SOURCE.LIB,VOL=SER=LIB007
```

```
//SYSUT2  DD  SYSOUT=B
//SYSIN  DD  *
  PUNCH MAXFLDS=1,MAXNAME=4,CDSEQ=100,                          X
                  CDINCR=10
  MEMBER NAME=EDIT
  RECORD FIELD=(4,77,,1)
  MEMBER NAME=SUM
  RECORD FIELD=(4,77,,1)
  MEMBER NAME=REFORM
  RECORD FIELD=(4,77,,1)
  MEMBER NAME=CONVERT
  RECORD FIELD=(4,77,,1)
/*
//SYSPRINT  DD  SYSOUT=A
//SYSUDUMP  DD  SYSOUT=A
//
```

Following an appropriate Job statement, utility program IEBPTPCH is called above. Dd statement SYSUT1 describes a disk input partitioned data set file. Dd statement SYSUT2 describes the new output punch file to system output area B. The control file for ddname SYSIN consists of Punch, Member, and Record statements. The Punch statement specifies that a maximum of one Field parameter exists in the control file, a maximum of four Name parameters exist in the control file, and a sequence number beginning with 100 and incremented by 10 should be generated in columns 73 to 80. The four Member statements specify that the EDIT, SUM, REFORM, and CONVERT members are to be punched. The Record statements move a 4-character field starting in column 77 to a field beginning in column 1 of the output area. It is presumed that the input data in columns 77 to 80 is valid and should be saved rather than simply overlaid by generated sequence numbers. The utility program writes the output record as structured. Utility program messages are written to the SYSPRINT ddname print file. A SYSUDUMP Dd statement and Null statement should also be provided.

In summary, utility program IEBPTPCH prints or punches sequential or partitioned data set files. Next to IEBGENER, this utility is perhaps the most frequently utilized of all by dp installation users. As can be seen from Figure 6.3, space does not permit a full display of all possible combinations of IEBPTPCH functions. Rather, the basic functions, those most common in all dp environments, have been discussed. The Utilities manual is also a handy detailed technical reference for more unique applications.

4. IEBUPDTE (Sequential and PDS Update)

   a. Purpose

      The purpose of utility program IEBUPDTE is to create and update partitioned data sets (PDS's) and/or their members. Sequential files can also be created and maintained. IEBUPDTE can also change files from one form of organization to another, i.e., sequential to partitioned and vice versa. However, the creation and updating of catalogued procedures are the most common functions. As a result, this utility program is very frequently utilized among those available to application and system programmers and analysts.

b. Files and Use

Standard utility ddnames and their functions are:

SYSUT1   - Optional Input Sequential or PDS File.
SYSUT2   - Output Sequential or PDS File.
SYSIN   - Utility Control and Data File.
SYSPRINT - Utility Message File.
SYSUDUMP - Storage Dump File.

Ddname SYSUT1 describes the old sequential or partitioned file. When creating a new output file, a SYSUT1 Dd statement is not required. Ddname SYSUT2 describes the existing or new updated output file. Both files may not exceed 80 characters in length. The SYSIN ddname file describes the utility control and data file, usually cards. Adding, replacing, and changing JCL procedures are typical specifications. As such, a SYSIN Dd Data statement must be coded. The ddname SYSPRINT file defines a utility message file for these activities. A SYSUDUMP Dd statement describes the storage dump file if this type of abnormal termination should occur.
The JCL example below creates a partitioned data set library and adds the first member:

```
//UTIL  JOB  99008148,DHR,MSGLEVEL=(1,1),CLASS=A
//STEP1  EXEC  PGM=IEBUPDTE,PARM='NEW'
//SYSUT2  DD  UNIT=3330,DISP=(NEW,CATLG,DELETE),
//          DSNAME=APROC.LIBRARY,VOL=SER=MOD007,
//          SPACE=(TRK,(100,10,10)),
//          DCB=(RECFM=FB,LRECL=080,BLKSIZE=3200)
//SYSIN  DD  DATA
./ ADD  NAME=PROC1,LIST=ALL
    - - - - Complete Member Here - - - -
./ ENDUP
/*
//SYSPRINT  DD  SYSOUT=A
//SYSUDUMP  DD  SYSOUT=A
//
```

Following an appropriate Job statement utility program IEBUPDTE

is called above. NEW is specified via a Parm parameter to indicate
the absence of a SYSUT1 input file. No other Exec statement parameters are necessary, as all other defaults are acceptable. Dd statement SYSUT2 describes the new PDS private library file to be created.
Note the detail description of the output file and its catalogued
disposition. Upon successful completion of this run, only the data
set name and disposition need be specified when accessing this
library. ADD has been specified within the SYSIN ddname control file.
The member (or set of JCL) which follows will be named PROC1. It is
80 characters in length and should contain sequence numbers for update
purposes in columns 73-80. A complete listing of the member along
with utility messages will be provided to the SYSPRINT ddname print file.
Finally, a SYSUDUMP Dd statement and Null statement are coded.

In order to more fully utilize the capabilities of this utility program, an expanded utility control file must be described. Figure 6.4
depicts parameter options and syntax for IEBUPDTE control file records.

Figure 6.4 Utility IEBUPDTE Control File Parameters

Function Statement:

```
./[Name] ⎧ADD  ⎫   [NAME=Member Name]
         ⎪CHANGE⎪  [,LIST=ALL]
         ⎨REPL ⎬   [,SEQFLD=xxx]
         ⎪REPRO⎪            ⎧PS⎫
         ⎩     ⎭   [,NEW=  ⎨  ⎬ ]
                            ⎩PØ⎭
                   [,MEMBER=Name Member]
                   [,COLUMN=yy]
                   [,UPDATE=INPLACE]
                   [,INHDR=Routine Name]
                   [,INTLR=Routine Name]
                   [,OUTHDR=Routine Name]
                   [,OUTTLR=Routine Name]
                   [,TOTAL=(Total Name,Size)]
                   [,LEVEL=zz]
                            ⎧0⎫
                   [,SOURCE=⎨ ⎬ ]
                            ⎩1⎭
                   [,SSI=System Status]
```

to specify the function to be performed,

where Name = an optional statement name;

ADD specifies addition;

CHANGE specifies change;

REPL specifies replace;

REPRO specifies reproduce (or copy);

236

Figure 6.4 Utility IEBUPDTE Control File Parameters (cont.)

Member Name indicates PDS name of member;

LIST=ALL indicates that a list of the member is desired;

xxx = the starting column and length of sequence

numbers, e.g., 738 default;

NEW for file organization changes only;

PS = change to physical sequential;

PO = change to partitioned organization;

Name Member indicates PDS member name when NEW is specified;

yy = starting column of changed data field;

UPDATE=INPLACE indicates that the data set is to be

updated in its same space;

Routine Name is the name of a routine to process

user labels;

Total Name is the name of a user totaling routine;

Size specifies storage required in bytes for user data;

zz = specifies an update directory entry level from 0 to FF;

SOURCE = specifies a user or vendor modification in the

directory entry of 0 or 1, respectively; and

System Status equals 8 hexadecimal characters of system status

information.

Detail Statement:

$$./[\text{Name}] \quad \text{NUMBER} \quad [\text{SEQ1}=\begin{Bmatrix} \text{aaaaaaaa} \\ \text{ALL} \end{Bmatrix}]$$

[,SEQ2=bbbbbbbb]

[,NEW1=cccccccc]

[,INCR=dddddddd]

[,INSERT=YES]

to renumber or delete records,

where aaaaaaaa = old sequence number of first record;

ALL specifies that all records should be sequenced;

bbbbbbbb = old sequence number of initial record;

cccccccc = new sequence number of final record;

237

Figure 6.4 Utility IEBUPDTE Control File Parameters (cont.)

```
            ddddddd = increment to be used for new sequence; and

                YES indicates that a block of records is to be inserted.

    Label Statement:


    ./[Name] LABEL


         to indicate that the data following are user labels.


    Alias Statement:


    ./[Name] ALIAS NAME=Alias Name


         to provide an alias name.


    Endup Statement:


    ./[Name] ENDUP


         to indicate the end of the utility control and data file.
```

A Function statement is mandatory for each member to be updated. Detail, Label, Alias, and Endup statements are optional but when used should be coded in the order described in Figure 6.4. Each must begin with a ./ (period slash) in columns 1 and 2 and a name or blank in column 3. Names, which follow standard naming conventions, are used as comments.

In addition to the utility control and data file specifications described in Figure 6.4, four items of information can also be provided via a Parm parameter. Its format is:

$$PARM = \left(\begin{Bmatrix} MOD \\ NEW \end{Bmatrix} [,Routine1] [,Routine\ 2] \right)$$

where MOD = Default specification, as input consists of the SYSUT1 ddname input file and a portion of the utility control file;

NEW = SYSUT1 ddname input file is not to be described;

Routine1 = Name of the routine to process user header label; and

Routine2 = Name of the routine to process user trailer label.

c. JCL Examples

The two JCL examples below replace an existing PDS catalogued procedure member as well as updating the same:

```
//UTIL   JOB   99008148,DHR,MSGLEVEL=(1,1),CLASS=A
//STEP1  EXEC  PGM=IEBUPDTE
//SYSUT1  DD   DSNAME=APROC.LIBRARY,DISP=SHR
//SYSUT2  DD   DSNAME=APROC.LIBRARY,DISP=SHR
//SYSIN   DD   DATA
./ REPL  NAME=PROC1,LIST=ALL
  -  -  -  -  Complete Member Here  -  -  -  -
./ ALIAS  NAME=MEM1
./ ENDUP
/*
//SYSPRINT  DD  SYSOUT=A
//SYSUDUMP  DD  SYSOUT=A
//
```

Following an appropriate Job statement, utility program IEBUPDTE is called above. Dd statements SYSUT1 and SYSUT2 both describe the private procedure library APROC.LIBRARY created and catalogued in the previous example. The control and data file for ddname SYSIN consists of Function (Replace), Alias, and Endup statements and the data (member) to be placed into the PDS. Because the procedural data (member) contains a // (slash slash) in columns 1 and 2, DD DATA rather than an asterisk (*) is coded. The actual data itself always follows Function and Detail statements but is placed before any Label and Alias statements for that member. The Replace statement indicates the member to be replaced and requests that a complete listing of the entire member be provided. The replacing member in the job stream should contain sequence numbers for update purposes. The Alias statement assigns an alternate name to the member. The Endup statement indicates the end of the control file. Utility program messages are written to the SYSPRINT ddname print file. A SYSUDUMP Dd statement and Null statement should also be provided. Upon successful completion of this run the JCL procedure named PROC1 with an alias of MEM1 will have replaced the current version of PROC1 in the partitioned APROC.LIBRARY data set. Another IEBUPDTE example is as follows:

```
//UTIL   JOB   99008148,DHR,MSGLEVEL=(1,1),CLASS=A
//STEP1  EXEC  PGM=IEBUPDTE
//SYSUT1  DD   DSNAME=APROC.LIBRARY,DISP=SHR
//SYSUT2  DD   DSNAME=APROC.LIBRARY,DISP=SHR
/SYSIN   DD   DATA
```

```
./ CHANGE   NAME=PROC1,LIST=ALL
./ NUMBER   SEQ1=ALL,NEW1=100,INCR=50
   -  -  -  - Member Statements Here  -  -  -  -
./ ENDUP
/*
//SYSPRINT   DD   SYSOUT=A
//SYSUDUMP   DD   SYSOUT=A
//
```

Following an appropriate Job statement, utility program IEBUPDTE is called above. Dd statements SYSUT1 and SYSUT2 both describe the previously created private procedure library APROC.LIBRARY. The control file for ddname SYSIN consists of Function (Change), Detail (Number), Endup statements, and the portions of the data (member) to be changed. Because the update data (member) portions contain // in columns 1 and 2, DD DATA rather than an asterisk (*) is coded. The actual update statements always follow Function and Detail statements but are placed before any Label and Alias statements for that member. The Change statement indicates the member to be changed and requests that a complete listing of the entire member be provided. The Number statement changes the sequence numbers after all updates have been posted. All statements in the member are to be resequenced, the first statement beginning with sequence number 00000100 and incrementing by 50 each line from that point. The actual member statements to be updated are determined by the sequence number coded in each update statement itself, that is, nonmatches are inserted while matches are overlayed in the old member. The Endup statement indicates the end of the control file. A SYSUDUMP Dd statement and Null statement should also be provided. Upon successful completion of this run the JCL procedure named PROC1 in the partitioned APROC. LIBRARY will have been changed based upon the update statements provided in the job stream.

In summary, utility program IEBUPDTE creates, adds, replaces, and changes sequential and partitioned data sets and/or their members. The updating of catalogued procedure libraries and members is a most common function. As can be seen from Figure 6.4, space has not permitted a full display of all possible combinations of IEBUPDTE functions; though those most common in all dp environments have been discussed. The Utilities manual is also a handy detailed technical reference for more unique applications.

D. OTHER DATA SET UTILITY PROGRAMS

Other utility programs classified as "data set" also perform creation, update, and manipulations of sequential and partitioned files. However, they are not utilized as frequently as the previously discussed data set utilities. This is not because they are less significant, but rather more unique to specific applications performed by selected technical user personnel. For this reason, their basic function and controls will be described along with a JCL example. Many details relating to control card use will not be covered. They are not pertinent to the day-to-day operations of most application and sys-

240

tem programmers and analysts. If necessary, a detailed description of all facets of these not-so-common utilities can be obtained from the Utilities manual.

1. IEBCOMPR (Compare)

a. Purpose

The purpose of utility program IEBCOMPR is to compare two files and verify that they are identical, i.e., that one is an exact duplicate of the other. Unequal compare conditions generate appropriate error messages. Typical examples include the comparison of critical data files, data base copies, system libraries, and backup installation software. Input/Output files may be either sequentially organized or partitioned.

b. Files and Use

Standard utility ddnames and their functions are:

SYSUT1   - First Input Sequential or PDS File.
SYSUT2   - Second Input Sequential or PDS File.
SYSIN   - Utility Control File.
SYSPRINT - Utility Message File.
SYSUDUMP - Storage Dump File.

Ddnames SYSUT1 and SYSUT2 describe the two files to be compared. They must both be either sequentially organized or partitioned. The SYSIN ddname file describes the utility control file. If file organization is sequential and no user routines are desired, the control file can be dummied. The ddname SYSPRINT file defines a utility message file for unequal comparisons. Ten successive errors will in fact terminate job step processing unless a user routine is provided.

The JCL example below compares and verifies an original tape file with its duplicative backup copy:

```
//UTIL   JOB  99008148,DHR,MSGLEVEL=(1,1),CLASS=C
//STEP1  EXEC  PGM=IEBCOMPR
//SYSUT1   DD   UNIT=2400,DISP=(OLD,KEEP),
//         DSNAME=ORIGINAL,VOL=SER=001873,
//         DCB=(RECFM=FB,LRECL=120,BLKSIZE=3200)
//SYSUT2   DD   UNIT=2400,DISP=(OLD,KEEP),
//         DSNAME=BACKUP,VOL=SER=024782,
//         DCB=(RECFM=FB,LRECL=120,BLKSIZE=6400)
//SYSIN  DD   DUMMY
//SYSPRINT  DD   SYSOUT=A
//SYSUDUMP   DD   SYSOUT=A
//
```

Following an appropriate Job statement, utility program IEBCOMPR is called above. Dd statements SYSUT1 and SYSUT2 describe two sequential tape files. However, data sets on two different devices such as card and disk can be compared. Different densities and label configurations are also allowed. As in the above example, blocksizes need not be identical. File organization must be the same as well as record format and logical record length. The SYSIN ddname control file is not needed and therefore is dummied. Sequential file organization is assumed; no user routines are to be provided. Unequal comparisons are indicated in the SYSPRINT ddname print file. Ten successive errors result in job step termination.

If Partitioned Data Set (PDS) files are compared, user routines provided, or additional test conditions desired, a utility control file must be described and coded. Figure 6.5 depicts parameter options and syntax for IEBCOMPR control file records.

Figure 6.5 Utility IEBCOMPR Control File Parameters

Compare Statement:

[Label] COMPARE [TYPORG= $\begin{Bmatrix} PS \\ PO \end{Bmatrix}$]

    to compare files,

    where PS = Physical Sequential (default); and

        PO = Partitioned Organization.

Exits Statement:

[Label] EXITS [INHDR=Routine Name]

            [,INTRL=Routine Name]

            [,ERROR=Routine Name]

            [,PRECOMP=Routine Name]

    to indicate user exit routines,

    where Routine Name is the name of a routine to process user

        input header labels (INHDR), process user input trailer

        labels (INTLR), receive control after an occurrence of

        an unequal comparison (ERROR), and/or process records

        prior to comparison (PRECOMP).

242

Figure 6.5 Utility IEBCOMPR Control File Parameters (cont.)

Labels Statement:

$$[\text{Label}]\ \text{LABEL}\ [\text{DATA}= \left\{ \begin{array}{l} \text{NO} \\ \text{YES} \\ \text{ALL} \\ \text{ONLY} \end{array} \right\}\ ]$$

to specify user label processing,

where NO specifies user labels are not to be processed;

YES means that they are;

ALL that they are to be processed regardless of

condition code; and

ONLY that user header label records are to be

processed only.

All control records are optional, should be coded in the order described in Figure 6.5, and must begin with a label or a blank in column 1.

In summary, utility program IEBCOMPR (Compare) verifies that two files are duplicative of each other. Unequal conditions generate appropriate error messages. This utility is utilized for applications where absolute file validity is a steadfast requirement, e.g., the transfer of data files to a new installation.

2. IEBDG (Data Generator)

a. Purpose

The purpose of utility program IEBDG is to generate test data in user-specified patterns. Test data records and format are also user-defined. This utility is used primarily when large and thorough volume system tests are required. Input/Output files may be either sequential or partitioned organization.

b. Files and Use

Standard utility ddnames and their functions are:

```
Ddname1  - Optional Input Sequential or Indexed File.
Ddname2  - Optional Input PDS File.
Ddname3  - Optional Output Sequential or Indexed File.
Ddname4  - Optional Output PDS File.
SYSIN    - Utility Control File.
SYSPRINT - Utility Message File.
SYSUDUMP - Storage Dump File.
```

Ddname1 and Ddname2 describe optional input files for test data generation. Specific ddnames are supplied via utility control records. Similarly with Ddname3 and Ddname4. Both, however, describe optional output files for the test data itself. One of these two files must be chosen and described on a Dd statement. The SYSIN ddname file describes the utility control file. This file describes the nature of the test data generation and pattern. The ddname SYSPRINT file defines a utility message file for print purposes.

The JCL example below generates a series from test data from control file specifications:

```
//UTIL    JOB   99008148,DHR,MSGLEVEL=(1,1),CLASS=C
//STEP1   EXEC  PGM=IEBDG
//TESTOUT  DD   UNIT=2400,DISP=(NEW,KEEP),
//          DSNAME=PATTERN1,VOL=SER=000903,
//          DCB=(RECFM=FB,LRECL=080,BLKSIZE=4000)
//SYSIN   DD   *
  DSD   OUTPUT=(TESTOUT)
  FD    NAME=IDENT,LENGTH=10,STARTLOC=1,
              PICTURE=10,P'0000000001',INDEX=1
  FD    NAME=ALPHNAME,LENGTH=50,STARTLOC=11,
              FORMAT=AL,ACTION=TR
  FD    NAME=RAWDATA,LENGTH=20,STARTLOC=61,
              PICTURE=20,P'98765432109876543210',INDEX=1234
  REPEAT  QUANTITY=100
  CREATE  QUANTITY=50,FILL='0',
              NAME=(IDENT,ALPHNAME,RAWDATA)
  END
/*
//SYSPRINT  DD   SYSOUT=A
//SYSUDUMP  DD   SYSOUT=A
//
```

Following an appropriate Job statement, utility program IEBDG is called above. Dd statement TESTOUT describes an output sequential tape file. Its ddname was specified in the SYSIN ddname utility control file via a Data Set Description (DSD) statement. Three Field Description (FD) statements are provided for the three fields of the 80-character output record. Each field is given a name, length, and starting location. The first and third fields are initialized to picture values given a picture length. Each field's output record value is indexed by 1 and 1234, respectively. The second field specifies an alphabetic A-through-Z-generated pattern to which each output occurrence is to be truncated 1 column on the right. A

utility statement continuation character is coded in column 72.
Any standard recognizable character is sufficient. The Repeat
statement specifies that the Create statement which follows should
be repeated 100 times. The Create statement indicates that 50 test
records should be generated each time, i.e., 50 times 100 repeats
equals 5,000 total test data records. Also, prior to writing of
the first record all output areas are zero-filled. This applies
to all fields specified in the Create statement. An End statement
signifies the end of the utility control file.

If additional test patterns are desired, input files are to be
used, the reformatting of data records is necessary, or user routines
are to be called, then a more detailed control file must be described
and coded. Figure 6.6 depicts further parameter options and syntax
for IEBDG control file records.

Figure 6.6 Utility IEBDG Control File Parameters

```
Data Set Description (DSD) Statement:



                          ⎧ (Ddname)        ⎫
[Label] DSD OUTPUT=       ⎨                 ⎬
                          ⎩ (Ddname,......) ⎭



     to specify output file ddnames,

     where Ddname is user-assigned name for output file.



[Label] FD NAME=Field Name,LENGTH=Size,

          [,STARTLOC=Start Column]
                     ⎧ 'Fill Characters'  ⎫
          [,FILL=    ⎨                    ⎬ ]
                     ⎩ X'Hex Characters'  ⎭

          [,FORMAT=Type[,CHARACTER=Character]]

                               ⎧ 'Picture Characters' ⎫
          [,PICTURE Length,    ⎨ P'P Number'           ⎬ ]
                               ⎩ B'B Number'           ⎭

          [,SIGN=Sign]

          [,ACTION=Code]

          [,INDEX=Index]

          [,CYCLE=Cycle]

          [,RANGE=Range]

          [,INPUT=Ddname]

          [,FROMLOC=End Column]
```

Figure 6.6 Utility IEBDG Control File Parameters (cont.)

to specify field characteristics,

where Field Name is name of field of interest;

Size = Length of Field;

Start Column is starting field column;

Fill Characters are Extended Binary Coded Decimal

Interchange Code (EBCDIC) initialization

characters;

Hex Characters are Hexadecimal initialization characters;

Type = AL - Alphabetic,

AN - Alphanumeric,

BI - Binary,

CO - Collating Sequence,

PD - Packed Decimal,

RA - Random Binary,

ZD - Zoned Decimal;

Character = Starting Character;

Length = Length of specification;

Picture Characters are EBCDIC characters;

P Number is to be converted to Packed;

B Number is to be converted to Binary;

Sign = plus (+) assumed, or minus (-);

Code = FX - Fixed contents,

RO - Roll contents,

SL - Shift left,

SR - Shift right,

TL = Truncate left,

TR - Truncate right,

WV - Waved contents;

Index = Number to add to each field occurrence;

Cycle = Number of characters within each Index to

be treated as a group;

Range = Maximum value;

Ddname is user-assigned name for input file; and

End Column is ending field column.

Figure 6.6 Utility IEBDG Control File Parameters (cont.)

Repeat Statement:

[Label] REPEAT QUANTITY=Quantity

        [,CREATE=Number]

    to indicate desired number of repetitions,

    where Quantity = Create statement repetitions desired; and

        Number = Number of Create statements.

Create Statement:

[Label] CREATE [QUANTITY=Quantity

$$[,FILL= \begin{Bmatrix} \text{'Fill Characters'} \\ \text{X'Hex Characters'} \end{Bmatrix}]$$

$$[,INPUT= \begin{Bmatrix} \text{Ddname} \\ \text{SYSIN(xxxx)} \end{Bmatrix}]$$

$$[,PICTURE=Length,Start\ Column, \begin{Bmatrix} \text{'Picture Characters'} \\ \text{P'P Number'} \\ \text{B'B Number'} \end{Bmatrix}]$$

$$[,NAME= \begin{Bmatrix} \text{Field Name} \\ \text{(Field Name,......)} \\ \text{(Field Name,COPY=Field1,Field2,......)} \end{Bmatrix}]$$

    [,EXIT=Routine Name]

    to define record characteristics,

    where Quantity = Number of output records;

   Fill Characters are EBCDIC initialization characters;

   Hex Characters are Hexadecimal initialization characters;

        Ddname is user-assigned name for input file;

        xxxx = Record Delimiter;

        Length = Length of specification;

    Start Column is starting field column;

  Picture Characters are EBCDIC characters;

        P Number is to be converted to Packed;

        B Number is to be converted to Binary;

Figure 6.6 Utility IEBDG Control File Parameters (cont.)

```
            Field Name is name of field of interest;

      Field1, Field2, etc. are to be treated as a group

                    for the Create statement; and
            Routine Name is name of user exit routine.


  End Statement:



  [Label] END



        to indicate the end of the utility control file.
```

All control records are optional, with the exception of the DSD statement, which is required. They should be coded in the order described in Figure 6.6, and must begin with a label or a blank in column 1.

In summary, utility program IEBDG (Data Generator) generates test data in user-specified patterns. Record format, field types, and quantity are also user-controlled.

3. IEBEDIT (Edit)

a. Purpose

The purpose of utility program IEBEDIT is to create and copy Job Control Language (JCL) statements. JCL syntax editing is also accomplished in the process. This utility is occasionally called upon during the creation of JCL input streams for large systems.

b. Files and Use

Standard utility ddnames and their function are:

```
SYSUT1    - Input Sequential File.
SYSUT2    - Output Sequential File.
SYSIN     - Utility Control File.
SYSPRINT  - Utility Message File.
SYSUDUMP  - Storage Dump File.
```

Ddnames SYSUT1 and SYSUT2 describe sequential input and output JCL files, respectively. The SYSIN ddname file describes the utility control file. This file directs the utility to copy, in whole or in part, one or more input job steps to the output file. The ddname SYSPRINT file defines a utility message file for print purposes.

The JCL example below copies various steps from a file containing an input job, thus creating a new JCL input stream:

```
//UTIL   JOB   99008148,DHR,MSGLEVEL=(1,1),CLASS=A

//STEP1  EXEC  PGM=IEBEDIT
```

```
//SYSUT1   DD   UNIT=2400,DISP=(OLD,KEEP),
//            DSNAME=STREAM1,VOL=SER=TPE007
//SYSUT2   DD   UNIT=SYSDA,DISP=(NEW,KEEP),
//            DSNAME=NEW.STREAM,VOL=SER=NET017,
//            SPACE=(CYL,1),
//            DCB=(RECFM=FB,LRECL=080,BLKSIZE=080)
//SYSIN  DD   *
 EDIT   START=JOB1,TYPE=INCLUDE,STEPNAME=(STEP1,STEP4,STEP5)
/*
//SYSPRINT  DD   SYSOUT=A
//SYSUDUMP  DD   SYSOUT=A
//
```

Following an appropriate Job statement, utility program IEBEDIT is called above. Ddnames SYSUT1 and SYSUT2 describe a sequential input tape and output disk file, respectively. An Edit statement is provided via the SYSIN ddname utility control file. It directs that JOB1's job related statements be copied along with STEP1, STEP4, and STEP5 to form a new JCL input stream.

If more than one job or a portion thereof is to be accessed and copied, a more detailed control file can be described and coded. Figure 6.7 depicts further parameter options and syntax for IEBEDIT control file records.

All control records are optional. If the SYSIN ddname file is dummied, all input JCL is merely copied to the output data set. When described, all control records must begin with a label or a blank in column 1.

In summary, utility program IEBEDIT (Edit) edits and copies JCL statements from an input file, thus creating a new JCL input stream file for future use.

4. IEBISAM (Index Sequential Access Method)

a. Purpose

The purpose of utility program IEBISAM is to copy, convert, and print data from an indexed sequential data set. This form of file organization is occasionally used in lieu of the traditional sequential approach. When a large number of sequential records must be read to search for a few occurrences of a given condition, it is sometimes more efficient to index the file into more than one search level to bypass many unrelated sequential records. The IEBISAM utility program interfaces with indexed sequential data sets for file maintenance and backup purposes.

b. Files and Use

Standard utility ddnames and their functions are:

Figure 6.7 Utility IEBEDIT Control File Parameters

```
Edit Statement:


[Label] EDIT [START=Jobname]
                       ┌ POSITION ┐
           [,TYPE=  ┤ INCLUDE   ├ ]
                       └ EXCLUDE   ┘

                       ┌ Stepname                         ┐
                       │ Stepname-Stepname                │
           [,STEPNAME= ┤ (Stepname,Stepname-Stepname)     ├ ,......]
                       └ (Stepname-Stepname,Stepname)     ┘

           [,NOPRINT]


    to specify JCL copy specifications,

    where Jobname is name of job to be copied;

         POSITION refers to a Stepname and all steps which follow;

          INCLUDE specifies that Stepname(s) are to be included;

          EXCLUDE specifies that Stepname(s) are to be excluded;

         Stepname is name or range of steps to be copied; and

          NOPRINT requests that the new input stream not be listed.
```

SYSUT1   - Input Sequential or Indexed File.
SYSUT2   - Output Sequential or Indexed File.
SYSPRINT - Utility Message File.
SYSUDUMP - Storage Dump File.

Ddnames SYSUT1 and SYSUT2 describe sequential or indexed sequential input and output files depending upon the function to be performed. Note the absence of a SYSIN ddname utility control file. All activities to be performed are indicated to the utility via the JCL Parm parameter. The ddname SYSPRINT file defines a utility message file for print purposes.

The JCL example below unloads an indexed sequential file. That is, a sequential tape backup copy of an indexed sequential disk data set is created.

```
//UTIL  JOB  99008148,DHR,MSGLEVEL=(1,1),CLASS=C

//STEP1  EXEC  PGM=IEBISAM,PARM=UNLOAD

//SYSUT1  DD  UNIT=3330,DISP=(OLD,KEEP),

//         DSNAME=INDEX.SEQFILE,VOL=SER=DISK99,
```

250

```
//          DCB=(DSORG=IS)
//SYSUT2  DD   UNIT=2400,DISP=(NEW,KEEP),
//          DSNAME=INDEX.BACKUP,VOL=SER=TAPE99,
//          DCB=(RECFM=FB,LRECL=080,BLKSIZE=3200)
//SYSPRINT  DD   SYSOUT=A
//SYSUDUMP  DD   SYSOUT=A
//
```

Following an appropriate Job statement, utility program IEBISAM
is called above. UNLOAD is provided to the program via a Parm parameter. This directs the utility to create a sequential output data
set from the indexed sequential input. Ddnames SYSUT1 and SYSUT2
describe the input disk and output tape files, respectively.

If other operations are desired or user exit routines are to be
called, other specifications must be made. Figure 6.8 depicts further parameter options and syntax for IEBISAM use.

Figure 6.8 Utility IEBISAM Parm Parameter Specifications

```
┌─────────────────────────────────────────────────────────────┐
│                                                               │
│   Parm Parameter:                                             │
│                                                               │
│                ⎧                                      ⎫       │
│                │ UNLOAD                               │       │
│                │                                      │       │
│                │ LOAD                                 │       │
│       PARM=   ⎨                                      ⎬       │
│                │ COPY                                 │       │
│                │                                      │       │
│                │ '[PRINTL][,N][,EXIT=Routine Name]'   │       │
│                ⎩                                      ⎭       │
│                                                               │
│                                                               │
│        to specify operations to be performed,                 │
│                                                               │
│      where UNLOAD specifies that an indexed sequential data set│
│                                                               │
│                 is to be unloaded into a sequential data set;  │
│                                                               │
│              LOAD specifies that a sequential copy is to be loaded│
│                                                               │
│                 into an indexed sequential data set;           │
│                                                               │
│              COPY specifies that an indexed sequential copy is to│
│                                                               │
│                 be made;                                       │
│                                                               │
│            PRINTL specifies that a hexadecimal print of the    │
│                                                               │
│                 indexed sequential input file is desired;      │
│                                                               │
│                 N specifies that a nonhexadecimal print of the │
│                                                               │
│                 indexed sequential input file is desired; and  │
│                                                               │
│      Routine Name is the name of a user routine which controls │
│                                                               │
│                 the operation to be performed.                 │
│                                                               │
└─────────────────────────────────────────────────────────────┘
```

If no Parm parameter is provided, UNLOAD is the default.

In summary, utility program IEBISAM (Index Sequential Access Method) copies, converts, and prints indexed sequential data sets. The conversion operation may be accomplished in either direction, that is, indexed sequential to sequential or sequential to indexed sequential. The utility is used for file maintenance and backup purposes.

5. IEBTCRIN (Tape Cartridge Input)

    a. Purpose

    The purpose of utility program IEBTCRIN is to read, edit, and produce a standard sequential output file from the Tape Cartridge Reader. The tape cartridge is assumed to have been created using specific Selectric typewriters or Data inscribers. The IEBTCRIN utility program checks each record for validity and maintains an appropriate error description field at the beginning of each record. Control is passed to user exit routines when error conditions are encountered.

    b. Files and Use

    Standard utility ddnames and their functions are:

    SYSUT1   - Input Tape Cartridge File.
    SYSUT2   - Good Record Output Sequential File.
    SYSUT3   - Error Record Output Sequential File.
    SYSIN   - Utility Control File.
    SYSPRINT - Utility Message File.
    SYSUDUMP - Storage Dump File.

    Ddname SYSUT1 describes the input tape and cartridge reader. Ddnames SYSUT2 and SYSUT3 describe the sequential output for good records and error records, respectively. The SYSIN ddname file describes the utility control file. This file describes the nature of the input records and the type of processing desired. The ddname SYSPRINT file defines a utility message file for print purposes.

    The JCL example below reads a tape cartridge file, performs a record check for basic data validity, and creates a good record and an error record file:

```
//UTIL   JOB   90008148,DHR,MSGLEVEL=(1,1),CLASS=C
//STEP1  EXEC   PGM=IEBTCRIN
//SYSUT1  DD   UNIT=TAPECART,DISP=(OLD,KEEP),
//          VOL=SER=CART07,DCB=(BUFL=2000)
//SYSUT2  DD   UNIT=2400,DISP=(NEW,KEEP),
//          DSNAME=GOODDATA,VOL=SER=TAPE07,
//          DCB=(RECFM=FB,LRECL=80,BLKSIZE=3200)
//SYSUT3  DD   UNIT=SYSDA,DISP=(NEW,KEEP),
```

```
//          DSNAME=ERRDATA,VOL=SER=PACK07,
//          DCB=(RECFM=FB,LRECL=84,BLKSIZE=3192)
//SYSIN   DD   *
 TCRGEN   TYPE=MTD1,EDIT=EDITD,VERCHK=VOKCHK,MAXLN=80
/*
//SYSPRINT   DD   SYSOUT=A
//SYSUDUMP   DD   SYSOUT=A
//
```

Following an appropriate Job statement, utility program IEBTCRIN
is called above. Ddname SYSUT1 describes tape cartridge input via
an installation-defined unit group named TAPECART. As data is not
physically blocked on tape cartridges, a buffer length was indicated
within the DCB specification. Ddnames SYSUT2 and SYSUT3 describe a
good record output tape file and an error record output disk file,
respectively. Ddname SYSIN describes the utility control file.
The Tape Cartridge Generate (TCRGEN) statement specifies that a
Magnetic Tape Data Inscriber (MTDI) created the input file. The
Edit Delete (EDITD) specification prevents Start of Record (SOR)
and End of Record (EOR) codes from being included in the output
file. A verification check is made for the presence of tape cartridge OK codes. The maximum-length record expected for good output is 80 characters.

If other functions are desired or user exit routines are to be
called, other utility control file specifications must be coded.
Figure 6.9 depicts further parameter options and syntax for IEBTCRIN
control file records.

Figure 6.9 Utility IEBTCRIN Control File Parameters

```
  ┌─────────────────────────────────────────────────────────────┐
  │                                                               │
  │   Tape Cartridge Generate Statement:                          │
  │                                                               │
  │                            ⎧ MTDI ⎫                           │
  │   [Label] TCRGEN  [TYPE=  ⎨      ⎬  ]                          │
  │                            ⎩ MTST ⎭                           │
  │                                                               │
  │                            ⎧ STDUC ⎫                          │
  │                            ⎪ STDLC ⎪                          │
  │                [,TRANS=  ⎨        ⎬  ]                         │
  │                            ⎪ Name  ⎪                          │
  │                            ⎩ NOTRAN⎭                          │
  │                            ⎧ EDITD ⎫                          │
  │                [,EDIT=  ⎨ EDITR  ⎬  ]                          │
  │                            ⎩ NOEDIT⎭                          │
  │                            ⎧ NOCHK ⎫                          │
  │                [,VERCHK=  ⎨       ⎬  ]                         │
  │                            ⎩ VOKCHK⎭                          │
```

253

Figure 6.9 Utility IEBTCRIN Control File Parameters (cont.)

[,MINLN=x]

[,MAXLN=y]

[,REPLACE=X'zz']

$$[,ERROPT= \left\{ \begin{array}{c} NORMAL \\ NOERR \end{array} \right\}]$$

to specify the nature of the input records and the type of

processing desired,

where MTDI = Magnetic Tape Data Inscriber;

MTST = Magnetic Tape Selectric Typewriter;

STDUC = Translated Standard Upper Case for MTST input;

STDLC = Translated Standard Lower Case for MTST input;

Name = name of user-translate table load module;

NOTRAN = No Translation;

EDITD indicates that Start of Record (SOR) and

End of Record (EOR) codes are not to be transferred

to output record;

EDITR indicates that SOR and EOR codes are to be transferred

to output records;

NOEDIT indicates that all data is to be transferred to

output record as is;

NOCHK specifies that no Verification OK (VOK) check is

to be made;

VOKCHK specifies that VOK check is to be made;

x = Minimum Record length;

y = Maximum Record length;

zz = Hexadecimal characters to use to replace an error

byte;

NORMAL indicates that the normal Error Option (ERROPT)

should be used; and

NOERR indicates that all records should be placed in

the SYSUT2 data set (none in SYSUT3).

Exits Statement:

[Label] EXITS [ERROR=Routine Name]

[,OUTREC=Routine Name]

Figure 6.9 Utility IEBTCRIN Control File Parameters (cont.)

```
                   [,OUTHDR2=Routine Name]

                   [,OUTHDR3=Routine Name]

                   [,OUTTLR2=Routine Name]

                   [,OUTTLR3=Routine Name]


              to indicate user exit routines,

          where Routine Name is name of user routine to process

                  error records, good records, good record user output

                  header labels, error record user output header labels,

                  good record user output trailer labels, and error record

                  user output trailer labels.
```

All control records are optional and must begin with a label or a blank in column 1.

In summary, utility program IEBTCRIN (Tape Cartridge Input) reads, edits, and creates a standard sequential file using the Tape Cartridge Reader with tape cartridges from Selectric typewriters or Data inscribers.

6. IEBUPDAT (Symbolic Update)

a. Purpose

The purpose of utility program IEBUPDAT is to create and update symbolic libraries and/or their members. A symbolic library consists of records which symbolize an 80-character card image. Procedure library maintenance is the typical application. It should be noted that utility program IEBUPDTE discussed previously also provides this function in addition to others.

b. Files and Use

Standard utility ddnames and their functions are:

```
SYSUT1   - Optional Input PDS File.
SYSUT2   - Output PDS File.
SYSIN    - Utility Control and Data File.
SYSPRINT - Utility Message File.
SYSUDUMP - Storage Dump File.
```

Ddname SYSUT1 describes the old partitioned file. When creating a new output file, a SYSUT1 Dd statement is not required. Ddname SYSUT2 describes the existing or new updated output file. Both files must be 80 characters in length. The SYSIN ddname file describes the utility control and data file. Adding, replacing, and changing JCL procedures are typical specifications. As such, a SYSIN Dd Data statement must be coded. The ddname SYSPRINT file describes a utility message file for these activities.

The JCL example below replaces an existing PDS catalogued procedure 80-character record member with a new version:

```
//UTIL    JOB   99008148,DHR,MSGLEVEL=(1,1),CLASS=A
//STEP1   EXEC  PGM=IEBUPDAT
//SYSUT1  DD    DSNAME=APROC.LIBRARY,DISP=SHR
//SYSUT2  DD    DSNAME=APROC.LIBRARY,DISP=SHR
//SYSIN   DD    DATA
./        REPL PROC1,01,0,1
  -  -  -  - Complete Member Here  -  -  -  -
./        ALIAS MEM1
./        ENDUP
/*
//SYSPRINT  DD   SYSOUT=A
//SYSUDUMP  DD   SYSOUT=A
//
```

Following an appropriate Job statement, utility program IEBUPDAT is called above. Dd statements SYSUT1 and SYSUT2 both describe procedure library APROC.LIBRARY. The control and data file for ddname SYSIN consists of Header (Replace), Alias, and Endup statements and the data (member) to be placed into the symbolic library. The actual data itself always follows Header, Number, and Delete statements but is placed before any Alias and Endup statements for that member. The Replace statement indicates the member to be replaced, run number, and modification source and requests that a complete listing of the entire member be provided. The replacing member in the job stream should contain sequence numbers in columns 73 to 80 for update purposes. The Alias statement assigns an alternate name to the member. The Endup statement indicates the end of the control file.

If other functions are desired, other utility control and data file specifications must be coded. Figure 6.10 depicts further parameter options and syntax for IEBUPDAT control file records.

Figure 6.10 Utility IEBUPDAT Control File Parameters

```
Header Statement:


          ⎧ ADD   ⎫
          ⎪       ⎪
          ⎪ CHNGE ⎪
./        ⎨       ⎬   Member Name,Run,Mod,List[,System Status]
          ⎪ REPL  ⎪
          ⎪       ⎪
          ⎩ REPRO ⎭
```

Figure 6.10 Utility IEBUPDAT Control File Parameters (cont.)

to specify the function to be performed,

where ADD specifies addition;

CHNGE specifies change;

REPL specifies replace;

REPRO specifies reproduce (or copy);

Member Name indicates PDS name of member;

Run = Run Number 00 to 99;

Mod = Modification Source of 0 for user and 1 for IBM;

List = 0 for no list of member,

1 for list of member; and

System Status is 8 hexadecimal characters of system status information.

Number Statement:

./   NUMBER aaaaaaaa,bbbbbbbb,cccccccc,dddddddd

to remember records,

where aaaaaaaa = old sequence number of initial record;

bbbbbbbb = old sequence number of final record;

cccccccc = new sequence number of first record; and

dddddddd = increment to be used for new sequence.

Delete Statement:

./   DELET aaaaaaaa,bbbbbbbb

to delete records,

where aaaaaaaa = old sequence number of initial record; and

bbbbbbbb = new sequence number of final record.

Alias Statement:

./   ALIAS Alias Name

to provide an alias name.

257

Figure 6.10 Utility IEBUPDAT Control File Parameters (cont.)

Endup Statement:

./   ENDUP

to indicate the end of the utility control and data file.

A Header statement should be coded for each member to be updated. Number, Delete, Alias, and Endup statements are optional but when used should be coded in the order described in Figure 6.10. Each must begin with a ./ (period slash) in columns 1 and 2 and blanks in columns 3 to 9.

In addition to the above described utility control and data file specifications, four items of information can also be provided via a Parm parameter. Its format is:

$$PARM = (\left\{ \begin{array}{c} MOD \\ NEW \end{array} \right\} [,Routine1][,Routine2])$$

where MOD = Default specification, as input consists of the SYSUT1 ddname input file and a portion of the utility control file;

NEW = SYSUT1 ddname input file is not to be described;

Routine1 = Name of the routine to process user header labels; and

Routine2 = Name of the routine to process user trailer labels.

In summary, utility program IEBUPDAT creates, adds, replaces, and changes symbolic libraries.

A significant topic in and by itself, a detailed description of the many functions of data set utilities can be obtained from the Utilities manual. Those data set utility applications common to all dp environments have been covered in this chapter.

E. DATA SET ALLOCATION PROGRAM

Though not part of the "official" group of programs commonly referred to as utilities, program IEFBR14 should be classified as such.

1. Purpose

The purpose of program IEFBR14 is twofold. Its main function is to allocate space for direct-access data sets. It can delete data sets as well. A secondary function is to test for JCL syntax prior to actual program execution. When substituted for a program name, IEFBR14 not only allocates appropriate disk files, but first automatically checks for syntactical JCL errors.

2. Files and Use

No standard ddnames are required to be coded. Rather, the ddname intended for use when the file is processed should be used. The JCL example below allocates space for a disk data set:

```
//UTIL    JOB   99008148,DHR,MSGLEVEL=(1,1),CLASS=A
//STEP1   EXEC  PGM=IEFBR14
//DISKFILE  DD  UNIT=3330,DISP=(NEW,KEEP),
//          DSNAME=NEWFILE,VOL=SER=PACK99,
//          SPACE=(TRK,20),
//          DCB=(RECFM=FB,LRECL=100,BLKSIZE=3200)
```

Following an appropriate Job statement, utility program IEFBR14 is called above. Dd statement DISKFILE describes an output sequential disk file for which 20 tracks are to be allocated. Though this function could be performed in a later job stream, allocating data space independent of test and production run JCL negates a need to change such job streams once allocated. In fact, some programmers initially change the name of the program being called in the JCL to IEFBR14. JCL syntax is checked, appropriate disk files are allocated, but actual processing does not commence. Then the program name is changed back to the original, JCL errors corrected, and the job resubmitted.

In summary, program IEFBR14 allocates space for direct-access data sets. It also checks for JCL syntax in the process.

F. DATA SET UTILITY WORKSHOP

All data set utilities which can be called have been discussed. A workshop is now provided to solidify a working knowledge of basic data set utility use and JCL job coding. Workshop answers can be found in Appendix E.

1. Reformat and Print Sequential File

An application program package we wish to utilize requires input records to be of a specific format. Our current file's format does not coincide exactly with the package's input requirements. However, we need only reformat our records to meet these requirements. Some reformatted data should also be printed for verification purposes. Code the Job statement, all Exec statements, and all Dd statements for the two-step job depicted by the system flowchart in Figure 6.11.

Pertinent Job statement information is displayed thereon. Choose your own jobname and programmer name, however. Only the program name need be coded on the Exec statements.

Pertinent Dd statement information is displayed as appropriate. Use 2400 for tape unit allocations, and 3330 for disk unit allocations. Code all three subparameters of the Disposition parameter for passed files, eventually keeping all tape and disk files. Choose your own permanent data set names. Use DD * for card files with no other parameters. Also, code no parameters other than SYSOUT for print files. Assume standard tape labels are utilized and therefore need not be described.

Utility program IEBGENER is to accomplish the following: (1) move the contents of the whole input record to the output record; (2) move the contents of input columns 10-15 to output columns 95-100; and (3) move blanks to output columns 10-15. Utility program IEBPTPCH is to accomplish the following: (1) print every other record in the input file, triple-spaced, until 250 have been printed; (2) print 'PARTIAL DATA FILE LISTING' beginning in column 20 at the top of each page; and (3) ensure that a solid line of data will be printed for each record.

To assist your coding efforts, follow the step-by-step instructions described below:

Figure 6.11 Sequential Reformat and Print System Flowchart

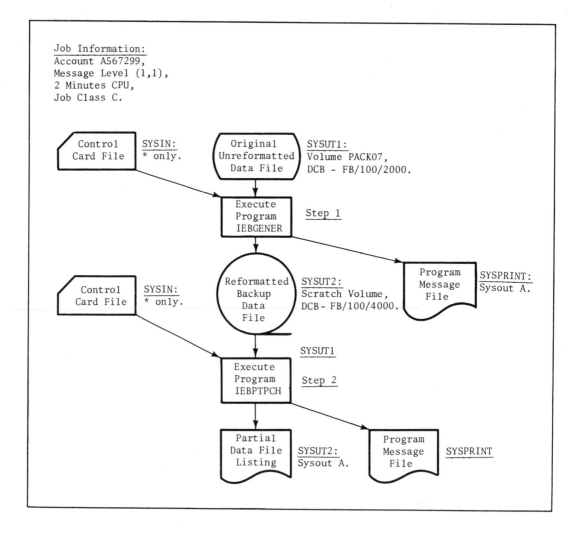

1. Code the Job statement.

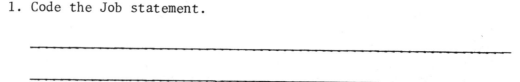

260

2. Code Step 1's Exec statement. Then code five Dd statements
-- the first for ddname SYSUT1, a second for ddname SYSUT2,
a third for ddname SYSIN followed by the utility control file
itself and a file delimiter, a fourth for ddname SYSPRINT,
and the fifth for ddname SYSUDUMP. Then code a step delimiter.

_____

_____

_____

_____

_____

_____

_____

_____

_____

_____

_____

_____

3. Code Step 2's Exec statement. Then code five Dd statements
-- the first for ddname SYSUT1, a second for ddname SYSUT2,
a third for ddname SYSIN followed by the utility control
file itself and a file delimiter, a fourth for ddname
SYSPRINT, and the fifth for ddname SYSUDUMP. Then code a
Null statement.

_____

_____

_____

_____

_____

_____

_____

_____

_____

_____

_____

_____

_____

_____

2. Update And Copy/Compress Procedure Library

You have the responsibility for maintaining a library of catalogued procedures unique to your office's application. Each week procedure content is updated as desired. Disk space for desired and duplicative members is freed, and the library is compressed and copied. Code the Job statement, all Exec statements, and all Dd statements for the two-step job depicted by the system flowchart in Figure 6.12.

Pertinent Job statement information is displayed thereon. Choose your own jobname and programmer name, however. Only the program name need be coded on the Exec statements.

Pertinent Dd statement information is displayed as appropriate. Use 3330 for disk unit allocations. Code shared Disposition parameters for disk library files. Choose your own library data set names. Use DD * for card files with no other parameters. Also, code no parameters other than SYSOUT for print files.

Utility program IEBUPDTE is to accomplish the following: (1) access member name PROC22 and change the record with sequence number 00000017 to //STEPX EXEC PGM=LEADZERO,REGION=40K; (2) change the record with sequence number 00000023 to //UNIT=SYSDA,DISP=SHR; (3) list the new updated member; and (4) resequence all statements by 10 beginning with 5. Utility program IEBCOPY is to accomplish the following: (1) provide ddnames OUT1 and IN1 for the same output and input library file, respectively; (2) remove all identically named members from the input library; and, (3) exclude member names REFORM, JCL17, and PROC07 from the copy/compress process.

To assist your coding efforts, follow the step-by-step instructions below:

1. Code the Job statement.

_____

_____

Figure 6.12 Procedure Update and Copy/Compress System Flowchart

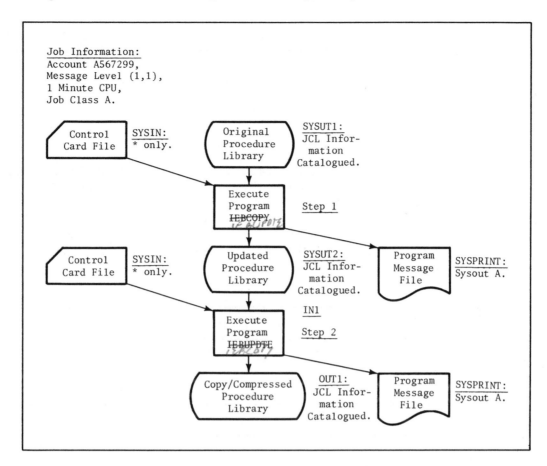

2. Code Step 1's Exec statement. Then code five Dd statements -- the first for ddname SYSUT1, a second for ddname SYSUT2, a third for ddname SYSIN followed by the utility control and data file itself and a file delimiter, a fourth for ddname SYSPRINT, and the fifth for ddname SYSUDUMP. Then code a step delimiter.

_____

_____

_____

_____

_____

_____

_____

_____

_____

_____

_____

_____

_____

3. Code Step 2's Exec statement. Then code seven Dd statements
   -- the first for ddname IN1, a second for ddname OUT1, a
   third for ddname SYSIN followed by the utility control file
   itself and a file delimiter, a fourth for ddname SYSPRINT,
   a fifth and sixth for ddnames SYSUT3 and SYSUT4 one-track
   work files, respectively, and the seventh for ddname SYSUDUMP.
   Then code a Null statement.

_____

_____

_____

_____

_____

_____

_____

_____

_____

_____

_____

7

System and Independent Utility Programs

A. SYSTEM UTILITY USE

As discussed in the previous chapter, utility programs are classified as either,

    Data Set;
    System; or
    Independent Utilities.

System utilities are those which access and print or otherwise manipulate system-related data sets. They perform functions necessary for the proper maintenance of system libraries and files. In general, they are system-oriented and more frequently utilized by technical installation personnel. System utility programs and a summary of their most common functions follow:

    IEHATLAS - Assign tracks.
    IEHDASDR - Initialize, dump, restore.
    IEHINITT - Create tape labels.
    IEHIOSUP - Modify supervisor control tables.
    IEHLIST   - List data set descriptive entries.
    IEHMOVE   - Copy, move, replace.
    IEHPROGM - Catalogue, connect volumes, create index, maintain
                 passwords.
    IEHUCAT   - Update system catalogues.
    IFHSTATR - List tape errors.

B. BASIC SYSTEM UTILITY PROGRAMS

Some system utilities can be considered basic to the performance of a programmer's or analyst's duties. That is, they are common to the needs of most application and system programmers and analysts. These are IEHINITT, IEHLIST, IEHMOVE, and IEHPROGM.

1. IEHINITT (Initialize Tape)

   a. Purpose

   The purpose of utility program IEHINITT is to create standard labels on tape volumes. This must be accomplished prior to the writing of actual data onto a reel or the data set itself. This procedure is sometimes referred to as the tape initialization process. It must always be accomplished after newly purchased tapes have been received and logged into the tape library. An initial volume label record and a tape mark are created. Only when data is eventually written to a file on the volume is the first header record filled, the tape mark written over, a second header record created, optional user header records created, and a tape mark placed prior to the beginning of actual data itself. Similar trailer records and tape marks are also placed behind the data. (Standard label record format and fields are described in detail in Chapter 8.)

   b. Files and Use

   Standard utility ddnames and their function are:

   Ddname1   - Input/Output Tape Volume.
   SYSIN   - Utility Control File.
   SYSPRINT   - Utility Message File.
   SYSUDUMP   - Storage Dump File.

   Ddname1 is a ddname which is specified by the user in the utility control file. The JCL need only describe a unit and density specification. More than one ddname and type description may be provided in the JCL, i.e., more than one tape may be labeled per job step. The SYSIN ddname file describes the control file, usually cards. The utility control file should not be dummied due to the necessity of providing a volume serial number to the operating system and the label itself. The ddname SYSPRINT file defines a utility message file for tape-labeling operations. A SYSUDUMP Dd statement describes the storage dump file if this type of abnormal termination should occur.
   The JCL example below labels a single-tape volume:

```
//SYST    JOB   ALPHAPROJ,CHAR,MSGLEVEL=(1,1),CLASS=C
//STEP1   EXEC  PGM=IEHINITT
//TAPELABL   DD UNIT=2400,DCB=DEN=3
//SYSIN   DD   *
TAPELABL   INITT   SER=TAPE54
/*
//SYSPRINT   DD   SYSOUT=A
//SYSUDUMP   DD   SYSOUT=A
//
```

Following an appropriate Job statement, utility program IEHINITT is called above. No other Exec statement parameters are necessary, as all defaults are acceptable. Dd statement TAPELABL (so named per utility control record) describes two tape characteristics -- 9-track, 1600 Bits per Inch (BPI). The SYSIN ddname control file contains one INITT (Initialize Tape) statement. Column 1 to 8 specify that ddname TAPELABL is to be utilized for the tape volume description. The serial number is TAPE54. Utility messages are provided by the SYSPRINT ddname print file. Finally, a SYSUDUMP Dd statement and Null statement are coded. Upon completion of this job, the above tape will contain appropriate initial volume, and tape mark records.

In order to more fully utilize this utility program, a more complete utility control file should be described. Figure 7.1 depicts further parameter options and syntax for IEHINITT records.

Figure 7.1 Utility IEHINITT Control File Parameters.

```
Initialize Tape Statement:


Ddname    INITT   SER=xxxxxx
                         ⎧ UNLOAD) ⎫
                  (,DISP=⎨          ⎬
                         ⎩ REWIND  ⎭

                  (,LABTYPE=AL)

                  (,NUMBTAPE=y)

                  (,OWNER='zzzzzzzzzz(zzzz)')



    to specify tape and label characteristics,

    where Ddname is a user-assigned ddname for the unit and

                 density description;

       xxxxxx = volume serial number of tape to be labeled;

        UNLOAD specifies that the tape is to be rewound and

               dismounced (default) upon completion;

        REWIND specifies that the tape is to be only rewound;

          AL = American National Standard (ANS) Label for

               ASCII volumes; BCD 7-track default; and EBCDIC

               9-track default;

           y = the number of volumes to be labeled with serial

               numbers automatically incremented; and

  zzzzzzzzzz(zzzz) is owner information; 10 bytes for EBCDIC and

               BCD, and 14 bytes for ANS labels.
```

267

At least one INITT statement must be provided as a ddname and serial number must be specified. More than one INITT statement can also be coded for one or more Dd statements. A Parm parameter specification can also be made such that PARM='LINECT=xx' where xx equals the number of print lines per page. The default is 60 for standard installation paper.

c. JCL Example

The two JCL examples below initialize a multiple number of volumes with varying tape characteristics:

```
//SYST  JOB  ALPHAPROJ,CHAR,MSGLEVEL=(1,1),CLASS=C

//STEP1  EXEC  PGM=IEHINITT

//TAPEINIT  DD UNIT=(2400,,DEFER),DCB=DEN=4

//SYSIN  DD  *

TAPEINIT  INITT  SER=0S001,NUMBTAPE=3

TAPEINIT  INITT  SER=TAPE36

/*

//SYSPRINT  DD  SYSOUT=A

//SYSUDUMP  DD  SYSOUT=A

//
```

Following an appropriate Job statements, utility program IEHINITT is called above. Dd statement TAPEINIT describes two basic tape characteristics -- 9-track, 6250 BPI. The SYSIN ddname control file contains two INITT statements. Columns 1 to 8 specify that ddname TAPEINIT is to be utilized for four-tape volume descriptions. The first three are 0S001, 0S002, and 0S003. The fourth volume serial is TAPE36. Utility messages are written to the SYSPRINT ddname print file. A SYSUDUMP Dd statement and Null statement should also be provided. Another IEHINITT example is as follows:

```
//SYST  JOB  ALPHAPROJ,CHAR,MSGLEVEL=(1,1),CLASS=C

//STEP1  EXEC  PGM=IEHINITT

//INITIAL1  DD  UNIT=(2400-2,,DEFER),DCB=DEN=1

//INITIAL2  DD  UNIT=(2400-2,3,DEFER),DCB=DEN=2

//SYSIN  DD  *

INITIAL1  INITT  SER=014576,OWNER='USDA GS'

INITIAL2  INITT  SER=TAPE07,NUMBTAPE=6,LABTYPE=AL

/*

//SYSPRINT  DD SYSOUT=A

//SYSUDUMP  DD  SYSOUT=A

//
```

Following an appropriate Job statement, utility program IEHINITT is called above. Dd statements INITIAL1 and INITIAL2 describe two basic tape characteristics -- 7-track and either 556 or 800 BPI. They also indicate that the mounting of each volume is to be deferred until needed. In addition, the second Dd statement requests that three tape drives be utilized. The SYSIN Ddname control file contains two INITT statements. Columns 1 to 8 specify that ddnames INITIAL1 and INITIAL2 are to be utilized for seven-tape volume descriptions. The first is 014576, for which some owner identification information is to be stored in the volume label. The next six volume serial numbers are TAPE07, TAPE08, TAPE09, TAPE10, TAPE11, and TAPE12. These ASCII tapes are to contain ANS tape lables. Utility messages are written to the SYSPRINT ddname print file. A SYSUDUMP statement and Null statement should also be provided.

In summary, utility program IEHINITT initializes tape volumes. A volume record, dummy header record, and tape mark are created as the initial label. This utility is more frequently utilized when new installation or user tapes have been received.

2. IEHLIST (List)

   a. Purpose

   The purpose of utility program IEHLIST is to list the contents of a Volume Table Of Contents (VTOC), Partitioned Data Set (PDS) directory, or data set Catalogue entries. These activities are performed frequently by both installation and user personnel as a part of file and disk management procedures. Like tape files, disk data sets also have a tendency to grow in size and number. In reality, a typical user may have control over many files which no longer need to be saved and should be scratched (deleted). Utility program IEHLIST is a tool which can be used to determine which data sets are currently available, and where they are located, as well as their nature and characteristics.

   b. Files and Use

   Standard utility ddnames and their functions are:

   Ddname1   - On-line Input Volume.
   Ddname2   - Mountable Input Volume.
   SYSIN   - Utility Control File.
   SYSPRINT - Utility Message File.
   SYSUDUMP - Storage Dump File.

   Ddname1 and Ddname2 can be any ddname as chosen by the user. The ddnames are not specified in the utility control file as with a few other utilities. The JCL need only describe a unit, disposition, and volume specification. Both statements may be provided in the JCL. More than one volume of each type may also be specified using control records. The SYSIN ddname file describes the control file, usually cards. The utility control file should not be dummied due to the necessity of providing a volume indication or data set name. The ddname SYSPRINT file defines a utility message file operation. A

SYSUDUMP Dd statement describes the storage dump file if this type of abnormal termination should occur.

The JCL example below lists the directory entries for the numbers of a Partitioned Data Set (PDS) and their characteristics:

```
//SYST    JOB   ALHAPROJ,CHAR,MSGLEVEL=(1,1),CLASS=A
//STEP1   EXEC PGM=IEHLIST
//FILE1   DD UNIT=3330,DISP=OLD,
//          VOL=SER=PACK18
//SYSIN   DD   *
 LISTPDS   DSNAME=A.PROG.LIBRARY
/*
//SYSPRINT  DD SYSOUT=A
//SYSUDUMP  DD SYSOUT=A
//
```

Following an appropriate Job statement, utility program IEHLIST is called above. No other Exec statement parameters are necessary, as all defaults are acceptable. Dd statements FILE1 describes an appropriate on-line unit and disk pack which contains the PDS of interest. The SYSIN ddname control file contains one List PDS statement which specifies the data set name of the PDS to be listed. Utility messages as well as a listing of member names and their characteristics are written to the SYSPRINT ddname print file. Finally, a SYSUDUMP Dd statement and Null statement are coded.

In order to more fully utilize this program, other utility control file statements should be described. Figure 7.2 depicts further parameter options and syntax for IEHLIST records.

Figure 7.2 Utility IEHLIST Control File Parameters

```
List Catalogue Statement:

[Label]    LISTCTLG  [VOL=Unit=Number]
                        [,NODE=Node]
       to list the contents of a catalogue,
     where Unit = Device Type;
         Number = Volume serial number; and
           Node = that portion of qualified dsname
                  structure for which a listing
                  is desired.


List Partitioned Data Set Statement:
```

Figure 7.2 Utility IEHLIST Control File Parameters (cont.)

```
[Label]   LISTPDS  DSNAME= ⎰ Dsname                    ⎱
                           ⎱ (Dsname,Dsname,.......)   ⎰

                         [,VOL=Unit=Number]

                         ⎡ ⎰ ,DUMP   ⎱ ⎤
                         ⎣ ⎱ ,FORMAT ⎰ ⎦
```

to list the contents of a PDS,

where Dsname is name of data set(s) for which members and their

characteristics are to be listed;

Unit = Device Type;

Number = Volume Serial Number;

DUMP requests a nonedited hexadecimal print; and

FORMAT requests an edited print form.

List Volume Table of Contents Statement:

```
[Label]   LISTVTOC  ⎡ ⎰ DUMP   ⎱ ⎤
                    ⎣ ⎱ FORMAT ⎰ ⎦

                      [,DATE=Julian]

                      [,DSNAME= ⎰ Dsname                    ⎱ ]
                                ⎱ (Dsname,Dsname,......)    ⎰

                      [,VOL=Unit=Number]
```

to list the Volume Table of Contents (VTOC),

where DUMP requests a nonedited hexadecimal print;

FORMAT requests an edited print form;

Julian = 3-digit day and 2-digit year (DDDYY) for which

expired data sets will be flagged;

Dsname is a name of data set(s) for which VTOC entries

are to be listed;

Unit = Device Type; and,

Number = Volume Serial Number.

More than one of the statements in Figure 7.2 may be coded, though they should all be of the same type, i.e., LISTCTLG, LISTPDS, or LISTVTOC. All must begin with a label or blank in column 1. Labels, which follow standard JCL naming conventions, are used as comments to delineate utility operations.

A Parm parameter specification can also be made such that PARM='LINECNT=xx', where xx equals the number of print lines per page.

271

The default is 58 for standard installation paper.

c. JCL Examples

The two JCL examples below list a Volume Table of Contents and a data set Catalogue:

```
//SYST   JOB   ALPHAPROJ,CHAR,MSGLEVEL=(1,1),CLASS=C
//STEP1  EXEC  PGM=IEHLIST
//VOL2   DD UNIT=3330,DISP=OLD,
//         VOL=SER=DISK84
//SYSIN  DD   *
 LISTVTOC   FORMAT,DATE=17578,VOL=3330=DISK84
/*
//SYSPRINT  DD   SYSOUT=A
//SYSUDUMP  DD   SYSOUT=A
//
```

Following an appropriate Job statement, utility program IEHLIST is called above. Dd statement VOL2 describes an appropriate mountable unit and disk pack which contains the VTOC of interest. The SYSIN ddname control file contains one LISTVTOC statement which specifies that an edited formatted reportlike print is desired, Those data sets with an expiration date prior to the 175th day of 1978 will be flagged with an asterisk. A device type and volume serial number are also indicated. Utility messages as well as a listing of the VTOC are written to the SYSPRINT ddname file. Finally, a SYSUDUMP Dd statement and Null statement are coded. Another IEHLIST example is as follows:

```
//SYST   JOB   ALPHAPROJ,CHAR,MSGLEVEL=(1,1),CLASS=C
//STEP1  EXEC  PGM=IEHLIST
//CATLG1  DD UNIT=3330,DISP=OLD,
//         VOL=SER=001872
//CATLG2  DD UNIT=3330,DISP=OLD,
//         VOL=SER=OS2307
//SYSIN DD   *
 LISTCTLG   VOL=3330=001872
 LISTCTLG   VOL=3330=OS2307,NODE=PROJECT.ALPHA
/*
//SYSPRINT  DD   SYSOUT=A
//SYSUDUMP  DD   SYSOUT=A
//
```

Following an appropriate Job statement, utility program IEHLIST is called above. Dd statement CATLG1 and CATLG2 describe appropriate on-line and mountable units and disk packs which contain the data set catalogues of interest. The SYSIN ddname control file **contains two** LISTCTLG statements. They specify on-line and mountable device types and volume serial numbers, respectively. The second listing will only contain information for those entries in the catalogue which comprise the qualified name PROJECT.ALPHA. Cataloguing data sets and the use of generation numbers will be detailed in the next chapter. Utility messages as well as a listing of the catalogues are written to the SYSPRINT ddname file. A SYSUDUMP Dd statement and Null statement should also be provided.

In summary, utility program IEHLIST lists the contents of the Volume Table Of Contents (VTOC), Partitioned Data Set (PDS) directory, and data set Catalogue entries. Portions of the above can also be listed for file management purposes if desired.

3. IEHMOVE (Move)

a. Purpose

The purpose of utility program IEHMOVE is to move and/or copy data sets, catalogues, and volumes. Operations which can be performed include merging, replacing, and/or deleting of programs, procedures, and other source data of interest. As such, this utility is most handy for maintaining system program and procedure libraries.

b. Files and Use

Standard ddnames and their functions are:

Ddname1	-	On-line Input/Output Volume.
Ddname2	-	Mountable Input/Volume.
Ddtape	-	Input/Out Tape Volume.
SYSIN	-	Utility Control File.
SYSPRINT	-	Utility Message File.
SYSUT1	-	Temporary Work File.
SYSUDUMP	-	Storage Dump File.

Ddname1 and Ddname2 can be any ddname as chosen by the user. The ddnames may or may not be specified in the utility control file depending upon the specific application. Both Dd statements may be provided in the JCL. In fact, more than two may be coded. The first Dd statement relates to on-line volumes; the remaining ones describe mountable volumes. Ddtape can also be any ddname as chosen by the user. The SYSIN ddname file describes the control file, usually cards. The utility control file should not be dummied. The ddname SYSPRINT file defines a utility message file for move and copy operations. Ddname SYSUT1 defines utility work space. A SYSUDUMP Dd statement describes the storage dump file if this type of abnormal termination should occur.

The JCL example below copies the contents of one volume to another:

273

```
//SYST   JOB   ALPHAPROJ,CHAR,MSGLEVEL=(1,1),CLASS=C
//STEP1   EXEC PGM=IEHMOVE
//VOL1   DD   UNIT=3330,DISP=OLD,
//          VOL=SER=ONLINE88
//TAPE1   DD   UNIT=2400,DISP=OLD,
//          VOL=SER=BACKUP01,
//          DCB=(RECFM=LRECL=80,BLKSIZE=1600,DEN=2)
//SYSIN  DD   *
 COPY   VOLUME=2400=BACKUP01,                              X
               TO=3330=ONLINE88,CATLG
/*
//SYSPRINT  DD SYSOUT=A
//SYSUT1   DD UNIT=3330,VOL=SER=WORK01
//SYSUDUMP  DD   SYSOUT=A
//
```

Following an appropriate Job statement, utility program IEHMOVE is called above. No other Exec statement parameters are necessary, as all defaults are acceptable. Dd statement VOL1 describes an appropriate on-line volume. Dd statement TAPE1 describes a backup tape for this on-line volume The SYSIN ddname control file contains one Copy Volume statement which specifies the tape device and volume to be used as source data. A move differs only from a copy in that with a "move" the source data is scratched. As can be seen, one must be careful in the use of the Move statement. These statements specify the on-line disk device and volume to which backup tape data sets will be copied and catalogued. Utility messages are provided by the SYSPRINT ddname print file. Finally, a SYSUDUMP Dd statement and Null statement are coded.

In order to more fully utilize this program, other utility control file statements should be described. Figure 7.3 depicts further parameter options and syntax for IEHMOVE records.

Figure 7.3 Utility IEHMOVE Control File Parameters

```
Copy/Move Catalogue Statement:

[Label]  ⎧COPY⎫  CATALOG[=Name]
         ⎩MOVE⎭  ,TO=Unit=Number

               [,CVOL=Unit=Number]

               [,FROM=Unit=Number]

               [,FROMDD=Ddname]

               [,TODD=Ddname]
```

274

Figure 7.3 Utility IEHMOVE Control File Parameters (cont.)

to copy or move data set catalogues,

   where Name = qualified name of catalogue entries;

           Unit = Device Type;

       Number = Volume Serial Number;

             CVOL is where initial catalogue search is to begin; and

FROMDD and TODD specify tape ddnames where Data Control

             Block (DCB) and other label information is to be

             obtained.

Copy/Move Data Set Name Statement:

[Label] { COPY   DSNAME=Dsname
         { MOVE   ,TO=Unit=Number

             [,FROM=Unit=Number]

             [,CVOL=Unit=Number]

             [,UNCATLG]

             [,CATLG]

             [,RENAME=Name]

             [,FROMDD=Ddname]

             [TODD=Ddname]

             [,UNLOAD]

   to copy or move a data set,

   where Dsname = name of data set to be copied or moved;

           Unit = Device Type;

       Number = Volume Serial Number;

             CVOL is where initial catalogue search is to begin;

UNCATLG and CATLG specify whether the source data is to

             be uncatalogued or the copied data catalogued;

       Name = New Data Set Name;

FROMDD and TODD specify tape ddnames where DCB

             and other label information is to be obtained; and

       UNLOAD specifies that an attempt to unload the data

             set should be made regardless of possible

             incompatible conditions.

275

Figure 7.3 Utility IEHMOVE Control File Parameters (cont.)

Copy/Move Partitioned Data Set Statement:

[Label] { COPY / MOVE } PDS=Dsname

,TO=Unit=Number

[,FROM=Unit=Number]

[,CVOL=Unit=Number]

[,EXPAND=xx]

[,UNCATLG]

[,CATLG]

[,RENAME=Name]

[,FROMDD=Ddname]

[,TODD=Ddname]

to copy or move partitioned data sets,

where Dsname = name of PDS;

Unit = Device Type;

Number = Volume Serial Number;

CVOL is where initial catalogue search is to begin;

xx = number of 256-byte records to be added to

PDS directory;

UNCATLG and CATLG specify whether the source data is to be

uncatalogued or the copied data catalogued;

Name = New PDS name; and

FROMDD and TODD specify tape ddnames where DCB and other

label information is to be obtained.

Copy/Move Data Set Group Statement:

[Label] { COPY / MOVE } DSGROUP[=Name]

,TO=Unit=Number

[,CVOL=Unit=Number]

[,PASSWORD]

[,UNCATLG]

[,DATLG]

[,TODD=Ddname]

[,UNLOAD]

to copy or move a group of data sets,

where Name = qualified name of catalogue entries;

Figure 7.3 Utility IEHMOVE Control File Parameters (cont.)

```
                 Unit = Device Type;

             Number = Volume Serial Number;

                 CVOL is where initial catalogue search is to begin;

          PASSWORD specifies that all protected and unprotected

                  data sets are to be moved or copied;

UNCATLG and CATLG specify whether the source data is to be

                  uncatalogued or the copied data catalogued;

             TODD specifies tape ddname where DCB and other label

                  information is to be obtained; and

           UNLOAD specifies that an attempt to unload the data

                  set should be made regardless of possible

                  incompatible conditions.
```

Include Statement:

```
[Label]    INCLUDE  DSNAME=Dsname

                      [,MEMBER=Member Name]

                      [,FROM=Unit=Number]

                      [,CVOL=Unit=Number]


    to include other sources in copy or move operations,

   where Dsname = Data Set Name to be included;

   Member Name = name of PDS member to be included;

          Unit = Device Type;

        Number = Volume Serial Number; and

          CVOL is where initial catalogue search is to begin.
```

Exclude Statement:

```
[Label]    EXCLUDE [ ⎧DSGROUP=Name          ⎫ ]
                     ⎩MEMBER=Member  Name⎭


    to exclude sources from copy or move operations,

   where Name = qualified name of catalogue entries; and

   Member Name = name of PDS members to be excluded.
```

Select Statement:

```
                         ⎧Member Name                        ⎫
                         ⎪                                   ⎪
                         ⎪(Member Name,......)               ⎪
[Label]   SELECT  MEMBER=⎨                                   ⎬
                         ⎪(Member Name,New Name)             ⎪
                         ⎪                                   ⎪
                         ⎩((Member Name,New Name),......)⎭
```

Figure 7.3 Utility IEHMOVE Control File Parameters (cont.)

to select PDS members to be moved or copied,

where Member Name=name of PDS member to be selected; and

New Name=new name of PDS member selected.

Copy/Move Volume Statement:

[Label] $\left\{ \begin{array}{l} COPY \\ MOVE \end{array} \right\}$ VOLUME=Unit=Number

,TO=Unit=Number

[,PASSWORD]

[,CATLG]

[,TODD=Ddname]

[,UNLOAD]

to copy or move volume data,

where Unit = Device Type;

Number = Volume Serial Number;

PASSWORD specifies that all protected and unprotected

data sets are to be moved or copied;

CATLG specifies that the copied data is to be catalogued;

TODD specifies tape ddname where DCB and other label

information to be obtained; and

UNLOAD specifies that an attempt to unload the data

set should be made regardless of possible

incompatible conditions.

Replace Statement:

[Label]   REPLACE   DSNAME=Dsname

,MEMBER=Member Name

[,FROM=Unit=Number]

[,CVOL=Unit=Number]

to replace copied or moved PDS members,

where Dsname = PDS name;

Member Name = name of PDS member;

Unit = Device Type;

Number = Volume Serial Number; and

CVOL is where initial catalogue search is to begin.

One of the first five operations should be chosen, that is, copy or move Catalogues, Data Sets, Data Set Groups, PDS's, or Volumes. Within this operation, a multiple number of statements may be coded. The Include, Exclude, Select, and Replace statements are completely. optional, however. All must begin with a label or blank in column 1. Labels, which follow standard JCL naming conventions, are used as comments to delineate utility operations.

Additional information can also be supplied via a Parm parameter. The format is:

$$PARM= \begin{cases} \text{'LINECT=xx'} \\ \text{'POWER=y'} \\ \text{'LINECT=xx,POWER=y'} \end{cases}$$

where xx specifies the number of print lines per page

(default=60); and

y equals the normal amount of SYSUT1 work space

increased y times (to the yth power).

c. JCL Examples

The two JCL examples below copy a data set catalogue and partitioned data sets to new volumes:

```
//SYST   JOB  ALPHAPROJ,CHAR,MSGLEVEL=(1,1),CLASS=C
//STEP1  EXEC  PGM=IEHMOVE
//CATLG1  DD   UNIT=3330,DISP=OLD,
//         VOL=SER=CATL07
//CATLG2  DD   UNIT=3330,DISP=OLD,
//         VOL=SER=DUPL07
//SYSIN   DD   *
  COPY   CATALOG=PROJECT.ALPHA,                              X
             TO=3330=DUPL07,                                 X
          FROM=3330=CATL07
  EXCLUDE  DSGROUP=PROJECT.ALPHA.PAST
/*
//SYSPRINT  DD  SYSOUT=A
//SYSUT1   DD   UNIT=3330,VOL=SER=WORK01
//SYSUDUMP  DD SYSOUT=A
//
```

Following an appropriate Job statement, utility program IEHMOVE is called above. Dd statement CATLG1 describes an appropriate on-line volume. Dd statement CATLG2 describes an appropriate mountable unit and disk pack. The SYSIN ddname control file contains one Copy statement and one Exclude statement. They specify that all qualified data set names within PROJECT.ALPHA be copied with the exception of any qualified by PROJECT.ALPHA.PAST. They are to be copied from on-line 3330 volume CATL07 to mountable 3330 volume DUPL07. Utility messages are written to the SYSPRINT ddname file. A SYSUT1 work file is also defined. Finally, a SYSUDUMP Dd statement and Null statement are coded. Another IEHMOVE example is as follows:

```
//SYST   JOB   ALPHAPROJ,CHAR,MSGLEVEL=(1,1),CLASS=C
//STEP1  EXEC  PGM=IEHMOVE
//PDS1   DD   UNIT=3330,DISP=OLD,
//          VOL=SER=PDS007
//PDS2   DD   UNIT=3330,DISP=OLD,
//          VOL=SER=LIB007
//BACKUP1  DD   UNIT=2400,DISP=OLD,

//          VOL=SER=TAPE07
//SYSIN   DD   *
  COPY   PDS=SYS.LIB,TO=2400=TAPE07,                              X
                FROM=3330=PDS0007,CATLG
  INCLUDE   DSNAME =USER.LIB,                                     X
                MEMBER=FILEMAIN,                                  X
                FROM=3330=LIB007
/*
//SYSPRINT  DD   SYSOUT=A
//SYSUT1   DD   UNIT=3330
//SYSUDUMP   DD   SYSOUT=A
//
```

Following an appropriate Job statement, utility program IEHMOVE is called above. Dd statement PDS1 describes an appropriate on-line volume. Dd statement PDS2 describes an appropriate mountable unit and disk pack. Dd statement BACKUP1 describes a 9-track tape and drive. The SYSIN ddname control file contains one Copy statement and one Exclude statement. They specify that the PDS named SYS.LIB from on-line 3330 volume PDS007 and the member named FILEMAN in the PDS named USER.LIB from mountable 3330 volume LIB007 are to be copied to backup tape volume TAPE07. Utility messages are written to the SYSPRINT ddname file. A SYSUT1 work file is also defined. Finally, a SYSUDUMP Dd statement and Null statement should also be provided.

In summary, utility program IEHMOVE moves or copies all or a portion of catalogues, data sets, data set groups, partitioned data sets, and volumes. Specific entries can also be included, excluded, selected, or

replaced. This utility effectively merges, replaces, and/or deletes
programs, procedures, and other source data of interest. It is primarily used for the maintenance of system program and procedure libraries.

4. IEHPROGM (Program Maintenance)

    a. Purpose

        The purpose of utility program IEHPROGM is to perform system-related
    data set maintenance. Deleting data sets and/or PDS members, catalogu-
    ing and uncataloguing data sets, renaming data sets, connecting volumes,
    creating indexes and generation data sets, and maintaining password
    libraries are the primary functions of this utility. As such, this
    utility is used somewhat frequently by application and system programm-
    ers and analysts.

    b. Files and Use

        Standard ddnames and their functions are:

        Ddname1   - On-line Input/Output Volume.
        Ddname2   - Mountable Input/Output volume.
        SYSIN   - Utility Control File.
        SYSPRINT   - Utility Message File.
        SYSUDUMP   - Storage Dump File.

        Ddname1 and Ddname2 can be any ddname as chosen by the user. The
    ddnames may or may not be specified in the utility control file depend-
    ing upon the specific application. Both Dd statements may be provided
    in the JCL. The first Dd statement relates to on-line volumes, the
    second to mountable volumes. The SYSIN ddname file describes the con-
    trol file, usually cards. The utility control file should not be dummied.
    The ddname SYSPRINT defines a utility message file for program maintenance
    purposes. A SYSUDUMP Dd statement describes the storage dump file if
    this type of abnormal termination should occur.
        The JCL example below creates a generation index table for catalogu-
    ing data sets:

        //SYST   JOB ALPHAPROJ,CHAR,MSGLEVEL=(1,1),CLASS=A

        //STEP1 EXEC PGM=IEHPROGM

        //INDEX1 DD   UNIT=3330,DISP=OLD,

        //   VOL=SER=SYS001

        //SYSIN DD   *

         BLDG   INDEX=PROJECT.ALPHA,ENTRIES=20

        /*

        //SYSPRINT DD   SYSOUT=A

        //SYSUDUMP DD   SYSOUT=A

        //

        Following an appropriate Job statement, utility program IEHPROGM is called above. No other Exec statement parameters are necessary, as all defaults are acceptable. Dd statement INDEX1 describes an appropriate on-line volume. The SYSIN ddname control file contains one Build Generation statement. An index name of PROJECT.ALPHA has been assigned. The index table will contain 20 positions for generation numbers. When the index table overflows, the oldest generation will be removed from the table but not scratched; the new generation will be inserted. (Cataloguing and creating generation data sets will be discussed in detail in Chapter 8.) Utility messages are provided by the SYSPRINT ddname print file. Finally, a SYSUDUMP Dd statement and Null statement are coded.

In order to more fully utilize this program, other utility control file statements should be described. Figure 7.4 depicts further parameter options and syntax for IEHPROGM records.

Figure 7.4 Utility IEHPROGM Control File Parameters

```
Add Statement:

[Label]   ADD   DSNAME=Dsname

              [,CPASWORD=Control Password]

              [,PASWORD2=New Password]

              [,DATA='Password Data']

              [,TYPE=Code]

              [,VOL=Unit=Number]


              to add password information to the Password data set,
            where Dsname = name of data set to be assigned a password;
        Control Password is data set's password for change purposes;
            New Password is password to be assigned;
            Password Data is additional password information up to
                      77 characters;
                  Code = 1 for Read/Write access, and Read/Write control
                         with password;
                         2 for Read Only access, and Read/Write control
                         without password;
                  Unit = Device Type; and
                Number = Volume Serial Number.

  Build Index Alias Statement:

  [Label]   BLDA   INDEX=Index Name
```

Figure 7.4 Utility IEHPROGM Control File Parameters (cont.)

```
                    ,ALIAS=Alias Name

                    [,CVOL=Unit=Number]


        to assign an alias to an index,

    where Index Name = name of index area;

         Alias Name = name of alias index;

              CVOL is where initial catalogue search is to begin;

         Unit = Device Type; and

         Number = Volume Serial Number.
```

Build Generation Statement:

```
[Label]    BLDG   INDEX=Index Name

                    ,ENTRIES=xxx

                    [,CVOL=Unit=Number]

                    [,DELETE]

                    [,EMPTY]



        to build a generation data set index table,

    where Index Name = name of index area;

              xxx = number of table positions (generations)

                    allowed from 1 to 255;

              CVOL is where initial catalogue search is to

                    begin;

         Unit = Device Type;

         Number = Volume Serial Number;

         DELETE indicates that data sets are to scratched

                    when renamed from table; and

         EMPTY indicates that all generations are to be

                    removed from table upon overflow.
```

Build Index Statement:

```
[Label]    BLDX   INDEX=Index Name

                    [,CVOL=Unit=Number]


    to build an index,

   where Index Name = qualified name of index area;
```

283

Figure 7.4 Utility IEHPROGM Control File Parameters (cont.)

CVOL is where initial catalogue search is to begin;

Unit = Device Type; and

Number = Volume Serial Number.

Catalogue Statement:

[Label]   CATLG   DSNAME=Dsname

,VOL=Unit=Number

[,CVOL=Unit=Number]

to catalogue a data set,

where Dsname = name of data set to be catalogued;

Unit = Device Type;

Number = Volume Serial Number; and

CVOL is where initial catalogue search is to begin.

Connect Statement:

[Label]   CONNECT   INDEX=Index Name

,VOL=Unit=Number

[,CVOL=Unit=Number]

to connect two volumes,

where Index Name = name of index area;

Unit = Device Type

Number = Volume Serial Number; and

CVOL is where initial catalogue search is to begin.

Delete Password Statement:

[Label]   DELETEP   DSNAME=Dsname

[,CPASWORD=Control Password]

[,PASSWORD1=Current Password]

[,VOL=Unit=Number]

to delete password information from the Password data set,

where Dsname = name of data set from which password is to be

deleted;

Control Password is data set password for change purposes;

Current Password is password currently assigned;

Figure 7.4 Utility IEHPROGM Control File Parameters (cont.)

```
                          Unit = Device Type; and

                        Number = Volume Serial Number.

   Delete Alias Statement:


   [Label]   DLTA   ALIAS=Alias Name

                        [,CVOL=Unit=Number]


      to delete an alias from an index,

     where Alias Name = name of alias index;

                      CVOL is where initial catalogue search is to begin;

                     Unit = Device Type; and

                   Number = Volume Serial Number.

   Delete Index Statement:


   [Label]    DLTX   INDEX=Index Name

                         [,CVOL=Unit=Number]


      to delete an index,

     where Index Name = qualified name of index area;

                      CVOL is where initial catalogue search is to begin;

                     Unit = Device Type; and

                   Number = Volume Serial Number.

   List Statement:


   [Label]    LIST   DSNAME=Dsname

                          ,PASWORD1=Current Password


      to list system-related password information,

     where Dsname = name of data set for which information

                       is to be listed; and

   Current Password is password currently assigned.



   Release Statement:


   [Label]    RELEASE   INDEX=Index Name

                           [,CVOL=Unit=Number]


      to release (disconnect) two volumes
```

Figure 7.4 Utility IEHPROGM Control File Parameters (cont.)

```
          where Index Name = name of index area;

                     CVOL is where initial catalogue search is to begin;

                Unit = Device Type; and

              Number = Volume Serial Number.


Rename Statement:


[Label]    RENAME   DSNAME=Dsname

                     ,VOL=Unit=Number

                     ,NEWNAME=New Name

                     [,MEMBER=Member Name]


     to rename data set name or alias,

   where Dsname = name of data set to be renamed or data

                     set which contains member to be renamed;

            Unit = Device Type;

          Number = Volume Serial Number;

        New Name = name to be assigned; and

     Member Name = name of member to be renamed.


Replace Statement:


[Label]    REPLACE   DSNAME=Dsname

                     [,CPASWORD=Control Password]

                     [,PASWORD1=Current Password]

                     [,PASWORD2=New Password]

                     [,DATA='Password Data']

                     [,TYPE=Code]

                     [,VOL=Unit=Number]


     to replace password information in the Password data set,

   where Dsname = name of data set to have password replaced;

 Control Password is data set password for change purposes;

 Current Password is password currently assigned;

     New Password is password to be assigned;

    Password Data is additional password information up to

                     77 characters;

                Code = 1 - Read/Write Access, Read/Write Control

                              with Password;
```

Figure 7.4 Utility IEHPROGM Control File Parameters (cont.)

```
                    2 - Read Only Access, Read/Write Control with

                        Password;

                    3 - Default to Read/Write Access, Read/Write

                        Control without Password;

            Unit = Device Type; and

         Number = Volume Serial Number.
```

Scratch Statement:

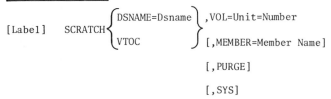

```
    to scratch a data set or member,

  where Dsname = name of data set to be scratched or

                 which contains member to be scratched;

          VTOC indicates that all Volume Table of Contents

               (VTOC) data sets are to be scratched;

          Unit = Device Type;

        Number = Volume Serial Number;

   Member Name = name of member to be scratched;

          PURGE indicates that data set is to be scratched

                only if expiration date has passed; and

          SYS specifies OS data sets that are to be scratched.
```

Uncatalogue Statement:

```
[Label]    UNCATLG   DSNAME=Dsname

                     [,VOL=Unit=Number]

    to uncatalogue a data set,

  where Dsname = name of data set to be uncatalogued;

          Unit = Device Type; and

        Number = Volume Serial Number.
```

One or more of the operations in Figure 7.4 should be chosen. Within an operation, a multiple number of statements may be coded. All must begin with a label or blank in column 1. Labels, which follow standard JCL naming conventions, are used to delineate utility operations.

Additional information can also be supplied via a Parm parameter. Its format is:

$$\text{PARM}='\text{LINECT=xx} \left\{ \begin{array}{l} \text{,PRINT} \\ \text{,NOPRINT} \end{array} \right\} \text{'}$$

where xx specifies the number of print lines per page
(default = 45); and
PRINT (default) or NOPRINT specifies whether or not utility control statements are to be listed in the SYSPRINT ddname file.

c. JCL examples

The two JCL examples below connect two volumes and maintain a password data set:

```
//SYST    JOB   ALPHAPROJ,CHAR,MSGLEVEL=(1,1),CLASS=C

//STEP1   EXEC  PGM=IEHPROGM

//VOL1    DD    UNIT=3330,DISP=OLD,

//              VOL=SER=PACK01

//VOL2    DD    UNIT=3330,DISP-OLD,

//              VOL=SER=PACK02

//SYSIN   DD    *

  CONNECT INDEX=PROJECT.ALPHA,                                    X

                VOL=3330=PACK02

  RENAME DSNAME=PROJECT.ALPHA.ONE,                                X

                VOL=3330=PACK02,                                  X

                NEWNAME=PROJECT.ALPHA.TWO

/*

//SYSPRINT  DD  SYSOUT=A

//SYSUDUMP  DD  SYSOUT=A

//
```

Following an appropriate Job statement, utility program IEHPROGM is called above. Dd statements VOL1 and VOL2 describe appropriate on-line and mountable units and disk packs, respectively. The SYSIN ddname control file contains one Connect statement and one Rename statement. An entry is made in the first volume (PACK01) that PROJECT.ALPHA

data sets can also be found on a second volume (PACK02). Also, a data
set named PROJECT.ALPHA.ONE on PACK02 is to be renamed PROJECT.ALPHA.
TWO. Utility messages are written to the SYSPRINT ddname file. Finally,
a SYSUDUMP Dd statement and Null statement are coded. Another IEHPROGM
example is as follows:

```
//SYST   JOB   ALPHAPROJ,CHAR,MSGLEVEL=(1,1),CLASS=A
//STEP1  EXEC  PGM=IEHPROGM
//PASS1  DD    UNIT=3330,DISP=OLD,
//            VOL=SER=DISK08
//SYSIN  DD   *
  ADD DSNAME=UNSECURE.DATA,                                      X
             PASWORD2=BETA,                                      X
             TYPE=2
  REPLACE DSNAME=SECURE.DATA,                                    X
             CPASWORD=AREWIDE,                                   X
             PASWORD1=SIGMA,                                     X
             PASWORD2=ZETA
  LIST   DSNAME=UNSECURE.DATA,                                   X
             PASWORD1=BETA
  LIST   DSNAME=SECURE.DATA,                                     X
             PASWORD1=ZETA
/*
//SYSPRINT  DD   SYSOUT=A
//SYSUDUMP  DD   SYSOUT=A
//
```

Following an appropriate Job statement, utility program IEHPROGM
is called above. Dd statement PASS1 describes an appropriate on-line
volume. The SYSIN ddname control file contains one Add statement, one
Replace statement, and two List statements. They specify that password
Beta is being added for data set UNSECURE.DATA for read-only access.
Also password ZETA is to replace password SIGMA for the SECURE.DATA
data set. To effect this change, control password AREAWIDE must be
specified. Originally, this was the first password assigned to the data
set. Two listings of system-related password information for these
data sets are also requested. Utility messages are written to the
SYSPRINT ddname file. Finally, a SYSUDUMP Dd statement and Null statement should also be provided.

In summary, utility program IEHPROGM performs system-related file
maintenance functions. Three primary functions are creating index and
generation tables, connecting and releasing two volumes, and maintaining
the Password data set. The utility also catalogues data sets as well
as renames and scratches data sets and/or their members. As such, it
is frequently used by application and system programmers and analysts.

C. OTHER SYSTEM UTILITY PROGRAMS

Other utility programs, classified as "system," also perform maintenance of system-related data sets and libraries. They are not utilized as frequently, however, as the previously discussed system utilities. This is not because they are less significant, but rather because they are more unique to specific applications performed by selected technical installation personnel. For this reason their basic function and controls will be described along with a JCL example. Many details relating to control card use will not be covered. They are not pertinent to the day-to-day operations of most application and system programmers and analysts. If necessary, a detailed description of all facets of these not-so-common utilities can be obtained from the Utilities Manual.

1. IEHATLAS   (Alternate Track Locate And Assign)

a. Purpose

A purpose of utility program IEHATLAS is to locate and assign an alternate track. This utility is called whenever a defective track has been uncovered and, in essence, prevents a user from having to completely re-create an otherwise seemingly good data set. The Volume Table of Contents (VTOC) for a given volume can also be reassigned.

b. Files and Use

Standard utility ddnames and their functions are:

```
SYSUT1    -  Input/Output Volume or File.
SYSIN     -  Utility Control File.
SYSPRINT  -  Utility Message File.
SYSUDUMP  -  Storage Dump File.
```

Ddname SYSUT1 describes the volume or file which contains the bad track as indicated by an error message in a previous run. The SYSIN ddname file describes the utility control file which describes the track of concern and data. The ddname SYSPRINT file defines a utility message file for track assignment and description.

The JCL example below assigns an alternate track, but only after an attempt has been made to salvage or write over the defective one:

```
//SYST   JOB   ALPHAPROJ,CHAR,MSGLEVEL=(1,1),CLASS=A

//STEP1  EXEC  PGM=IEHATLAS

//SYSUT1  DD   UNIT=3330,DISP=(OLD,KEEP),

//          DSNAME=DISKDATA,VOL=SER=PACK17

//SYSIN  DD   *

 TRACK=00000054000702000018

404040F0F2F1F7F3C9C440D5E4D4C2C5D940

/*

//SYSPRINT  DD   SYSOUT=A

//SYSUDUMP  DD   SYSOUT=A

//
```

Following an appropriate Job statements, utility program IEHATLAS is called above. Dd statement SYSUT1 describes the data set and volume which contains the defective track. The SYSIN ddname control file specifies that a defective record can be located at Cylinder 54, Track 7, Record 2. The data to be replaced is 18 bytes in length. It is to be stored in Character Format (unpacked) and follows the Track statement. Track descriptions are provided in the SYSPRINT ddname print file.

If VTOC's are to be reassigned or other options utilized, an expanded utility control file must be described and coded. Figure 7.5 depicts parameter options and syntax for IEHATLAS control file records.

Figure 7.5 Utility IEHATLAS Control File Parameters


```
Track or Vtoc Statements:

 TRACK=aaaabbbbccccddeeffff[S]

 VTOC=aaaabbbbccccddeeffff


 to describe a track or VTOC,

where aaaa = Data Cell Bin Number;

      bbbb = Cylinder Number;

      cccc = Track Number;

        dd = Record Number;

        ee = Key Length;

      ffff = Data Length; and

           S indicates special write for track overflows.
```


Either a Track or Vtoc control statement must be coded and must contain a blank in column 1.

2. IEHDASDR (Direct Access Storage Device Restore)

   a. Purpose

   The purpose of utility program IEHDASDR is to dump or restore the contents of a direct-access device for backup and recovery purposes. In addition, this utility initializes direct-access volumes, analyzes tracks for defects, and can be used to change volume serial numbers.

   b. Files and Use

   Standard utility ddnames and their functions are:

291

```
Ddname1   -  Input/Output Direct Access Volume.
Ddtape    -  Input/Output Tape Volume.
SYSIN     -  Utility Control File.
SYSPRINT  -  Utility Message File.
SYSUDUMP  -  Storage Dump File.
```

Ddname1 can be any ddname as chosen by the user. Ddtape can also be any ddname as chosen by the user. These ddnames are specified in the utility control file and may both be provided depending upon the specific application. The SYSIN ddname file describes the utility control file used to perform analyze, dump, format, and restore functions. The ddname SYSPRINT file defines a utility message file for these operations.

The JCL example below dumps the contents of a direct-access volume to tape:

```
//SYST    JOB   ALPHAPROJ,RAR,MSGLEVEL=(1,1),CLASS=A

//STEP1   EXEC   PGM=IEHDASDR

//DISKFILE   DD   UNIT=3330,DISP=(OLD,KEEP),

//          VOL=SER=DISK07

//TAPECOPY   DD   UNIT=2400,DISP=(NEW,KEEP),

//          DSNAME=BACKUP,VOL=SER=012398

//SYSIN   DD   *

 DUMP FROMDD=DISKFILE,TODD=TAPECOPY

/*

//SYSPRINT   DD   SYSOUT=A

//SYSUDUMP   DD   SYSOUT=A

//
```

Following an appropriate Job statement, utility program IEHDASDR is called above. Dd statement DISKFILE describes the disk volume to be copied. Dd statement TAPECOPY describes the tape volume which is to receive disk contents. The SYSIN ddname control file specifies the ddnames of the disk and tape files. The contents of the volume defined by ddname DISKFILE is to be copied (dumped) to the volume defined by ddname TAPECOPY. Copy, restore, initialize, and other utility messages are provided in the SYSPRINT ddname print file.

If analyzing, formatting, labeling, assigning tracks, and restoring functions are to be performed, an expanded utility control file must be described and coded. Figure 7.6 depicts parameter options and syntax for IEHDASDR control file records.

One or more of the statements in Figure 7.6 must be coded and must contain a label or blank in column 1.

Figure 7.6 Utility IEHDASDR Control File Parameters

Analyze Statement:

$$
\text{[Label]} \quad \text{ANALYZE} \quad \text{TODD=} \left\{ \begin{array}{l} \text{Address} \\ \text{(Address, ...)} \\ \text{Ddname} \\ \text{(Ddname, ...)} \end{array} \right\}
$$

,VTOC=xxxxx

,EXTENT=yyyyy

[,NEWVOLID=Number]

[,IPLDD=Iplname]

$$
\left[,\text{FLAGTEST=} \left\{ \begin{array}{l} \text{YES} \\ \text{NO} \end{array} \right\} \right]
$$

$$
\left[,\text{PASSES=} \left\{ \begin{array}{l} \text{zzz} \\ 0 \end{array} \right\} \right]
$$

[,OWNERID=Idname]

$$
\left[,\text{PURGE=} \left\{ \begin{array}{l} \text{YES} \\ \text{NO} \end{array} \right\} \right]
$$

to analyze direct-access recording surfaces,

where TODD specifies Channel and Unit Address or
        Ddname of volume to be analyzed;

   xxxxx = Beginning Track Address;

   yyyyy = VTOC Length in tracks;

  Number = New Volume Serial Number;

 Iplname = Ddname for IPL Program;

 FLAGTEST specifies whether check for defective
        tracks should be made;

     zzz = Number of analyzing passes to be made of
        recording surface where 0 equals a bypass
        of analysis check;

  Idname = 1 to 10 characters of owner volume
        identification; and

    PURGE specifies whether or not unexpired data sets
        may be scratched.

293

Figure 7.6 Utility IEHDASDR Control File Parameters (cont.)

Dump Statement:

[Label]　　DUMP　　FROMDD=Ddname

$$,\text{TODD}=\begin{Bmatrix} \text{Ddname} \\ (\text{Ddname},\ldots\ldots) \end{Bmatrix}$$

$$[\,,\text{CPYVOLID}=\begin{Bmatrix} \text{YES} \\ \text{NO} \end{Bmatrix}]$$

[,BEGIN=aaaabbbb]

[,END=aaaabbbb]

$$[\,,\text{PURGE}=\begin{Bmatrix} \text{YES} \\ \text{NO} \end{Bmatrix}]$$

to dump the contents of a volume,

where FROMDD and TODD specify the ddnames of the input

and putput files;

CPYVOLID specifies whether or not output

volumes are to receive serial

numbers also;

aaaa = Cylinder Number;

bbbb = Head Number; and

PURGE specifies whether or not unexpired

data sets may be scratched.

Format Statement:

$$[\text{Label}]\quad\text{FORMAT}\quad\text{TODD}=\begin{Bmatrix} \text{Ddname} \\ (\text{Ddname},\ldots\ldots) \end{Bmatrix}$$

,VTOC=xxxxx

,EXTENT=yyyyy

[,IPLDD=Iplname]

[,OWNERID=Idname]

$$[\,,\text{PURGE}=\begin{Bmatrix} \text{YES} \\ \text{NO} \end{Bmatrix}]$$

to initialize volumes,

where TODD specifies Ddname of volume to be formatted;

xxxxx = beginning of VTOC relative address;

yyyyy = VTOC length in tracks;

Iplname = Ddname for IPL Program;

Figure 7.6 Utility IEHDASDR Control File Parameters (cont.)

```
                    Idname = 1 to 10 characters of owner identification; and

                    PURGE specifies whether or not unexpired data sets may

                    be scratched.


Get Alternate Statement:

[Label]    GETALT   TODD=Ddname

                    ,TRACK=aaaabbbb


           to assign alternate track,

           where TODD specifies Ddname of volume where alternate

                    track is to be assigned;

                aaaa = Cylinder Number; and

                bbbb = Head number.



Initial Program Load Text Statement:

[Label]    IPLTXT


           to indicate that IPL text follows.



Label Statement:

                                  ⎧ Address ⎫
[Label]    LABEL    TODD=         ⎨         ⎬
                                  ⎩ Ddname  ⎭

                    ,NEWVOLID=Number

                    [,OWNERID=Idname]


           to change volume serial number,

           where TODD specifies Channel and Unit Address or

                    Ddname of volume serial to be changed;

                Number = New  Volume Serial Number; and

                Idname = 1 to 10 characters of owner volume

                    identification.



Restore Statement:

                              ⎧ Ddname       ⎫
[Label]    RESTORE TODD=      ⎨              ⎬
                              ⎩ (Ddname,.....)⎭
```

295

Figure 7.6 Utility IEHDASDR Control File Parameters (cont.)

```
               ,FROMDD=Ddname
                               ⎧ Yes ⎫
               [,CPYVOLID=     ⎨     ⎬  ]
                               ⎩ NO  ⎭

                            ⎧ YES ⎫
               [,PURGE=      ⎨     ⎬ ]
                            ⎩ NO  ⎭


     to restore the contents of a volume,

  where TODD and FROMDD specify the ddnames of output

                    and input files;

     CPYVOLID specifies whether or not output

              volume is to receive serial

              number also; and

     PURGE specifies whether or not unexpired

              data sets may be scratched.
```

Additional information can also be supplied via a Parm parameter. Its format is:

$$
PARM= \left\{ \begin{array}{l} \text{'LINECT=xx'} \\ \text{'N=n'} \\ \text{'LINECT=xx,N=n'} \end{array} \right\}
$$

where xx specifies the number of print lines per page
(default = 58); and

n equals the number of similar utility functions which
can be accomplished concurrently (maximum = 6).

In summary, utility program IEHDASDR dumps, restores, initializes, and analyzes volume contents. This utility also changes volume serial numbers if desired.

3. IEHIOSUP (Input/Output Supervisor Update)

a. Purpose

The purpose of utility program IEHIOSUP is to update entries to the control tables of the Supervisor Call (SVC) library. This utility must be executed whenever the SVC library is moved or changed for any reason.

b. Files and Use

Standard utility ddnames and their functions are:

SYSUT1   - Input Update Control File.
SYSPRINT - Utility Message File.
SYSUDUMP - Storage Dump File.

Ddname SYSUT1 describes the SYS1.SVCLIB data set which contains the

296

control tables for the SVC library. No utility control file is defined. The ddname SYSPRINT file defines the utility message file for any errors encountered during the update process.

The JCL example below updates the control tables for the Supervisor Call (SVC) library:

```
//SYST    JOB   ALPHAPROJ,RAR,MSGLEVEL=(1,1),CLASS=A

//STEP1   EXEC  PGM=IEHIOSUP

//SYSUT1  DD    UNIT=3330,DISP=(OLD,KEEP),

//        DSN=SYS1.SVCLIB,VOL=SER=SYS007

//SYSPRINT  DD  SYSOUT=A

//SYSUDUMP  DD  SYSOUT=A

//
```

Following an appropriate Job statement, utility program IEHIOSUP is called above. Dd statement SYSUT1 describes the data set which contains SVC control table information. A SYSIN ddname utility control file is not provided. Utility messages are written to the SYSPRINT ddname print file. If the SVC library is part of a Time Sharing Option (TSO) environment, PARM=TSO must be provided via the Exec statement.

In summary, utility program IEHIOSUP updates the selected entries in the control tables for the Supervisor Call (SVC) library.

4. IEHUCAT (Update Catalogue)

a. Purpose

The purpose of utility program IEHUCAT is to update OS system catalogues to that compatible with a Multiple Virtual Storage (MVS) environment. This utility is generally executed during the process of conversion to MVS.

b. Files and Use

Standard utility ddnames and their functions are:

```
SYSUT1    -   Input SMF File.
Ddname    -   Optional Input Volume(s).
SYSPRINT  -   Utility Message File.
SYSUDUMP  -   Storage Dump File.
```

Ddname SYSUT1 describes the SYS1.MANX or SYS1.MANY disk file from the System Management Facilities (SMF) system. Ddname can be any ddname as chosen by the user. It may occur multiple times and describes additional volumes containing system catalogues on other than the system residence volume. No utility control file is defined. The ddname SYSPRINT defines a utility message file for catalogue update purposes.

The JCL example below updates system catalogue SYSCTLG on the system residence volume:

```
//SYST   JOB   ALPHAPROJ,RAR,MSGLEVEL=(1,1),CLASS=A
//STEP1  EXEC  PGM=IEHUCAT
//SYSUT1  DD   UNIT=3330,DISP=SHR,
//            DSNAME=SYS1.MANX,VOL=SER=DISK01
//SYSPRINT DD  SYSOUT=A
//SYSUDUMP DD  SYSOUT=A
//
```

Following an appropriate Job statement, utility program IEHUCAT is called above. Dd statement SYSUT1 describes the SMF file as relates to the system residence volume. Utility update messages are provided in the SYSPRINT ddname print file.

Additional information can also be supplied via a Parm parameter. Its format is:

$$PARM= \begin{Bmatrix} \text{'LIST'} \\ \text{'NOLIST'} \end{Bmatrix} \begin{bmatrix} \text{,CVOL(Number,Type)} \end{bmatrix}$$

where LIST provides all utility messages;

NOLIST supplies utility error messages only;

Number=Volume Serial Number of optional catalogue

volume (CVOL); and

Type=Device Type.

In summary, utility program IEHUCAT updates OS system catalogues to meet converted MVS requirements.

5. IFHSTATR (Statistic Type Records)

   a. Purpose

   The purpose of utility program IFHSTATR is to print error records from a System Management Facilities (SMF) error statistics file. An appropriate report is formatted.

   b. Files and Use.

   Standard utility ddnames and their function are:

   SYSUT1   - Input SMF File.
   SYSUT2   - Utility Report File.
   SYSUDUMP - Storage Dump File.

   Ddname SYSUT1 describes the IFASMFDP or SYS1.MAN tape or the SYS1.MANX or SYS1.MANY disk file from the SMF system. No utility control file is defined. Ddname SYSUT2 describes the file to which an error report will be written.

   The JCL example below creates an error statistics report:

```
//SYST   JOB   ALPHAPROJ,RAR,MSGLEVEL=(1,1),CLASS=A
//STEP1  EXEC  PGM=IFHSTATR
//SYSUT1  DD    UNIT=2400,DISP=(OLD,KEEP),
//             DSNAME=SYS1.MAN,VOL=SER=TAPE07
//SYSUT2  DD    SYSOUT=(C,,1432)
//SYSUDUMP DD   SYSOUT=A
//
```

Following an appropriate Job statement, utility program IFHSTATR is called above. Dd statement SYSUT1 describes a tape data set which contains SMF error statistic records. A SYSIN ddname utility control file is not provided. Utility report messages are provided in the SYSPRINT ddname print file.

In summary, utility program IFHSTATR creates an error report from statistics provided by the SMF system.

A major topic in and by itself, a detailed description of the many functions of system utilities can be obtained from the Utilities Manual. Those system utility applications common to all dp environments have been covered in this chapter.

D. INDEPENDENT UTILITY USE

As discussed previously, utility programs are classified as either:

    Data Set;
    System; or
    Independent Utilities.

Independent utilities are those which operate independent of or outside the Operating System. They do support the Operating System, however. They perform functions necessary to the proper maintenance of system volumes. In general, they are system-oriented and more frequently utilized by technical installation personnel. Some of their functions overlap with system utilities. Independent utility programs and a summary of their most common functions are as follows:

    IBCDASDI - Initialize, assign tracks.
    IBCDMPRS - Dump, restore.
    IBCRCVRP - Recover, replace tracks.
    ICAPRTBL - Load forms and character set.

E. INDEPENDENT UTILITY PROGRAMS

1. IBCDASDI (Direct Access Storage Device and Initialization)

a. Purpose

The purpose of utility program IBCDASDI is to initialize direct-access volumes and/or assign alternate tracks. In this process the Volume Table of Contents (VTOC) and volume labels are created.

b. Files and Use

Because IBCDASDI is an independent utility, standard JCL is not used.
Rather, this utility program is directed solely by control statements.
Figure 7.7 depicts parameter options and syntax for IBCDASDI control
file records.

Figure 7.7 Utility IBCDASDI Control File Parameters

Job Statement:

[Label]   JOB   [Comment]

        to indicate the beginning of a set of utility

        control statements.

Message Statement:

[Label]   MSG TODEV=Device Type

                ,TOADDR=abb

        to describe the operator's message file,

        where Device Type relates to equipment model number;

                a = Channel Number; and

                bb = Unit Number.

Direct Access Definition Statement:

[Label]   DADEF TODEV=Device Type

                  ,TOADDR=abb

                  [,IPL=YES]

                  [,VOLID={ Number
                           SCRATCH }]

                  [,FLAGTEST=NO]

                  [,PASSES=xxx]

                  [,BIN=y]

                  [,MODEL=z]

        to define direct-access volume,

        where Device Type relates to equipment model number;

300

Figure 7.7 Utility IBCDASDI Control File Parameters (cont.)

a = Channel Number;

bb = Unit Number;

IPL indicates that an IPL program is to be
written;

Number = Volume Serial Number;

FLAGTEST specifies whether check for defective
tracks should be made;

xxx = Number of analyzing passes to be made
of recording surface;

BYPASS specifies no track check;

y = Data Cell Bin Number; and

z = Model 1 or 2.

Volume Definition Statement:

[Label]   VLD   NEWVOLID=Number

$$[,VOLPASS= \begin{Bmatrix} 0 \\ 1 \end{Bmatrix}]$$

[,OWNERID=Idname]

[,ADDLABEL=n]

to identify volume,

where   Number=Volume Serial Number;

VOLPASS specifies volume security (1) or no
security (0);

Idname = 1 to 10 characters of owner volume
identification; and

n = number of labels.

Volume Table of Contents Definition Statement:

[Label]   VTOC   STRTADR=xxxxx
,EXTENT=yyyy

to define Volume Table of Contents,

where xxxxx = Beginning Track Address; and

yyyy = VTOC length in tracks.

301

Figure 7.7 Utility IBCDASDI Control File Parameters (cont.)

<u>Initial Program Load Text Statement</u>:

[Label]   IPLTXT

    to indicate that IPL text follows.

<u>Get Alternate Statement</u>:

[Label]   GETALT   TODEV=Device Type

                ,TOADDR=abb

                ,TRACK=ccccdddd

                ,VOLID=Number

                [,FLAGTEST=NO]

                [,PASSES=xxx]

                [,BYPASS=YES]

                [,BIN=y]

                [,MODEL=z]

    to assign and define alternate tracks,

    where Device Type relates to equipment model number;

             a = Channel Number;

          bb = Unit Number;

       cccc = Cylinder Number;

       dddd = Head Number;

   Number = Volume Serial Number;

   FLAGTEST specifies whether check for defective

            tracks should be made;

     xxx = Number of analyzing passes to be made of

            recording surface;

   BYPASS specifies no track check;

      y = Data Cell Bin Number; and

      z = Model 1 and 2.

<u>End Statement</u> :

[Label]   END   [Comment]

Figure 7.7 Utility IBCDASDI Control File Parameters (cont.)

```
          to signify the end of a utility control statement job.


Last Card Statement:

LASTCARD

          to signify the end of a set of utility control statement jobs.
```

One or more of the statements in Figure 7.7 must be coded in the order indicated and must contain a label or blank in column 1 with the exception of the Last Card statement, which must begin in column 1.

The control statement example below initializes a direct-access volume for system use:

```
SYST   JOB

MSG    TODEV=1443,TOADDR=007

DADEF  TODEV=3330,TOADDR=105,                                 X

          VOLIX=DISK96

VLD    NEWVOLID=PACK96,                                       X

          OWNERID=ALPHAPROJ

VTOCD  STRTADR=00001,                                         X

          EXTENT=7

END
```

Following the Job control statement, a message file for the operator is defined. Next, the disk to be initialized is described followed by volume identification. Finally, the location and length of the VTOC are defined.

In summary, utility program IBCDASDI initializes direct-access volumes. In addition to defining the VTOC, alternate tracks can also be assigned.

2. IBCDMPRS (Dump And Restore)

a. Purpose

The purpose of utility program IBCDMPRS is to dump and restore the contents of a direct-access device and/or tape.

b. Files and Use

Being independent utility, standard JCL is not used. Rather, this utility program is directed solely to control statements. Figure 7.8 depicts parameter options and syntax for IBCDMPRS control file records.

Figure 7.8 Utility IBCDMPRS Control File Parameters

Job Statement:

[Label]   JOB   [Comment]

    to indicate the beginning of a set of utility control
    statements.

Message Statement:

[Label]   MSG   TODEV=Device Type
                  ,TOADDR=abb

    to describe the operator's message file,
    where Device Type relates to equipment model numbers;
                  a = Channel Number; and
                 bb = Unit Number.

Dump Statement:

[Label]   DUMP   FROMDEV=Device Type
                   ,FROMADDR=abb
                   ,TODEV=Device Type
                   ,TOADDR=abb
                   [,VOLID=Number(,Number)]
                   [,MODE=xx]
                   [,BIN=y]
                   [,MODEL=z]

    to indicate lower and upper limits to dump volume contents,
    to dump the contents of a volume,
    where FROMDEV and TODEV specify the Device Types of the
                        input and output files;
                     a = Channel Number;
                    bb = Unit Number;
                Number = Volume Serial Number;
                    xx = Density Indicator;
                     y = Data Cell Bin Number; and
                     z = Model 1 and 2.

304

Figure 7.8 Utility IBCDMPRS Control File Parameters (cont.)

Volume Dump Restore Limit Statement:

[Label]   VDRL   BEGIN=xxxxx

                       ,END=yyyyy

        to indicate lower and upper limits to dump volume contents,

     where xxxxx = Beginning Track Address; and

            yyyyy = Ending Track Address.

Restore Statement:

[Label]   RESTORE   FROMDEV=Device Type

                        ,FROMADDR=abb

                        ,TODEV=Device Type

                        ,TOADDR=abb

                        ,VOLID=Number

                        [,MODE=xx]

                        [,BIN=y]

                        [,MODEL=z]

        to restore the contents of a volume,

        where FROMDEV and TODEV specify the Device Types of the

                              input and output files;

                        a = Channel Number;

                       bb = Unit Number;

                  Number = Volume Serial Number;

                       xx = Density Indicator;

                        y = Data Cell Bin Number; and

                        z = Model 1 and 2.

End Statement:

[Label]   END   [Comment]

        to signify the end of utility control statements.

One or more of the statements in Figure 7.8 must be coded in the order indicated and must contain a label or blank in column 1.

The control statement example below restores the contents of a tape volume to disk:

```
SYST    JOB

MSG     TODEV=1443,TOADDR=007

RESTORE FROMDD=1400,FROMADDR=402,                              X

              TODEV=3330,TOADDR=206,                           X

              VOLID=PACK23

END
```

Following the Job control statement, a message file for the operator is defined. Next, the tape which contains the data to be restored and the disk and volume to which restored data will be sent are described.

In summary, utility program IBCDMPRS dumps and restores tape and disk volume contents.

3. IBCRCVRP (Recover/Replace)

a. Purpose

The purpose of utility program IBCRCVRP is to recover good data from a defective track and/or replace data on a defective track. This utility also assigns alternate tracks and/or merges good data with replacement data.

b. Files and Use

Because IBCRCVRP is independent utility, standard JCL is not used. Rather, this utility program is directed solely by control statements. Figure 7.9 depicts parameter options and systax for IBCRCVRP control file records.

Figure 7.9 Utility IBCRCVRP Control File Parameters

```
Job Statement:

[Label]   JOB   [Comment]


      to indicate the beginning of a set of utility control statements.

Message Statement:

[Label]   MSG   TODEV=Device Type

              ,TOADDR=abb

              [,MODE=xx]
```

Figure 7.9 Utility IBCRCVRP Control File Parameters (cont.)

to describe the operator's message file,

where Device Type relates to equipment model number;

a = Channel Number;

bb = Unit Number; and

xx = Density Indicator.

Recover Statement:

[Label]   RECOVER   FROMDEV=Device Type

,FROMADDR=abb

,TODEV=Device Type

,TOADDR=abb

,VOLID=Number

,TRACK=ccccddddeeee

[,MODE=xx]

to recover good data from a defective track,

where FROMDEV and TODEV specify the Device Types of the

input and output files;

a = Channel Number;

bb = Unit Number;

Number = Volume Serial Number;

cccc = Bin Address;

dddd = Cylinder Address;

eeee = Head Address

xx = Density Indicator.

Replace Statement:

[Label]   REPLACE   FROMDEV=Device Type

,FROMADDR=abb

,TODEV=Device Type

,TOADDR=abb

,VOLID=Number

,TRACK=ccccddddeeee

[,MODE=xx]

to replace data on a defective track,

307

Figure 7.9 Utility IBCRCVRP Control File Parameters (cont.)

where FROMDEV and TODEV specify the Device Types of the

input and output files;

a = Channel Number;

bb = Volume Serial Number;

Number = Volume Serial Number;

cccc = Bin Address;

dddd = Cylinder Address;

eeee = Head Address; and

xx = Density Indicator.

List Statement:

[Label]   LIST   TODEV=Device Type

,TOADDR=abb

[,MODE=xx]

to list the contents of a defective track,

where TODEV specifies the Device Type of the output files;

a = Channel Number;

bb = Unit Number; and

xx = Density Indicator.

Insert Statement:

[Label]   INSERT   [FROMDEV=Device Type]

[,FROMADDRR=abb]

$$\left\{ \begin{array}{l} ,RECORD=ccc \\ ,RECORD=LAST \end{array} \right\}$$

,COUNT=ddddeeeeffgghhhh

[,MODE=xx]

[,OVERFLOW=YES]

to insert data,

where FROMDEV specifies the Device Type of the input file;

a = Channel Number;

bb = Unit Number;

Figure 7.9 Utility IBCRCVRP Control File Parameters (cont.)

```
                ccc = Record Number of bad data from a previous

                       error message;

                LAST refers to last record on track;

               dddd = Cylinder Number;

               eeee = Head Number;

                 ff = Record Number;

                 gg = Key Length;

               hhhh = Data Length;

                 xx = Density Indicator; and

           OVERFLOW refers to location of record.



  End Statement:


  [Label]   END   [Comment]



      to signify the end of utility control statements.
```

One or more of the statements in Figure 7.9 must be coded in the order indicated and must contain a label or blank in column 1.

The control statement example below recovers bad data from a defective track:

```
SYST   JOB

MSG       TODEV=1443,TOADDR=007

RECOVER FROMDEV=3330,FROMADDR=202,                              X

             TODEV=2400,TOADDR=406,                             X

             VOLID=PACK33,                                      X

             TRACK=000000760012

LIST      TODEV=1443,TOADDR=007

END
```

Following the Job control statement, a message file for the operator is defined. Next, the disk, volume, and defective track which contains the data to be recovered and the tape to which the recovered data will be sent are described. A list of the contents of the defective track is also requested.

In summary, utility program IBCRCVRP recovers and/or replaces data from defective tracks.

4. ICAPRTBL (Print Buffer Load)

   a. Purpose

      The purpose of utility program ICAPRTBL is to load Model 3211 Printer
   buffers. They are the Universal Character Set (UCS) buffer and the Forms
   Control buffer (FCB).

   b. Files and Use

      Because ICAPRTBL is an independent utility, standard JCL is not used.
   Rather, this utility program is directed solely by control statements.
   Figure 7.10 depicts parameter options and syntax for ICAPRTBL control
   file records.

Figure 7.10 Utility ICAPRTBL Control File Parameters

Job Statement:

[Label]   JOB   [Comment]

     to indicate the beginning of a set of utility controlstatements.

Definition Statement:

DFN ADDR=abb,FOLD=$\begin{Bmatrix} Y \\ N \end{Bmatrix}$

     to define Model 3211 printer characteristics,

   where a = Channel Number;

      bb = Unit Number; and

      FOLD specifies whether lower-case letters may be printed

         as upper-case (Y) or not (N).

Universal Character Set Statement:

Name UCS Characters

     to specify UCS buffer image,

     where Name provides a print train reference; and

       Characters specifies buffer content in columns 16 to 71.

Figure 7.10 Utility ICAPRTBL Control File Parameters (cont.)

```
Forms Control Buffer Statement;


[Name]    FCB   LPI={ 6
                     { 8

             ,LNCH=((a,b)[,(a,b),......]

             ,FORMEND=x


        to specify FCB buffer image,

        where Name is a reference;

            LPI = Lines per Inch;

              LNCH specifies Line and Channel Number; and

            x = number of lines per page.


  End Statement:


  [Label]   END   [Comment]


        to signify the end of utility control statements.
```

One or more of the statements in Figure 7.10 must be coded in the order indicated and must contain a label, name, or blank in column 1.

The control statement example below loads UCS and FCB images into their respective buffer areas:

SYST JOB

DFN ADDR=204,FOLD=Y

UNI   UCS   ABCDEFGHIJKLMNOPQRSTUVWXYZ0123456789?:"¼)(*&¢%$#@

    FCB   LPI=6,   X

            LNCH=((6,1),(8,2),(10,3),(12,4),   X

            (22,5),(32,6),(42,7),(52,8),   X

            (60,9),(62,10),(64,11),(66,12))

  END

Following the Job control statement, a definition of the Model 3211 printer is provided. Next, a UCS buffer image is coded in column 16 to 64. A FCB image is also provided.

In summary, utility program ICAPRTBL loads UCS and FCB images into buffer areas for the Model 3211 Printer.

A primary topic in and by itself, a detailed description of all functions of independent utilities can be obtained from the Utilities Manual. Those independent utility applications somewhat common to all dp installation environments have been covered in this chapter.

F. SYSTEM AND INDEPENDENT UTILITY WORKSHOP

All system and independent utilities which can be called have been discussed.
A workshop is now provided to solidify a working knowledge of basic system
and independent utility use and job control coding. Workshop answers
can be found in Appendix E.

1. Update and Copy Program Library

You have the responsibility for maintaining a library of executable
program load modules for your office's many applications. Due to system
disk problems, you have been advised by the dp facility to reload the
program library from your backup tape copy. You decide to perform some
library maintenance at the same time. Code the Job statement, all Exec
statements, and all Dd statements for the three-step job depicted by
the system flowchart in Figure 7.11.

Pertinent Job statement information is displayed thereon. Choose
your own jobname and programmer name, however.

Figure 7.11 Update and Copy System Flowchart

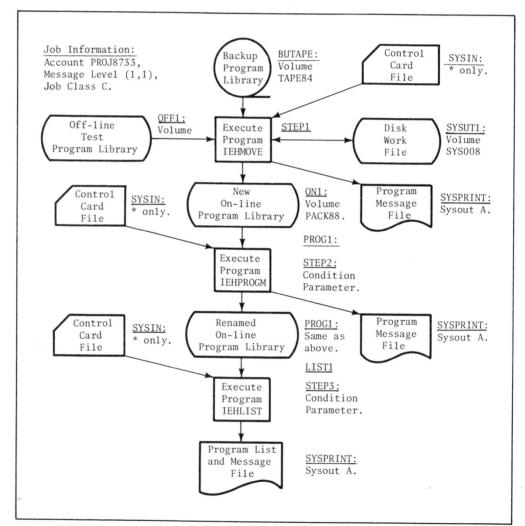

Pertinent Exec and Dd statement information is displayed as appropriate. Use 3330 for disk allocations. Code old Disposition parameters for disk library files. Choose your own library data set names. Use DD * for card files with no other parameters. Also, code no parameters other than SYSOUT for print files.

Utility program IEHMOVE is to accomplish the following: (1) copy backup program library tape to on-line disk; (2) exclude two members from this process -- ADJUST and RESUM; and (3) replace member AEDIT with a member of the same name from an off-line test program library. Utility program IEHPROGM is to accomplish the following: (1) rename the new program library; and (2) catalogue the new program library. Utility program IEHLIST is to list the member names in the new program library. Neither IEHPROGM nor IEHLIST are to be executed if 4 is less than the condition code returned from the first step (IEHMOVE).

To assist your coding efforts, follow the step-by-step instructions below:

1. Code the Job statement.

_____

_____

_____

2. Code Step1's Exec statement. Then code seven Dd statements -- the first for ddname ON1, a second for ddname OFF1, a third for ddname BUTAPE, a fourth for ddname SYSIN followed by the utility control file itself and a file delimiter, a fifth for ddname SYSUT1, a sixth for ddname SYSPRINT, and the seventh for ddname SYSUDUMP. Then code a step delimiter.

_____

_____

_____

_____

_____

_____

_____

_____

_____

_____

_____

_____

_____

_____

_____

_____

_____

_____

_____

_____

3. Code Step2's Exec statement with a Condition parameter. Then code four Dd statements -- the first for ddname PROG1 (input and output), a second for ddname SYSIN followed by the utility control file itself and a file delimiter, a third for ddname SYSPRINT, and the fourth of ddname SYSUDUMP. Then code a step delimiter.

_____

_____

_____

_____

_____

_____

_____

_____

_____

_____

_____

4. Code Step3's Exec statement with a Condition parameter. Then
   code four Dd statements -- the first for ddname LIST1, a second
   for ddname SYSIN followed by the utility control file itself and
   a file delimiter, a third for ddname SYSPRINT, and the fourth for
   ddname SYSUDUMP. Then code a Null statement.

_____

_____

_____

_____

_____

_____

_____

_____

2. Independent Disk Volume Dump

   The contents of a critical installation disk pack need to be dumped to
   tape. Code the control statements necessary to accomplish this task as
   depicted by the flowchart in Figure 7.12.
        Code Job, Message, Dump, and End statements. Choose your own channel
   and unit numbers.
        To assist your coding efforts, follow the step-by-step instructions
   below:

Figure 7.12 Independent Disk Volume Dump Flowchart

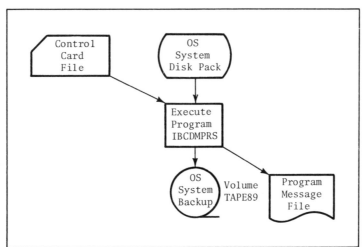

315

1. Code the Job statement.

_____

2. Code a Message statement.

_____

3. Code the Dump statement.

_____

_____

_____

4. Code an End statement.

_____

8

Advanced JCL Considerations

A. LABEL PROCESSING AND LAYOUT

As indicated in an earlier chapter, most data sets follow standard label principles. Labels describe the characteristics of a data set. This information is verified against program and JCL specifications prior to and after the actual processing of user data. Conflicts result in termination of the user task.

1. Standard Tape Labels

Standard tape labels consist of 80-character header and trailer label records. Figure 8.1 depicts standard tape label organization.

Header label records begin just beyond a tape's leader and reflective spot. They consist of a volume record and two header records. Though infrequently utilized, up to 8 optional user header label records can also be created. A single magnetic tape mark symbolizes the end of the header label and the beginning of the actual data to be processed. Similarly, another tape mark indicates the end of actual data and the beginning of the trailer label. The trailer label consists of two End of Volume (EOV) records if this condition is reached prior to the file's end. Two End of File (EOF) records are eventually created, however. Up to eight optional user trailer label records can also be created. A single tape mark then symbolizes the end of the trailer label. Two consecutive tape marks indicate the end of the complete data set, including labels.

Detailed characteristics of a tape data set are stored within the 80-character header and trailer label records. Figure 8.2 depicts specific label record format and field layout.

Figure 8.1 Standard Tape Label Organization

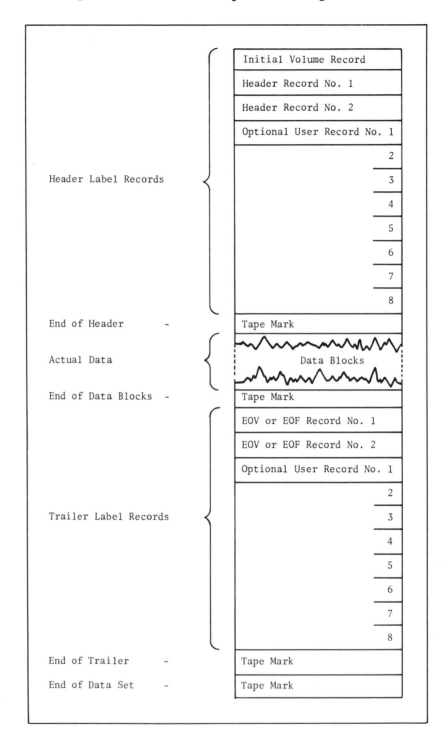

Figure 8.2 Standard Tape Label Fields

Initial Volume Records:

Label Identification (VOL)	-	3 Bytes
Record Number (1)	-	1 Byte
Volume Serial Number	-	6 Bytes
Reserved	-	31 Bytes
Owner Identification	-	10 Bytes
Blank	-	29 Bytes

Figure 8.2 Standard Tape Label Fields (cont.)

Header and Trailer Record Number 1:

Header/Trailer Identification (HDR, EOV, EOF)	-	3 Bytes
Record Number (1)	-	1 Byte
Data Set Name	-	17 Bytes
Data Set Volume Serial Number	-	6 Bytes
Volume Sequence Number	-	4 Bytes
Data Set Sequence Number	-	4 Bytes
Generation Data Set Number	-	4 Bytes
Generation Version Number	-	2 Bytes
Creation Date	-	6 Bytes
Expiration Date	-	6 Bytes
Data Set Security Indicator	-	1 Byte
Block Count	-	6 Bytes
Reserved	-	13 Bytes
Blank	-	7 Bytes

320

Figure 8.2 Standard Tape Label Fields (cont.)

Header and Trailer Record Number 2:

Header/Trailer Identification (HDR, EOV, EOF)	-	3 Bytes
Record Number (2)	-	1 Byte
Record Format (F, V, U)	-	1 Byte
Block Size or Block Factor	-	5 Bytes
Logical Record Length	-	5 Bytes
Density Indicator	-	1 Byte
Data Set Position Number	-	1 Byte
Jobname/Stepname	-	17 Bytes
Blank	-	4 Bytes
Blocking Indicator	-	1 Byte
Reserved	-	41 Bytes

Figure 8.2 Standard Tape Label Fields (cont.)

Optional User Header and Trailer Records:

User Label Identification (UHL, UTL)	-	3 Bytes
Record Number (1 to 8)	-	1 Byte
User Specifications	-	76 Bytes

The Initial Volume Record contains Label Identification (VOL), Record Number (1), Volume Serial Number (6 digits), and an Owner Identification field.

Header and Trailer Record Number 1 contains Header/Trailer Identification (HDR, EOV, EOF), Record Number (1), Data Set Name (rightmost 17 characters), Data Set Volume Serial Number for the first (and/or only) volume, Volume Sequence Number (1 to 9999) for multivolume data sets, Data Set Sequence Number (1 to 9999) for multidata set volumes, Generation Data Set Numbers (1 to 9999), and Version Numbers (1 to 99) if this feature is utilized, Julian Creation and Expiration Dates (bxxyyy) where b = blank, xx = year, and yyy = day), Data Set Security Indicator (1 for security, 0 for no security), and a Block Count (0's in header, 1 to 999999 in trailer) of the number of data blocks created.

Header and Trailer Record Number 2 contains Header/Trailer Identification (HDR, EOV, EOF), Record Number (2), Record Format (F for Fixed, V for Variable, U for Undefined), Block Size or

Block Factor (number of logical records per physical block),
Logical Record Length, Density Indicator (0 for 200, 1 for 556,
2 for 800, 3 for 1600, and 4 for 6250 BPI), Jobname and Stepname
with a / (slash) separator, and a Blocking Indicator (B for
Blocked).

Optional User Header and Trailer Records contain User Label
Identification (UHL, UTL), Record Number (1 to 8), and desired User
Specifications.

It should be pointed out that standard label principles are
used for direct-access device data sets as well. For example, a
disk contains a volume label which points to a Volume Table of
Contents (VTOC). The VTOC and Data Set Control Block (DSCB) area
contain descriptions and locations of each data set which reside
on the pack. Regardless of the type of physical device utilized, label-
processing principles can be applied.

2. Other Label Types

Coding LABEL=(,SL) on a Dd statement indicates that standard labels
are to be utilized for the data set of interest. In the absence
of this coding, standard labels are assumed. It is for this reason
that whenever a different label configuration is encountered, a Label
parameter must be coded.

American National Standard (ANS) labels are of different format
-- LABEL=(,AL) should be coded. Other labels considered to be nonstandard would be coded LABEL=(,NSL). Whenever optional user labels
are programmed, (,SUL) or (,AUL) should be coded. If label processing
is to be bypassed, code LABEL=(,BLP). Finally, in the absence of all
label records, LABEL=(,NL) should be indicated.

Tape mark sequence is of prime importance to successful recognition of label configurations. Labels created by other vendors may
have multiple leading, trailing, and interspersed tape mark throughout the label records. This situation makes it difficult for the
system to recognize and separate label records from data records. It
is for this reason that whenever a data tape is requested from another
dp facility and/or vendor, a nonlabeled file should be created for
ease of use and safety's sake.

B. SEVEN-TRACK TAPE PROCESSING

The utilization of 7-track tapes and drives is still a somewhat common
occurrence. Most 9-track-oriented dp facilities have at least one
7-track device available for such situations.

1. Common Seven-Track Tape Parameter Specifications

Up to this point in the text we have assumed 9-track tape usage to
be common. Also assumed were standard labels, simple or qualified
data set names, 1600 Bits per Inch (BPI) track density, odd parity,
and no translation or data conversion required. When processing 7-
track tapes, it is quite possible that few or none of the above defaults or assumptions will suffice.

UNIT=2400-1, 2400-2, or an appropriate 7-track group name is required in lieu of UNIT=2400, 2400-3, or 2400-4. Many 7-track data sets are nonlabeled. LABEL=(,NL) would therefore be necessary. Due to the absence of labels, a data set name is not required for verification purposes, as one could not have been created and saved within the label itself. Thus, Dsname parameters are treated as comments. Densities of 200, 556, and 800 BPI are common, as 7-track 1600 and 6250 BPI are neither technically feasible nor available. Binary Coded Decimal (BCD) representation in lieu of the Extended Binary Coded Decimal Interchange Code (EBCDIC) is also a common occurrence. Even parity tape files also occur on a somewhat frequent basis -- especially with other computer vendors. That is, a parity bit is either turned on or off within each byte of data, thus creating a consistent even or odd number of "on" bits for each byte throughout the file as requested by the user.

2. Seven-Track Tape JCL Example

Assume the following input file is to be processed:

7-track, nonlabeled, 800 BPI, even parity, and BCD code

Sample JCL for this file could be coded as follows:

```
//SYSUT1   DD   UNIT=2400-2,DISP=(OLD,KEEP),
//              LABEL=(,NL),VOL=SER=TAPE07,
//              DCB=(RECFM=FB,LRECL=080,BLKSIZE=3200,DEN=2,TRTCH=ET)
```

where 2400-2 = 7-track drive with data conversion capabilities;

NL = No Labels;

DEN = 0 for 200 BPI,

1 for 556 BPI,

2 for 800 BPI;

TRTCH = C for odd parity and no translation but with conversion,

E for even parity and no translation nor conversion,

T for odd parity and translation but no conversion,

ET for even parity and translation but no conversion.

The term "translation" refers to BCD-to-EBCDIC interpretation when reading and EBCDIC-to-BCD interpretation when writing. The term "conversion" refers to a feature of a special tape drive which internally converts from a 7-track to 9-track basis.

All of the above JCL considerations must be accounted for when processing 7-track tape files and other files whose characteristics deviate from operating standards.

C. DD STATEMENT CONSIDERATIONS

Some aspects of Dd statements were not considered part of JCL basics. Because of their occasional use they should be discussed, however.

1. Blocking Card and Print Files

At most installations a Logical Record Length and Blocksize subparameter need not be coded as part of the DCB parameter. A default card and print record length and blocksize are in effect. On some occasions one may wish to change card file blocksize, as well as print file record length and blocksize. Consider the following four Dd statement card files:

```
//SYSIN  DD  *
//SYSIN  DD  *,DCB=BLKSIZE=0080
//SYSIN  DD  *,DCB=BLKSIZE=1600
//SYSIN  DD  *,DCB=BLKSIZE=3200
```

What is the significance of the difference among the above four Dd statements? Remember that card files are blocked to temporary input disk files during the JCL input reader/interpreter process prior to actual job processing. The first statement above assumes a default blocksize, perhaps 1600. Card reader logical record length is fixed at 80 characters. The second statement assumes that the card file consists of only one card record. No need to waste main storage buffer requirements with a blocksize larger than the file itself! The third example merely blocks a card file. This may be the same as the default, and therefore an unnecessary specification, however. The fourth example blocks a card file at a higher and more efficient level than previous examples. By the way, if a data card file is placed into a job stream with no Dd statement, a DD * statement for ddname SYSIN is assumed and generated.

Consider the following four Dd statement print files:

```
//SYSOUT  DD  SYSOUT=A
//SYSOUT  DD  SYSOUT=B,DCB=BLKSIZE=2640
//SYSOUT  DD  SYSOUT=(C,,1434),DCB=(LRECL=100,BLKSIZE=4000)
//SYSOUT  DD  SYSOUT=(C,,1482),DCB=(RECFM=FBA,LRECL=80,BLKSIZE=4000)
```

Print files are also blocked to temporary output disk files during job processing prior to actual printing of the file itself. The first statement above assumes default DCB characteristics. The operating program must create print records of a standard logical length, e.g., 121, 133, or 160. In addition, column 1 must contain a carriage control character. A default blocksize is also assumed, perhaps 1330. The second statement modifies an installation's blocksize default. The third statement changes both logical record and blocksize print length. File definitions in the operating program must agree. The fourth example also modifies logical record length and blocksize. The Record Format parameter merely reiterates an FBA print default, that is,

fixed block with a standard carriage control character in column 1.
Whether deviating from installation standards or not, one must ensure that program and JCL specifications and/or defaults coincide
with each other.

2. File Organization

Unless specified, a file of sequential organization is assumed, that
is, DSORG=PS with the DCB parameter. Indexed Sequential, Direct, and
Partitioned forms of data set organization can also be defined. The
following Dd statement creates an indexed sequential disk file:

```
//INDEX1   DD   UNIT=3330,DISP=(NEW,KEEP),
//             DSNAME=INDX.FILE1(INDEX),VOL=SER=PACK01,
//             SPACE=(CYL,2,,CONTIG),
//             DCB=(CYLOFL=2,DSORG=IS,OPTCK=Y)
//          DD   UNIT=3330,DISP=(NEW,KEEP),
//             DSNAME=INDX.FILE(PRIME),VOL=SER=PACK01,
//             SPACE=(CYL,100,,CONTIG)
//             DCB=(CYLOFL=2,DSORG=IS,OPTCD=Y)
//          DD   UNIT=3330,DISP=(NEW,KEEP),
//             DSNAME=INDX.FILE(OVFLOW),VOL=SER=PACK01,
//             SPACE=(CYL,10,,CONTIG),
//             DCB=(CTLOFL=2,DSORG=IS,OPTCD=Y)
```

The above-described file specifies the indexed sequential form of
file organization. Ten cylinders are required for the index area, 100
for the prime area, and 10 for the overflow area. All cylinders are
to be contiguous with each other. Two tracks per cylinder are desig-
nated for overflow purposes. The following Dd statement creates a
directly organized random-access disk file:

```
//DIRECT1   DD   UNIT=3330,DISP=(NEW,KEEP),
//             DSNAME=ACCS.FILE1,VOL=SER=PACK02,
//             SPACE=(CYL,(100,20),RLSE),
//             DCB=DSORG=DA
```

The above-described file specifies the direct form of file organization. All unused cylinders are to be released upon completion of
the executing step. The following Dd statement creates a partitioned
disk data set:

```
//PARTION1   DD   UNIT=3330,DISP=(NEW,KEEP),
//             DSNAME=PART.FILE1,VOL=SER=PACK03,
//             SPACE=(CYL,(100,20,10),MXIG),
//             DCB=DSORG=PO
```

The above described file specifies the partitioned form of file organization. Ten 256-byte blocks are required for the directory. The data set is to be allocated to the largest contiguous area available on the volume.

It should be pointed out that these alternative forms of file organization are more of a system and programming challenge than one of JCL complexity.

3. Job Catalogue

It has been recommended throughout the text that five basic keyword parameters be coded to describe tape and disk files regardless of whether or not they absolutely had to be coded on each specific Dd statement itself. This practice enables one to more easily read and logically follow a given set of JCL even though some parameter information may have already been described in the program or assumed by the system itself. These keywords are the Unit, Disposition, Data Set Name, Volume, and Data Control Block parameters.

On occasion it is desirable to limit the coding of JCL to only those parameters necessary for successful execution of a given task. Creating a large job stream and the cataloguing of a set of JCL are two examples where the benefits of JCL brevity may outweigh the desire for JCL readability. In this case, knowledge of job catalogues are required.

A job catalogue merely stores the characteristics of each "passed" data set for each job being executed. The following parameter information is stored by Data Set Name:

Unit;
Volume(s); and
Data Set Sequence Number (tape).

Therefore, if a file is created in Step 1 and passed to Step 2 for further processing, only the Date Set Name and Disposition need be specified. DCB characteristics are accessed from the Label or VTOC. Disposition characteristics are not stored in job catalogues, as these specifications may change each step. For example:

```
//JOBCAT  JOB  ALPHPROJ,DHR,MSGLEVEL=(1,1)
//JOBLIB  DD  DSNAME=APROG.LIBRARY,DISP=SHR
//STEP1  EXEC  PGM=USERPROG,REGION=60K,TIME=1
//INPUT1  DD  UNIT=2400,DISP=(OLD,KEEP),
//        DSNAME=OLDFILE,VOL=SER=TAPE88,
//        DCB=(RECFM=FB,LRECL=100,BLKSIZE=4000)
//OUTPUT1  DD  UNIT=2400,DISP=(NEW,PASS),
//        DSNAME=NEWFILE1,VOL=SER=TAPE01,LABEL=(1,SL),
//        DCB=(RECFM=VB,LRECL=80,BLKSIZE=3204)
```

```
//OUTPUT2  DD   UNIT=3330,DISP=(NEW,PASS),
//           DSNAME=NEWFILE2,VOL=SER=DISK02,
//           SPACE=(2400,(100,10),RLSE),
//           DCB=(RECFM=FB,LRECL=120,BLKSIZE=2400)
/*
//STEP2   EXEC  PGM=PROGRM1,REGION=40K,TIME=1
//IN1   DD   DSNAME=NEWFILE1,DISP=(OLD,KEEP)
//IN2   DD   DSNAME=NEWFILE2,DISP=(OLD,KEEP)
//OUT1  DD   SYSOUT=A
//
```

Following an appropriate Job statement a user program is called in Step 1. Tape and disk output files are created from an input tape. All files are fully described in Step1's JCL. Note the brevity in Step 2, however. Only a Data Set Name and Disposition parameter have been coded for the two input files passed from Step 1. This is because any other necessary file descriptions can be obtained from this job's catalogue or file labels. The catalogue for this job contained two data set entries -- one for each file in a "passed" state. These entries were:

Data Set Name	-	NEWFILE1	NEWFILE2
Unit	-	2400	3330
Volume	-	TAPE01	DISK02
Data Set Sequence Number	-	1	--

The above specifications do not need to be coded in the JCL, as each data set's characteristics were stored in the job catalogue and label records. These entries are deleted at the end of the job of interest. Some job catalogue information may in fact be redundant with program file definitions. Nevertheless, the job catalogue is always available as needed whenever only minimum JCL is desired to be coded.

D. INSTREAM PROCEDURES

1. Purpose

An instream procedure is just like a catalogued procedure -- except that it's not catalogued! That is, an instream procedure is a set of JCL contained within a job stream and given a name for calling purposes. As such, it does not reside in procedure libraries for general use.

Like catalogued procedures, instream procedures can be used to minimize the duplicative coding of lengthy JCL for applications common to many users. An instream procedure can be called many times within the same job. More typically, however, instream procedures are used to test JCL prior to it being catalogued. That is, one must be sure that a given procedure functions as intended, and then catalogued, prior to its widespread use.

2. Instream Procedure Statements

a. PROC (Procedure) Statement

The PROC statement identifies the instream procedure of interest. It is divided into four fields of varying size, as depicted in Figure 8.3.

Figure 8.3 Proc Statement Overview

The // is followed by a name to be assigned to the instream procedure. All JCL identifier names are 1 to 8 alphanumeric characters in length and follow standard naming conventions and rules. The symbol 'PROC' follows the Procname after at least one blank. The Operand Field follows the symbol 'PROC' after at least one blank. This field can be used to specify symbolic parameter values to be covered later in the text. The optional Comment Field follows the Operand Field after at least one blank.

b. PEND (Procedure End) Statement

The PEND statement indicates the end of the instream procedure of interest. It is divided into three fields of varying size, as depicted in Figure 8.4.

Figure 8.4 Pend Statement Overview

The // is followed by an optional Procedure End statement name. All JCL names are 1 to 8 alphanumeric characters in length and follow standard naming conventions and rules. The symbol 'PEND' follows the optional Pendname after at least one blank. The optional Comment Field follows the word 'PEND' after at least one blank.

3. Instream Procedure Example

A job example which calls an instream procedure and tests a set of JCL prior to cataloguing is depicted below:

```
//JOBPROC   JOB   ALPHPROJ,DHR,MSGLEVEL=(1,1)
//PROCTEST  PROC
```

```
//ST1    EXEC   PGM=LEADZERO                              ⎫
//RECIN   DD    UNIT=2400,DISP=(OLD,KEEP)                 ⎪
//RECOUT  DD    UNIT=2400,DISP=(NEW,KEEP),                ⎪  Instream
//              DCB=(RECFM=FB,LRECL=080,BLKSIZE=3200)     ⎬  Procedure
//MSGOUT  DD    SYSOUT=A                                  ⎭
// PEND
/*
//STEP1   EXEC   PROC=PROCTEST
//ST1.RECIN   DD   DSNAME=TESTCARD,VOL=SER=TAPE08
//ST1.RECOUT  DD   DSNAME=TESTZERO,VOL=SER=TAPE09
//
```

Following an appropriate Job statement a Proc statement is
defined. An instream procedure to be called PROCTEST follows.
The procedure calls a leading zero program which processes input
and output data tapes and a message file. The Pend statement
signifies the end of the instream procedure. Step 1 then calls
instream procedure PROCTEST. Data set name and volume serial
number information is provided to both the RECIN and RECOUT
ddname files in the ST1 (first) step of the instream procedure.

Procedures can be tested in this way until finally error-
free and ready to be catalogued. The techniques of creating and
loading partitioned library data sets have been covered in the
preceding utility chapters. The PROC statement is also occasionally utilized as the first statement in a catalogued procedure to assign values to symbolic values.

E. SYMBOLIC PARAMETERS

1. Purpose And Use

A Symbolic Parameter is simply a parameter represented by a
symbol rather than the actual value. The actual value will
most likely be provided at execution time. Symbolic Parameters
are utilized when a simplication of JCL modifications is desired,
especially for non-JCL user-oriented personnel.

Symbolic parameters are indicated as such by an ampersand
(&), followed by 1 to 7 alpha and/or numeric characters, e.g.,
UNIT=&DEVICE, VOL=SER=&NUMBER, etc. Of course, &DEVICE is not
a valid unit device type, group name, or address. Rather, the
ampersand indicates that this value is to be represented by
the symbol 'DEVICE'. Similarly, the volume serial number is
to be represented by the symbol 'NUMBER'. All symbols are
user-chosen and should follow standard naming conventions and
rules. When a job containing symbolic parameters is submitted,
actual values are supplied via an Exec or Proc statement, e.g.,
DEVICE=3330,NUMBER=PACK87, etc. This type of descriptive
approach is found not only in user-coded JCL, but in catalogued
procedures as well.

330

2. Symbolic Parameter Example

Assume the following catalogued procedure named SYMBOL contains symbolic parameters as indicated:

```
//ST1    EXEC   PGM=LEADZERO,TIME=&MINUTES
//RECIN   DD    UNIT=&DEVICE,DISP=(OLD,KEEP)
//RECOUT  DD    UNIT=&DEVICE,DISP=(NEW,KEEP),
//              DSNAME=&FILEOUT,VOL=SER=&NUMBER,
//              DCB=(RECFM=FB,LRECL=80,BLKSIZE=&BLOCK)
//MSGOUT  DD    &PRINT
```

The following job stream could be used to call and modify the above procedure:

```
//ASYM   JOB   ALPHPROJ,DHR,MSGLEVEL=(1,1)
//STEP1  EXEC  PROC=SYMBOL,MINUTES=2,
//             DEVICE=2400,FILEOUT=TESTZERO,
//             NUMBER=TAPE09,BLOCK=3200,
//             PRINT='SYSOUT=A'
//ST1.RECIN  DD   DSNAME=TESTCARD,VOL=SER=TAPE08
```

Following an appropriate Job statement, procedure SYMBOL is called. Actual parameters and values 2, 2400, TESTZERO, TAPE09, 3200, and SYSOUT=A are provided for the symbols MINUTES, DEVICE, FILEOUT, NUMBER, BLOCK, and PRINT, respectively. A data set name and volume serial number are also provided to the RECIN ddname file in the ST1 (first) step of the procedure. They could have been accounted for via symbolic parameters if so designed.

Similarly, the first statement in the catalogued procedure itself could have been a Proc statement. Symbolic parameter values can be provided thereon. For example:

```
// PROC  MINUTES=2,DEVICE=2400,
//       FILEOUT=TESTZERO,NUMBER=TAPE09,BLOCK=3200,
//       PRINT='SYSOUT=A'
```

The above statement essentially sets default values for the symbolic parameters in the procedure to follow. The existence of JCL parameters can be nullified by coding an equal sign with no value, e.g., MINUTES=, BLOCK=, etc,. The use of symbolic parameters is a somewhat frequent occurrence in many dp environments.

F. MULTIVOLUMES AND DATA SETS

The creation of large data sets spanning more than one volume, the stringing together (concatenation) of data sets as one file for processing, and the stacking of more than one data set on a given volume are all techniques which at one time or another must be utilized by application and system programmers and analysts.

1. Multivolume Data Sets

The use of more than one volume to store a data set is a frequent occurrence in most dp environments. Assume, for example, that two tape volumes will be needed on output to contain a large data set to be created. Some installations require no specific volume request for output files; i.e., scratch tape(s) will be mounted as needed. In this case, when the first tape volume is filled, a second scratch volume would be called and mounted. Other installations require specific volume serial number requests for output files, e.g., VOL=SER=001804 or VOL=SER=(TAPE17,TAPE54). In this case, when volume TAPE17 is filled (1 of 2), the second volume TAPE54 (2 of 2) would be called and mounted. Upon successful completion of the step of interest, an initial portion of the file will reside on the first volume, the remaining portion on the second volume. There is no particular technical limit to the maximum number of volumes one may utilize for a multivolume data set. Practically speaking, however, more than three volumes can be cumbersome and should be avoided by splitting the file if possible.

On input the Volume parameter would also reflect multivolume use, that is, VOL=SER=(TAPE17,TAPE54). The first and second volumes should not be interchanged when coding these volume serial numbers. Abnormal termination would be likely. The following example depicts JCL for a three-volume file:

```
//MASTFILE  DD  UNIT=2400,DISP=(OLD,KEEP),
//          DSNAME=MASTER.FILE,VOL=SER=(OS2701,TAPE48,007699),
//          DCB=(RECFM=FB.LRECL=160,BLKSIZE=3200)
```

The use of 6250 BPI tapes will also reduce the frequency of multivolume files. Due to the vulnerability of multivolume files to error occurrences, the utilization of multivolume data sets should be minimized to the most reasonable extent possible.

2. Data Set Concatenation

The concatenation of data sets is a frequent occurrence in all dp environments. Concatenation is the technique of stringing together more than one data set for the purpose of processing as if they were all one program file. Assume, for example, that six bimonthly data sets (some with multivolume use) have been created over the past year for a given application. They now need to be brought together for an annual summary run. This concept is depicted in Figure 8.5.

In order to code concatenations one must first describe the initial file to be processed. The second, third, etc. files to

Figure 8.5 The Concatenation of Data Sets

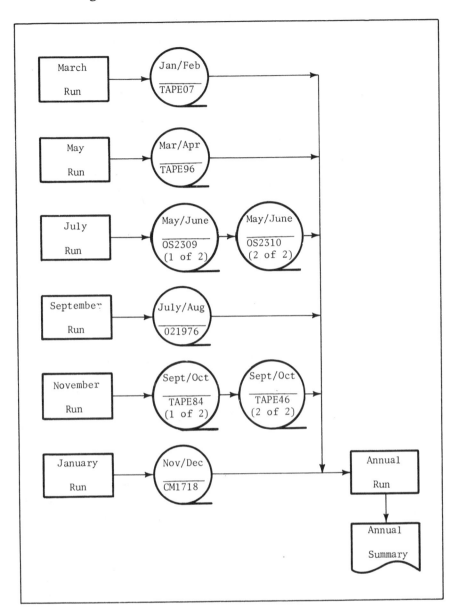

be processed are described next in sequential order; however, the Ddname (columes 3 to 10) must be left blank. The Affinity keyword should also be used in subsequent occurrences of the Unit parameter. This prevents multiple drives from being unnecessarily allocated, as only one drive is needed, that is, only one data set is processed at a time. The following example depicts JCL necessary to accomplish the annual run concatenation in Figure 8.5. For coding brevity, DCB information is assumed to be accessed from standard label content.

```
//CONCAT  JOB  ALPHPROJ,DHR,MSGLEVEL=(1,1),
//         CLASS=M,TIME=10
//STEP1  EXEC  PGM=SUMMARY,REGION=100K
//INPUT1  DD  UNIT=2400,DISP=(OLD,KEEP),
```

```
//          DSNAME=JANFEB,VOL=SER=TAPE07
//          DD   UNIT=AFF=INPUT1,DISP=(OLD,KEEP),
//          DSNAME=MARAPR,VOL=SER=TAPE96
//          DD   UNIT=AFF=INPUT1,DISP=(OLD,KEEP),
//          DSNAME=MAYJUNE,VOL=SER=(OS2309,OS2310)
//          DD   UNIT=AFF=INPUT1,DISP=(OLD,KEEP),
//          DSNAME=JULYAUG,VOL=SER=021976
//          DD   UNIT=AFF=INPUT1,DISP=(OLD,KEEP),
//          DSNAME=SEPTOCT,VOL=SER=(TAPE84,TAPE46)
//          DD   UNIT=AFF=INPUT1,DISP=(OLD,KEEP),
//          DSNAME=NOVDEC,VOL=SER=CM1718
//OUTPUT1   DD   SYSOUT=(C,,1484)
//SYSUDUMP  DD   SYSOUT=A
//
```

Following an appropriate Job statement a summary program is called. Each data set is coded as a separate Dd statement. After initial file description, subsequent Dd statements omit the coding of the ddname. This denotes that concatenation with the previous data set is desired. Upon completion of processing for the first file (JANFEB on TAPE07), the volume will be dismounted, data set MARAPR on volume TAPE96 called and mounted, and processing resumed. This procedure continues until the last file (NOVDEC on CM1718) has been processed. Subsequent Dd statements also specify a ddname for the Unit parameter, i.e., UNIT= AFF=INPUT1. This means that the same physical device which was allocated for the first file should be utilized for the current file. Coding UNIT=2400 on all Dd statements would have allocated six separate tape drives in this example, even though only one is needed. As can be seen for data sets MAYJUNE and SEPTOCT, multivolume files can also be concatenated.

If a concatenation contained within a catalogued procedure needs to be modified, leave the Dd statement for unmodified files blank. That is,

```
//ST1.INDATA  DD
//            DD   DSNAME=SECOND,DISP=(OLD,KEEP)
```

modifies the second file of a concatenation for ddname INDATA contained within the ST1 step of the procedure. The first file description remains unchanged.

Given some experience, the technique of concatenation is soon mastered.

3. Stacking Data Sets

The technique of stacking data sets is a frequent occurrence in most dp environments. This refers to the placement of more than one data

set on a reel of tape. After all, we usually have 2,400 feet of
tape for data set use regardless of whether we need it or not!
Though installation tape rental fees appear nominal, a $1-per-month
per-tape charge for 500 reels amounts to an annual cost of $6,000
for tape rental. To save costs and release unused tape space, data
sets to be saved (history files) should usually be stacked on each
given reel. Assume, for example, that two files are to reside on
the same reel of tape. This concept is depicted in Figure 8.6.

Figure 8.6 The Stacking of Data Sets

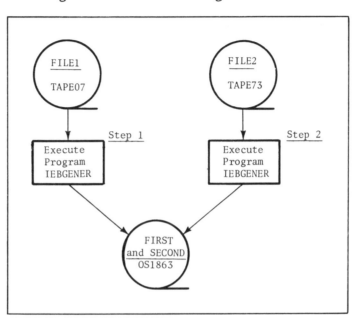

In order to code the JCL necessary to stack data sets, the Data
Set Sequence Number field of the Label parameter must be incremented
for each file to be stacked. LABEL=(1,SL) and LABEL=(,SL) are identical specifications, that is, the data set of interest is the first
data set on the volume, and this file contains standard labels.
Coding (2,SL), (3,SL), etc. would place or access the 2nd, 3rd, etc.
data set on the volume of interest. The Retain keyword of the
Volume parameter should also be used for stacked output to prevent
needless repetitive dismounting and mounting of the private volume
being stacked. The following example depicts JCL necessary to
accomplish the stacking run in Figure 8.6. For coding brevity,
DCB information is assumed to be accessed from standard label content.

```
//STACK   JOB   ALPHPROJ,DHR,MSGLEVEL=(1,1),
//        CLASS=C,TIME=5
//STEP1  EXEC   PGM=IEBGENER
//SYSUT1  DD    UNIT=2400,DISP=(OLD,KEEP),LABEL=(,SL),
//        DSNAME=FILE1,VOL=SER=TAPE07
```

```
//SYSUT2   DD   UNIT=2400,DISP=(NEW,KEEP),LABEL=(1,SL),
//              DSNAME=FIRST,VOL=SER=(PRIVATE,RETAIN,SER=OS1863)
//SYSIN  DD  DUMMY
//SYSPRINT  DD   SYSOUT=A
//SYSUDUMP  DD   SYSOUT=A
/*
//STEP2   EXEC   PGM=IEBGENER
//SYSUT1  DD   UNIT=2400,DISP=(OLD,KEEP),LABEL=(,SL),
//              DSNAME=FILE2,VOL=SER=TAPE73
//SYSUT2   DD   UNIT=2400,DISP=(NEW,KEEP),LABEL=(2,SL),
//              DSNAME=SECOND,VOL=SER=OS1863
//SYSIN  DD  DUMMY
//SYSPRINT  DD   SYSOUT=A
//SYSUDUMP  DD   SYSOUT=A
//
```

Following an appropriate Job statement, utility program IEBGENER
is called in both steps to accomplish the stacking exercise. Ddnames
SYSUT1 and SYSUT2 in Step 1 describe the input and output tape files
for the initial data set to be stacked. Label specifications of
(,SL) and (1,SL), respectively, both ask for the first data set on
each volume. Note the Retain keyword on the Volume parameter of the
first output file. Though not absolutely necessary, this specification prevents the needless dismounting, then mounting again, of the
same private reel in Step 2. Also note that the Keep disposition
is correct -- Disposition parameters refer to data set use, not
volume use.

Ddnames SYSUT1 and SYSUT2 in Step 2 describe the input and output
tape files for the second data set to be stacked. The output label
specification of (2,SL) indicates that the data set is to be written
as the second file on tape OS1863. Standard labels are also to be
created and utilized for the file. Upon successful completion of
this run, tape volume OS1863 will contain two separate and distinct
standard labeled data sets.

Of course, this process can be repeated -- one step for each data
set to be stacked. Be reminded that it is not wise to stack data
sets which need to be later updated. Adding one record, for example,
would cause all files behind it to be restacked. This is why the
stacking of data sets is generally limited to history files and
others of a saved and static nature.

G. BACKWARD REFERENCE

1. Purpose and Use

    On various occasions a file will need to be accessed for processing

purposes but its data set name is not known. Yet a file's presence
and purpose within a job stream is known and desired. In this situation, the file can only be referred to, but not by data set name.
The ddname for the file of interest and/or the stepname within which
the file is described are known. A reference to a previous file
and/or step can therefore be made. Backward references are also
sometimes used to minimize repetitious coding of JCL subparameter
information.

Backward references are signified by coding the pertinent keyword, an equal (=) sign, and an asterisk followed by a period (*.).
If a previous file being referred to is in the same step as the
backward reference, the appropriate ddname is then coded, e.g.,
DCB=*.INPUT1. Similarly, if the file being referred to is in a
previous JCL-coded step from the backward reference, the appropriate stepname followed by a period and ddname are then coded, e.g.,
DSNAME=*.STEP1.OUTPUT1. Finally, if the file being referred to is
in a procedure step previous to the backward reference, the appropriate JCL-coded stepname followed by a period, the procedure stepname followed by a period, and ddname are then coded, e.g., VOL=
REF=*.STEP1.GO.RAWDATA. Note that the Volume Reference (REF) keyword is utilized for referback purposes in lieu of the Volume
Serial (SER) keyword. Referbacks can also be used with the Program
(PGM) keyword, e.g., PGM=*.LKED.SYSLMOD, as in many catalogued procedures.

2. Referback JCL Examples

The technique of backward reference can be utilized for the following
JCL parameters:

    Data Control Block (DCB);
    Data Set Name (DSNAME or DSN);
    Program (PGM); and
    Volume Reference (VOL=REF).

The following three-step job utilizes all four keywords and referback syntax:

    //REFER   JOB   ALPHPROJ,DHR,MSGLEVEL=(1,1),
    //   CLASS=C,TIME=5
    //STEP1   EXEC   PROC=LKED
    //LKED.SYSIN   DD   DSNAME=A.PROGRAM.LIBRARY(SUM),DISP=SHR
    /*
    //STEP2   EXEC   PGM=*.STEP1.LKED.SYSLMOD,
    //   REGION=80K,TIME=3,COND=(4,LT,STEP1.LKED)
    //DATAIN   DD   UNIT=2400,DISP=(OLD,KEEP),
    //   DSNAME=AMASTER,VOL=SER=001531,
    //   DCB=(RECFM=FB,LRECL=100,BLKSIZE=4000)
    //DATAOUT   DD   UNIT=SYSDA,DISP=(NEW,PASS),

```
//          SPACE=(TRK,40,RLSE),
//          DCB=*.DATAIN
/*
//STEP3  EXEC  PGM=AEDIT,
//          REGION=120K,TIME=3,COND=((4,LT,STEP1,LKED),(4,LT,STEP2))
//DISKIN  DD  DSNAME=*.STEP2.DATAOUT,DISP=(OLD,KEEP)
//DISKOUT  DD  UNIT=SYSDA,DISP=(NEW,KEEP),
//          DSNAME=GOODATA,VOL=REF=*.DISKIN,
//          SPACE=(TRK,40,RLSE),
//          DCB=(RECFM=VB,LRECL=120,BLKSIZE=3204)
//
```

Following an appropriate Job statement, the linkage editor catalogued procedure is called. An object module is to be converted to
a 100% machine-executable load module. In Step 2 the PGM keyword
parameter refers back to the SYSLMOD ddname load module file in the
procedure step name LKED in the JCL-coded step named STEP1. Similarly, Step 2's ddname DATAOUT file references back to the same
step's DATAIN file for DCB information. In Step 3, a Dsname referback is made to Step 2's ddname DATAOUT file from the DISKIN ddname
file. Whatever data set name was generated by the system in Step 2
will be picked up for reference in Step 3. Finally, Step 3's
ddname DISKOUT file refers back to the same volume utilized for
the input file. Whichever disk pack was assigned by the system in
Step 2 for this previous data set will also be used for the GOODATA
file.

As can be seen, the constant use of referbacks can be confusing
to the JCL coder. Though many programmers and analysts utilize the
backward reference to minimize coding efforts, it is the author's
opinion that referbacks should only be coded when absolutely necessary. To do otherwise results in a coded JCL flow which becomes
difficult and cumbersome to follow. Nevertheless, when specific
characteristics or parameter values are not known but must be specified anyway, the technique of backward reference should be utilized.

H. GENERATION DATA SETS

1. Purpose and Use

The technique of creating and saving generation data sets is frequently utilized in many dp environments. They are used to minimize
JCL coding and modifications for operational jobs of a repetitive
nature. A generation consists of more than one file of the same
data set name. They are accessed by coding a generation number within parentheses behind the data set name according to the following
format:

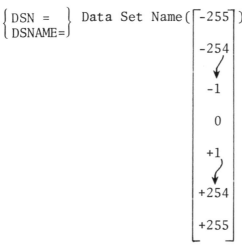

$\left\{\begin{array}{l}\text{DSN} = \\ \text{DSNAME=}\end{array}\right\}$ Data Set Name $\left(\begin{array}{c}-255 \\ -254 \\ \downarrow \\ -1 \\ 0 \\ +1 \\ \downarrow \\ +254 \\ +255\end{array}\right)$

The most recent or current data set is indicated by a generation number of zero (0), e.g., DSNAME=UPDATE(0). A new generation of the same data set name is created by coding +1 to +255, e.g., DSNAME= UPDATE(+1). A past generation data set is denoted by coding -1 to -255, e.g., DSNAME=UPDATE(-4). In all cases, generation numbers farthest from zero (0) indicate the oldest (-255) or the newest (+255) generation of this data set.

2. The System Catalogue

Prior to the decision to create a generation data set, system utility program IEHPROGM needs to be called to set up a generation table of a given size in the System Catalogue. A systemwide catalogue named SYSCTLG stores the characteristics of each data set for which CATLG was indicated in the Disposition parameter, e.g., DISP=(NEW,CATLG, DELETE). The following parameter information is stored by Data Set Name:

    Unit;
    Volume(s); and
    Data Set Sequence Number (tape).

Upon cataloguing, only the Data Set Name and Disposition must be specified. DCB characteristics are accessed from the Label or VTOC. Disposition characteristics are not stored in the System Catalogue, as these specifications may change each step. The System Catalogue will release the characteristics of a data set under two conditions: (1) UNCATLG is coded in the Disposition parameter; or (2) generation table size is exceeded. Perhaps an array of 10 generation positions has been set up in a generation table for data set UPDATE. When the 11th and succeeding generations are created, the oldest generation (in the 10th position) will be removed. The 9th will be moved to the 10th, 4th to 5th, 1st to 2nd, etc. The most current generation (zero or 0) will then be placed into the 1st position of the table. That is, only 10 generations (from 0 to 9) of the same data set name will be maintained in the System Catalogue in this example. Remember that just because a file has been removed from the System Catalogue doesn't mean it will be deleted or scratched. Rather, this only means that a more complete JCL description of the data set is necessary to access the file of concern. This concept is similar in principle to that of job catalogues discussed previously in this chapter.

3. Generation Data Set Examples

The following set of JCL updates the current master file and creates a new generation:

```
//GENER   JOB   ALPHAPROJ,DHR,MSGLEVEL=(1,1),
//        CLASS=C,TIME=5
//JOBLIB   DD   DSNAME=APROG.LIBRARY,DISP=SHR
//STEP1   EXEC   PGM=USERMOD,REGION=80K
//OLDMAST   DD   DSNAME=UPDATE(0),DISP=(OLD,KEEP)
//UPDATES   DD   UNIT=2400,DISP=(OLD,KEEP),
//        DSNAME=CARDDATA,VOL=SER=TAPE12,
//        DCB=(RECFM=FB,LRECL=080,BLKSIZE=3200)
//NEWMAST   DD   DSNAME=UPDATE(+1),DISP=(NEW,CATLG,DELETE)
//SYSUDUMP   DD   SYSOUT=A
//
```

Following an appropriate Job statement a user program is called in Step 1. Characteristics for the most current master are accessed from the System Catalogue by referring to the zero (0) or latest generation. The updates themselves are supplied via a completely JCL-described noncatalogued tape file. Characteristics for the new master are obtained from the current generation (with the exception of the volume serial number, which can be coded or system-assigned). When the job has reached a normal end, the plus one (+1) or newest generation becomes the current (0) generation. The original current (0) generation becomes the minus one (-1) generation, etc. Changing JCL is thus minimized if not prevented altogether. In the above example, no JCL would ever need to be modified if the next set of updated records were to be placed on the same volume. Assuming normal execution, the maintenance of generation data sets take care of themselves.

I. JCL SECURITY CONSIDERATIONS

Though by its nature Job Control Language itself suffers from a minimum of security-oriented considerations when compared to on-line text-editing interactive control languages, three items of security concern can be discussed.

1. Password Security

When standard labels are created, a data set password feature can be utilized. The process is as follows:

a. Execute system utility program IEHPROGM and specify to the
    password library a series of 8-character user passwords for
    each data set on each volume. Communicate password combina-
    tions to installation operations management.
b. Create labeled data set and secure by specifying the keyword
    PASSWORD in the Label parameter, e.g., LABEL=(1,SL,PASSWORD).
    This turns a security switch "on" in a Header label record.
c. Upon mounting of the volume, a prompt is given to the com-
    puter operator asking that the password be specified.
d. If the appropriate password is correctly keyed via the
    operator's console, processing of the data set begins.

Certainly this form of password security is not a foolproof
method. All passwords must be communicated among various user and
operations personnel. Bypassing label processing by coding LABEL=
(1,BLP) on input, for example, is also valid at some installations.
Nevertheless, password procedures have merit. A check with the installation should be made to ascertain if improved password techniques are being utilized, however.

2. Data Set Name Masking

The masking of data set names is an inhibitor to the breaking of
security-conscious dp environments. The process is as follows:

a. Create labeled data set and secure by keying valid multi-
    punch (nonprintable) characters (EBCDIC, BCD, ASCII, etc.).
    Their punchcard codes can be obtained from the System 360
    or 370 Reference Data Cards.
b. Job control listings for this data set will reflect a
    blank or nonprintable data set name, e.g., DSNAME='   ',
    though the volume serial number may well be recognized.
c. During input label processing an abnormal termination of
    the job will occur due to a conflict between whatever data
    set name was specified by the user and that residing in
    the header label in multipunch form.

Of course, this form of data set security is not a foolproof
method either. Given the appropriate volume, multipunch combinations of a given data set name can be obtained from the resulting
abnormal termination's storage dump or some utility program prints
of header label records. Bypassing label processing by coding
LABEL=(1,BLP) on input, for example, is also valid at some installations. Nevertheless, this procedure should be considered a
bothersome step and can lengthen the time necessary to break a
security system.

3. Preventing Accidental Volume Scratching

The specification of Retention Period (RETPD) or Expiration Date
(EXPDT) on the LABEL parameter in installations with automated
tape library procedures minimizes the accidental loss of critical
data sets. This technique has been discussed previously. Bypassing label processing by coding LABEL=(1,BLP) on input, for ex-

ample, is also unfortunately valid at some installations. Nevertheless, this process can be of assistance to security-conscious dp environments.

J. ADVANCED JCL WORKSHOP

A workshop is now provided to solidify a working knowledge of advanced JCL techniques. Workshop answers can be found in Appendix E.

1. JCL Syntax and Coding Project

a. Syntax Check

Review, analyze, and correct the following ten JCL statements for syntactical and/or logic coding errors. A given statement may contain none, one, or more than one error.

```
1. //IN   DD   DSN=XYZ,DISP=(OLD,KEEP),LABEL=(,NOL)


2. //IN1   DD   UNIT=2400=2,DISP=(OLD,PASS),

   //        LABEL=(1,NL),VOL=SER=TAPE07,

   //        DCB=(DEN=3,RECFM=VB,LRECL=100,BLKSIZE=3204,TRTCH=CT)


3. //CARDIN  DD   *,DCB=BLKSIZE=040


4. //OUT1   DD   UNIT=2400,DISP=(NEW,KEEP),

   //        DSNAME=DATA1,VOL=RETAIN=SER=002404,

   //        LABEL=(0,SL)


5. //INPUT1   DD   DSNAME=ABC


6. //MASTIN   DD   UNIT=2400,DISP=(OLD,KEEP),

   //        DSNAME=MAST1,VOL=SER=(TAPE89,TAPE86),
```

```
//          DCB=*.STEP2.MASTOUT


7. //ST4    EXEC  PGM=AEDIT,TIME=MINUTE

   //IN1    DD    UNIT=&&DEVICES,DISP=(OLD,KEEP),

   //            DSN=&SYMBOL.NAME


8. //MASTIN  DD   UNIT=SYSDA,DISP=(OLD,KEEP),

   //            DSNAME=FILE1,VOL=REF=PACK13

   //MASTIN  DD   UNIT=SYSDA,DISP=(OLD,KEEP),

   //            DSNAME=FILE2,VOL=SER=PACK66


9. //STEP1   EXEC  PGM=*.STEP1.OUT1


10. //OLDFILE  DD  DSNAME=DATA(0),DISP=(NEW,CATLG,DELETE)
```

b. Advanced JCL Coding Project

Code the Job statement, Exec statements, and all Dd statements for
the two-step job depicted by the system flowchart in Figure 8.7.
Pertinent Job statement information (Account, Message Level, Time,
and Class) is displayed thereon. Choose your own jobname and programmer name, however.
Pertinent Exec statement information (Program or Procedure Name,
Region, and Time) are displayed as appropriate thereon. Choose your
own stepnames, however. Code the first step as an instream procedure.
Include three symbolic parameters -- program REFORM main storage requirements, input tape blocksize, and output disk data set name.
Supply valid symbolic parameter information when the instream procedure is called.
Pertinent Dd statement information (Ddname, Unit, Disposition,
Volume, Space, DCB, and Sysout) are displayed as appropriate. Use
2400-2 for concatenated 7-track tape allocations, 2400 for 9-track
tape allocations, and 3330 for disk allocations. Code minimum JCL
for passed and/or catalogued files. In the second step use a data
set name referback to the first step's output disk file. The genera-

tion data sets in the second step are to be catalogued. Choose your own data set names. Insert a Joblib statement after the Job statement. Insert a Sysudump Dd statement at the end of each step.

To assist your coding efforts, follow the step-by-step instructions below:

Figure 8.7 Advanced JCL Coding System Flowchart

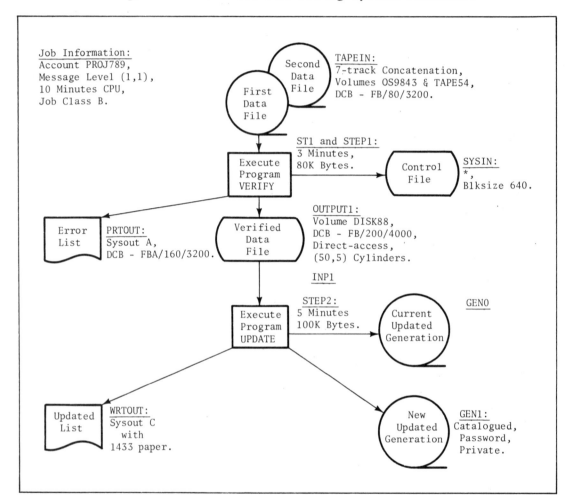

1. Code the Job statement and Joblib statement using a shared program library name.

_____

_____

_____

2. Code the first step (ST1) as an instream procedure using Proc and Pend statements. Code a Time parameter and a symbolic Region parameter. Code five Dd statements -- the first for a 7-track concatenation with ddname TAPEIN consisting of symbolic blocksizes and your own specifications, a second for

344

ddname SYSIN, a third for ddname PRTOUT, a fourth for direct-access ddname OUTPUT1 with a symbolic data set name, and the fifth for a user storage dump file.

_____

_____

_____

_____

_____

_____

_____

_____

_____

_____

_____

_____

_____

_____

_____

_____

3. Code Step 1's Exec statement calling the previously coded in-stream procedure. Provide appropriate information for the three symbolic parameters in the procedure.

_____

_____

_____

4. Code Step 2's Exec statement with Region and Time parameters. Code five Dd statements -- the first with a data set name backward reference for ddname INP1, a second for current generation ddname GEN0, a third for new generation ddname GEN1, a fourth for ddname WRTOUT, and the fifth for a user storage dump file. Then code a Null statement to indicate an end-of-job condition.

_____

_____

_____

_____

_____

_____

_____

_____

_____

_____

_____

A

JCL Syntax Reference Summary (JCL Reference Card)

A most handy reference for JCL coding purposes is the Syntax Reference Summary. It is reproduced in Figure A.1 and can be used as a later reference throughout the text.

Figure A.1 JCL Syntax Reference Summary Card

OS/360 Job Control Language: Syntax Reference Summary

Requests for copies of this and other IBM publications should be made to your IBM representative or to the IBM branch office serving your locality. Please direct any comments on the contents of this publication to the address below. All comments and suggestions become the property of IBM.

Information About Syntax Illustrations

- Upper case letters, numbers, parentheses, and punctuation marks must be coded as shown. Never code brackets, braces, or ellipses.
- Lower case items represent variables.
- Items or groups of items within brackets are optional; code one or none.
- Braces group alternative items; code one.
- An ellipsis (...) indicates that the preceding item or group of items can be coded more than once in succession.

GX28-6783-0

Seventh Edition (March, 1972)

This reference summary supersedes X20-1746-5. Effective system level is OS Release 21. Information contained in this summary is extracted from GC28-6704-2. Changes or additions are marked by a vertical line to the left of the change.

IBM Corporation, Publications Development, Dept. D58, Bldg. 706-2, PO Box 390, Poughkeepsie, New York 12602

//jobname JOB

[([account #] [,accounting information,...])]

[programmer's name]

[CLASS=jobclass]

[COND=((code,operator),...)]

[MSGCLASS=output class]

$$[\text{MSGLEVEL}=(\begin{bmatrix}0\\1\\2\end{bmatrix}\begin{bmatrix},0\\,1\end{bmatrix})]$$

[NOTIFY=user identification]

[PRTY=priority]

$$[\text{RD}=\begin{Bmatrix}R\\RNC\\NC\\NR\end{Bmatrix}]$$

$$[\text{REGION}=(\begin{Bmatrix}\text{valueK}\\\text{value}_0\text{K}\end{Bmatrix}[,\text{value}_1\text{K}])]$$

$$[\text{RESTART}=(\begin{Bmatrix}*\\\text{stepname}[.\text{procstepname}]\end{Bmatrix}[,\text{checkid}])]$$

$$[\text{ROLL}=(\begin{Bmatrix}\text{YES}\\\text{NO}\end{Bmatrix}\begin{Bmatrix},\text{YES}\\,\text{NO}\end{Bmatrix})]$$

$$[\text{TIME}=\begin{Bmatrix}(\text{minutes,seconds})\\1440\end{Bmatrix}]$$

[TYPRUN=HOLD]

//stepname EXEC

$$\begin{Bmatrix}\text{PGM}=\begin{Bmatrix}\text{program name}\\*.\text{stepname}[.\text{procstepname}].\text{ddname}\end{Bmatrix}\\[\text{PROC}=]\text{procedure name}\end{Bmatrix}$$

[ACCT[.procstepname]=(accounting information,...)]

[COND[.procstepname]=

$$(\begin{bmatrix}(\text{code,operator})\\(\text{code,operator,stepname}[.\text{procstepname}])\end{bmatrix}[,...]$$

$$...[,]\begin{bmatrix}\text{EVEN}\\\text{ONLY}\end{bmatrix})]$$

[DPRTY[.procstepname]=(value1,value2)]

[PARM[.procstepname]=value]

$$[\text{RD}[.\text{procstepname}]=\begin{Bmatrix}R\\RNC\\NC\\NR\end{Bmatrix}]$$

$$[\text{REGION}[.\text{procstepname}]=(\begin{Bmatrix}\text{valueK}\\\text{value}_0\text{K}\end{Bmatrix}[,\text{value}_1\text{K}])]$$

$$[\text{ROLL}[.\text{procstepname}]=(\begin{Bmatrix}\text{YES}\\\text{NO}\end{Bmatrix}\begin{Bmatrix},\text{YES}\\,\text{NO}\end{Bmatrix})]$$

$$[\text{TIME}[.\text{procstepname}]=\begin{Bmatrix}(\text{minutes,seconds})\\1440\end{Bmatrix}]$$

$$//\begin{bmatrix}\text{ddname}\\\text{procstepname.ddname}\\\text{JOBLIB}\\\text{STEPLIB}\\\text{SYSABEND}\\\text{SYSUDUMP}\\\text{SYSCHK}\end{bmatrix}\text{DD}$$

$$\begin{bmatrix}*\\\text{DATA}\end{bmatrix}[,\text{DLM}=xx]$$

[DUMMY]

[DYNAM]

[AFF=ddname]

$$[\text{DCB}=([\begin{Bmatrix}\text{dsname}\\*.\text{ddname}\\*.\text{stepname.ddname}\\*.\text{stepname.procstepname.ddname}\end{Bmatrix}][,\text{attributes}])]^{\dagger}$$

[DDNAME=ddname]

† See "Glossary of DCB Subparameters" in OS JCL Reference.

$$[\text{DISP}=(\begin{bmatrix}\text{NEW}\\\text{OLD}\\\text{SHR}\\\text{MOD}\end{bmatrix}\begin{bmatrix},\text{DELETE}\\,\text{KEEP}\\,\text{PASS}\\,\text{CATLG}\\,\text{UNCATLG}\end{bmatrix}\begin{bmatrix},\text{DELETE}\\,\text{KEEP}\\,\text{CATLG}\\,\text{UNCATLG}\end{bmatrix})]$$

$$[\begin{Bmatrix}\text{DSNAME}\\\text{DSN}\end{Bmatrix}=\begin{Bmatrix}\text{dsname}\\\text{dsname(member name)}\\\text{dsname(generation number)}\\\text{dsname(area name)}\\\&\&\text{dsname}\\\&\&\text{dsname(member name)}\\\&\&\text{dsname(area name)}\\*.\text{ddname}\\*.\text{stepname.ddname}\\*.\text{stepname.procstepname.ddname}\end{Bmatrix}]$$

$$[\text{FCB}=(\text{image-id}\begin{bmatrix},\text{ALIGN}\\,\text{VERIFY}\end{bmatrix})]$$

$$[\text{LABEL}=([\text{seq}\#]\begin{bmatrix},\text{SL}\\,\text{SUL}\\,\text{AL}\\,\text{AUL}\\,\text{NSL}\\,\text{NL}\\,\text{BLP}\\,\text{LTM}\\,\end{bmatrix}\begin{bmatrix},\text{PASSWORD}\\,\text{NOPWREAD}\end{bmatrix}\begin{bmatrix},\text{IN}\\,\text{OUT}\end{bmatrix}[,]\begin{bmatrix},\text{EXPDT}=\text{yyydd}\\,\text{RETPD}=\text{nnnn}\end{bmatrix})]$$

[OUTLIM=number]

[QNAME=process name]

$$\begin{bmatrix}(\text{SPACE}=(\begin{Bmatrix}\text{TRK}\\\text{CYL}\\\text{blocklength}\end{Bmatrix},(\text{primary}\begin{bmatrix},\text{secondary}\end{bmatrix}\\\begin{bmatrix},\text{directory}\\,\text{index}\end{bmatrix})\begin{bmatrix},\text{RLSE}\end{bmatrix}\begin{bmatrix},\text{CONTIG}\\,\text{MXIG}\\,\text{ALX}\end{bmatrix}[,\text{ROUND}])\\\\\text{SPACE}=(\text{ABSTR},(\text{primary,address}\begin{bmatrix},\text{directory}\\,\text{index}\end{bmatrix}))\end{bmatrix}$$

$$\left[SPLIT= \begin{Bmatrix} (n,CYL,(primary\,[,secondary]\,)) \\ n \\ (percent,blocklength,(primary\,[,secondary]\,)) \\ percent \end{Bmatrix} \right]$$

$$\left[SUBALLOC= \left(\begin{Bmatrix} TRK \\ CYL \\ blocklength \end{Bmatrix} ,(primary \begin{bmatrix} ,secondary \\ , \end{bmatrix} \right. \right.$$

$$\left. \left. [,directory]\,) \begin{Bmatrix} ,ddname \\ ,stepname\,[.procstepname]\,.ddname \end{Bmatrix} \right) \right]$$

$$\left[SYSOUT=(classname \begin{bmatrix} ,program\ name \\ , \end{bmatrix} [,form\,\#]) \right.$$

$$\left. [,]\,[OUTLIM=number]\, \right]$$

[TERM=TS]

$$\left[UCS=(character\ set\ code \begin{bmatrix} ,FOLD \\ , \end{bmatrix} \left[,VERFY \right]\,) \right]$$

$$\left[\begin{Bmatrix} UNIT=\left(\begin{bmatrix} unit\ address \\ device\ type \\ group\ name \end{bmatrix} \begin{bmatrix} ,unit\ count \\ ,P \\ , \end{bmatrix} [,DEFER] \right. \\ [,SEP=(ddname,...)]\,) \\ UNIT=AFF=ddname \end{Bmatrix} \right]$$

$$\left[\begin{Bmatrix} VOLUME \\ VOL \end{Bmatrix} =([PRIVATE] \begin{bmatrix} ,RETAIN \\ , \end{bmatrix} \begin{bmatrix} ,volume\ seq\,\# \\ , \end{bmatrix} [,vol\ count] \right.$$

$$\left. [,] \begin{bmatrix} SER=(serial\ number,...) \\ REF=dsname \\ REF=*.ddname \\ REF=*.stepname\,[.procstepname]\,.ddname \end{bmatrix}) \right]$$

IBM

International Business Machines Corporation
Data Processing Division
1133 Westchester Avenue, White Plains, New York 10604
(U.S.A. only)

IBM World Trade Corporation
821 United Nations Plaza, New York, New York 10017
(International)

PRINTED IN U.S.A.

B

Catalogued Procedure Listings (In Alphabetical Order)

1. ASSEMBLER (F-Level)

   The following ASSEMBLER Level-F procedures can also be considered comparable to other ASSEMBLER programming levels.

   ASMFC (Assemble Only):

   ```
   //ASM EXEC PGM=IEUASM,REGION=80K,
   //        PARM='LIST'
   //SYSPRINT DD SYSOUT=A
   //SYSPUNCH DD SYSOUT=B
   //SYSUT1 DD UNIT=SYSDA,DSNAME=&SYSUT1,SPACE=(3200,(80,80))
   //SYSUT2 DD UNIT=SYSDA,DSNAME=&SYSUT2,SPACE=(3200,(80,80))
   //SYSUT3 DD UNIT=SYSDA,DSNAME=&SYSUT3,SPACE=(3200,(80,80))
   //SYSLIB DD DSNAME=SYS1.MACLIB,DISP=SHR
   ```

   ASMFCG (Assemble and Load):

   ```
   //ASM EXEC PGM=IEUASM,REGION=80K,
   //        PARM='LOAD,LIST,XREF'
   //SYSPRINT DD SYSOUT=A
   //SYSPUNCH DD SYSOUT=B
   //SYSUT1 DD UNIT=SYSDA,DSNAME=&SYSUT1,SPACE=(3200,(80,80))
   //SYSUT2 DD UNIT=SYSDA,DSNAME=&SYSUT2,SPACE=(3200,(80,80))
   ```

```
//SYSUT3 DD UNIT=SYSDA,DSNAME=&SYSUT3,SPACE=(3200,(80,80))
//SYSLIB DD DSNAME=SYS1.MACLIB,DISP=SHR
//SYSGO DD UNIT=SYSDA,DISP=(MOD,PASS),
//         DSNAME=&LOADSET,DCB=BLKSIZE=3200,
//         SPACE=(3200,(10,10),RLSE)
//GO EXEC PGM=LOADER,REGION=100K,
//         PARM='MAP,LET,NOCALL',
//         COND=(4,LT,ASM)
//SYSLOUT DD SYSOUT=A
//SYSLIN DD DSNAME=&LOADSET,DISP=(OLD,DELETE)
//SYSUDUMP DD SYSOUT=A
```

ASMFCL (Assemble and Link):

```
//ASM EXEC PGM=IEUASM,REGION=80K,
//         PARM='LOAD,LIST,XREF'
//SYSPRINT DD SYSOUT=A
//SYSPUNCH DD SYSOUT=B
//SYSUT1 DD UNIT=SYSDA,DSNAME=&SYSUT1,SPACE=(3200,(80,80))
//SYSUT2 DD UNIT=SYSDA,DSNAME=&SYSUT2,SPACE=(3200,(80,80))
//SYSUT3 DD UNIT=SYSDA,DSNAME=&SYSUT3,SPACE=(3200,(80,80))
//SYSLIB DD DSNAME=SYS1.MACLIB,DISP=SHR
//SYSGO DD UNIT=SYSDA,DISP=(MOD,PASS),
//         DSNAME=&LOADSET,DCB=BLKSIZE=3200,
//         SPACE=(3200,(10,10),RLSE)
//LKED EXEC PGM=IEWL,REGION=100K,
//         PARM='LET,LIST,XREF,NCAL',
//         COND=(4,LT,ASM)
//SYSPRINT DD SYSOUT=A
//SYSUT1 DD UNIT=SYSDA,DSNAME=&SYSUT1,SPACE=(1024,(50,50))
//SYSLIN DD DSNAME=&LOADSET,DISP=(OLD,DELETE)
//         DD DDNAME=SYSIN
//SYSLMOD DD UNIT=SYSDA,DISP=(MOD,PASS),
//         DSNAME=&GOSET(GO),DCB=BLKSIZE=1024,
//         SPACE=(1024,(50,20),RLSE)
```

ASMFCLG (Assemble, Link, and Execute):

```
//ASM EXEC PGM=IEUASM,REGION=80K
//         PARM='LOAD,LIST,XREF'
//SYSPRINT DD SYSOUT=A
//SYSPUNCH DD SYSOUT=B
//SYSUT1 DD UNIT=SYSDA,DSNAME=&SYSUT1,SPACE=(3200,(80,80))
//SYSUT2 DD UNIT=SYSDA,DSNAME=&SYSUT2,SPACE=(3200,(80,80))
//SYSUT3 DD UNIT=SYSDA,DSNAME=&SYSUT3,SPACE=(3200,(80,80))
//SYSLIB DD DSNAME=SYS1.MACLIB,DISP=SHR
//SYSGO DD UNIT==SYSDA,DISP=(MOD,PASS),
//         DSNAME=&LOADSET,DCB=BLKSIZE=3200,
//         SPACE=(3200,(10,10),RLSE)
//LKED EXEC PGM=IEWL,REGION=100K,
//         PARM='LET,LIST,XREF,NCAL',
//         COND=(4,LT,ASM)
//SYSPRINT DD SYSOUT=A
//SYSUT1 DD UNIT=SYSDA,DSNAME=&SYSUT1,SPACE=(1024,(50,20))
//SYSLIN DD DSNAME=&LOADSET,DISP=(OLD,DELETE)
//         DD DDNAME=SYSIN
//SYSLMOD DD UNIT=SYSDA,DISP=(MOD,PASS),
//         DSNAME=&GOSET(GO),DCB=BLKSIZE=1024,
//         SPACE=(1024,(50,20),RLSE)
//GO EXEC PGM=*.LKED.SYSLMOD,
//         COND=((4,LT,ASM),(4,LT.LKED))
//SYSUDUMP DD SYSOUT=A
```

ASMFLG (Link and Execute):

```
//LKED  EXEC  PGM=IEWL,REGION=100K,
//          PARM='LET,LIST,XREF,NCAL'
//SYSPRINT  DD  SYSOUT=A
//SYSUT1  DD  UNIT=SYSDA,DSNAME=&SYSUT1,SPACE=(1024,(50,20))
//SYSLIN  DD  DDNAME=SYSIN
//SYSLMOD  DD  UNIT=SYSDA,DISP=(MOD,PASS),
//          DSNAME=&GOSET(GO),DCB=BLKSIZE=1024,
//          SPACE=(1024,(50,20,1),RLSE)
//GO  EXEC  PGM=*.LKED.SYSLMOD,
//          COND=(4,LT,LKED)
//SYSUDUMP  DD  SYSOUT=A
```

2. COBOL (ANS)

The following ANS COBOL procedures can also be considered comparable to other COBOL programming levels.

COBUC (Compile Only):

```
//COB     EXEC PGM=IKFCBLOO,REGION=130K,
//             PARM='NOLOAD'
//STEPLIB DD DSNAME=SYS1.COBLIB,DISP=SHR
//SYSPRINT DD SYSOUT=A
//SYSPUNCH DD SYSOUT=B
//SYSUT1  DD UNIT=SYSDA,DSNAME=&SYSUT1,SPACE=(460,(700,300),RLSE)
//SYSUT2  DD UNIT=SYSDA,DSNAME=&SYSUT2,SPACE=(460,(700,300),RLSE)
//SYSUT3  DD UNIT=SYSDA,DSNAME=&SYSUT3,SPACE=(460,(700,300),RLSE)
//SYSUT4  DD UNIT=SYSDA,DSNAME=&SYSUT4,SPACE=(460,(700,300),RLSE)
```

COBUCG (Compile and Load):

```
//COB     EXEC PGM=IKFCBLOO,REGION=130K
//STEPLIB DD DSNAME=SYS1.COBLIB,DISP=SHR
//SYSPRINT DD SYSOUT=A
//SYSPUNCH DD SYSOUT=B
//SYSUT1  DD UNIT=SYSDA,DSNAME=&SYSUT1,SPACE=(460,(700,300),RLSE)
//SYSUT2  DD UNIT=SYSDA,DSNAME=&SYSUT2,SPACE=(460,(700,300),RLSE)
//SYSUT3  DD UNIT=SYSDA,DSNAME=&SYSUT3,SPACE=(460,(700,300),RLSE)
//SYSUT4  DD UNIT=SYSDA,DSNAME=&SYSUT4,SPACE=(460,(700,300),RLSE)
//SYSLIN  DD UNIT=SYSDA,DISP=(MOD,PASS),
//             DSNAME=&LOADSET,DCB=BLKSIZE=3200,
//             SPACE=(3200,(20,20),RLSE)
//GO      EXEC PGM=LOADER,REGION=100K,
//             PARM='MAP,LET',
//             COND=(4,LT,COB)
//SYSLOUT DD SYSOUT=A
//SYSLIB  DD DSNAME=SYS1.COBLIB,DISP=SHR
//SYSLIN  DD DSNAME=&LOADSET,DISP=(OLD,DELETE)
//SYSUDUMP DD SYSOUT=A
//SYSOUT  DD SYSOUT=A
```

COBUCL (Compile and Link):

```
//COB     EXEC PGM=IKFCBLOO,REGION=130K
//STEPLIB DD DSNAME=SYS1.COBLIB,DISP=SHR
//SYSPRINT DD SYSOUT=A
```

```
//SYSPUNCH DD SYSOUT=B
//SYSUT1 DD UNIT=SYSDA,DSNAME=&SYSUT1,SPACE=(460,(700,300),RLSE)
//SYSUT2 DD UNIT=SYSDA,DSNAME=&SYSUT2,SPACE=(460,(700,300),RLSE)
//SYSUT3 DD UNIT=SYSDA,DSNAME=&SYSUT3,SPACE=(460,(700,300),RLSE)
//SYSUT4 DD UNIT=SYSDA,DSNAME=&SYSUT4,SPACE=(460,(700,300),RLSE)
//SYSLIN DD UNIT=SYSDA,DISP=(MOD,PASS),
//         DSNAME=&LOADSET,DCB=BLKSIZE=3200,
//         SPACE=(3200,(20,20),RLSE)
//LKED EXEC PGM=IEWL,REGION=100K,
//         PARM='LET,LIST,XREF',
//         COND=(4,LT,COB)
//SYSPRINT DD SYSOUT=A
//SYSUT1 DD UNIT=SYSDA,DSNAME=&SYSUT1,SPACE=(1024,(50,20))
//SYSLIN DD DSNAME=&LOADSET,DISP=(OLD,DELETE)
//         DD DDNAME=SYSIN
//SYSLIB DD DSNAME=SYS1.COBLIB,DISP=SHR
//SYSLMOD DD UNIT=SYSDA,DISP=(NEW,PASS),
//         DSNAME=&GOSET(RUN),DCB=BLKSIZE=1024,
//         SPACE=(1024,(50,20,1),RLSE)

COBUCLG (Compile, Link, and Execute:
//COB EXEC PGM=IKFCBLOO,REGION=130K
//STEPLIB DD DSNAME=SYS1.COBLIB,DISP=SHR
//SYSPRINT DD SYSOUT=A
//SYSPUNCH DD SYSOUT=B
//SYSUT1 DD UNIT=SYSDA,DSNAME=&SYSUT1,SPACE=(460,(700,300),RLSE)
//SYSUT2 DD UNIT=SYSDA,DSNAME=&SYSUT2,SPACE=(460,(700,300),RLSE)
//SYSUT3 DD UNIT=SYSDA,DSNAME=&SYSUT3,SPACE=(460,(700,300),RLSE)
//SYSUT4 DD UNIT=SYSDA,DSNAME=&SYSUT4,SPACE=(460,(700,300),RLSE)
//SYSLIN DD UNIT=SYSDA,DISP=(MOD,PASS),
//         DSNAME=&LOADSET,DCB=BLKSIZE=3200,
//         SPACE=(3200,(20,20),RLSE)
//LKED EXEC PGM=IEWL,REGION=100K,
//         PARM='LET,LIST,XREF',
//         COND=(4,LT,COB)
//SYSPRINT DD SYSOUT=A
//SYSUT1 DD UNIT=SYSDA,DSNAME=&SYSUT1,SPACE=(1024,(50,20))
```

```
//SYSLIN DD DSNAME=&LOADSET,DISP=(OLD,DELETE)
//        DD DDNAME=SYSIN
//SYSLIB DD DSNAME=SYS1.COBLIB,DISP=SHR
//SYSLMOD DD UNIT=SYSDA,DISP=(NEW,PASS),
//        DSNAME=&GOSET(RUN),DCB=BLKSIZE=1024,
//        SPACE=(1024,(50,20,1),RLSE)
//GO EXEC PGM=*.LKED.SYSLMOD,
//        COND=((4,LT,COB),(4,LT,LKED))
//SYSUDUMP DD SYSOUT=A
//SYSOUT DD SYSOUT=A
```

COBULG (Link and Execute):

```
//LKED   EXEC  PGM=IEWL,REGION=100K,
//        PARM='LET,LIST,XREF'
//SYSPRINT  DD  SYSOUT=A
//SYSUT1   DD   UNIT=SYSDA,DSNAME=&SYSUT1,SPACE=(1024,(50,20))
//SYSLIN   DD   DDNAME=SYSIN
//SYSLIB   DD   DSNAME=SYS1.COBLIB,DISP=SHR
//SYSLMOD  DD   UNIT=SYSDA,DISP=(NEW,PASS),
//        DSNAME=&GOSET(RUN),DCB=BLKSIZE=1024,
//        SPACE=(1024,(50,20,1),RLSE)
//GO   EXEC  PGM=*.LKED.SYSLMOD,
//        COND=(4,LT,LKED)
//SYSUDUMP   DD   SYSOUT=A
//SYSOUT   DD   SYSOUT=A
```

3. FORTRAN (G1-Level)

The following FORTRAN Level-G1 procedures can also be considered comparable to other FORTRAN programming levels.

FTG1C (Compile Only):

```
//FORT EXEC PGM=IGIFORT,REGION=130K
//STEPLIB DD DSNAME=SYS1.FORTLIB,DISP=SHR
//SYSPRINT DD SYSOUT=A
//SYSPUNCH DD SYSOUT=B
//SYSLIN DD UNIT=SYSDA,DISP=(MOD,PASS),
//        DSNAME=&LOADSET,DCB=BLKSIZE=3200,
//        SPACE=(3200,(60,60),RLSE)
```

FTG1CG (Compile and Load):

```
//FORT EXEC PGM=IGIFORT,REGION=130K
//STEPLIB DD DSNAME=SYS1.FORTLIB,DISP=SHR
//SYSPRINT DD SYSOUT=A
//SYSPUNCH DD SYSOUT=B
//SYSLIN DD UNIT=SYSDA,DISP=(MOD,PASS),
//         DSNAME=&LOADSET,DCB=BLKSIZE=3200,
//         SPACE=(3200,(60,60),RLSE)
//GO EXEC PGM=LOADER,REGION=100K,
//         PARM='MAP,LET',
//         COND=(4,LT,FORT)
//SYSLOUT DD SYSOUT=A
//SYSLIB DD DSNAME=SYS1.FORTLIB,DISP=SHR
//SYSLIN DD DSNAME=&LOADSET,DISP=(OLD,DELETE)
//SYSUDUMP DD SYSOUT=A
//FT05F001 DD DDNAME=SYSIN
//FT06F001 DD SYSOUT=A
//FT07F001 DD SYSOUT=B
```

FTG1CL (Compile and Link):

```
//FORT EXEC PGM=IGIFORT,REGION=130K
//STEPLIB DD DSNAME=SYS1.FORTLIB,DISP=SHR
//SYSPRINT DD SYSOUT=A
//SYSPUNCH DD SYSOUT=B
//SYSLIN DD UNIT=SYSDA,DISP=(MOD,PASS),
//         DSNAME=&LOADSET,DCB=BLKSIZE=3200,
//         SPACE=(3200,(60,60),RLSE)
//LKED EXEC PGM=IEWL,REGION=100K,
//         PARM='LET,LIST,XREF',
//         COND=(4,LT,FORT)
//SYSPRINT DD SYSOUT=A
//SYSUT1 DD UNIT=SYSDA,DSNAME=&SYSUT1,SPACE=(1024,(20,20))
//SYSLIN DD DSNAME=&LOADSET,DISP=(OLD,DELETE)
//         DD DDNAME=SYSIN
//SYSLIB DD DSNAME=SYS1.FORTLIB,DISP=SHR
//SYSLMOD DD UNIT=SYSDA,DISP=(NEW,PASS),
//         DSNAME=&GOSET(MAIN),DCB=BLKSIZE=1024,
//         SPACE=((1024,(20,20),1),RLSE)
```

FTG1CLG (Compile, Link, and Execute):

```
//FORT EXEC PGM=IGIFORT,REGION=130K
//STEPLIB DD DSNAME=SYS1.FORTLIB,DISP=SHR
//SYSPRINT DD SYSOUT=A
//SYSPUNCH DD SYSOUT=B
//        DSNAME=&LOADSET,DCB=BLKSIZE=3200,
//        SPACE=(3200,(60,60),RLSE)
//LKED EXEC PGM=IEWL,REGION=100K,
//        PARM='LET,LIST,XREF',
//        COND=(4,LT,FORT)
//SYSPRINT DD SYSOUT=A
//SYSUT1 DD UNIT=SYSDA,DSNAME=&SYSUT1,SPACE=(1024,(20,20))
//SYSLIN DD DSNAME=&LOADSET,DISP=(OLD,DELETE)
//        DD DDNAME=SYSIN
//SYSLIB DD DSNAME=SYS1.FORTLIB,DISP=SHR
//SYSLMOD DD UNIT=SYSDA,DISP=(NEW,PASS),
//        DSNAME=&GOSET(MAIN),DCB=BLKSIZE=1024,
//        SPACE=(1024,(20,20,1),RLSE)
//GO EXEC PGM=*.LKED.SYSLMOD,
//        COND=((4,LT,COB),(4,LT,LKED))
//SYSUDUMP DD SYSOUT=A
//FT05F001 DD DDNAME=SYSIN
//FT06F001 DD SYSOUT=A
//FT07F001 DD SYSOUT=B
```

FTG1LG (Link and Execute):

```
//LKED  EXEC  PGM=IEWL,REGION=100K,
//        PARM='LET,LIST,XREF'
//SYSPRINT  DD  SYSOUT=A
//SYSUT1  DD  UNIT=SYSDA,DSNAME=&SYSUT1,SPACE=(1024,(50,20))
//SYSLIN  DD  DDNAME=SYSIN
//SYSLMOD  DD  UNIT=SYSDA,DISP=(NEW,PASS),
//        DSNAME=&GOSET(MAIN),DCB=BLKSIZE=1024,
//        SPACE=(1024,(50,20,1),RLSE)
//GO  EXEC  PGM=*.LKED.SYSLMOD,
//        COND=(4,LT,LKED)
```

```
//SYSUDUMP   DD   SYSOUT=A
//FT05F001   DD   DDNAME=SYSIN
//FT06F001   DD   SYSOUT=A
//FT07F001   DD   SYSOUT=B
```

4. LINKAGE EDITOR

LKED (Link Only):

```
//LKED EXEC PGM=IEWL,REGION=100K,
//        PARM='XREF,LIST,LET,NCAL'
//SYSPRINT DD SYSOUT=A
//SYSUT1 DD UNIT=SYSDA,DSNAME=&SYSUT1,SPACE=(1024,(200,20))
//SYSLIN DD DDNAME=SYSIN
//SYSLMOD DD UNIT=SYSDA,DISP=(MOD,PASS),
//        DSNAME=&GOSET(GO),DCB=BLKSIZE=1024,
//        SPACE=(1024,(200,20))
```

5. PL/1 (F-Level)

The following PROGRAMMING LANGUAGE/1 (PL/1) Level-F procedures can also be considered comparable to other PL/1 programming levels.

PL1LFC (Compile Only):

```
//PL1L EXEC PGM=IEMMA,REGION=100K,
//        PARM='NOLOAD'
//SYSPRINT DD SYSOUT=A
//SYSPUNCH DD SYSOUT=B
//SYSUT3 DD UNIT=SYSDA,
//        DSNAME=&SYSUT3,DCB=BLKSIZE=3200,
//        SPACE=(3200,(10,10))
//SYSUT1 DD UNIT=SYSDA,
//        DSNAME=&SYSUT1,DCB=BLKSIZE=1024,
//        SPACE=(1024,(60,60))
```

FL1LFCG (Compile and Load):

```
//PL1L EXEC PGM=IEMMA,REGION=100K
//SYSPRINT DD SYSOUT=A
//SYSPUNCH DD SYSOUT=B
```

```
//SYSUT3 DD UNIT=SYSDA,
//         DSNAME=&SYSUT3,DCB=BLKSIZE=3200,
//         SPACE=(3200,(10,10))
//SYSUT1 DD UNIT=SYSDA,
//         DSNAME=&SYSUT1,DCB=BLKSIZE=1024,
//         SPACE=(1024,(60,60))
//SYSLIN DD UNIT=SYSDA,DISP=(MOD,PASS),
//         DSNAME=&LOADSET,DCB=BLKSIZE=3200,
//         SPACE=(3200,(10,10),RLSE)
//GO EXEC PGM=LOADER,REGION=100K,
//         PARM='MAP,LET',
//         COND=(4,LT,PL1L)
//SYSLOUT DD SYSOUT=A
//SYSLIB DD DSNAME=SYS1.PL1LIB,DISP=SHR
//SYSLIN DD DSNAME=&LOADSET,DISP=(OLD,DELETE)
//SYSUDUMP DD SYSOUT=A
//SYSPRINT DD SYSOUT=A
```

PL1LFCL (Compile and Link):

```
//PL1L EXEC PGM=IEMMA,REGION=100K
//SYSPRINT DD SYSOUT=A
//SYSPUNCH DD SYSOUT=B
//SYSUT3 DD UNIT=SYSDA,
//         DSNAME=&SYSUT3,DCB=BLKSIZE=3200,
//         SPACE=(3200,(10,10))
//SYSUT1 DD UNIT=SYSDA,
//         DSNAME=&SYSUT1,DCB=BLKSIZE=1024,
//         SPACE=(1024,(60,60))
//SYSLIN DD UNIT=SYSDA,DISP=(MOD,PASS),
//         DSNAME=&LOADSET,DCB=BLKSIZE=3200,
//         SPACE=(3200,(10,10),RLSE)
//LKED EXEC PGM=IEWL,REGION=100K,
//         PARM='LET,LIST,XREF',
//         COND=(4,LT,PL1L)
//SYSPRINT DD SYSOUT=A
//SYSUT1 DD UNIT=SYSDA,DSNAME=&SYSUT1,SPACE=(1024,(200,20))
//SYSLIN DD DSNAME=&LOADSET,DISP=(OLD,DELETE)
```

```
//        DD DDNAME=SYSIN
//SYSLIB DD DSNAME=SYS1.PL1LIB,DISP=SHR
//SYSLMOD DD UNIT=SYSDA,DISP=(MOD,PASS),
//        DSNAME=&GOSET(GO),DCB=BLKSIZE=1024,
//        SPACE=(1024,(50,20),RLSE)
```

PL1LFCLG (Compile, Link, and Execute):
```
//PL1L EXEC PGM=IEMMA,REGION=100K
//SYSPRINT DD SYSOUT=A
//SYSPUNCH DD SYSOUT=B
//SYSUT3 DD UNIT=SYSDA,
//        DSNAME=&SYSUT3,DCB=BLKSIZE=3200,
//        SPACE=(3200,(10,10))
//SYSUT1 DD UNIT=SYSDA,
//        DSNAME=&SYSUT1,DCB=BLKSIZE=1024,
//        SPACE=(1024,(60,60))
//SYSLIN DD UNIT=SYSDA,DISP=(MOD,PASS),
//        DSNAME=&LOADSET,DCB=BLKSIZE=3200,
//        SPACE=(3200,(10,10),RLSE)
//LKED EXEC PGM=IEWL,REGION=100K,
//        PARM='LET,LIST,XREF',
//        COND=(4,LT,PL1L)
//SYSPRINT DD SYSOUT=A
//SYSUT1 DD UNIT=SYSDA,DSNAME=&SYSUT1,SPACE=(1024,(200,20))
//SYSLIN DD DSNAME=&LOADSET,DISP=(OLD,DELETE)
//        DD DDNAME=SYSIN
//SYSLIB DD DSNAME=SYS1.PL1LIB,DISP=SHR
//SYSLMOD DD UNIT=SYSDA,DISP=(MOD,PASS),
//        DSNAME=&GOSET(GO),DCB=BLKSIZE=1024,
//        SPACE=(1024,(50,20,1),RLSE)
//GO EXEC PGM=*.LKED.SYSLMOD,
//        COND=((4,LT,PL1L),(4,LT,LKED))
//SYSUDUMP DD SYSOUT=A
//SYSPRINT DD SYSOUT=A
```

PL1LFLG (Link and Execute):
```
//LKED  EXEC  PGM=IEWL,REGION=100K,
//        PARM='LET,LIST,XREF'
```

```
//SYSPRINT  DD  SYSOUT=A
//SYSUT1   DD   UNIT=SYSDA,DSNAME=&SYSUT1,SPACE=(1024,(50,20))
//SYSLIN   DD   DDNAME=SYSIN
//SYSLIB   DD   DSNAME=SYS1.PL1LIB,DISP=SHR
//SYSLMOD   DD   UNIT=SYSDA,DISP=(MOD,PASS),
//         DSNAME=&GOSET(GO),DCB=BLKSIZE=1024,
//         SPACE=(1024,(50,20,1),RLSE)
//GO  EXEC  PGM=*.LKED.SYSLMOD,
//        COND=(4,LT,LKED)
//SYSUDUMP  DD  SYSOUT=A
//SYSPRINT  DD  SYSOUT=A
```

6. SORT / MERGE

SORT (With Linkage):
```
//SORT EXEC PGM=IERRCO00,REGION=98K
//SYSOUT DD SYSOUT=A
//SORTLIB DD DSNAME=SYS1.SORTLIB,DISP=SHR
//SYSPRINT DD DUMMY
//SYSLMOD DD DSNAME=&GOSET,UNIT=SYSDA,SPACE=(3600,(20,20,1))
//SYSLIN DD DSNAME=&LOADSET,UNIT=SYSDA,SPACE=(80,(10,10))
//SYSUT1 DD DSNAME=&SYSUT1,SPACE=(1000,(60,20)),
//        UNIT=(SYSDA,SEP=(SORTLIB,SYSLMOD,SYSLIN))
```

SORTD (Sort Only):
```
//SORT EXEC PGM=IERRCO00,REGION=26K
//SYSOUT DD SYSOUT=A
//SORTLIB DD DSNAME=SYS1.SORTLIB,DISP=SHR
```

Installation-Defined:
```
//SORT EXEC PGM=IERRCO00,REGION=98K
//SYSOUT DD SYSOUT=A
//SORTLIB DD DSNAME=SYS1.SORTLIB,DISP=SHR
//SORTWK01 DD UNIT=SYSDA,SPACE=(TRK,(100),,CONTIG)
//SORTWK02 DD UNIT=SYSDA,SPACE=(TRK,(100),,CONTIG)
//SORTWK03 DD UNIT=SYSDA,SPACE=(TRK,(100),,CONTIG)
//SORTWK04 DD UNIT=SYSDA,SPACE=(TRK,(100),,CONTIG)
//SORTWK05 DD UNIT=SYSDA,SPACE=(TRK,(100),,CONTIG)
```

C

Compiler, Assembler, Linkage Editor, Loader, and Sort/Merge Parameter Options (A Desk Reference)

1. COBOL COMPILERS

Figure C.1 COBOL Compiler Parm Parameter Specifications

Compiler Default	Compiler Option	Item Description
APOST	QUOTE	Indicates that either the apostrophe (') or quote (") is valid program character code.
BUF=xxxxxx	BUF=yyyyyy	Compiler buffer main storage allocation, where xxxxxx = installation default (minimum 2768) and yyyyyy = user specification.
FLAGW	FLAGE	Specifies that Warning (W) messages or Error (E) messages only are to be printed.
LIB	NOLIB	Indicates whether or not to open the Copy Library for compiler access.

LINECNT=60	LINECNT=yy	Number of print lines per page, where yy = user specification.
LOAD	NOLOAD	Specifies whether the program object module is (LOAD) or is not (NOLOAD) to be created in the SYSLIN ddname disk file.
NOBATCH	BATCH	Indicates whether a single program (NOBATCH) or a group of programs (BATCH) are to be compiled this step.
NOCLIST	CLIST	Specifies that a Condensed Listing (CLIST) of the source program's assembly language representation is to be provided. Option recommended.
NODECK	DECK	Specifies whether a program object deck is or is not to be created in the SYSPUNCH ddname punch file.
NODMAP	DMAP	Specifies that a Data Map (DMAP) listing of program variables is to be provided. Option recommended.
NODYNAM	DYNAM	Provides for dynamic (DYNAM) allocation of program modules at execution time rather than being link-edited to form a single load module.
NOFLOW	FLOW FLOW=yy	Specifies whether error facility procedure name trace messages are (FLOW or FLOW=yy) or are not (NOFLOW) to be written to the SYSDBOUT ddname print file. Default is generally 99 procedures, though yy=user specification.

NONAME	NAME	Coupled with the BATCH option, NAME specifies that a separate object module is to be created for each program compiled. NONAME specifies a single module is to be created.
NONUM	NUM	Specifies that program line numbers (NUM) should be printed rather than compiler-generated program source statement numbers.
NOOPTIMIZE	OPTIMIZE	Generates a nonoptimized or optimized program object module.
NOPMAP	PMAP	Specifies that a Procedure Map (PMAP) listing of program assignments, tables, and an assembly language representation of the source program are to be provided. Option recommended after all testing completed.
NOPRINT	PRINT PRINT (*) PRINT (Dsname)	For Time Sharing Option (TSO) only. Indicates whether source program listing is not to be printed (NOPRINT), written to secondary storage (PRINT), routed to terminal (PRINT (*)), or written to the specified data set name file (PRINT (Dsname)).
NORESIDENT	RESIDENT	Specifies that the source program library feature should be utilized.
NOSTATE	STATE	Prints, when possible, the program source statement (STATE) number being executed upon abnormal termination, Option recommended.

NOSUPMAP	SUPMAP	Indicates if creation of the object module should be suppressed (SUPMAP) upon occurrence of compiler-discovered source program errors.
NOSYMDMP	SYMDMP	Requests a symbolic dump (SYMSMP) of specific program, data, and buffer areas.
NOSYNTAX	SYNTAX NOCSTNTAX CSYNTAX	Indicates whether the source program is to be edited for syntax errors (C or greater) only (SYNTAX), or conditional errors (E or greater) only (CSYNTAX). If error is found, creation of object module is suspended.
NOTERM	TERM	For Time Sharing Option (TSO) only. Indicates that progress messages and diagnostics are to be printed to a SYSTERM ddname terminal (TERM) data set.
NOTRUNC	TRUNC	Allows truncation (TRUNC) when moving Usage Computational items, i.e., the Binary form of data representation.
NOXREF	XREF	Specifies that an unsorted Cross-Reference Table (XREF) is desired. Option recommended.
SEQ	NOSEQ	Avoids the checking of source statement number sequence (NOSEQ).
SIZE=xxxxxx	SIZE=yyyyyy	Compiler main storage allocation, where xxxxxx = installation default (e.g., 020000) and yyyyyy = user specification.

SOURCE	NOSOURCE	Specifies that a source program listing is not (NOSOURCE) to be provided.
SPACE1	SPACE2 SPACE3	Indicates that the source program listing is to be single-, double-, or triple-spaced, respectively.
SYST	SYSx	Defines ddname for debug and display output as SYSOUT or SYSOUTx where x = 0 to 9, or A to Z excluding T.
VERB	NOVERB	Specifies that procedure verbs are not to be listed (NOVERB) in the Procedure Map or Condensed Listing.
ZWB	NOZWB	Specifies that the compiler should not drop the sign (NOZWB) from any signed external decimal fields if they are to be compared with any alphanumeric fields.

2. FORTRAN COMPILERS

Figure C.2 FORTRAN Compiler Parm Parameter Specifications

Compiler Default	Compiler Option	Item Description
EBCDIC	BCD	Indicates that the source program is written in Binary Coded Decimal (BCD) or the Extended Binary Coded Decimal Interchange Code (EBCDIC).
LINECNT=50	LINECNT=yy	Number of print lines per page, where yy = user specification.

LOAD	NOLOAD	Specifies whether the program object module is (LOAD) or is not (NOLOAD) to be created in the SYSLIN ddname disk file.
NAME=MAIN	NAME=yyyyyy	Provides a name to the program object module, where yyyyyy = user specification.
NODECK	DECK	Specifies that the program object module is to be punched (DECK) from the SYSPUNCH ddname punch card file.
NOEDIT (H Level Only)	EDIT	Indicates that a structured source program listing depicting program loop and logical conditions (EDIT) should be provided.
NOID	ID	Specifies that internal source statement numbers (ID) for external call instructions should be printed in the trace tables.
NOLIST	LIST	Specifies that an assembly language representation (LIST) of the source program should be provided. Option recommended.
NOMAP	MAP	Specifies that a location map (MAP) of program variable names, subprograms, and format statements is to be provided. Option recommended.
NOXREF (H Level Only)	XREF	Specifies that a Cross-Reference Table (XREF) is desired. Option recommended.
SOURCE	NOSOURCE	Specifies that a source program listing is not (NOSOURCE) to be provided.

OPT=0 (H Level Only)	OPT=1 OPT=2	Indicates that no optimizing (0), single-loop optimizing (1), or multiple-loop optimizing (2) techniques are to be utilized when creating the program object module.
SIZE=xxxxK (H Level Only)	SIZE=yyyyK	Compiler main storage allocation, where xxxx = installation default (e.g., 0020K) and yyyy = user specification.

3. PL/1 COMPILERS

Figure C.3 PL/1 Compiler Parm Parameter Specifications

Compiler Default	Compiler Option	Item Description
CHARSET(60 EBCDIC)	CHARSET(48) CHARSET(60) CHARSET(48 BCD) CHARSET(48 EBCDIC) CHARSET(60 BCD)	Indicates whether the 48- or 60-character set is to be utilized, and if the Binary Coded Decimal (BCD) or Extended Binary Coded Decimal Interchange Code (EBCDIC) form of data representation is to be used.
--	CONTROL('Password')	Specifies that compiler options deleted at this dp facility are to be available for this compile, where Password is user-coded and conforms to the installation's control password.
FLAG(I)	FLAG(W) FLAG(E) FLAG(S)	Specifies at what error level appropriate messages should begin to be provided, where

		I=all, W=warning, E=standard error, S=severe error, and FLAG above =FLAG(W).
INSOURCE	NOINSOURCE	Specifies only when the preprocessor is used that a source program listing including preprocessor statements is not (NOINSOURCE) to be provided.
LINECNT=55	LINECNT=yy	Number of print lines per page, where yy = user specification.
LMESSAGE	SMESSAGE	Indicates that compiler messages are to be provided in long (L) or short (S) form.
MARGINS(2,72,0) for Fixed-Length Records MARGINS(10,100,0) for Variable-Length Records	MARGINS(x,y,z)	Specifies location of PL/1 source program statements, where x = user left-hand column, y = user right-hand column, and z = ANS control character column or a zero for its absence.
--	NAME('Name')	Indicates that a Linkage Editor Name statement should be created where Name=user Program Name.
NOAGGREGATE	AGGREGATE	Indicates that an aggregate-length table (AGGREGATE) is to be provided.
NOATTRIBUTES	ATTRIBUTES	Indicates that an indentifier attributes table (ATTRIBUTES) is to be provided.
NOCOMPILE(S)	NOCOMPILE(W) NOCOMPILE(E)	Specifies at what error level compilation should begin to be

	COMPILE	discontinued, where W = warning,
	NOCOMPILE	E = standard error, E = severe error,
		NOCOMPILE = stop after syntax
		check, and COMPILE = do not
		discontinue compilation if
		possible.
NOCOUNT	COUNT	Indicates that a count of each
		source statement's execution
		is to be maintained when the
		program is executed.
NODECK	DECK	Specifies whether a program
		object deck is or is not to be
		created in the SYSPUNCH ddname
		punch card file.
NODUMP	DUMP	Specifies that a main storage
		dump should be written to the
		ddname SYSPRINT print file if the
		compile step abnormally terminates.
NOESD	ESD	Specifies that an External
		Symbol Dictionary (ESD) is to
		be provided.
NOFLOW	FLOW	Indicates that a flow of
	FLOW(x,y)	program control is to be
		provided (FLOW) for a default
		maximum of 25 entries and 10
		procedures, where x = user number
		of entries specification and y =
		user number of procedures
		specification.

NOGONUMBER	GONUMBER	Print, when possible, the program source statement number (GONUMBER) being executed upon abnormal termination using additional line number information for analysis.
NOGOSTMT	GOSTMT	Print, when possible, the program source statement number (GOSTMT) being executed upon abnormal termination. Option recommended.
NOIMPRECISE	IMPRECISE	Specifies that program object module should be modified to improve upon identification of specific System 360 Model 91 or 195 interrupts.
NOINCLUDE	INCLUDE	Indicates that the compiler is to use PL/1 preprocessor %INCLUDE statements (INCLUDE) rather than calling the preprocessor itself.
NOLIST	LIST LIST(x) LIST(x,y)	Specifies that an assembly language representation of the source program in lieu of a Table of Offsets should be provided, where x=number of first source statement desired, and y=number of last source statement desired. Option recommended after all testing completed. NOLIST, SOURCE, and NOSTMT may also need to be provided to obtain a Table of Offsets.

NOMACRO	MACRO	Specifies that the PL/1 preprocessor is to process the source program (MACRO).
NOMAP	MAP	Specifies that a location map (MAP) of the program is to be provided. Option recommended.
NOMARGIN1	MARGIN1('x')	Specifies that a left- and right-hand margin indicator (MARGIN1) should be printed, where x = the character to be used.
NOMDECK	MDECK	Specifies whether a macro program deck from the PL/1 preprocessor is or is not to be created in the SYSPUNCH ddname punchcard file.
NONEST	NEST	Specifies that nested program loops should be fully identified in the source listing.
NONUMBER	NUMBER	Specifies that source program sequence numbers should be used for compiler program listings.
NOOFFSET	OFFSET	Specifies that a statement and line number table of offsets should be provided. Option recommended. NOLIST, SOURCE, and NOSTMT may also need to be provided to obtain a Table of Offsets.
NOOPTIMIZE	OPTIMIZE(0) OPTIMIZE(TIME)	Generates a nonoptimized or optimized program object module,

	OPTIMIZE(2)	where 0 = nonoptimized, TIME and 2 = optimized.
NOSEQUENCE	SEQUENCE(x,y)	Specific location of PL/1 statement sequence numbers, where x = user left-hand column, and y = user right-hand column.
NOSTORAGE	STORAGE	Indicates that main storage requirements (STORAGE) for the program object module should be provided.
NOSYNTAX(S)	NOSYNTAX(W) NOSYNTAX(E) SYNTAX	Specifies at what error level syntax checking should stop (NOSYNTAX), where W = warning, E = standard unrecoverable error, S = severe error, and SYNTAX = do not stop if possible.
NOTERMINAL	TERMINAL(Options)	Time Sharing Options (TSO) only. Specifies which components of compiler output are to be routed to the terminal, where Options = various compiler options in this table.
NOXREF	XREF	Specifies that a Cross-Reference Table is desired. Option recommended.
OBJECT	NOOBJECT	Specifies whether the program object module is or is not to be created in the SYSLIN ddname disk file.

373

OPTIONS	NOOPTIONS	Indicates that a listing of compiler defaults and options in effect should be provided.
SIZE(MAX)	SIZE(yyyyyyyy) SIZE(yyyyyK) SIZE(-yyyyyy) SIZE(-yyyK)	Limits the amount of main storage to be used by the compiler, where y's = bytes of main storage, K = 1024 bytes of main storage, MAX directs compiler to obtain as much main storage as possible, and the- ('-') specifies MAX with a release of the number of bytes indicated.
SOURCE	NOSOURCE	Specifies that a source program listing including preprocessor statements is not (NOSOURCE) to be provided. NOLIST, SOURCE, and NOSTMT may also need to be provided to obtain a Table of Offsets.
STMT	NOSTMT	Indicates that each source statement is to be counted and that this number is to be used to identify statements in various compiler outputs, NOLIST, SOURCE, and NOSTMT may also need to be provided to obtain a Table of Offsets.

4. ASSEMBLERS

Figure C.4 ASSEMBLER Parm Parameter Specifications

Assembler Default	Assembler Option	Item Description
ALGN	NOALGN	Indicates that the alignment error

374

		diagnostic message should not be provided (NOALGN).
DECK	NODECK	Specifies whether a program object deck is or is not to be created in the SYSPUNCH ddname punchcard file.
LINECNT=55	LINECNT=yy	Number of print lines per page, where yy = user specification.
LIST	NOLIST	Specifies that the assembler language source listing should not be provided (NOLIST).
NOLOAD	LOAD	Specifies whether the program object module is or is not to be created in the SYSGO ddname disk file.
NONUM	NUM	Specifies that program line numbers (NUM) written to ddname SYSTERM should be printed.
NORENT	RENT	Indicates that additional edit checks should be made for reenterable program code errors (RENT).
NOSTMT	STMT	Indicates that diagnostic messages written to ddname SYSTERM are to contain source statement numbers.
NOTERM	TERM	Indicates that progress messages and diagnostics are to be printed to a SYSTERM ddname terminal (TERM) data set.
NOTEST	TEST	Indicates that the program object module

		is to contain a table for a test translator routine (TEST).
OS	DOS	Specifies that the assembler program is to operate as if it were in a Disk Operating System (DOS) environment.
XREF	NOXREF	Specifies that a Cross-Reference Table is not desired (NOXREF).

5. LINKAGE EDITOR

Figure C.5 Linkage Editor Parm Parameter Specifications

Linkage Editor*	Item Description
DC	Downward Compatible (DC). Must be specified if program load modules created by the Level-F linkage are desired to be processed by the Level-E linkage editor.
DCBS	Data Control Block Size (DCBS). Allows blocksize to be specified via JCL to the Data Control Block area for the ddname SYSLMOD load module file.
HIAR	Hierarchy (HIAR). Assigns the hierarchy format attribute. Used when main storage hierarchy is supported by the Operating System.
LET	Let (LET). Program load module will be marked executable though one or more error conditions which may make execution impossible have been encountered.

*Linkage Editor defaults are denoted by the absence of a coded option.

LIST	List (LIST). Provides a list of Linkage Editor Control Statements utilized.
MAP	Map (MAP). Provides a map listing of the relative location and length of each program and subprogram module.
NCAL	No Call (NCAL). Automatic calls to SYSLIB ddname libraries will not be made to resolve external references. The LIBRARY statement also cannot be used. The program load module is marked as executable, however.
NE	Not Editable (NE). Output load module will not contain an External Symbol Dictionary. Saves space but cannot be reprocessed by the linkage editor.
OL	Only Loadable (OL). Program module can be placed in main storage by a LOAD macro only. Saves space but LINK, XCTL, and ATTACH macros cannot be used.
OVLY	Overlay (OVLY). Must be specified if the program overlay-processing feature is to be utilized.
REFR	Refreshable (REFR). Refreshable program modules can be replaced by a new copy during execution.
RENT REUS	Program Reusability Attributes: Reenterable (RENT) and Serially Reusable (REUS). Reenterable modules can be executed by more than one task at the same time. Serially reusable modules can be executed by only one task at the same time.

377

Nonreusable modules must request a new copy for each task to be executed.

SCTR	Scatter (SCTR). Program load modules with Scatter Format need not be loaded in one contiguous area of main storage, i.e., dynamic loading. Opposite of block loading.
SIZE=(xxxxxx, yyyyyy) SIZE=(xxxK,yyyK)	Main Storage Allocation (SIZE), where xxxxxx and xxxK = maximum number of bytes to be allocated for the linkage editor program including buffers, while yyyyyy and yyyK = maximum number of bytes to be allocated for buffer area only.
TERM	Terminal (TERM). Indicates that progress messages and diagnostics are to be printed to a SYSTERM ddname terminal data set.
TEST	Test (TEST). Program load module is to be tested using the Operating System's test translator (TESTRAN) or the Time Sharing Option's (TSO) test command.
XCAL	Exclusive Call (XCAL). Program load module will be marked as executable though a warning message will be given for all valid exclusive references made between overlay segments.
XREF	Cross-Reference Table (XREF). Provides a Cross-Reference Table of the output load module in addition to a map (MAP) listing.

6. LOADER

Figure C.6 Loader Parm Parameter Specifications

Loader Default	Loader Option	Item Description
CALL	NCAL NOCALL	No Call (NCAL or NOCALL). Automatic calls to SYSLIB ddname libraries will not be made to resolve external references.
--	EP=Name	Entry Point (EP). Name indicates the external name for an entry point in the program to be executed.
NAME=**GO	NAME=Name	Name indicates a program name to identify the program to be executed.
NOFLOW	FLOW FLOW=yy	Specifies whether error facility procedure name trace messages are (FLOW or FLOW=yy) or are not (NOFLOW) to be written to the SYSDBOUT ddname print file. Default is generally 99 procedures, though yy = user specification. If this program option is coded here rather than at compile time, a slash (/) must be coded prior to the specification. It must also be positioned last among the options coded, e.g., PARM.GO='NOCALL,NORES, /FLOW'.
NOLET	LET	Executable program module will be allowed (LET) to continue even though one or more errors occurred during the loader process.

NOMAP	MAP	Provides a map listing of the relative location and length of each program and subprogram module.
NOTERM	TERM	Terminal (TERM). Indicates that progress messages and diagnostics are to be printed to a SYSTERM ddname terminal data set.
PRINT	NOPRINT	Indicates that diagnostic messages are to be printed to the SYSLOUT ddname print file.
RES	NORES	No Resident Search (NORES). Automatic calls to the link pack queue area will not be made.
SIZE=100K	SIZE=yyyyyK	Main Storage Allocation (SIZE), where yyyyK = maximum number of bytes to be allocated for loader use including buffers.

7. SORT/MERGE PROGRAM

Figure C.7 Sort/Merge Parm Parameter Specifications

Sort/Merge Option*	Item Description
BALN	Balance (BALN). Utilizes the Balanced Tape or Direct Access Technique for sort work distribution.
CORE=yyyyyy	Main Storage Allocation (CORE), where yyyyyy = number of bytes to be allocated for the sort/merge program including buffers.

CRCX	Criss Cross (CRCX). Utilizes the Criss Cross Direct Access Technique for sort work distribution.
DIAG	Diagnostics (DIAG). Creates detailed diagnostic messages for use in solving severe sort/merge problems.
MSG= $\begin{cases} AC \\ AP \\ CC \\ CP \\ NO \end{cases}$	Message (MSG). Modifies installation message default, where AC=All Messages to Console, AP=All Messages to Printer, CC=Critical Messages to Console, CP=Critical Messages to Printer, and NO=No Messages.
OSCL	Oscillating (OSCL). Utilizes the Oscillating Tape Technique for sort work distribution.
POLY	Polyphase (POLY). Utilizes the Polyphase Tape Technique for sort work distribution.

*Sort/Merge defaults are denoted by the absence of a coded option.

D

JCL and Utility Program Glossary (42 Common Terms)

The following gloassary is intended to clarify terminology frequently used when discussing JCL coding and Utility procedures.

Assembler - A program which translates an assembly source program to a relocatable object module on a 1-for-1 machine language basis. Macro statements generate more than one assembly statement. Nevertheless, one machine language statement is created from each assembly statement.

Backward Reference - The technique of referring back to a previous file, procedure step, and/or JCL step by coding appropriate ddnames, procedure stepnames, and/or JCL stepnames rather than the actual parameter value itself. All referbacks are preceded by an asterisk and period (*.) after the keyword's equal (=) sign.

Buffer - An area of main storage into which blocks of data are moved one at a time during processing. Data is transferred from a physical device through a channel to a buffer for program use on input. On output, data is created from the program to a buffer through a channel to a physical device.

Catalogue - An area of storage, usually disk, where the characteristics of data sets are stored and accessed by name. These characteristics as described by JCL include Unit, Volume(s), and Data Set Sequence Number (tape).

Central Processing Unit (CPU) - That portion of a computer system which interprets and controls the execution of program machine instructions as opposed to input/output work.

Compiler - A program which translates a high-level language source program to a relocatable object module on a greater than 1-for-1 machine language basis. Most higher-level language statements generate more than one assembly/machine language statement.

Concatenation - The technique of "stringing" together two or more independent data sets for the purpose of processing as if they were all one program file.

Data Set - A JCL term synonymous with "file," that is, a collection of related records. Label identification records are included in this term. A data set name, assigned by the programmer/analyst when the file was created, is stored in the label and is so referenced.

Ddname - A name which identifies each logical program file and the physical files described in the JCL. The ddname is the only link between program and JCL file description. It can also be used for referback purposes.

DD Statement - One of three basic types of JCL Statements (JOB, EXEC, DD). The DD (Data Definition) statement describes the characteristics of a data set and must be coded for each file to be processed.

Dump - A printed representation of the contents of main storage at a given moment in time. Used for file- and/or program-debugging purposes.

EXEC Statement - One of three basic types of JCL Statements (JOB, EXEC, DD). The EXEC (Execute) statement describes the characteristics of the program or procedure to be called and must be coded for each step of a given job.

File Organization - The technique of arranging a collection of records in the most effective processing manner. The four basic types are: Physical Sequential, Indexed Sequential, Direct Access, and Partitioned Organization.

Generation Data Sets - Data sets used in creating, saving, and cataloguing more than one file of the same name though of different generations. They are used to minimize JCL modifications and coding.

Input/Output (I/O) - A term used to describe activities which relate to the transfer of data into or out of a buffer area. At these moments in time the Central Processing Unit (CPU) is not being utilized to execute the program of concern.

Job - A set of JCL consisting of one or more steps as described by the programmer/analyst. Jobs are delineated from one another by the occurrence of a Job statement.

Job Classification System - A method of grouping jobs with similar characteristics into the same job class. Jobs with dissimilar characteristics, that is, different job classes, provide a good processing mix and tend to increase total thruput.

Job Control Language (JCL) - JCL is the interface between the user and the Operating System. It is the communication tool used to activate and coordinate the many hardware and software facilities available to accomplish a given data processing task.

Jobname - A name which identifies a particular job. Dp installations generally apply additional naming rules and conventions to jobnames.

JOB Statement - One of three basic types of JCL Statements (JOB, EXEC, DD). The JOB statement describes conditions and characteristics of the job to be processed.

Keyword Parameter - A JCL parameter signified by the presence of a special set of system-recognizable characters, usually followed by an equal sign and one or more value specifications.

Label - A series of records placed before and after the actual data to be processed. Labels contain the characteristics of a data set and are used for verification purposes. DCB information can also be obtained from the label records.

Library - A Partitioned Data Set (PDS) where programs, procedures, and/or data may be stored as members, generally on disk. Three types of libraries may be accessed: Temporary, System, and Private.

Linkage Editor - A program which "links" or attaches object modules and routines, thus satisfying external references to form a re-locatable executable load module. Program names may be assigned here and the module saved. Overlay tree structures can also be defined to the linkage editor and appropriate segment references satisfied. The linkage editor is not specific to a unique source programming language.

Loader - A program which combines the basic functions of the linkage editor with the loading and execution of a program module into one step. Program names may not be assigned, nor their modules saved. Overlay capabilities are also not available.

Member - A portion or subdivision of a Partitioned Data Set (PDS). Members, which are named, may consist of programs, procedures, and/or data. PDS's are commonly referred to as libraries; thus the term "library member."

Multivolume Data Set - A data set so large that it requires more than one storage volume, that is, 1 of 2, 2 of 2, etc.

Object Module - A set of machine language instructions to be executed as a program upon completion of the linkage or loader process.

Operating System - A group of programs (system software) which control, process, translate, and service a computer configuration (hardware), by automatically supervising a computer's operation to the fullest extent possible, thus maximizing thruput of user programs (application software) and file processing.

OS Components - The components of the Operating System (OS) are the Control Program and Processing Programs. The Control Program performs Job, Task, and Data Management functions. Processing Programs include Assemblers, Compilers, the Linkage Editor, Loader, Sort/Merge, and other service programs.

OS Configurations - The configurations (options, types) of the operating system (OS) available to an installation are Primary Control Program (PCP), Multiprogramming with a Fixed number of Tasks (MFT), Multiprogramming with a Variable number of Tasks (MVT), and the Virtual Storage (VS) feature.

OS Interruptions - An interrupt occurs whenever a particular processing activity is halted such that another of higher priority can begin. The five classes of interrupts in priority order are Machine Check, Supervisor Call, Program, External, and Input/Output.

Partitioned Data Set (PDS) - A file which has the capability of being partitioned (or subdivided) into separate members. PDS's are commonly referred to as libraries where programs, procedures, and/or data may be stored.

Positional Parameter - A JCL parameter whose value is signified by its presence in a specific or relative location of a JCL statement.

Procedure - A set of JCL given a name for calling purposes and designed to perform a specific set of functions. Procedures, both catalogued and instream, reduce repetitive coding for common and frequently called applications.

Program - A set of machine language instructions executed under the control of the Operating System. Also referred to as Load Module, Executable Module, and Executable Routine.

Stacking Data Sets - The technique of placing more than one independent file on a given tape volume to lessen storage costs. Generally used for storing files of a historic nature, that is, those subject to minimal change.

Step - A set of JCL which calls, loads, and executes a program load module. Steps are delineated from one another by the occurrence of an Exec statement.

Stepname - A name which identifies a particular step of a given job. Used primarily for referback purposes.

Symbolic Parameter - A parameter and/or its value which is represented by a symbol rather than the actual code itself. Used as a means of simplifying the technical nature of JCL coding for non-JCL user personnel.

<u>Utility</u> - Relatively small and simple programs which perform common functions on a somewhat frequent basis, i.e., print, punch, copy, allocate, etc. Utility programs are classified as either Data Set, System, or Independent Utilities.

<u>Virtual Storage</u> - A feature of the Operating System where main storage requirements are allocated by segments (or pages) as needed by the processing program, thus creating an appearance to the user of unlimited or "virtual" storage.

E

Workshop Answers (Chapters 2 - 8)

Chapter 2 - Job Statement Workshop

Syntax Check:

1. //RUN?   JOB   A5438,CFT,TIME=1,30,MSGLEVEL=(1,1)

      ✓   ✓
     Illegal Character   Code (1,30)

2. //RUN1   JAB   A5438,PROJ1,CFT,CLASS=D   NEED 1484 PAPER

            ✓ ✓
        JOB Misspelled   Code (A5438,PROJ1)

3. //#RUN   JOB   (A5438,PROJ1),CFT,COND=((8,LE),(8,GT))

                                    ✓
                              Illogical Condition

4. //#@$15678   JOB 456,'ARS',CLASS=G,MSGLEVEL=(1,1)

   OK - No Apparent Errors

5. //123456   JOB   456,ARS,CLASE=A,COND=(8,AND)

      ✓   ✓   ✓
    1st Character   Misspelled Illegal
    Numeric   Keyword   Operator

6. //A12345678   JOB   456,ARS,MSGLEVEL=(1,2),TIME=2

            ✓   ✓
     Jobname Too Long   Illegal Specification

7. //XAMPLE JOB XYZ,DHR,CLASS=J,PRTY=13,TYPRUN=SCAN

                                             ✓
                                    Reserved Specification

8. //SAMPLE JOB XYZ,'D R',PRTY=6,TYPRUN=HELD

                                     ✓
                               HOLD Misspelled

9. //EXAMPLE JOB XYZ,DHR,CLASS=B,COND=(4,LT)

   OK - No Apparent Errors

10. //$123 JOB (XYZ,123),D*R,CLASS=X,COND=(0,GT),

                      ✓   ✓
               Code 'D*R'   Illogical Condition

   //MSGLEVEL=(1,1),TIME=(,45),PRIORITY=9,TYPRUN=HOLD

        ✓   ✓
   Code Blank Column 3   PRTY Misspelled

Job Statement Coding:

   1. //ANSWER1 JOB PH1234,DHR,MSGLEVEL=(1,1),
      //   CLASS=C,TIME=3

   2. //ANSWER2 JOB PH1234,DHR,MSGLEVEL=(1,1),
      //   CLASS=A,TIME=(,45),COND=(8,LE)   COND=(8,LT)

                                                       F probably better

   3. //ANSWER3 JOB PH1234,DHR,MSGLEVEL=(1,1),
      //   CLASS=E,TYPRUN=SCAN

   4. //ANSWER4 JOB PH1234,DHR,MSGLEVEL=(1,1),
      //   CLASS=B

   5. //ANSWER5 JOB PH1234,DHR,MSGLEVEL=(1,1),
      //   CLASS=G,PRTY=6   PRTY=8

   6. //ANSWER6 JOB (PH1234,UPDATE),'D R',MSGLEVEL=(1,1),
      //   CLASS=H,COND=(12,EQ)   COND=(12,LE)

   7. //ANSWER7 JOB PH1234,UPDATE),'D R',MSGLEVEL=(1,1),
      //   CLASS=D,PRTY=12

   8. //ANSWER8 JOB (PH1234,UPDATE),'D R',MSGLEVEL=(1,1),
      //   CLASS=I,TYPRUN=HOLD

   9. //ANSWER9 JOB (PH1234,UPDATE),'D R',MSGLEVEL=(1,1),
      //   CLASS=F,TIME=15

   10. //ANSWER0 JOB (PH1234,UPDATE),'D R',MSGLEVEL=(1,1),
       //   TIME=(12,30),PRTY=8,COND=(4,LT)

                                               ✓

Chapter 3 - Exec Statement Workshop

Syntax Check:

1. //STEP& EXEC PGM=ALOAD,TIME=2,30,REGION=40K

   √   √
   Illegal Character   Code (2,30)

2. //STEP2 EXAC PGM=AAA999,PARM=ON,YES,COND=(4,LT)

      √   √
      EXEC Misspelled   Code (ON,YES)

3. //#STEP EXEC PROC=SORTW,COND=((4,LT),(4,GE))

                                      √
                                      Illogical Condition

4. //$@#12345 EXEC COBUCL,PARM=(CLIST,DMAP,XREF)
   OK - No Apparent Errors

5. //7654321 EXEC PGM=EXAM,TYME=1,COND=(12,OR)

   √   √   √
   1st Character   Misspelled   Illegal
   Numeric   Keyword   Operator

6. //Z12345678 EXEC PROC=ABC,TIME=(2,64),REGION=80K

        √   √
        Stepname Too Long   Illegal Specification

7. //   EXEC PGM=IEBGENER,COND=(8,LT,STEP10)

                                      √
                                      Illegal Forward Reference

8. //EIGHTH EXEC REGION=140K,TIME=3

                      √
                      No Program or Procedure Called

9. //EXAMPLE EXEC FTG1C,PARM=(LIST,MAP)
   OK - No Apparent Errors

10. //STEP10 EXEC PGM=AEDIT,PARM=10%,REGION=50K

                                √   √
                                Code '10%' No Continuation Comma
    //   CONDITION=(4,LT,STEP2),TIME=(,45)

                      √
                      COND Misspelled

389

Exec Statement Coding:

1. //STEP1 EXEC PROC=TAPE

2. //STEP2 EXEC PGM=AEDIT,REGION=70K,
   //   TIME=3

3. //STEP3 EXEC PGM=IEBPTPCH

4. //STEP4 EXEC PGM=AMATCH,TIME=1,
   //   COND=(4,LT,STEP2)

5. //STEP5 EXEC PROC=COBUC,PARM=(DMAP,PMAP)

6. //STEP6 EXEC PROC=LKED,PARM=(XREF,LIST,LET),
   //   COND=((*,LE,STEP5),(12,EQ))

7. //STEP7 EXEC PGM=AREFORM,REGION=200K,
   //   TIME=(1,30),PARM=(YES,OFF,'A*B')

8. //STEP8 EXEC PROC=FTG1CLG,PARM=(LIST,MAP),
   //   TIME=5

9. //STEP9 EXEC PGM=IEBGENER,COND=(8,LT,STEP8)

10. //   EXEC PGM=FINEE,REGION=120K,
    //   TIME=4,COND=(4,LT),PARM='4+8'

Chapter 4 - Dd Statement Workshop

Syntax Check:

1. //INPUT% DD UNIT=SYSDA,DISP=OLD,KEEP,

   Illegal Character   Code (OLD,KEEP)

   //   DSN=MASTER,VOL=SER=018762

   OK - No Apparent Errors

2. //SYSUT2 DB DSN=INDATA,

   DD Misspelled

   //   LABEL=1,SL,DISP=SHR

   Code (1,SL)

3. //SYSIN DD *,DCB=BLKSIZE=4800

   OK - No Apparent Errors

4. //OUTPUT1 DD UNIT=2400,DISP=(KEEP,PASS,DELETE),

   Illegal Status

390

```
//          DSN=AFILE.ONE,VOL=SER=TAPE18
                                      ↙
                              No Continuation Comma
//          DCB=(RECFM=FB,LRECL=80,BLKSIZE=3160)
                        ↑                  ↙
                        E            Block Size Not a Multiple
                        ✗
```

5. //2INPUT   DD   UNIT=3330,DISP=(NEW,PASS),
```
      ↙
   1st Character Numeric
```
```
//          SPICE=(4000,20,RLSE),
                    ↙
              Misspelled Keyword
```
```
//          DSN=&&TEMPFILE,VOL=SER=PACK77,
```
 OK - No Apparent Errors
```
//          DCB=(RECFM=AB,LRECL=100,BLKSIZE=4000)
                      ↙
              Illegal Specification
```

6. //APRINTOUT   DD   SYSOUT=(C,1484)   NEED SPECIAL PAPER
```
              ↙            ↙
        Ddname Too Long   Two Commas Necessary
```

7. //   DD   DISP=(MOD,KEEP),DSN=.STEP1.GO.OUTPUT2
```
      ↙                         ↙
   No Ddname                Referback Needs *.
```

8. //CARDIN   DD   DATA,UNIT=2400
```
                  ↙
            Illogical Card File Specification
```

9. //PROGOUT   DD   UNIT=DISK,DISP=(NEW,CATLG,DELETE),

//   LABEL=(1,SL),VOLUME=SER=DISK02,

//   DSN=A.PRGM.LIBRY(MEMBER),

//   DCB=(RECFM=VB,BLKSIZE=3204)

   OK - No Apparent Errors

10. //SYSPRINT   DD   STSTEMOUT=*
```
                    ↙
              Misspelled  Illegal Sysout Class
              Keyword
```

Dd Statement and Job Coding Project:

```
1. //EDITSUM   JOB   99008148,DANHR,MSGLEVEL=(1,1),
   //          TIME=15,CLASS=E
   //*         THIS JOB REQUIRES 5000 LINES OF 1062 PAPER.
   //JOBLIB   DD   DSNAME=A.PRGM.LIBRY,DISP=SHR
2. //STEP1   EXEC   PGM=AEDIT,TIME=5,REGION=100K
   //INPUT1   DD   UNIT=3330,DISP=(OLD,KEEP),
   //         DSN=RAWDATA,VOL=SER=001545,
   //         DCB=(RECFM=FB,LRECL=80,BLKSIZE=3200)
   //OUTPUT1   DD   UNIT=2400,DISP=(NEW,PASS),
   //         DSN=GOODDATA,
   //         DCB=(RECFM=VB,LRECL=160,BLKSIZE=3204)
   //MSGOUT   DD   SYSOUT=A
   //SYSUDUMP   DD   SYSOUT=A
   /*
3. //STEP2   EXEC   PROC=SORTW,PARM=('CORE=30000')
   //SYSIN   DD   *
     -  -  -  - Control Card File Here -  -  -  -
   /*
   //SORTIN   DD   UNIT=2400,DISP=(OLD,KEEP),
   //         DSN=GOODDATA,
   //         DCB=(RECFM=VB,LRECL=160,BLKSIZE=3204)
   //SORTOUT   DD   UNIT=SYSDA,DISP=(NEW,PASS),
   //         DSN=&&TEMPDATA,VOL=SER=PACK88,   .
   //         SPACE=(CYL,5,RLSE),
   //         DCB=(RECFM=VB,LRECL=160,BLKSIZE=3204)
   /*
4. //STEP3   EXEC   PGM=ASUM,TIME=15,REGION=60K,
   //         COND=(8,LT,STEP1)
   //TAPEIN   DD   UNIT=2400,DISP=(OLD,KEEP),
   //         DSN=PASTDATA,VOL=SER=002309,
   //         DCB=(RECFM=FB,LRECL=120,BLKSIZE=2400)
   //DISKIN   DD   UNIT=SYSDA,DISP=(OLD,DELETE),
   //         DSN=&&TEMPDATA,VOL=SER=PACK88,
   //         DCB=(RECFM=VB,LRECL=160,BLKSIZE=3204)
   //PRINT1   DD   SYSOUT=(C,,1062)
```

```
//PRTMSG    DD   SYSOUT=A
//SYSUDUMP  DD   SYSOUT=A
//
```

Chapter 5 - Catalogued Procedures Workshop

Program Test Environment:

```
1. //TEST1   JOB   99008148,DANHR,MSGLEVEL=(1,1),
   //        TIME=3,CLASS=C
2. //STEP1   EXEC  PROC=SORTW
   //SORT.SORTIN   DD   UNIT=2400,DISP=(OLD,KEEP),
   //        DSNAME=UNSORT.DATA,VOL=SER=TAPE54,
   //        DCB=(RECFM=FB,LRECL=80,BLKSIZE=2400)
   //SORT.SORTOUT  DD   UNIT=SYSDA,DISP=(NEW,PASS),
   //        DSNAME=&&SORTED.DATA,VOL=SER=SCRTCH,
   //        SPACE=(TRK,(10,1),RLSE),
   //        DCB=(RECFM=FB,LRECL=80,BLKSIZE=2400)
   //SORT.SYSIN  DD   *
    SORT   FIELDS=(20,8,A,3,4,D),FORMAT=CH
   /*
3. //STEP2   EXEC  PROC=COBUCLG,
   //        PARM.COB='CLIST,DMAP,XREF',
   //        REGION.GO=80K,
   //        TIME.GO=1,
   //        COND=(8,LT,STEP1.SORT)
4. //COB.SYSIN  DD   *
      - - - - ANS COBOL Program Here - - - -
   /*
   //GO.DATAIN  DD   UNIT=SYSDA,DISP=(OLD,DELETE),
   //        DSNAME=&&SORTED.DATA,
   //        DCB=(RECFM=FB,LRECL=080,BLKSIZE=2400)
   //GO.MASTIN  DD   UNIT=2400,DISP=(OLD,KEEP),
   //        DSNAME=SORTED.MASTER,VOL=SER=018534,
   //        DCB=(RECFM=VB,LRECL=100,BLKSIZE=3204)
   //GO.DATAOUT  DD   UNIT=3330,DISP=(NEW,KEEP),
```

```
//         DSNAME=GOOD.DATA,VOL=SER=TEST01,
//         SPACE=(TRK,(10,1),RLSE),
//         DCB=(RECFM=FB,LRECL=080,BLKSIZE=4800)
//GO.MSGOUT  DD   SYSOUT=A
//
```

Production Run Environment:

```
1. //RUN1   JOB  99008148,DANHR,MSGLEVEL=(1,1),
   //       TIME=15,CLASS=E
   //*      JOB REQUIRES 3000 LINES OF 1473 PAPER.
   //JOBLIB  DD  DSNAME=PROG.LIB1,DISP=SHR
2. //STEP1  EXEC  PROC=FTG1CL,
   //       PARM.FORT='LIST,MAP'
   //FORT.SYSIN  DD  *
     - - - - FORTRAN (G1) Program Here - - - -
   /*
   //LKED.SYSIN  DD  *
    NAME   STAT(R)
   /*
   //LKED.SYSLMOD  DD  DSNAME=PROG.LIB1,DISP=SHR
   /*
3. //STEP2  EXEC  PROC=SORTD
   //SORT.SORTIN01  DD  UNIT=3330,DISP=(OLD,KEEP),
   //       DSNAME=GOOD.DATA1,VOL=SER=PACK11,
   //       DCB=(RECFM=FB,LRECL=080,BLKSIZE=4800)
   //SORT.SORTIN02  DD  UNIT=3330,DISP=(OLD,KEEP),
   //       DSNAME=GOOD.DATA2,VOL=SER=PACK12,
   //       DCB=(RECFM=FB,LRECL=080,BLKSIZE=4800)
   //SORT.SYSIN  DD  *
    MERGE  FIELDS=(10,4,D,28,10,A),FORMAT=CH
   /*
4. //STEP4  EXEC  PGM=STAT,
   //       REGION=130K,
   //       TIME=5,
   //       COND=(4,LT,STEP1,LKED)
   //FT01F001  DD  UNIT=2400,DISP=(OLD,KEEP),
   //       DSNAME=MERGE.DATA,
```

```
//          DCB=(RECFM=FB,LRECL=080,BLKSIZE=4800)
//FT09F001  DD   SYSOUT=(C,,1473)
//FT06F001  DD   SYSOUT=A
//SYSUDUMP  DD   SYSOUT=A
//
```

Chapter 6 - Data Set Utility Programs

Reformat and Print Sequential File:

```
1. //JOB1   A567299,DHR,MSGLEVEL=(1,1),
   //          TIME=2,CLASS=C
2. //STEP1  EXEC  PGM=IEBGENER
   //SYSUT1  DD   UNIT=3330,DISP=(OLD,KEEP),
   //          DSNAME=ORIGINAL,VOL=SER=PACK07,
   //          DCB=(RECFM=FB,LRECL=100,BLKSIZE=2000)
   //SYSUT2  DD   UNIT=2400,DISP=(NEW,PASS),
   //          DSNAME=REFORMAT,
   //          DCB=(RECFM=FB,LRECL=100,BLKSIZE=4000)
   //SYSIN   DD   *
    GENERATE  MAXFLDS=3,MAXLITS=6
    RECORD  FIELD=(100,1,,1),
               FIELD=(6,15,,95),
               FIELD=(6,'       ',,10)
    /*
   //SYSPRINT  DD   SYSOUT=A
   //SYSUDUMP  DD   SYSOUT=A
    /*
3. //STEP2  EXEC  PGM=IEBPTPCH
   //SYSUT1  DD   UNIT=2400,DISP=(OLD,KEEP),
   //          DSNAME=REFORMAT,
   //          DCB=(RECFM=FB,LRECL=100,BLKSIZE=4000)
   //SYSUT2  DD   SYSOUT=A
   //SYSIN   DD   *
    PRINT  MAXFLDS=1,CNTRL=3,
               STOPAFT=250,SKIP=2
    TITLE  ITEM=('PARTIAL DATA FILE LISTING',20)
    RECORD  FIELD=(100,1,,1)
     /*
```

```
//SYSPRINT   DD   SYSOUT=A
//SYSUDUMP   DD   SYSOUT=A
//
```

Update and Copy/Compress Procedure Library:

```
1. //JOB2   A567299,DHR,MSGLEVEL=(1,1),
   //        TIME=1,CLASS=A
2. //STEP1   EXEC   PGM=IEBUPDTE
   //SYSUT1   DD   DSNAME=PROCE.DURE.LIBRARY,DISP=SHR
   //SYSUT2   DD   DSNAME=PROCE.DURE.LIBRARY,DISP=SHR
   //SYSIN   DD   DATA
   ./ CHANGE   NAME=PROC22,LIST=ALL
   /
   ./ NUMBER   SEQ1=ALL,NEW1=5,INCR=10
   //STEPX EXEC PGM=LEADZERO,REGION=40K
   //        UNIT=SYSDA,DISP=SHR
   ./ ENDUP
   /*
   //SYSPRINT   DD   SYSOUT=A
   //SYSUDUMP   DD   SYSOUT=A
   /*
3. //STEP2   EXEC   PGM=IEBCOPY
   //IN1   DD   DSNAME=PROCE.DURE.LIBRARY,DISP=SHR
   //OUT1   DD   DSNAME=PROCE.DURE.LIBRARY,DISP=SHR
   //SYSIN   DD   *
    COPY   OUTDD=OUT1,INDD=(IN1,R)
    EXCLUDE   MEMBER=(REFORM,JCL17,PROC07)
   /*
   //SYSPRINT   DD   SYSOUT=A
   //SYSUT3   DD   UNIT=SYSDA,SPACE=(TRK,1)
   //SYSUT4   DD   UNIT=SYSDA,SPACE=(TRK,1)
   //SYSUDUMP   DD   SYSOUT=A
   //
```

Chapter 7 - System and Independent Utility Program

Update and Copy Program Library:

```
1. //JOB1   PROJ8733,DHR,MSGLEVEL=(1,1),
```

```
//          CLASS=C
2. //STEP1   PGM=IEHMOVE
   //ON1    DD   UNIT=3330,DISP=(OLD,KEEP),
   //          VOL=SER=PACK88
   //OFF1   DD   UNIT=3330,DISP=(OLD,KEEP),
   //          VOL=SER=TEMP99
   //BUTAPE  DD   UNIT=2400,DISP=(OLD,KEEP),
   //          VOL=SER=TAPE84
   //SYSIN  DD   *
    COPY  PDS=APROG.LIB,TO=3330=PACK88,                              X
                  FROM=2400=TAPE84
    EXCLUDE   MEMBER=ADJUST
    EXCLUDE   MEMBER=RESUM
    REPLACE   DSNAME=APROG.LIB,                                      X
                  MEMBER=AEDIT
   /*
   //SYSPRINT   DD   SYSOUT=A
   //SYSUT1   DD   UNIT=3330,DISP=(NEW,DELETE),
   //          VOL=SER=TEMP99
   //SYSUDUMP   DD   SYSOUT=A
   /*
3. //STEP2  EXEC  PGM=IEHPROGM,COND=(4,LT,STEP1)
   //PROG1   DD   UNIT=3330,DISP=(OLD,KEEP),
   //          VOL=SER=PACK88
   //SYSIN   DD   *

    RENAME   DSNAME=APROG.LIB,                                       X
                  VOL=3330=PACK88,                                   X
                  NEWNAME=GOOD.PROGRAM.LIBRARY
     CATLG  DSNAME=GOOD.PROGRAM.LIBRARY,                             X
                  VOL=3330=PACK88
   /*
   //SYSPRINT   DD   SYSOUT=A
   //SYSUDUMP   DD   SYSOUT=A
   //
4. //STEP3  EXEC  PGM=IEHLIST,COND=(4,LT,STEP1)
   //LIST1   DD   UNIT=3330,DISP=(OLD,KEEP),
```

```
//          VOL=SER=PACK88
//SYSIN   DD   *
 LISTPDS   DSNAME=GOOD.PROGRAM.LIBRARY
 /*
//SYSPRINT   DD   SYSOUT=A
//SYSUDUMP   DD   SYSOUT=A
//
```

Independent Disk Volume Dump:

1. ADUMP   JOB

2. MSG   TODEV=1443,TOADDR=208

3. DUMP   FROMDEV=3330,FROMADDR=404,   X
                  TODEV=2400,TOADDR=602,   X
                  VOLID=TAPE89

4. END

Chapter 8 - Advanced JCL Workshop

Syntax Check:

1. //IN   DD   DSN=XYZ,DISP=(OLD,KEEP),LABEL=(,NOL)

                             √ Illegal Specification

2. //INL   DD   UNIT=2400-2,DISP=(OLD,PASS),

  OK - No Apparent Errors

  //   LABEL=(1,NL),VOL=SER=TAPE07,

  OK - No Apparent Errors

  //   DCB=(DEN=3,RECFM=FB,LRECL=100,BLKSIZE=3204,TRTCH=CT)

                √ Erroneous 7-track specification   √ Illegal Specification

3. //CARDIN   DD   *,DCB=BLKSIZE=40

                √ Invalid Blocksize

4. //OUT1   DD   UNIT=2400,DISP=(NEW,KEEP),

  OK - No Apparent Errors

  //   DSNAME=DATA1,VOL=RETAIN=SER=002404,

                √ Illegal Keyword Use

  //   LABEL=(0,SL)   √

                Invalid Data Set Sequence Number

```
5. //INPUT1   DD   DSNAME=ABC
                        ✓
                           Illogical Disposition
6. //MASTIN   DD   UNIT=2400,DISP=(OLD,KEEP),

   //           DSNAME=MAST1,VOL=SER=(TAPE89,TAPE86),

   //           DCB=*.STEP2.MASTOUT

    OK  -  No Apparent Errors
7. //ST4   EXEC   PGM=AEDIT,TIME=MINUTE
                           ✓
                              Erroneous Symbolic Parameter
   //IN1   DD   UNIT=&&DEVICES,DISP=(OLD,KEEP),
                      ✓
                        Erroneous Symbolic Parameter
   //           DSN=&SYMBOL.NAME
    OK  -  No Apparent Errors
8. //MASTIN   DD   UNIT=SYSDA,DISP=(OLD,KEEP),
    OK  -  No Apparent Errors
   //           DSNAME=FILE1,VOL=REF=PACK13
                              ✓
                                 Illogical Referback
   //MASTIN   DD   UNIT=SYSDA,DISP=(OLD,KEEP),
              ✓
         Ddname Repeated; Concatenation Error?
   //           DSNAME=FILE2,VOL=SER=PACK66
    OK  -  No Apparent Errors
9. //STEP1   EXEC   PGM=*.STEP1.OUT1
                         ✓
                           Stepname Referback Error
10. //OLDFILE   DD   DSNAME=DATA(0),DISP=(NEW,CATLG,DELETE)
                            ✓
                              Illogical Disposition
```

Advanced JCL Coding Project:

```
1. //ADVANCE   JOB   PROJ789,DHR,MSGLEVEL=(1,1),
   //           TIME=10,CLASS=B
   //JOBLIB   DD   DSNAME=APROG.LIBRARY,DISP=SHR
```

```
2. //INSTREAM  PROC
   //ST1 EXEC PGM=VERIFY,TIME=3,
   //         REGION=&CORE
   //TAPEIN  DD  UNIT=2400-2,DISP=(OLD,KEEP),
   //        DSNAME=FILE1,VOL=SER=OS9843,
   //        DCB=(RECFM=FB,LRECL=80,BLKSIZE=&BLOCK,DEN=2,TRTCH=ET)
   //         DD  UNIT=2400-2,DISP=(OLD,KEEP),
   //        DSNAME=FILE2,VOL=SER=TAPE54,
   //        DCB=(RECFM=FB,LRECL=80,BLKSIZE=&BLOCK,DEN=2,TRTCH=ET)
   //SYSIN  DD  DSNAME=CAT.CONTROL.FILE,DISP=(OLD,KEEP)
   //PRTOUT  DD  SYSOUT=A,
   //        DCB=(RECFM=FBA,LRECL=160,BLKSIZE=3200)
   //OUTPUT1  DD  UNIT=3330,DISP=(NEW,PASS),
   //        DSNAME=&NAME,VOL=SER=DISK88,
   //        DCB=(RECFM=FB,LRECL=200,BLKSIZE=4000,DSORG=DA),
   //        SPACE=(CYL,(50,5))
   //SYSUDUMP  /DD/  SYSOUT=A
   //     PEND
3. //STEP3  EXEC  PROC=INSTREAM,
   //        CORE=80K,BLOCK=3200,
   //        NAME=VERIFIED.DATA.FILE
4. //STEP2  EXEC  PGM=UPDATE,
   //        TIME=5,REGION=100K
   //INP1  DD  DSNAME=*.STEP1.ST1.OUTPUT1,DISP=(OLD,KEEP)
   //GENO  DD  DSNAME=UPDATA(0),DISP=(OLD,KEEP)
   //GEN1  DD  DSNAME=UPDATA(+1),DISP=(NEW,CATLG,DELETE),
   //        LABEL=(1,SL,PASSWORD),VOL=SER=PRIVATE
   //WRTOUT  DD  SYSOUT=(C,,1433)
   //SYSUDUMP  DD  SYSOUT=A
   //
```

Index